D1715660

The Enduring Struggle

ALSO BY JOHN NORRIS:

Mary McGrory: The First Queen of Journalism
Disaster Gypsies
Collision Course

The Enduring Struggle

The History of the U.S. Agency
for International Development
and America's Uneasy
Transformation of the World

John Norris

ROWMAN & LITTLEFIELD
Lanham • Boulder • New York • London

Published by Rowman & Littlefield
A wholly owned subsidiary of The Rowman & Littlefield Publishing Group, Inc.
4501 Forbes Boulevard, Suite 200, Lanham, Maryland 20706
www.rowman.com

6 Tinworth Street, London SE11 5AL, United Kingdom

British Library Cataloguing in Publication Information Available

Library of Congress Cataloging-in-Publication Data

ISBN: 978-1-5381-5466-3 (cloth)
ISBN: 978-1-5381-5467-0 (electronic)

To Brenda, Ian, Eliza, Phoebe, and Salty
who fill my heart with light, love, and laughter.

Now the trumpet summons us again—not as a call to bear arms, though arms we need—not as a call to battle, though embattled we are—but a call to bear the burden of a long twilight struggle, year in and year out, "rejoicing in hope, patient in tribulation"—a struggle against the common enemies of man: tyranny, poverty, disease, and war itself.

—President John F. Kennedy
Inaugural Address
January 20, 1961

Contents

Contents

ix

Introduction

Why a history of the United States Agency for International Development, or AID?

Because there is perhaps no better reflection of how America engages with the world than its foreign assistance program. For years, the United States was virtually alone in embracing the notion that there was merit in attempting to lift people thousands of miles away out of poverty. For most of human history, this was simply something that nations did not do.

The spirit of the United States has deeply imbued this endeavor; a restless, entrepreneurial, sometimes arrogant conviction that the face of the world could be transformed by assisting like-minded nations and encouraging them to embrace free markets and free ideas.

No other area of presidential decision-making in the modern era has affected more people, more profoundly, and with so little fanfare than the foreign aid program. It is an area where the ambitions, worldview, and grievances of American presidents from John F. Kennedy to Donald Trump have been projected in broad brushstrokes on the canvas of developing countries. The results have ranged from the triumphal to the tragic, with a great deal in between.

Foreign aid propelled the eradication of smallpox and unleashed technological innovations that helped feed millions of people when the specter of famine loomed. US foreign aid also propped up dozens of despots as they clung to power and untenably placed aid workers on the front lines of ill-conceived wars in Vietnam and Iraq, dispensing millions of dollars in projects that were doomed to fail. America's aid program has been propelled by genuine altruism, self-interest, and strategic gamesmanship—often all at the same time.

Throughout, the American public has looked to foreign aid with antipathy and ambivalence driven in no small part by the mistaken belief that such assistance is the single largest item in the federal budget when, at less than 1 percent of all discretionary spending, it is far from being so. The instinctive generosity of the American public has continually wrestled against an abiding fear that foreigners were somehow taking advantage of American goodwill.

Public perception has often been disproportionately shaped by highly vocal members of Congress across the decades that have vied to outdo one another with ever-more-lavish denunciations of foreign aid, claiming that American tax dollars were being flushed down "ratholes," or that supporters of international development wanted to, as a Texas congressman so memorably described it, put "Ghana ahead of grandma."

But the political lines around foreign aid have not always been neatly drawn. Almost all Republican presidents, with one highly notable exception, have embraced foreign aid, while their party has remained content to run against it from Congress when they don't hold the White House. The largest increases in foreign aid have come under Republican presidents, notably Ronald Reagan and George W. Bush, rather than Democrats. Quiet partnership between Democrats and Republicans has repeatedly rescued the aid program at key moments when its future has looked most dire.

In President Kennedy's inaugural address, and then in subsequently creating AID, Kennedy challenged the American people and the world to join a shared struggle against "tyranny, poverty, disease, and war itself." AID's history over more than sixty years is the story not only of that long, uneven struggle, but an abiding reflection of ourselves.

1

Tipping Points

ANGER AND UNREST

From Washington, DC, it was easy to imagine that the entire developing world was slipping toward chaos in 1960. The collapse of colonialism was accelerating. Twenty-one new countries had been recognized since World War II, and a remarkable nineteen more would emerge in 1960 alone.[1]

Soviet premier Nikita Khrushchev, while not eager for a direct military confrontation with the West, viewed the mass of countries emerging from under the brutal yoke of colonial rule as fruit ripe to be picked by socialism.[2] Khrushchev embraced his predecessor Joseph Stalin's belief that the "backs of the British, the West, will be broken not on the River Thames, but on the Yangtze and the Ganges."[3]

A competition for influence in the developing world had come to parallel the escalating arms race, and opportunities for missteps and dangerous miscalculations by the United States, China, and the Soviet Union abounded.[4]

In the spring of 1958, Vice President Richard Nixon set off on a tour of Latin America. It was a disaster. At the airport in Venezuela, demonstrators showered spit and chewing tobacco down upon Nixon and his wife Patricia. By the time Nixon's motorcade reached downtown Caracas, an angry mob had assaulted the cars with rocks and bottles. Nixon's military aide, General Don Hughes, recalled, "The hate on their faces was unbelievable."[5] The 101st Airborne Division was scrambled in case Nixon had to be evacuated by force. Unsettling images of the fracas were featured on the cover of *Life* magazine.

On New Year's Day 1959 came a thunderbolt. Cuban dictator Fulgencio Batista, long supported by the United States, abandoned his fight against insurgents in the countryside and fled Havana at three in the morning with suitcases full of cash. Rebel leader Fidel Castro quickly consolidated his hold on power. Castro nationalized more than $1 billion in US holdings ranging from casinos to sugar plantations. He also established favorable relations with Moscow, creating a major Soviet outpost just 103 miles from the coast of Florida.

No one watched the unfolding events with keener interest than an ambitious young politician from Massachusetts: John F. Kennedy. JFK's worldview had been shaped by several formative events, including a trip to Argentina as a student, his World War II service in the Pacific Theater, and occasional, somewhat debauched, junkets to Cuba. But the evolution of his views on the developing world had come into sharp relief during a seven-week, 25,000-mile congressional trip in 1951 during which Kennedy traveled to Israel, Pakistan, India, Malaysia, Thailand, Korea, Japan, and what was known then as French Indochina, and later as Vietnam.[6]

Kennedy walked away from his trip with an affinity for those in Asia, the Middle East, Africa, and Latin America fighting to establish their own nations and identity. Kennedy became openly critical of colonialism in Algeria and Indochina, and sharply reversed his earlier opposition to foreign aid programs.[7] Kennedy's support for independence movements was controversial, and it was frequently cited at the time as an example of his lack of maturity on foreign policy.[8]

Kennedy argued that communism could not be combatted purely through the force of arms and called for Washington to build "non-communist sentiments" through other means, such as economic assistance.[9] Kennedy's own father, Joseph, took such strong exception to his son's idea of courting the people of newly independent states that he openly ridiculed it: "Perhaps, our next effort will be to ally to ourselves the Eskimos of the North Pole and the Penguins of the Antarctic." The views of father and son were so bitterly divided that they refused to discuss foreign policy with one another after Joseph's remarks.

The practice of the United States offering foreign assistance to other countries was not new, dating back to 1794 when Treasury Secretary Alexander Hamilton helped secure $15,000 of assistance for Haitian refugees displaced during that country's bloody independence struggle. During rancorous congressional debate, several representatives argued vehemently that sending American taxpayer dollars abroad was unconstitutional.[10]

Other efforts followed. Thousands of bushels of corn and flour were sent to Venezuela in 1812 following deadly earthquakes. Assistance was provided to Greeks as they tried to break away from the Ottoman Empire.[11] In the 1840s, Americans directed more than $1 million to help blunt the Irish potato famine. And although impossible to disentangle from the complex legacy of US involvement in building the Panama Canal, army physicians William Gorgas and Walter Reed helped spearhead the successful effort to wipe out yellow fever in the Panama Canal Zone in the early 1900s, a landmark achievement in public health.[12]

But it was World War I that marked a true sea change in the US approach to foreign aid, largely because of the remarkable efforts of one man: Herbert Hoover. While Hoover is often ranked as one of the worst US presidents because of his missteps during the Great Depression, his actions before assuming the presidency led one of his contemporaries to argue that Hoover "fed more people and saved more lives than any other man in human history."[13]

Hoover, a successful US businessman living in London during World War I, founded and led the Commission for Relief in Belgium, delivering food to millions of desperate Belgians trapped between the German occupation and a British naval blockade. It was something that had never been done before: a private American citizen leading a massive humanitarian effort to a desperate nation caught between major powers at war. Newton Baker, the US Secretary of War, described Hoover's "unconquerable determination to keep the Belgians from starving," as he "scolded, threatened, and out-bullied every human obstacle."[14]

After the war, Hoover mounted an equally impressive and far more controversial effort to stave off mass starvation in Soviet Russia. As Hoover biographer George Nash argued, it was Hoover who gave birth to the notion that "when there is a humanitarian tragedy in the world, whether from war or from famine or revolution or a typhoon or an earthquake, that Americans will be there to organize the relief."[15]

World War II fundamentally tested that proposition. In 1940, President Franklin D. Roosevelt was alarmed that the United Kingdom could no longer afford its vital purchases of weapons and supplies from the United States. Constrained by legislation requiring that all trade with warring nations be done on a cash basis, FDR launched a major effort to let London "borrow" the materiel it so desperately needed to keep Hitler's forces at bay. Roosevelt compared the effort to lending a hose to a neighbor when their house was on fire—you didn't want him to pay for the hose, you just wanted it back when he was done.[16] During the war, the United States provided substantial assistance to help both neighbors in the Western Hemisphere and citizens in areas liberated from the fascists.

By the end of World War II, Europe and large parts of Asia were decimated. Fifty to eighty million people around the globe had died during the war. The United States was in an unparalleled position of economic and military dominance. Although having only 6 percent of the world's population, the United States suddenly accounted for about 50 percent of the global economy.[17]

The United States used this postwar dominance to help shape multilateral institutions and instruments in a remarkably visionary way, helping to establish the United Nations, the World Bank, the International Monetary Fund, and the World Health Organization.[18] Washington viewed this global architecture as an essential foundation for more peaceful and prosperous relations between states and as important instruments in lowering trade barriers and building up the economic connectivity between what were still largely closed economies.[19]

The strategy was straightforward: Expanding the pool of countries that were free market democracies would help the US economy, produce reliable allies, reduce sources of conflict, and serve as an important bulwark against extremism.[20]

When he announced the "Truman Doctrine" in 1947—the idea of assisting free nations, with both economic and military support, to fend off threats of communism and aggression—President Harry Truman was reacting to fears that Greece and

Turkey were about to fall to Soviet influence. These concerns pushed Truman and his secretary of state, General George Marshall, to begin planning a much larger recovery effort for badly battered Europe.

Marshall's instruction to George Kennan—head of policy planning at the State Department, whom he tasked with developing these plans—was direct: "Avoid trivia."[21] As Kennan and his staff dove into their work, they argued that while communism was an enduring threat, "the present crisis results in large part from the disruptive effect of the war on the economic, political, and social structure of Europe."[22]

Their answer: the massive package of economic assistance that came to be known as the Marshall Plan. It was an unprecedented step to revive the economies of competitors following war, but these were economies that were vital to the health of American industry and trade.[23] President Truman was heavily influenced in his thinking toward postwar Europe not only by the State Department but by former president Herbert Hoover, whom he had dispatched on an extensive assessment tour of the region in 1946. As Hoover declared at the time, "[T]he final voice of victory is the guns, but the first voice of peace is food."[24]

With the passage of time, most simply remember the scale of the Marshall Plan, its lasting success, and the stirring invocation of Marshall's June 1947 speech at Harvard University: "Our policy is directed not against any country or doctrine but against hunger, poverty, desperation, and chaos."

But Truman and his advisers recognized that trying to get approval for the plan would be politically fraught. Truman insisted that the effort be dubbed the Marshall Plan not out of humility, but because he was certain it was more likely to find support from congressional Republicans if his own name was not attached to it.[25] Some of Truman's advisers also wanted it named after Marshall rather than the president because they feared it would fail.

Congress was hostile to the emerging plan, and the public, indifferent. The influential isolationist Republican senator, Robert Taft of Ohio, denounced the plan as welfare for Europeans and demanded that the United States stop playing "Santa Claus."[26] Republican representative Howard Buffett of Nebraska dubbed the Marshall Plan "Operation Rathole." Media outlets as diverse as the *Daily Worker* on the left, and the powerful McCormick and Hearst newspaper chains on the right, blasted the proposal. The Truman administration responded with a massive publicity campaign, with Secretary Marshall—a beloved war hero—barnstorming the country to court labor groups, business associations, congregations, and student groups.[27]

Despite this, the plan's fate remained uncertain in Congress until the 1948 Soviet-backed coup in Czechoslovakia. Suddenly, the Marshall Plan looked like a much-needed weapon against communist expansion. It was soon approved with bipartisan support.[28] Senator Taft, who had so strongly opposed the Marshall Plan initially, voted in favor of it.

The aid to Europe relied heavily on commodities, but as one history of the Marshall Plan pointed out, this was not "primarily an enterprise for delivering orange juice and baby chicks," but instead was an "investment for productivity and modernization: tractors for farms, steel plate for shipbuilding, iron for locomotives, coal to turn generators."[29] Substantial technical assistance was provided to rebuild factories and recapitalize European banks so they could fund reconstruction. Assistance was also conditioned on a willingness to lower barriers to trade and other reforms.

The results of the Marshall Plan are well known. Former British foreign secretary Ernest Bevin likened the Marshall Plan to "a lifeline for sinking men," and author Greg Behrman called the Marshall Plan "one of the most successful foreign policy enterprises in the annals of US history."[30]

As the United States carried out the Marshall Plan, it also undertook a patchwork of other foreign aid efforts around the globe, all of which were driven by security imperatives with little in the way of country-led planning.[31]

Hoping what had been achieved through the Marshall Plan might be applied more broadly, President Truman's 1949 inaugural address proposed a "bold new program" for the growth of "underdeveloped areas."[32] Given concerns about containing China, much of the aid at this time was directed to Asia in places like Korea, Thailand, and Indochina.[33] Ben Hardy, one of the wordsmiths behind what came to be known as the "Point Four" speech, called Truman's determination to lift up the developing world, "a ringing declaration of democratic principles that would fire the imagination of the masses of people throughout the world."[34] (Ironically, this emphasis on foreign aid was an eleventh-hour addition to a speech that was largely dominated by an emphasis on more-traditional security concerns.)

Truman, in his autobiography, said that the reports he had received from the developing world indicated "a great many people were still living in an age almost a thousand years behind the times," in what he called, "the curse of colonialism."[35]

Henry Bennett, who was appointed to direct much of this aid, promised in 1951 that "results can be had quickly," and predicted towering breakthroughs: famine would be eliminated in India by 1956; malaria eradicated within a decade; "hunger, poverty, and ignorance" would end around the globe for all practical purposes within fifty years.[36]

But Bennett, like many others, misapplied the lessons of the Marshall Plan to the developing world. The European recovery was an effort to resuscitate modern economies led by a set of highly motivated and well-organized governments. Europe's educational base was strong and incentives for opening trade were high. Efforts to rebuild Europe's roads, dams, rail lines, and power plants were absolutely appropriate to the European context. Equally true, the Marshall Plan was the wrong template to apply to most of the developing world where institutions were weak, public services scant, illiteracy high, and economies largely dependent on subsistence agriculture.

Under President Dwight Eisenhower, US assistance became more military in nature throughout the mid-1950s, as it shifted from Europe to Asia, with South Korea and Taiwan—the very front lines against Communist China—the largest recipients.[37] During the height of the Marshall Plan, economic assistance had outpaced military aid on a four-to-one basis; by 1954 that figure was reversed.[38] A commission on foreign aid reported to President Eisenhower that demands were increasing from poor countries for general economic aid, but commission members declared, "We recognize no such right."[39]

THE UGLY AMERICAN

By the time John Kennedy started examining foreign aid programs as he eyed his White House run, there was a growing chorus of dissatisfaction with them.

Nothing crystallized these discontents more starkly than one of the most popular pieces of American fiction at the time, the 1958 novel *The Ugly American*, by William J. Lederer and Eugene Burdick. *The Ugly American* detailed the bumbling exploits of Americans in a fictional Asian country outflanked at every turn by shrewd communists, and the book scorched its way up the best-seller list where it remained for a seventy-six-week run.[40]

The book was a searing indictment of US diplomacy and aid at a time when it felt like the United States was on the losing end of the Cold War. As the book argued, misguided, out-of-touch US diplomats were not only failing to win hearts and minds in the developing world, they were also spending "billions on the wrong aid projects." The *New York Herald Tribune* found it such a damning critique that it breathlessly intoned, "If this were not a free country, this book would be banned."[41]

The Ugly American took on almost totemic importance in the debate about the US approach to the developing world, even as aid officials in the Eisenhower administration strongly objected to its content, calling the novel, "a grotesque cartoon" detailing "errors of the past."[42]

While not the most balanced view, the book was progressive in some important ways, particularly its contention that programs would only succeed if the people who administered them rejected paternalism and became steeped in local cultures, languages, and politics. The book made a convincing case that people weren't poor because they were lazy or backward, but because of the systems in which they were trapped.

Senator Kennedy was so enthusiastic about *The Ugly American* that he not only purchased copies for all of his Senate colleagues, he took out a full-page ad in the *New York Times* praising its depiction of Americans working overseas.[43]

And it was not just *The Ugly American* that was raising concerns about foreign aid. No less than six different major studies of the aid program were conducted during the late 1950s, many of them highly critical, even as such assistance was becoming a core element of US foreign policy.[44]

Many of the studies were coming to grips with the hard fact that offering a country foreign aid did not necessarily buy America love, admiration, or sympathetic votes at the United Nations. Many of the new leaders in the developing world had led independence movements, and one report at the time noted their "resentment of real or fancied attempts at outside interference" by the United States.[45]

As Michael Todaro and Stephen Smith argued, economists at the time "had no readily available conceptual apparatus with which to analyze the process of economic growth in largely agrarian societies characterized by the virtual absence of modern economic structures."[46] Countries were being asked to industrialize out of thin air, with "big push" projects that would allow them to turn subsistence farmers into efficient factory workers as if by alchemy.[47] Although there was a nascent group of thoughtful development economists emerging during this period, their voices remained on the margins.

Responsibilities for the US assistance program were diffuse, scattered across multiple competing agencies that had cropped up since the Marshall Plan and operating under overlapping and sometimes contradictory legislative mandates.[48] Public support for aid was waning, as was the morale of those working abroad. As one report of this period argued, finding and retaining qualified "shirt-sleeve ambassadors" should have "first claim" on the attention of aid officials.[49]

Even for its supporters, the aid program had drifted into considerable disarray through the 1950s. And if its real problems were not severe enough, foreign aid had to fight off more than its share of misinformation. One enduring myth: US assistance had been used to purchase suits for Greek morticians.[50] The story was sufficiently stubborn that the Eisenhower administration was compelled to provide the House Foreign Affairs Committee with detailed procurement records indicating that there was no financing of any kind for civilian clothing in Greece, much less garb for undertakers.

AID AND THE ELECTION

Around this time, Senator Kennedy began to assemble a kitchen cabinet to advise him on how best to overhaul the structure and policies of US foreign aid. Chester Bowles, a congressman and former ambassador to India, was an active participant.[51] Also crucial was Fred Holborn, a young Harvard-educated academic and the son of refugees from Nazi Germany, who served as JFK's key congressional aide on Algeria and India.[52]

India held half the population of the non-communist world. With China having already fallen to communism, the ability to steer India more firmly toward free markets and maintain it as a democracy was considered essential by US national security experts.[53]

Fred Holborn reached out to two MIT academics who were making a splash with new theories on foreign assistance: Walt Rostow and Max Millikan. The two had cochaired a presidential review of the aid program, and Rostow had served on George Kennan's staff at the State Department during the formulation of the Marshall Plan. Rostow and Millikan's 1956 findings on aid made the front page of the *New York Times* and were debated at Eisenhower's National Security Council.[54]

The pair argued that the battle for the developing world would be fought on economic rather than military grounds, and that economic growth and reform were essential if Washington wanted its gravitational pull to exceed Moscow's.[55] The authors rejected the idea that aid should be used to buy influence and deconstructed the idea that communism sprang from hunger.[56] Their prime recommendation: "The United States should launch at the earliest possible moment a long-term program for sustained economic growth in the free world."[57]

Rostow and Millikan wanted to inject capital and technical assistance into countries meeting "fairly high standards of eligibility" that would use such investments well. The notion of directing assistance based on economic prospects rather than on geo-strategic priorities was radical for the time.[58]

According to Rostow, the aim of foreign aid should be to help countries rapidly achieve an industrial take-off that would allow these economies to become self-sustaining.[59] The best means to do this would be through systemic economic reforms coupled with lending for big-ticket infrastructure projects like roads and power grids.

Millikan and Rostow believed that it would be necessary for the United States and other major industrial countries to open their markets to goods and services from the developing world, a useful reminder that the prospects for the developing world are often imbedded within larger and much more powerful currents, such as trade.[60] As noted economist and Kennedy insider John Kenneth Galbraith remarked in a moment of frankness, "[I]t is doubtful that many of us, if pressed, would insist that economic development was simply a matter of external aid. But nothing could be more convenient than to believe this, for once we admit that it is not the case, we become entrapped in a succession of grievously complex problems."[61]

While the Eisenhower administration largely failed to act upon recommendations from Millikan and Rostow, Kennedy embraced them—in part because it made him look tough on communism during his 1960 presidential race against Vice President Richard Nixon.

"The gap between the developed and underdeveloped worlds," Kennedy argued on the floor of Congress, was a "challenge to which we have responded most sporadically, most timidly, and most inadequately."[62] Kennedy was eager to step onto the world stage and shape geopolitics.

It was no surprise that Kennedy and Rostow emerged as kindred spirits. Both were intellectual, but neither was content with an ivory tower. Kennedy appreciated Rostow's intelligence and impatience to change the world both at home and abroad. Rostow was struck by what he called Kennedy's "remarkable computer of a mind."[63] Rostow's influence on Kennedy is striking, and it was Rostow who first stressed the "New Frontier" language that would become a centerpiece of Kennedy's campaign.[64]

The debate about foreign aid played a prominent role in the 1960 presidential race, in no small part because of spiraling Cold War tensions. In May 1960, the Soviets downed the U-2 spy plane of an American pilot, Francis Gary Powers, as it flew over their territory. The fallout from the U-2 episode quickly derailed a planned US–Soviet summit and negotiations on nuclear weapons.

On October 7, 1960, during the second Kennedy–Nixon presidential debate, the candidates squared off on the issue of foreign aid. Kennedy cited a poll that found most people in other countries thought the Soviet Union would be ahead of the United States militarily by 1970. He argued that too much aid to the developing world had been surplus military equipment, when long-term loans would produce greater growth and allow recipients to maintain their self-respect. "Unless we begin to identify ourselves not only with the anti-communist fight, but also with the fight against poverty and hunger, these people are going to begin to turn to the communists as an example."

Kennedy continued to push hard on the topic of foreign aid as the campaign came down its homestretch. On November 2, just six days from the election, at a major campaign rally in San Francisco, Kennedy again stressed his impatience with the status quo. "But the harsh facts of the matter are that in three vital areas we have been ill-staffed and ill-represented in the struggle for peace—in our disarmament planning—in our diplomatic and Foreign Service—and in our technical assistance to underdeveloped countries. In all three areas we have failed to realize that times have changed."[65]

Kennedy referenced *The Ugly American*, and made the case that while the public tended to hear about the aid workers who were either extremely competent or incompetent, "most of our personnel are somewhere in between. Most could be doing a better job—and most must do a better job if we are to survive."[66]

On November 8, 1960, the United States voted for its next president. The results were excruciatingly close, so much so that Richard Nixon did not concede until the afternoon of the next day. At the age of forty-three, John Fitzgerald Kennedy had become the youngest American elected as president.

Just days after the election, Kennedy received a report on foreign economic policy prepared by his advisers. Among the recommendations was the idea of creating "a Central Foreign Assistance Agency" with a director that was not located within the Department of State.[67]

What followed was a flurry of appointments that would have an enormous impact on the future course of the US assistance program. Dean Rusk, a seasoned diplomatic veteran and president of the Rockefeller Foundation, was nominated as Kennedy's secretary of state.[68] George Ball, who had been closely involved in negotiating the Marshall Plan, was assigned to lead a task force on reorganizing aid.[69]

And in a move that would have a number of long-term ramifications, Kennedy tapped David E. Bell, who had an unusually good understanding of international development by dint of having served on a field team in Pakistan with the Ford Foundation, to be his director of the Bureau of the Budget.[70]

As the Kennedy transition moved frenetically, relations with Cuba continued to deteriorate. On January 3, 1961, the United States broke diplomatic relations with Havana and imposed an embargo on Cuba little more than a month later.

WHAT SHAPE THE NEW FRONTIER?

On January 20, 1961, a throng of close to one million strong stood in a fresh, wet snow on the National Mall for President Kennedy's inaugural address: "To those peoples in the huts and villages of half the globe struggling to break the bonds of mass misery, we pledge our best efforts to help them help themselves, for whatever period is required—not because the communists may be doing it, not because we seek their votes, but because it is right."[71]

In Kennedy's first meeting with the National Security Council after becoming president, he directed the Bureau of the Budget to develop recommendations on foreign aid, and this effort was essentially co-joined with the work of George Ball, David Bell, and Henry Labouisse (who was in charge of much of the existing aid program).[72]

One key finding emerged from this initial work: Existing aid programs had been "designed primarily as an instrument against communism rather than for constructive economic and social advancement."[73] Beyond this broad understanding, some key issues remained.[74] Should aid be organized by region or by the type of assistance being delivered? Should the existing foreign aid agencies be merged, or should they be preserved? Should aid come mostly in the forms of loans or grants? Should the State Department be in charge of these programs? How could aid be shaped to fit Rostow's concept of development?

George Ball delivered his memo on reorganizing foreign assistance to the president on March 4.[75] The working group was in clear agreement that almost all foreign aid functions should be housed within a single new government agency, and that instead of a series of disconnected projects, development strategies should approach the challenges in recipient countries holistically.

The memo maintained that this new aid agency had to be field-driven, carrying out its responsibilities through the establishment of country "missions" staffed by a mix of US and local personnel. This field presence would allow for continual dialogue with host country governments by staff that were expert in economics and the local culture.

Kennedy's advisers also argued that the new agency should direct programs on a multiyear basis permitting, as David Bell put it, "the developing country to undertake the kind of difficult political measures, such as raising taxes or accomplishing a land reform program, which needed to be undertaken."[76]

There was also general concurrence that international economic assistance should be divorced from military aid; the tendency to commingle the two had led to too many assistance efforts that made neither economic nor strategic sense.[77] Aid should *not* be conditioned on support for US policies. As Arthur Schlesinger recalled Kennedy arguing, "If we undertake this effort in the wrong spirit, or for the wrong reasons, or in the wrong way, then any and all financial measures will be in vain."[78]

A meeting on March 6, chaired by White House counsel and presidential speechwriter Ted Sorensen, fleshed out some of the key areas where major disagreements remained, including the issue of food aid.[79] Food aid, which shipped American food surpluses overseas for use in foreign aid programs, was of enormous importance to US farmers at the time. In 1956, food aid purchases by the US government accounted for 22 percent of all US cotton exports and 27 percent of all wheat exports—a huge market share.[80]

Even though Kennedy and others were starting to see the key goal of food aid as addressing global hunger rather than just dumping America's surpluses, the Department of Agriculture was reluctant to relinquish control of the program.[81] Pork-barrel politics also played a role: A 1953 law specified that at least 50 percent of the food sent overseas as part of this program had to be sent on US-flagged vessels, even when it entailed considerably greater expense.[82]

Although Kennedy and his team were inclined to give the new aid agency full responsibility for food aid, political considerations won the day. "It was quite clear that the Agriculture committees would strongly oppose any such move," David Bell explained, "and this $1 to $2 billion worth of resources . . . might well not be provided in the future."[83]

March 13, 1961, brought a very full day for President Kennedy on the foreign aid front. In the Fish Room at the White House (so named because of the large stuffed blue sailfish that graced its wall), Kennedy chaired a discussion on the reform effort along with Secretary of State Dean Rusk and National Security Adviser McGeorge Bundy.[84]

One important question to be resolved was the relationship of the new aid agency to the secretary of state and the State Department. "There was a strong feeling," David Bell explained, "that aid decisions had been improperly subordinated in the previous arrangement to the views and judgments of the State Department's Assistant Secretaries and office chiefs."[85]

It was ultimately decided that the head of the new aid agency should report to the secretary of state, but not through any intervening layer of State Department officials. President Kennedy felt strongly about this position, although many in the State Department bristled at not having a closer hold on assistance programs.

That evening, President Kennedy hosted ambassadors from across Central and South America at the White House. His wife, Jackie, "radiant in a silk print dress," gave a tour of the White House to the ambassadors and their spouses.[86] In his remarks, Kennedy cited everyone from Simon Bolivar to Thomas Paine as he argued that having millions of people in Latin America "suffer the daily degradations of poverty and hunger" was unacceptable.[87] Kennedy called for a "vast new ten-year plan for the Americas" that was "unparalleled in magnitude and nobility of purpose."

This bold new aid effort would be called the "Alliance for Progress." Kennedy called his vision "an alliance of free governments" working to "eliminate tyranny from a hemisphere in which it has no rightful place." Kennedy pushed Latin America to embrace major social reforms and insisted that transformation of the region would have to be led by Latin America itself. He called for a high-level meeting of ministers to hammer out the details of the plan. After the speech, the Venezuelan ambassador grabbed the arm of Kennedy special adviser Arthur Schlesinger and proclaimed with excitement, "We have not heard such words since Franklin Roosevelt."[88]

The *New York Times* observed of the evening, "President Kennedy has now fired the first shots in a historic battle which, more than any other issue barring war, will engage Congress and the nation next year. It is a battle to create alongside of the North Atlantic Alliance another, larger and equally powerful 'Alliance for Progress' to win the Cold War that will be decided in the main in the economic field."[89] Although Fidel Castro insisted that Kennedy was trying to "buy" Latin America, a reporter in the region noted, "[T]he consensus, even among cynics, is that the President has opened a new chapter in the relationship of North and South America."[90]

Kennedy's speech was remarkably ambitious, all the more so for the fact that he was unveiling a major new aid initiative at the same time that he was restructuring the entire foreign assistance machinery—and secretly planning a covert invasion of Cuba to be launched just a month later.

On March 22, 1961, Kennedy's foreign aid message was delivered to Congress.[91] It called for the 1960s to be a "Decade of Development," and began with three assertions: Existing programs and concepts were "largely unsatisfactory and unsuited for our needs"; the collapse of the developing world would be disastrous for national security and "offensive to our conscience"; and that the 1960s represented a unique moment to move the people of the developing world into self-sustaining growth.[92] The message included some tough language, saying that assistance programs had become "bureaucratically fragmented, awkward and slow," across "a haphazard and irrational structure covering at least four departments and several other agencies."

The president wanted a single agency in charge of foreign aid in Washington and in the field, a "new agency with new personnel," drawn from both existing staff and the best people across the country. Aid would be delivered on the basis of clear and carefully thought through country plans tailored to meet local needs. It would be distinct from military aid because "development must be seen on its own merits."

Kennedy emphasized the need for long-term financing, and urged that the program be built around loans, although grants would sometimes be necessary. He urged a special focus on countries that were willing to mobilize their own resources and embrace reform.

The message also stressed that one of the key ambitions of the US assistance program should be to encourage increased aid spending by other industrialized nations. Indeed, Kennedy and his team successfully internationalized the push for international development. A formal body on development assistance was subsequently established within the Organization for Economic Cooperation and Development and chaired by the United States.[93] This gave the United States considerable long-term influence in setting the global aid agenda. In December 1961, with strong urging from Washington, the United Nations formally declared the 1960s as the "Decade of Development."

Initial congressional reactions to Kennedy's plans were mixed, but largely positive. A number of Republican senators praised the plan, including Jacob Javits of New York, who called the president's message "perceptive and statesmanlike."[94] On the House side, traditionally more opposed to aid programs, the Speaker of the House, Sam Rayburn of Texas, said he was reserving judgment but agreed that a fresh approach was needed.[95]

CONFRONTATION

Less than a month later, President Kennedy faced a foreign policy fiasco that threatened to undermine confidence in his entire presidency. The botched Bay of Pigs invasion of Cuba, where CIA-backed exiles met rapid defeat on Castro's shores, was a humiliating debacle. As a result, Castro's position in Cuba, and across Latin America, was strengthened, as were the links between Havana and Moscow.

In late May 1961, Kennedy met with Khrushchev in Vienna for a hastily planned summit. It too was a shambles, with Khrushchev suggesting that a standoff over Berlin could escalate to war. Kennedy was shocked at Khrushchev's aggressiveness as he tried to take advantage of what Khrushchev viewed as the new president's inexperience and weakness. Tensions between the United States and the Soviet Union had reached such a pitch that Kennedy argued that "any prudent family" should build a fallout shelter.[96]

The eroding foreign policy situation lent momentum to the president's push on foreign aid. Congress sped through Kennedy's request for an additional $500 million in aid for Latin America.[97] And on May 26, Democratic senator William Fulbright of Arkansas introduced the "Act for International Development," the key vehicle for creating a new aid agency.[98] But if Congress was willing to accept foreign aid as part of the price of facing global communism, it was not going to give the White House carte blanche in its design.

The largest and most immediate setback to Kennedy's vision came just days before the legislation was formally introduced. Sam Rayburn, the immensely powerful Democratic Speaker of the House, flatly rejected the notion of separate votes on military and economic aid.[99] Rayburn insisted that congressional support for foreign aid would evaporate if the security and economic dimensions were presented to Congress separately. The administration was forced into an embarrassing climb-down as it informed both the Department of Defense and the aid task force that the bills for economic and military aid would be recombined.

At the White House, long lists of potential names for the new agency were discussed.[100] However, since the legislation was titled the Act for International Development, staffers had fallen into the habit of calling it the "Agency for International Development," or, more simply, "AID." The name stuck. (One subsequent AID chief was not a fan of the name, saying, "It's just too goddamned Madison Avenue.")[101]

Senior administration officials aggressively worked Capitol Hill to make their case for the aid legislation. Secretary of State Dean Rusk told the House Foreign Affairs Committee, "There is nothing that the Communists want more than to see the Yanks go home—not only from Western Europe, but from the Mediterranean, South Asia, the Far East, Latin America, Africa, everywhere. If we Yanks go home, the communists will begin to take over."[102]

Secretary of the Treasury Douglas Dillon informed Congress that 80 percent of economic aid would be spent on American goods and services.[103] Henry Labouisse noted the concerted push to get other industrialized nations to ramp up their own foreign assistance programs.[104] Chester Bowles appealed to the sense of national pride: "We are only 6 percent of the world's people, but we are, by all odds, the greatest and most positive force, the most affirmative force in world affairs."[105]

But security was always the trump card, and Kennedy himself declared, "It was fitting that Congress opened its hearings on our new foreign military and economic aid programs in Washington at the very time that Mr. Khrushchev's words in Vienna were demonstrating as nothing else could the need for that very program."[106]

While concerns about Cuba, the Soviets, and China obviously gave the bill impetus, foreign assistance was never an easy issue on the Hill. Democratic senator Hubert Humphrey of Minnesota, an ardent supporter of international food aid, expressed the sentiment of many: "I am probably going to support the foreign aid program. However, I do it just like I go to see the dentist; I am just not happy about it."[107]

There was, however, at least a modest outside constituency for foreign assistance. Farmers liked that food aid purchased their surpluses. Organized labor saw aid as helping to boost domestic manufacturing. Church groups saw helping the poor as merciful.

The *New York Times* editorial board was likewise convinced. "The need for the revised foreign aid program President Kennedy has outlined is great; and Congress should act swiftly and favorably."[108]

One particular aspect of the legislation engendered fierce pushback from Congress. Eighty-three members of the House wrote to the chairman of the House Foreign Affairs Committee protesting the proposal that the agency would get multiyear appropriations, including thirty congressmen that had voted for aid in previous years.[109] William Gaud, who ran one of the agency's regional bureaus at the time, saw it as a grievous setback. "An AID program should be a long-term proposition if it is to achieve its ends," he argued, but instead, "We spend the whole bloody year fighting before the Congress, you might say for our lives, and for the amount of money that we need."[110]

President Kennedy was deeply irritated with the loss of long-term authority. As David Bell explained, "He could not understand the continuous carping and restrictive attitude of so many members of Congress. He saw that attitude as limiting the office of the president and the powers of the president in dealing with a turbulent, complicated, dynamic world."[111]

PUNTA DEL ESTE

Kennedy's efforts to tame that turbulent world were front and center in August 1961 as senior officials from across the Americas gathered to debate the future of the Alliance for Progress over two weeks at Punta del Este, a picturesque beach resort in Uruguay. It was winter in the southern hemisphere, and a chill pervaded the drafty rooms.[112]

The US delegation was led by Treasury Secretary Douglas Dillion, a wealthy Republican Wall Street financier with a distinguished war record, expensive taste in French art, and impeccably tailored business suits. In sharp contrast, the Cuban delegation was led by Che Guevara, the Argentine who had helped lead the Cuban revolution and who attended the sessions in fatigues and his trademark beret. The two men seemed to embody the very real fork in the road that lay ahead for Latin America.

Kennedy had been informed prior to the meeting that Argentina, Mexico, Brazil, and Chile would only make a sharp break with Cuba if Washington was willing to put major funding on the table.[113] Much of the region was badly in debt as a result of both poor economic policies and falling commodity prices.

A message from President Kennedy, which was delivered by Dillon to begin the proceedings, promised that the United States would allocate more than $1 billion of aid to the region in the Alliance's first year. Secretary Dillon, based on hasty back-of-the-envelope calculations during his flight, said that Latin America could expect $20 billion in funding over the next decade if they lived up to their reform commitments.[114]

Over the next ten days, delegates hashed out two foundational documents—the Punta del Este Declaration and the Charter of Punta del Este—which established the Alliance for Progress. And if Latin America leaders wanted assurances that American money would flow if they were to isolate Castro, Kennedy wanted assurances that Latin American governments would commit to fundamental economic and social reforms.

The delegates embraced highly specific targets for the Alliance. All countries should achieve annual growth of no less than 2.5 percent. Infant mortality should be halved. Adult illiteracy should be eliminated within a decade. Domestic prices were to be stabilized, industry and agriculture accelerated. A whole series of infectious diseases were to be tamed.

A thread of social justice was woven through the discussions. There were calls for more equitable distribution of income and changes in property ownership—always a sticky issue in a region where large landowners controlled the commanding heights of the economy.

As William Gaud observed, what was genuinely new about the Alliance for Progress "was its explicit recognition of a relationship between the United States' attainment of its objectives and the fate of landless peasants, hungry people in urban hovels, illiterate and diseased children, and young men and women without skills or employment opportunities."[115]

As authors Elliott and Victoria Morss argued, "It was a sophisticated development strategy aimed at substituting social reform for revolution."[116] President Kennedy had encouraged everyone involved to think big, and they had.

The interactions between the US and Cuban delegations remained largely civil. Guevara raised a number of points during the negotiations, but they were more constructive than argumentative. That changed on the conference's final day as the agreements were to be put to a vote. Before a packed room, Guevara unleashed a blistering tirade, denouncing the Alliance as little more than an "instrument of economic imperialism."

The ministers in attendance sat in silence, awaiting Douglas Dillon's response. In measured tones, the Treasury Secretary said that the United States would never "betray the thousands of patriotic Cubans who are still waiting and struggling for the freedom of their country," while congratulating the delegates for "a spirit of unity and serious effort." The only acceptable culmination to the conference, Dillon insisted, was to "now undertake the hard and steady work of making a reality of our dreams."[117]

The room erupted in applause as Dillon finished speaking. Guevara did not reply.[118] All of the countries represented at the conference voted in favor of the Charter and Declaration of Punta del Este—except for Cuba.

The nations of Latin America and the United States had made an enormous mutual commitment. As one veteran Latin America hand observed, "It was truly a remarkable undertaking—if not the most blatant example of hubris seen in modern life."[119]

AID IS BORN

The day after the Punta del Este conference ended, the US Senate passed the new legislative charter for foreign assistance by a vote of 66–24, with the House soon following suit. The Foreign Assistance Act of 1961 was signed by President Kennedy on Labor Day, as the president tried to manage a bit of a break at his Hyannis Port compound.[120]

The US Agency for International Development, or AID, had officially been born, with Congress requiring the merger of the preexisting assistance agencies into AID within sixty days.[121]

Veteran aid watchers James Hagen and Vernon Ruttan captured the moment:

> After years of attempting to identify a philosophy for the foreign aid program, Congress spelled one out with uncharacteristic clarity. It would be designed to result in better lives for the masses of poor in developing countries so that they would then be less likely to look to communism for relief. In order for the program to work, it would have to be substantial, consistent over a long term, and with no strings attached, except that the recipient governments would need to carry out the social, political, and economic

reforms necessary for self-sustaining growth to be possible. By assisting the recipients to develop, the United States could enjoy the kind of world neighborhood that would afford the greatest security and wealth for all its members.[122]

President Kennedy was clear that he wanted new blood to lead AID. Kennedy's initial choice, financier George Woods of the First Boston Corporation, dropped out of consideration. The search then turned to Fowler Hamilton, a Rhodes Scholar and accomplished New York lawyer with an impressive résumé.

During World War II, Hamilton had directed the US Embassy's Economic Warfare Division in London. His legal work had focused on international law as he represented American companies engaged in Latin America, Europe, and Africa.[123] Although he had hoped to be appointed the head of the Central Intelligence Agency, Hamilton accepted the job at AID after some initial hesitation.[124]

There was also the looming question of whom Kennedy and Hamilton would choose to run the Alliance for Progress. Teodoro Moscoso was selected for the position in October 1961. Moscoso was a Puerto Rican businessman who had played a critical role in "Operation Bootstrap" to industrialize Puerto Rico during the 1950s, an endeavor that was so successful that many had taken to dubbing the island an "economic miracle."[125] Moscoso had also briefly served as ambassador to Venezuela at the start of Kennedy's term.

As David Bell commented, "The President saw Moscoso as combining the assets of a person who had been a very important part of the economic renaissance of Puerto Rico, an effective American Ambassador, and a person politically sensitive to his fingertips to the kinds of changes and kinds of leaders who are needed in Latin America."[126] Kennedy fundamentally believed that dynamic growth in Latin America could only be unleashed by a radical shift away from traditional rule to modern liberal systems led by a new generation of leaders.

The *Washington Post* hailed the appointment, saying that the administration "could not have picked a more qualified director for Latin American aid than Teodoro Moscoso."[127] The *Post*'s endorsement struck a xenophobic note, however. "Whatever handicap he may carry as a Puerto Rican is more than compensated by the special skills he brings to the job."

Numerous AID staffers recall that Moscoso kept a clock on the wall of his office that was set at 11:59 in perpetuity. His message: With the influence of Castro and communism, it was one minute to midnight in Latin America, and unless his team acted with the utmost urgency, everything could implode.[128]

On November 3, 1961, President Kennedy formally established the Agency for International Development as the executor of US foreign assistance programs.[129] It is telling that some of Kennedy's first actions in office were to create AID and the Peace Corps while more than doubling the size of US Army Special Forces.[130] Kennedy wanted the United States to rise to meet the world. His was an expeditionary approach, born from an insistence that helping the developing world was the right thing to do from a moral, economic, and strategic perspective.

But in understanding AID's roots, it is vital to understand that very few people shared Kennedy's belief that the United States should provide foreign aid because of the inherent worth of development. "Looking back at the intellectual struggle for development aid of the 1950s," Walt Rostow reflected, "I would underline a chastening fact. The path-breaking victories did not come because, at last, we persuaded the opposition that we were right. They came about because of a series of crises."[131]

In December 1961, President Kennedy and his wife visited Latin America where they were greeted by raucous, welcoming crowds in Venezuela, a pointed contrast with Richard Nixon's ill-fated trip three years before. With Jackie Kennedy addressing crowds in Spanish, and JFK repeatedly emphasizing the importance of land reform and social justice, the moment seemed bright.

2

The Foot of the Mountain

WHEN EVERYTHING NEEDS TO BE DONE

In 1961, average life expectancy in Indonesia was thirty-two years of age; in Pakistan, only thirty.[1]

Ethiopia had slightly more than one doctor for every 100,000 of its people, the equivalent of having only 94 doctors to take care of the 8.5 million people living in New York City today.[2]

In Latin America, 15 of every 100 children died before their fifth birthday.[3]

In the Philippines, Rwanda, and Kenya, the average woman had more than seven children during her lifetime.

In Nepal, government officials in rural areas were often not heard from for six months at a time because getting to their posts often required a thirty-day walk.[4]

In the newly independent Republic of the Congo, devastated by outlandishly savage colonial rule, there was not a single Congolese university graduate prior to 1956. No one in the entire country had voted in an election prior to 1957. At independence in 1960, there were no black officers in the army, no native Congolese doctors or engineers, and a grand total of three African managers in the entire civil service to run a country larger than the United States east of the Mississippi.[5] The security guard at the AID compound was armed with a bow and arrow.[6]

Harvey Gutman, a program officer with AID, recalled arriving in Lomé, Togo, in 1961, a place of which he said, "Knowledge of the city's existence was then largely confined to *New York Times* crossword addicts."[7] The government dispatcher responsible for shipping Gutman's personal effects had assumed "Lomé" was a typographical error and shipped his household goods to Rome. He was only reunited with his belongings fifteen months later after they took another detour to Laos, where Gutman had previously been posted.

One of Gutman's early responsibilities was to oversee the transfer of a shipment of US tractors to the government. He ensured that the machines were in good working order, and that each was emblazoned with the now universally recognized AID logo of two hands clasped in partnership. The day before the tractors were to be delivered, dozens of Togolese gathered to look at the machines. Gutman noticed that several people were fixated on the AID emblems. Gutman asked a bystander what he thought they meant. Without hesitation the man replied, "Two whites congratulating one another on having pushed off these machines on Africans."

For Gutman, this raised an intriguing question: With AID's work taking place in Asia, Latin America, and Africa, why did the hands on the emblem look so Caucasian? He sent an inquiry to Washington asking why one of the hands couldn't be shaded. Two months later, he received a ten-page airgram that had been cleared by a dozen people. Gutman was informed that unfortunately it had been impossible for Washington to achieve a consensus regarding "hues and shadings."

Gutman also faced his share of challenges in dealing with the Togolese government. He called on the minister of health, a young French-trained physician and avowed Marxist. Gutman indicated that AID was eager to include Togo in a regional immunization effort. The minister immediately asked whether the vaccine had been tested in the United States. It had not. The minister queried whether AID was trying to use African children as guinea pigs. Gutman reassured the minister that the vaccines were safe.

Assuming the vaccines saved the lives of thousands of children, asked the minister, would the United States feed and clothe them? Would US assistance build schools and buy textbooks for this population boom? Gutman gently countered that the question of whether more Togolese children lived or died was of sufficient import that perhaps Togo's president should review the matter. Togo's president, Sylvanus Olympio, ultimately approved the vaccination campaign, but in doing so, argued like his minister that if the health plan worked, it would indeed demand an expansion of US assistance.

Back in Washington, Fowler Hamilton had quickly realized that his new agency had both far too many people and far too few. AID had been created from a mishmash of existing organizations, and Hamilton only had a month to select 6,500 civil servants to transfer to AID from the 17,500 employed by its predecessors.[8]

Hamilton and his staff had an enormous job not only in managing that transition, but in finding the right profile of staffers. Many of the foreign aid programs before AID had focused on technical issues in agriculture, and Hamilton noted that of the twenty-one mission directors he had inherited in Latin America, more than half were former county extension agents and Department of Agriculture staff.[9] Hamilton felt they were the "salt of the earth," but ill-equipped to deal with loans, infrastructure, and broad theories of economic development.

With AID shifting from a technical focus to overall country strategies, considerable disruption was inevitable. Yet, one disgruntled veteran of the technical programs decried the "fanciful contention that brilliant new policies, bright new administrators, and brand-new organization" would improve results.[10]

Never having been a colonial power, the United States had a relatively shallow talent pool of people with experience in the developing world. "The job that Fowler Hamilton had to do was to take this goddamned mess and try to make something of it," said William Gaud in characteristically colorful language.[11] Gaud added, "[W]e were just as green as grass, and we knew damn little about this business."

Living and working in the developing world of 1961 was not easy. One AID officer who took a position in Sierra Leone with his family not long after the agency was founded recalled being "a bit apprehensive" because the material he read on the country kept describing it as a "white man's graveyard."[12] In Vietnam, 40 percent of the AID staff visited the dispensary each month for treatment of illnesses ranging from dysentery to dengue fever.[13] "AID personnel must frequently live in environments of squalor, disease, and hardship," the Foreign Policy Association complained at the time, "and through it all they are expected to smile; to perform as trained economists, capable administrators, smooth diplomats, and shrewd politicians."[14]

Hamilton echoed those concerns, saying that he defied anyone to easily find candidates who would earn "a salary about equivalent to that of a fellow driving a beer truck in New York or Washington" to go to Central America to help establish free trade.[15]

General Lucius Clay, who had administered occupied Germany after World War II and was viewed as an influential conservative policy voice by President Kennedy, declared at the White House, "You ought to bring in businessmen."[16] Vice President Lyndon Johnson threw his weight behind this idea, saying that the fifty largest companies in the United States should send their best vice presidents to AID.[17] Defense Secretary Robert McNamara, who was a highly successful businessman in his own right, was cool to the idea. When asked, he said, "90 percent of the ones you get won't be any good at all."

Ignoring McNamara's advice, the administration launched a recruiting effort dubbed "Operation Tycoon." Operation Tycoon reached out to major US corporations to try and bring promising young business leaders to spend at least two years at AID, usually in the role of a mission director. After an intensive six-week training course in development economics and comparative cultures, the roughly thirty Operation Tycoon recruits were given a high-profile send-off by President Kennedy in the Rose Garden.[18]

At a later congressional hearing, Republican congressman Walter Judd of Minnesota, who had been a medical missionary in China, asked one of the Tycoon recruits, Jake Lingle, about the program.

"Mr. Lingle, I understand you're bringing in all these businessmen to run AID."

"That's right, sir," Lingle replied enthusiastically, "we're going to put it on a businesslike basis."

"I don't know if you know, Mr. Lingle, but I am a physician," responded the congressman, "and if I had a brain tumor, I would want a tumor specialist to remove it, not some businessman. You've got people who really know development, and you're firing them and bringing in people who know nothing about development."[19]

Although Operation Tycoon generated considerable positive press at the time, very few of its recruits stayed with the agency for any period of time.

Yet, the notion of being more "businesslike" was pervasive. Melbourne Spector, who was head of personnel at AID at the time, remembered one of his very first encounters with Fowler Hamilton. "Let me tell you how I'm going to run this agency," Fowler said. "I want every person working for AID throughout the world to keep a time sheet the way I do in my office in New York, as a Wall Street lawyer, and I want them all sent to me." Spector and the others exchanged worried glances.[20]

Hamilton's focus on accounting for time also featured prominently in a newspaper profile of him early in his tenure:

> His secretary made a tabulation of what he did in his first month on the job, accounting for every ten minutes, the way lawyers do in charging their clients. He attended ninety-six conferences, thirty-five official luncheons and dinners . . . He spent 259 hours on the job, a better than 9-hour-day average in twenty-eight working days, including Saturdays. For this he was paid $1,345 or $5.20 an hour which is low pay for a guy running a $2 billion business with 12,000 employees.[21]

Hamilton approached his work in such a lawyerly fashion that he took to referring to President Kennedy as "my client."[22] Hamilton, something of an insomniac, usually arrived at the office at six in the morning with half a dozen "dictatapes" of ideas and instructions that had come to him during the night.[23]

THE ALLIANCE ON THE BRINK

No issue on the foreign aid front in the early days was keeping staffers up later at night than the Alliance for Progress.

Posters appeared on every staff member's desk: "It Is Five Minutes to Midnight." There were constant demands from the White House for information, country strategy papers, and weekly progress reports. New staff immersed themselves in the writings of Walt Rostow and Argentine economist Raúl Prebisch.

"I would argue that no international development program with which I am familiar ever inspired such a high level of interest and enthusiasm at the outset," said Peter Askin, who joined the Latin America Bureau as assistant desk officer for Guatemala in 1962. "It is hard to fully describe the excitement, euphoria, and satisfaction that I felt at the time."[24]

In Latin America and elsewhere, AID was driving a combination of policy reforms; efforts to strengthen public administration; and investments in developing banks and credit unions, housing, and big infrastructure projects.[25] Most often, this was harnessed under broad industrialization plans designed to replace imports with domestic production. Many hoped that this recipe, when combined with measures like the spread of democracy, malaria eradication efforts, and land and labor reforms, would encourage stability while lifting the poor out of poverty.

Enthusiasm was not limited to Washington. The raw ambition of the Alliance for Progress appealed to a great many young leaders across South and Central America. Large numbers of economists from the region were brought to prestigious US universities like MIT, the University of Chicago, and Harvard to study under leading thinkers like Milton Friedman and Arnold Harberger through what were known as "participant training" programs. Many more students received training in economics and agronomy at local universities funded by the United States, and AID invested heavily in improving postsecondary education across the region.

The Alliance was pushing Latin American governments to formally plan and organize in ways that they largely had not in the past, and although proposed social reforms and infrastructure projects dominated the headlines, the accompanying investments in people and institutions were critical.

President Kennedy took to teasing Walt Rostow, saying that every time he met with a leader from Latin America they would invoke Rostow's concept of "take-off." It happened so frequently that staffers would literally time how long it took for a foreign leader to work a "take-off" reference into their meetings with Kennedy. As President Kennedy, smoking a cigar, emerged from a lunch with President Victor Paz Estenssoro of Bolivia, he quietly murmured to Rostow, "There goes the take-off again."[26]

However, the grand ambition of Punta del Este almost immediately crashed into hard political realities. Brazilian president Janio Quadros resigned just ten days after the Alliance for Progress was formally agreed upon, propelling his country into extended chaos.[27] Within a year, the governments of Argentina and Peru were toppled by military coups. With Brazil, Chile, Colombia, the Dominican Republic, and Costa Rica the highest-priority countries for the Alliance, turbulent politics in most of these states led to considerable difficulties for the development agenda.

The Kennedy administration was torn between its democratic ideals and the realpolitik of trying to oppose any further spread of communism in the region.

"We were concerned that the conditions in Latin America were so inequitable," said Lawrence Harrison, who joined AID's Latin America bureau in 1962, "that what happened in Cuba would naturally happen elsewhere."[28] Any government that was anti-communist was seen as an ally, which led to Washington backing authoritarians like the Somoza family in Nicaragua. (The eldest of the Somoza family had first risen to power in Nicaragua after a highly implausible 107,201- to 100-vote win in a presidential election.)[29] President Kennedy and his team quickly realized that creating systems that would broadly resist the temptations of communism was not synonymous with efforts to lift up the poor.[30]

Washington's reaction to the series of coups and juntas across Latin America was inconsistent: some were condemned, others tolerated, some actively encouraged, fueling concerns that the commitment to social justice embodied in the Alliance was being sacrificed on the altar of the Cold War.

Soviet publications in Spanish and Portuguese were quick to dismiss the Alliance as just another form of "Yankee imperialism," saying, "[N]o amount of propaganda can conceal the fact that Washington aid plays the same part, and pursues the same aims, as old-fashioned colonialist methods."[31]

The focus on Latin America reached a crescendo with the Cuban Missile Crisis in October 1962. The events that followed pushed the United States and the Soviet Union closer to a nuclear exchange than at any other point in history, and Kennedy's military advisers pushed hard for a quick military strike on the missile sites being constructed in the Cuban countryside.

President Kennedy instead decided to "quarantine" Cuba, demanding that the Soviets dismantle the sites and remove all offensive weapons from the island.

As Moscow remained defiant, US Strategic Forces were placed at DEFCON 2— the highest level of readiness seen since World War II. Fidel Castro, in a remarkably dangerous move, wrote to Soviet premier Nikita Khrushchev encouraging Moscow to launch a first-strike nuclear attack against the United States if Washington moved to invade Cuba—as it was considering at the time.

After a number of dramatic turns, the Soviets agreed to dismantle the missile sites and weapons and remove them from Cuba. The United States secretly agreed to remove missiles it had positioned in Turkey. Kennedy's resolve and creativity in defusing the Cuban Missile Crisis were seen both at home and abroad as a historic triumph.

But even after the crisis ebbed, concerns about security remained intense, leading the United States to fund the training of police across a whole series of developing countries. A particular focus was placed on issues like crowd control and efforts to infiltrate anti-communist groups under the broad mantra of these "public safety" programs.[32] AID and the CIA collaborated to train and equip police, eager to use local law enforcement as a source of intelligence and as a blunt force against leftist insurgencies.[33]

While never a huge part of the budget, AID's experience in police training led to a lasting black eye for the agency. Although the extent of AID's activities in public safety has still not been fully declassified, they included both important efforts to professionalize Latin American law enforcement agencies and serious abuses. The most notorious case involved Dan Mitrione, a former FBI officer and head of AID's public safety office in Uruguay.[34] Mitrione trained Uruguayan police, already well known for their abuses in countering violent leftist guerrillas. At a minimum, Mitrione observed and condoned torture in Uruguay.[35] Secondhand evidence suggests that Mitrione was directly engaged in recommending methods of torture. Mitrione was later kidnapped and killed by leftist guerrillas, and the military government responded by unleashing death squads in a series of reprisal killings.

The excesses of the public safety programs felt like a Cold War overreaction. The pull of Castro and communism in Latin America had been badly undercut by the Missile Crisis and its resolution. Soviet security guarantees seemed hollow, and although the ideological struggle between communism and capitalism remained intense in South and Central America, Moscow's influence in the region had crested. Congress ultimately banned the use of foreign assistance funds for training foreign police, a prohibition that remained in place for years.[36]

The White House was heavily engaged in almost every aspect of AID's work in Latin America. As David Bell said of JFK, "It almost seemed as though he wanted to know the progress in building each school, signing each loan."[37] There were a number of desk officers at AID and the State Department who were taken aback to be put on the phone directly with President Kennedy as he requested updates on everything from election results to crop harvests. "It was distressing to him," said Bell, "that the Alliance seemed to be as slow-moving as it was."

AID was trying to mount ambitious programs in Latin America in the middle of a major reorganization, a process that Arthur Schlesinger likened to "performing surgery on a man while he hauls a trunk upstairs."[38] Schlesinger noted that the president grew "exceedingly impatient," as AID worked through repeated assessment missions and feasibility studies. Some of this stemmed from the natural disruption of new personnel and a new organizational chart. But Fowler Hamilton's limited development experience and the maze of standards and requirements imposed on AID by Congress through the new Foreign Assistance Act of 1961 did not help.

Guatemala offers a good example of the mixed results of AID's work during this period. David Jickling recalls the talented cohort of fifty to seventy young people who were sent to a US university, Loyola in Chicago, for training.[39] "They often were schoolteachers, young bright people who often had been studying in secondary school in another town and had come back to the village," said Jickling, "These were the potential leaders." Many came back from studying abroad highly enthusiastic and eager for social progress only to grow frustrated with life under a highly repressive military government.

AID had viewed these young people as ideal change agents, but many of them were targeted by the military government because they were regarded as threats. AID had not only trained the Loyola students; it had likely trained some of the police who abducted and killed them.

But other work made a lasting impact. In Guatemala's case, AID's focus on developing the country's road system and providing agricultural extension services had a ripple effect across the economy that lasts to this day. Small farmers began to escape the trap of only producing low-value subsistence crops, such as corn and beans, and moved into planting high-value fruits, vegetables, and coffee, gaining access to export markets in the process.

Because of road improvements, crops reached urban centers, the national airport, and the country's major port more rapidly. AID began this work in the 1960s, and it was instrumental in building links from Guatemala's highland Indian communities to East Coast suburban consumers in the United States.

In Brazil—a flagship effort for the Alliance—Donor Lion of AID cabled back to headquarters about the agency's work in northeastern Brazil, the poorest part of that country: "The program attacks the underlying structural, economic, and institutional problems which underlie the social tensions and endemic poverty of the sugar zone of Northeast Brazil. Almost six million people inhabit this zone, or about one out of every fifteen Brazilians. It reflects many of the basic themes we have been stressing—self-help, rural and agricultural modernization, human resources strengthening." Lion noted with pride that AID staff were the "prime movers and the basic ideological and conceptual contributors to the program," yet "it is considered (and rightly), by the Brazilians, as a Brazilian program."[40]

Yet across Latin America, Kennedy's vision of growing democracy and social justice remained blunted by the hold of military governments, in part because the United States never fully came to terms with the class and power structures that kept these governments in place.

INTO AFRICA

AID's involvement in Africa started at almost zero. For much of the 1950s, American diplomatic representation on the continent was run out of offices in London or Paris rather than embassies on the ground.[41] The State Department did not establish an Africa bureau until 1957, and only about 3 percent of US assistance was directed to the region in 1960.[42] There were more American Foreign Service officers in West Germany than on the entire continent. As Arthur Schlesinger argued, with the exception of Liberia, which was founded by former US slaves, "Our very sense of the continent below the Mediterranean was vague and dim. No historic ties bound us to black Africa except the slave trade, and here we had done our best to repress the memory."[43]

Kennedy's term began with African leaders still reeling from the assassination of Patrice Lumumba, the first elected prime minister of Congo. Coming less than seven months after that country's independence, the murder was widely attributed to Belgium or Belgian-backed separatists. It would come out years after the fact that President Eisenhower had greenlit an earlier CIA assassination attempt on Lumumba using poisoned toothpaste that was never implemented.[44] For Africans, it was unclear whether the new American president would continue to embrace national independence movements or side with his European allies instead.

"There was no practical alternative to providing technical and economic assistance to the newly independent countries," said Maurice Williams, who played a wide variety of roles in AID over the years. "[H]ow else could an advanced country like the U.S. have established meaningful diplomatic relations with them without expanding their opportunities for self-betterment and advancement?"[45] And while early US assistance to Africa was plagued by mistakes born of unfamiliarity, Williams argued that early investments in health and education were of considerable enduring value.

One of the president's very first appointments at the State Department was G. Mennen "Soapy" Williams, whom Kennedy tapped to run the Africa bureau. AID, realizing that it would likely be engaged with Africa for years to come, trained a corps of officers, most of whom already had proficiency in French or Portuguese, to specialize in Africa.[46] The United States, eager to send the message that it still supported independence movements, sent gifts to new states as they emerged, such as a mobile health van to Togo and a $100,000 pledge to help construct an Institute for Foreign Affairs in Nigeria.[47] When Soapy Williams was criticized in the European press for saying that "Africa was for the Africans," Kennedy defended him while simultaneously poking fun of the Europeans: "I don't know who else Africa would be for."[48]

The greatest asset that the administration brought to the table was Kennedy himself. "African leaders flowed through the White House in what appeared an unending stream," observed Arthur Schlesinger, "eleven in 1961, ten in 1962 and in 1963, when the supply was nearing the point of exhaustion, seven."[49]

African leaders were impressed with Kennedy's willingness to talk to them as political equals. "It was astonishing to see how he could establish a rapport," said David Bell. "President Kennedy made it evident to each and all of these persons—I don't believe he ever had a failure along these lines—that he understood the problems they confronted, was sympathetic to them, and wanted the United States to be as helpful as possible."[50]

As Schlesinger said, the African leaders tended to leave the meetings with "a conviction that Kennedy's America, even if it could not do everything at once, was basically with them."[51]

Tony Schwarzwalder, a loan officer at AID working on Africa projects at the time, recalls sitting down with senior staffers trying to determine which African countries were poised for potential success based on Rostow's stages of development theory.[52] Some of the countries they agreed to target for fast-track economic development included Mauritania, Liberia, and Gabon. "But it was strictly based on raw materials," recalled Schwarzwalder. "Mauritania had bauxite. Liberia had rubber. There was not a single appreciation for human resources, politics, or the transition from colonialism."

In Guinea, rich with bauxite, the political tug-of-war for resources led to a whole series of failed international efforts. The Dutch provided forty thousand prefabricated houses that sat ruined at the airport. Another European donor financed Mercedes trucks that were abandoned because they didn't provide spare parts. The Soviets built a radio station in Guinea to broadcast to all of West Africa, but the signal didn't even reach the capital of Conakry.[53]

No situation was more emblematic of the twentieth-century scramble for Africa than that of Ghana. Ghana was the first African state to achieve independence, in 1957. It was led by Kwame Nkrumah who, along with Julius Nyerere in Tanzania and Jomo Kenyatta in Kenya, represented the bright, charismatic voice of African independence and pan-Africanism. Nkrumah's backstory was compelling. From modest roots, he had worked his way through college in Pennsylvania, where he became fixated on politics, race relations, and the struggle for independence.

As economists Anne Krueger and Vernon Ruttan note, Ghana was one of the best-positioned African states at independence. "Its physical infrastructure and educational establishment were reasonably well-developed, and its per capita income was the highest in black Africa."[54] Ghana exported considerable minerals, timber, and cocoa. However, Nkrumah was a dedicated socialist who felt that capitalism was "too complicated a system for a newly independent nation."[55]

Kennedy met with Nkrumah at the White House in early March 1961. The crown jewel of Nkrumah's vision for his country's economy was a massive dam on the Volta River to power a bauxite smelting plant that would transform Ghana into a major aluminum exporter and provide cheap energy to the public. He pushed Kennedy to support the project.

In July 1961 Kennedy wrote to Nkrumah that he was "delighted" to back the Volta project, a decision clearly based more on foreign policy imperatives and US business interests than the dam's potential to drive development.[56] However, Nkrumah's increasingly erratic and authoritarian behavior, as well as his continued overtures to both the Soviet Union and China, had Kennedy rethinking the commitment. Kennedy's father called his son to complain: "What the hell are you up to with that Communist?"[57] The CIA speculated that Nkrumah was at risk of becoming "an African Castro."[58] The deal was on the verge of collapse.

Enter the young Queen Elizabeth II. Eager to maintain British influence, she made a high-profile trip to Ghana despite intense concern from her own parliament about security in the capital of Accra. Elizabeth was greeted joyously by Ghanaians, and her trip was widely viewed as a triumph.

Immediately after the queen's trip concluded, British prime minister Harold Macmillan telephoned JFK. "I have risked my Queen, you must risk your money." Kennedy vowed that he would match the queen's "brave contribution."[59]

Despite the warning signs, the Kennedy administration and AID, working with the World Bank and the UK, pushed forward on the Volta dam. However, the administration included a notable proviso: The American company Kaiser Aluminum and Chemical Corporation, which was contracted to build the aluminum smelting plant, would be granted highly favorable electric rates for thirty years, with an option to renew these rates for another twenty.[60] Kaiser was also granted a ten-year tax holiday. The Ghanaians agreed to the terms.

When the dam was completed in 1965, it created the largest man-made body of water in the world, covering 3.6 percent of Ghana's total territory.[61] The dam has helped drive substantial industrial development in Ghana over time, with companies attracted to the relatively low power rates. But the government also displaced about eighty thousand people during the dam's construction, and little consideration was given to the project's environmental impact.

A *Washington Post* report from 1980 found that thirteen years after its completion, the dam was generating 90 percent of the electricity in Ghana, but 70 percent of the total output was consumed by the smelting plant, leaving most citizens reliant on more expensive electricity generated by imported fuel.[62] Kaiser Aluminum, rather than relying on bauxite from Ghana to supply the smelter, instead imported most of its bauxite from Jamaica before shipping out the finished aluminum. Job creation from the project was modest.

Under Nkrumah, Ghana went from having almost $2 billion in foreign exchange reserves when he came to power to being more than $1.5 billion in debt. While on an overseas trip to China and North Vietnam, Nkrumah was overthrown by a military coup in 1966. It would be almost another quarter-century before lasting civilian government would reemerge in Ghana.

Hariadene Johnson recalls working for AID in Ghana at the time. She said the view of many of the British expatriates in Ghana was "that somehow the U.S. had done them wrong by pressuring them to turn loose the African colonies before they were really ready for self-government."[63] Nkrumah's tenure gave them plenty of ammunition with which to make their case. "You learn how to self-govern by doing it," Johnson countered. "[Y]ou make your mistakes, and you learn from them."

ASIA AT A CROSSROADS

The lion's share of AID investments under Kennedy continued to be directed to Asia. As a memo from this period to AID's leadership argued, "If the Indian sub-continent were subverted and taken over by Communists, this fact could decisively swing most of Asia, Africa and Latin America into the Communist camp on the grounds that 'the wave of the future' points to Peking. Hitler's early successes had a similar effect in Europe."[64]

India relied on both US and Soviet assistance during this period. Soviet support to India focused on industrialization and large, centrally controlled projects like the Bhilai Steel Plant. US programs took a different tack as they encouraged a fundamental economic reorientation in both India and Pakistan.

India and Pakistan viewed capitalism warily. They were suspicious of foreign investment, and were eager to maintain governmental control of their economies.[65]

The Kennedy administration significantly ramped up its commitment to India, dedicating more than seven times the aid that had been offered during the Eisenhower years. Kennedy also appointed John Kenneth Galbraith, a close confidant and well-regarded economist, as his ambassador to New Delhi. Sam Butterfield of the agency observed, "Within AID, India aid was one of the glamour programs of the 1960s."[66] India seemed perfectly aligned with Walt Rostow's vision of a country where a commitment to reform, an infusion of aid, and efforts to build institutions could produce a dramatic economic lift-off.

American advisers in India and Pakistan pushed for the governments to loosen their grip on the private sector, particularly in agriculture. Many government officials in the region were disdainful of agriculture, seeing it as a backwards sector that was largely fit for peasants. AID argued that invigorating agriculture was not only key to employment, but to feeding populations that were growing with alarming speed. AID made the case that farming could be a genuine engine of growth if the governments were willing to relinquish some of their tight central control and embrace more-open trade. Job number one for AID officials during this period was to cultivate an emerging core of reformers within the two governments who shared this worldview.

The efforts in India and Pakistan were deeply complicated by the hostility between the two countries and the considerable unease, particularly in India, of being seen as reliant on outside support. "Foreign aid is as unpopular in the countries that receive it as in the countries that give it," India's ambassador to the United States, B. K. Nehru, observed.[67]

The rivalry between India and Pakistan following their bitter split in 1947 and conflict over Kashmir shaded almost all assistance efforts to these two countries. Both countries viewed US assistance to the other as a measure of bad faith. Senior staffers at the White House, AID, and the State Department were usually viewed as falling within pro-India or pro-Pakistan camps.

But as a memo to David Bell during this era argued, despite qualms about American policy in Vietnam, neither India nor Pakistan had joined in "accusing America of imperialism and new-colonialism."[68] And while relations between Washington and these two capitals were never easy, "almost all conceivable changes could only be for the worse." India and Pakistan were increasingly positioned to make important gains, but key political battles clearly lay ahead in both countries, as well as in Washington, if this progress was to be fully realized.

AID's most dynamic program in its early days may well have been in Taiwan. Taiwan's largely agrarian economy and private sector were relatively undeveloped at the time, with only two significant exports: rice and sugar.[69] But Taiwan was poised at a unique moment. As author Michael Pillsbury argued, Taiwanese president Chiang Kai-shek believed strongly that reconquering China would require transforming Taiwan into an economic "showcase" with the industrial might needed to take on Chairman Mao Zedong and the communists.[70]

Starting in 1960, and then continuing under AID after 1961, the United States launched an intensive dialogue with Taipei on economic policy. The United States offered Taiwan $55 million in initial grants if, and only if, it was willing to undertake sweeping reforms on nineteen points confidentially conveyed to the government, including the setting of realistic exchange rates, the elimination of subsidies and price controls, tax reform, an emphasis on promoting exports, and a general push to improve and professionalize public administration.[71]

Taiwanese minister of economic affairs, K. Y. Yin, while initially cool toward capitalism, began to view trade and industrialization as essential to Taiwan's struggle.[72] Yin, with US backing, created a series of quasi-independent institutions, including the Industrial Development and Investment Center and the China Development Corporation. These institutions would direct how AID funds would be spent and were staffed by a mixture of Taiwanese and US officials. AID officers took part in board meetings of these organizations, engaged in a lively debate about economic policy, and, along with their like-minded Taiwanese colleagues, effectively squeezed out opponents of economic reform.[73]

Many of these Taiwanese officials had also studied in the United States, again underscoring the importance of participant training programs in shaping the ground for reform.

Taiwan launched an aggressive land reform initiative, spreading productive assets more widely. The government, with US backing, also developed several export processing zones. Initial efforts were so successful that additional zones were soon added.[74] Some reform measures were simple but powerful, such as encouraging Taiwan to set prices for rail services and utilities that were high enough that these enterprises could become solvent.[75]

US investments in Taiwan were large. Between 1951 and 1965 the United States pumped $1.5 billion of aid into Taiwan's economy. US funding constituted almost 50 percent of Taiwan's public investment during that period, as the country rapidly built out its infrastructure and extricated the government from the economy.[76] It has to be noted that the United States was willing to accept working with a military dictatorship in Taiwan, and it never stressed the importance of democracy in Taiwan the way it did (however unevenly) through the Alliance for Progress.

Taiwan's gross national product leapt from $900 million in the early 1950s to $2.4 billion in 1965.[77] One independent estimate calculated that it would have taken Taiwan's economy an additional thirty years to hit that level of GNP without US assistance.[78] Perhaps the most telling sign of Taiwan's success: By 1963 AID's leadership decided that it needed to put in place clear criteria for winding down its program, which was completed by 1965.[79] Taiwan would remain a key security and trading partner for the United States moving forward.

Michael Pillsbury makes the case that the US success in Taiwan can be attributed to high-level ownership in both Washington and Taipei, and the important role of Western-trained technical experts in influential roles.[80] But more than anything, Taiwan would seem to demonstrate that successful development isn't formulaic. The policy prescriptions were sound, but they were only advanced because of an adroit understanding of how to push reform through an inherently political process. Chiang Kai-shek viewed economic development as a strategic imperative, the United States made long-term investments in people and not just infrastructure, and both AID and the government were willing to work through hard choices as they occurred.

If Taiwan deserves to be remembered as a signature investment by AID during its formative years, so does Vietnam, but for entirely different, and far less salutary, reasons.

Just days after Kennedy was sworn in as president, Walt Rostow, who had been appointed as JFK's deputy special assistant for national security affairs, turned his attention to the still-simmering conflict in Vietnam. There were already about one thousand American forces deployed to that country, and concern was growing that Northern communist forces would overwhelm South Vietnam.

Rostow, who was staunchly and hawkishly anti-communist, was particularly taken with a memo that had been prepared by Colonel Edward Lansdale for the incoming administration. Lansdale was unconventional as military officers went, and his reputation had been bolstered by his involvement with a successful counterinsurgency campaign in the Philippines. Rostow appreciated Lansdale's fresh thinking on how to deal with Vietnam and the fact that Lansdale had clearly immersed himself in Vietnam's politics and culture. (Lansdale had been the basis for one of the more-heroic characters portrayed in *The Ugly American*.)

Lansdale was invited to a senior-level meeting at the White House on January 28, 1961, along with key officials from the State Department, Department of Defense, and AID. Two key decisions emerged. First, Kennedy wanted to "draw a line in the sand" in Vietnam by opposing the spread of communism. Second, the administration would adopt Lansdale's counterinsurgency campaign concept.[81]

Lansdale believed that ramped-up economic and military assistance needed to flow directly to Vietnamese villagers in the countryside. He felt that villagers not only needed to see the tangible benefits of assistance, they also needed a cause to believe in—the democratization and independence of Vietnam.

"It appealed to President Kennedy very much," David Bell explained. "President Kennedy and his brother saw the situation in the less-developed countries in most parts of the world as a highly dynamic, indeed a revolutionary situation in which, if the United States was to be influential, we had to influence the rising generation of leadership."[82] Adopting an assistance-driven counterinsurgency approach was a major shift for AID, and few fully thought through its implications.

AID established a new Office of Rural Affairs in Vietnam headed by Rufus Phillips (who had been recommended by Lansdale), with Bert Fraleigh, a career AID officer, as his deputy. Phillips was a close associate of Lansdale and had spent time both in the US military and the CIA, and his appointment was emblematic of a period when the lines between intelligence, military, and aid operations were often cloudy.

Phillips recalled his first interaction with the AID bureaucracy in Saigon, an experience he found so foreign that he likened it to stepping off the moon. "Everything was centralized, from the top down. Not only did they appear incapable of understanding the bottom-up idea of village development, but they seemed to perceive it as a threat to their own programs."[83] Before the creation of the Rural Affairs office, only three of AID's 110 staffers were posted outside of the capital.[84] In essence, from that point forward, there were two very distinct AID programs in Vietnam: one focused on traditional assistance in the capital, and one an unorthodox approach to working in the countryside.

Rural Affairs officers, all volunteers, and American military advisers were inserted at the province level across Vietnam, often living under the most basic conditions in the hamlets they were trying to assist.

The "strategic hamlets" were provided with barbed wire, bamboo spikes, and wooden towers to harden their defenses. At the provincial level, a Rural Affairs officer, US military representative, and the Vietnamese province chief jointly determined how best to direct assistance, with a heavy emphasis placed on improving agriculture, since it was so central to the livelihoods of most Vietnamese.

A particularly popular program gave farmers surplus corn, Yorkshire piglets, and basic supplies to build pigpens. The pigs were considerably larger and healthier than the varieties common to Vietnam, and even the North Vietnamese communists adopted a similar effort seeing how well it worked in the South.[85] The AID officer in charge of the effort, Harvey Neese, was affectionately known in the countryside as "Mr. Pig."[86] At a subsequent presentation for the National Security Council, a senior AID official noted with pride that the average market weight of a hog in Vietnam had soared from 130 to 220 pounds.[87]

Across Vietnam, roads, ports, and schools were built, agricultural extension services expanded, and public health services considerably modernized.[88]

But the Rural Affairs office was buffeted from all directions.

In Washington, numerous senior officials at the Departments of State and Defense simply did not see utility in working with the villagers. A February 1962 State Department memo to Rostow argued that any civic action undertaken should be in the form of packages "involving little or no local effort," and complaining that the Vietnamese only wanted things done by "American machines" (which had not been the experience of Rural Affairs officers).[89] The same memo argued that AID should drop its focus on long-term economic development and that the assistance program should be oriented almost completely toward directing support for the war, and be "run by a military officer answering directly to the military commander." Both US and Vietnamese military hierarchies continued to view the conflict largely as a matter of killing as many Viet Cong as possible.

Rufus Phillips argued persuasively that although the White House had embraced a counterinsurgency strategy, "Neither the new secretary of defense, Robert McNamara, nor the regular military brass understood Lansdale's emphasis on a people-first approach."[90] As Phillips, still very much a Lansdale loyalist, contended, "[T]he official American view of the war missed its single most influential component—a South Vietnamese political cause worth fighting for."[91]

Princeton Lyman, who had a distinguished career at both AID and the State Department, wrote in a classified memo at the time, "We still saw ourselves as the troops marching through conquered territory during and after WWII, handing out Hershey bars to the cheers of the local population. So, the thought was that as long as we handed out enough 'candy bars'—schools, hospitals, clinics, etc.—at some point everyone would come out and cheer."[92] Washington was trying to achieve results without understanding the underlying structural changes needed to make them possible.

The United States simply could not sort out Vietnamese national politics. President Ngo Dinh Diem remained inflexible, treating potential allies in the fight against communism with a heavy hand. Diem's refusal to share power with the country's large Buddhist population triggered growing political upheaval that sapped important momentum from the military campaign. A number of the key players around Diem were corrupt and loathed by the public. The Kennedy administration vacillated between showering Diem with praise (Vice President Johnson had called Diem the "Winston Churchill of Asia" during a visit to Saigon) and contemplating pushing him out of power.[93]

Splits among senior US officials regarding the situation sharpened to the point where at a 1963 meeting on Vietnam with Secretary of State Rusk, Secretary of Defense McNamara, and other major players, President Kennedy asked two of his briefers, "The two of you did visit the same country, didn't you?"[94]

As David Bell scribbled in his notebook during a meeting with US Special Forces: "Weapons, gadgets, and guns can't substitute for a cause and a program."[95]

THE OTHER END OF PENNSYLVANIA AVENUE

AID's honeymoon with Congress after its creation was short-lived. While all agreed that economic development was a long-term endeavor, there was little patience with AID on Capitol Hill. One of the agency's most implacable opponents was Congressman Otto Passman, who represented Louisiana's 5th District and was sometimes referred to as "Otto the Terrible" by frustrated administration officials.[96]

Passman, who chaired the subcommittee on foreign aid appropriations, called foreign aid "the greatest give-away in history," and claimed it was the first time that a nation had tried to achieve security by sacrificing its wealth.[97] Passman delighted in tormenting agency officials. He kept the head of one of AID's regional bureaus on the stand for approximately one hundred hours of questioning, and he regularly struck from the record statements by witnesses that he thought were too friendly to foreign aid.[98]

When Passman made a two-day visit to Saigon, the AID mission estimated that it spent 328 man-days preparing papers and making arrangements for his trip.[99] In South Korea, Passman was noted for his regular brothel visits when in Seoul.[100]

While Passman was the most notorious thorn in the administration's side on foreign assistance, he was far from the only source of congressional pressure. Many in Congress expressed dismay that aid programs were causing too much money to flow out of the United States, which pushed AID to ensure that more and more of its money was spent in the United States as it tried to promote development abroad. "We tied our aid," said William Gaud. "[W]e required that the money be spent here. As a result, well over 90 percent, 94 to 95 percent, of all of our funds are spent here in the United States."[101]

This also meant that US assistance dollars didn't go as far. "If Pakistan needs steel and we are financing it on a loan, instead of buying that steel from Japan or Italy or Belgium where it is cheaper," explained Gaud, "it is bought here in the United States, sometimes at a premium of 30 or 40 or 50 percent." The aid program was made less effective, but domestic constituencies were placated to a degree.

AID also began to rely far more on loans than grants to aid recipients. In the early 1950s, loans only made up about 10 percent of assistance; by the early 1960s that figure approached 60 percent.[102] Although most of these were loans below market rates with lengthy grace periods, it still meant that eventually substantial sums flowed back into the US treasury. Kennedy felt that these highly concessional loans were a more dignified (and politically palatable) vehicle for engaging the developing world.

The number of countries receiving US assistance leapt from forty-two in 1950 to ninety-five by 1962.[103] However, half of the total assistance was directed to just six countries.

At times, AID gave its critics easy fodder. In 1962, AID put out a contract for one thousand television sets, powered by battery, that could be used for education in remote villages lacking electricity. But as author Jacob Rubin observed, "The coupling of these two words, 'jungle' and 'television,' lent itself to almost endless ridicule for AID."[104]

AID's deputy, Frank Coffin, complained in a commencement address in Nebraska that Congress wanted the impossible from foreign assistance. "We expect it to 'buy friends.' We expect it to produce favorable votes by all countries we help on all issues in the United Nations. We expect it to cause all nations we help to sever all relations with the Sino-Soviet bloc." Coffin's summation: "This I submit is too large an order to expect from 7/10s of 1 per cent of our gross national product."[105]

In a speech before the Economic Club of New York, President Kennedy declared, "I would like to cut out foreign aid. It is very unpopular," adding, "But I must say I am reminded of Mr. Robert Frost's motto about not taking down a fence until you know why it is put up."[106]

TRANSITION AND TRAGEDY

William Gaud recalled going to several White House meetings with Fowler Hamilton and Teodoro Moscoso to discuss the Alliance for Progress which "didn't work out well at all."[107] Gaud was alarmed when the conversation degenerated into minutiae, with Moscoso complaining that he did not have enough secretaries and contract officers. "The rest of us, I may say, were pretty goddamned fed up," commented Gaud.

Hamilton was also not well served by his deputy, Frank Coffin. Hamilton preferred to be the face of AID and leave its management to others. But Coffin, also a lawyer, often obsessed about details to the point of paralysis.[108] As David Bell observed from his perch at the White House, Coffin did not leave the Kennedy team with an image of AID as "a hard driving, fast moving, effectively managed enterprise."[109] Just the opposite, in fact.

Bell thought Hamilton was miscast from the start and suggested that President Kennedy made a strategic blunder by not appointing someone of greater stature to the post.[110]

Fowler Hamilton, well aware of a mounting whisper campaign against him directed by the White House staff, resigned before he could be fired—just fifteen months into his tenure. He returned to his law practice in New York. On November 17, 1962, he received a thank-you note from President Kennedy for his service, remarkable only for its brevity and impersonal nature.

Kennedy was again faced with deciding who would run the US foreign assistance program, a role that had seen such high turnover since the Marshall Plan that Soviet propagandists highlighted it as a weakness of the West.[111]

Kennedy approached his budget director, David Bell, about running AID.[112] After contemplating several days, Bell accepted the position, with his appointment announced on November 28, 1962.[113] Bell was self-deprecating about his credentials, "Certainly, I could make no case that I was less qualified than the ordinary government person for this job."[114] He did however allow that he was the first person to run the program who had both an academic background in the topic and direct experience in developing countries.[115]

Bell was a shrewd administrator from the outset. He commissioned a detailed analysis of Taiwan's rapid economic progress and the role of US assistance in that breakthrough. He brought in top-notch economists to run AID's policy shop—first, Gus Ranis, a well-known Yale economist, and later, Hollis Chenery from Harvard. He set aside one Saturday morning each month for his leadership team to meet with economists from around the country to debate policy.[116] He pushed the agency to better evaluate its programs and determine the proper conditions for graduating countries from aid. Princeton Lyman said of Bell, "He fostered an intellectual atmosphere that has never been equaled."[117]

Not long after his appointment, Bell received a sly, short note from President Kennedy: "I'm sure that my troubles with AID are over, and I hope that yours never begin."[118]

In January 1963, at President Kennedy's behest, General Lucius Clay launched a major review of AID. Arthur Schlesinger described the thinking behind the review in a nutshell, saying JFK "resorted to the familiar device of a blue-ribbon panel of bonded conservatives set up to cast a presumably cold eye on the aid effort and then to recommend its continuance as essential."[119]

It was Kennedy's hope that the Clay Committee, as it came to be known, would help cut off what looked like an impending assault on the AID budget, led by Congressman Otto Passman. Bell was uneasy with the Clay Committee, feeling that Kennedy was guilty of a "certain naiveté" in thinking that a "consensus could be formed on foreign aid if only enough energy and brains were put into the effort."[120]

Bell and his team worked closely with the committee and viewed getting its more conservative members to embrace a largely constructive tone as a significant accomplishment.[121]

The topline message of the Clay Committee report, when it was released in March of 1963, was positive. "It is our belief that, sharpened up, tightened and properly carried out, there is no greater return than the return that is obtained from our foreign aid programs," said General Clay.[122]

The report leveled some fair criticism at the program, with Clay arguing that some of the countries where AID was working "are either not ready to move forward economically or the amount of aid which we are providing is not really sufficient to move them in that direction."[123] The report also decried the tendency to use aid as gifts to foreign heads of state and as a gambit to head off Soviet influence.[124]

The report argued, and David Bell very much agreed, that Washington needed to be far tougher in demanding reforms and results from recipient countries, even in cases where that might create tensions. However, the policy recommendations in the report were quickly overshadowed by a tempest about the aid budget. Both the report and General Clay in his briefing were rather ambiguous with regard to their position on funding. Reporters interpreted Clay's comments as advocating a $500 million reduction in foreign assistance.

Seizing on the opportunity, Otto Passman declared that he was "surprised and pleased" by the report and vowed to champion its aim to cut aid.[125]

The morning after Clay's press conference, when suggestions that Clay wanted the budget cut by $500 million appeared in the newspapers, Bell received a "furious call" from President Kennedy, who was "astonished and angry that the committee had recommended a cutback."[126] And even though Bell and Clay later flew to Hyannis Port and got Clay to issue a solid endorsement of the aid budget, the damage was done.[127]

Congress hammered the president's foreign assistance account. The president had requested $4.9 billion in funding for 1964, but ultimately only $3.2 billion was approved. It was easily the largest cut in the history of the aid program, taking the budget down to 1958 levels.

Business Week called the budget "the President's worst drubbing by the House."[128] Worryingly for the administration, it lost a number of traditional supporters of the aid program in the battle. When Teodoro Moscoso arrived in Peru after a key budget vote, Peru's president asked him if the United States was backing out of the Alliance for Progress.[129]

"Should we scrap the Alliance for Progress, which is our best answer to the threat of communism in this hemisphere?" asked an aggrieved President Kennedy. "Should we deny help to India, the largest free power in Asia, as she seeks to strengthen herself against communist China? Do we wish to dismantle our joint defenses in Korea, Taiwan, Pakistan, Iran, Turkey, and Greece, countries along the very rim of communist power?"[130]

Senator Gale McGee, a Democrat from Wyoming and confidant of Kennedy, conducted his own review of AID during this period. He observed that many of the agency's "false starts, miscalculations, and mistakes" were perhaps the inevitable result of America's lack of experience and "the hasty manner" in which programs had been established.[131] A joke started making the rounds in Washington that the constant scrutiny of aid programs was akin to someone who constantly removed all the dirt from a plant to see how well its roots were growing.[132]

Walt Rostow wrote a memo to David Bell in the fall of 1963 wondering how to get back on track at a time when "there is still in the country, if not in Congress, the notion that we are lonely suckers in the aid business, carrying the white man's burden alone."[133] Rostow noted that liberal support for AID had eroded in Congress in part because of the military coups in Latin America, creating growing sentiment to "break AID into fragments."

Rostow took a long view. He pointed out that as a result of US prodding, Europe, Japan, Australia, New Zealand, and Israel had all become new foreign assistance donors.[134] He also argued that the process of political modernization in Latin America was naturally uneven, and that "we may have to take a certain amount of military government without panic and hair-pulling as part of an historical sequence whose main trend has been, on the whole, in the right direction." His proposed solution: getting the president to make the case that foreign aid was part of a unified national security strategy.

The idea of a unified approach to national security was not proving easy in Vietnam, where US ambassador Henry Cabot Lodge had become increasingly fed up with President Diem. At one point, a clearly disgruntled Lodge complained, "They have not done anything I asked. Why should I keep asking?"[135] Lodge pushed hard to have US assistance suspended to bring greater pressure on the government.

Vietnamese generals began plotting a coup to depose Diem, with the CIA and Ambassador Lodge enthusiastic about its prospects. The White House was deeply ambivalent about such a move, wanting to ensure that Diem would not be harmed if he was ousted. In a confused back-and-forth over a weekend, with many key players left out of the loop, the White House deferred to Lodge's judgment about moving against Diem. Lodge eagerly took the mixed signals as a green light.

On November 1, 1963, Vietnamese generals toppled South Vietnam's first elected government. After their capture at a Catholic church, Diem and his brother were stabbed and shot to death by rebel military officers as they were transported in the back of an armored personnel carrier.

The fallout from the coup and murder of the two men was far-reaching. By having directly supported the coup, the United States found itself more vested than ever before in Vietnam. Instead of creating greater stability in the government, the coup triggered a long struggle for power between rival military factions.

The coup brought the efforts of the Rural Affairs office to a halt. The generals who had engineered the coup did not favor aid at the hamlet level, and paramilitary outfits protecting many of the villages were disbanded. A new AID mission director also arrived in Saigon and insisted that all programming again be run out of the capital. The Viet Cong began attacking the suddenly vulnerable villages.

Just days after the coup, President Kennedy took several minutes to dictate his thoughts about the events in Vietnam into a tape recorder. "I feel we must bear a good deal of responsibility for it," said Kennedy of the coup. The president ruefully observed that he should not have given his consent to Lodge without having more closely consulted the Pentagon.[136]

As Kennedy spoke, his young son, John Jr., appeared at his knee. Just shy of his third birthday, John Jr.'s voice is small, but clear, on the recording. The president briefly diverted from the weight of world affairs to quiz his son about the seasons.[137]

Returning to his thoughts as John Jr. played, President Kennedy speculated as to whether the public would soon turn on the new government "as oppressive and undemocratic." And Kennedy lamented of the late President Diem, "The way he was killed made it particularly abhorrent."

Just eighteen days later, on November 22, 1963, a sniper's bullet barked out in Dallas, Texas, killing President Kennedy. The assassination was shocking and shattering, and it cast America and much of the world into despair. The bright promise of the new frontier had been extinguished in a moment.

Vice President Lyndon Johnson had been thrust into the presidency under the worst possible circumstances. Johnson delayed moving into the White House for an extra day because Jackie Kennedy wanted to hold a reception for the many Latin America heads of state who attended the funeral. As the presidents and prime ministers went by to shake hands with Mrs. Kennedy, she said to each, "Jack loved Latin America. Jack loved Latin America."[138]

David Bell marveled that Kennedy, born into wealth and aristocracy, was instinctively on the side of the poor around the globe.[139] Said Bell of JFK: "It seemed to me that sometimes he acted as though the problems elsewhere in the world were more challenging, more interesting, more difficult, more worthy of attention than most of the problems in the United States, which was, after all, wealthy, strong, and secure."[140]

In Guinea, President Ahmed Sékou Touré declared, "I have lost my only true friend in the outside world." The African magazine *Transition* grieved the loss of Kennedy, noting, "His death leaves us unprepared and in the darkness."[141]

Gordon Evans of AID recalled traveling deep into the forests of the Ashanti region of Ghana after Kennedy's assassination.[142] Evans called upon a lesser chief in the smoky interior of his large adobe hut. Evans spoke to the chief through an interpreter. The first thing the chief did was to stand up with all of the fifteen or twenty villagers present and declare, "We shall have two minutes of silence in the memory of American President John F. Kennedy."

Robert Nooter of AID remembered that when he first arrived at his post in Uruguay, graffiti proclaiming "*Yanqui fuera,*" or "Yankee Go Home," was ubiquitous. Yet, when Kennedy was killed, there was an enormous outpouring of sympathy. Uruguayans formed a lengthy line outside his home to pay their respects. "That moment changed the atmosphere about the United States more than anything that I can think of," said Nooter. "We were no longer the Yankee oppressor. We were now wounded and vulnerable ourselves."[143]

3

Larger than Life

AFTER THE DIRGE

The image of Lyndon Johnson being sworn into the presidency aboard *Air Force One*, standing next to Jackie Kennedy blank-faced with shock, remains seared in America's national consciousness. For Johnson, who had so long yearned to be president, it was an almost unimaginable way to achieve the position he had always wanted.

Even amid the outpouring of grief and the frenetic scramble of transition, President Johnson was quick to get to work. Foreign policy—an area in which JFK had evinced little trust in Johnson—would be an intense and unsettled focus of his presidency from its first day to its last.

Less than two days after the Kennedy assassination, with numerous heads of state still in Washington for the funeral, Johnson assembled his senior national security team to discuss Vietnam. Johnson thought that the US support for President Diem's assassination had been a mistake, with a State Department officer summarizing LBJ's view as, "Diem may have been a son of a bitch, but he was our son of a bitch."[1]

In the days after Kennedy's death, Johnson was determined to project an image of strength, stability, and fealty to Kennedy's vision. In Vietnam, that meant remaining bullish on the conflict despite abundant signs that LBJ thought it was one in which the United States should not have been ensnared in the first place. And while President Johnson hewed closely to existing Kennedy policies, he was not shy about putting his own stamp on them, with foreign aid being no exception.

Ambassador to Vietnam Henry Cabot Lodge Jr.'s notes from the initial meeting on Vietnam underscore Johnson's shifting tone. LBJ wanted "so-called social reforms" to be a lower priority. In Johnson's view, "It was too much to expect young and underdeveloped countries to establish peace and order against well-trained and disciplined guerrillas, to create modern democratic political institutions, and to organize strong economies at the same time."[2] CIA director John McCone was more blunt, saying Johnson was not interested in "do-gooders."[3]

Johnson's lack of appetite for social reform was also evident in his approach to Latin America and the Alliance for Progress. A military coup had toppled the government of the Dominican Republic in September 1963, and while Kennedy had suspended aid, he had done so reluctantly, as its military was staunchly anti-communist. Trying to stabilize the situation in the Dominican Republic was a preoccupation in LBJ's early days, and as author William Walker observed, the situation only "further confirmed Johnson's difficulty adhering to the more idealistic tenets" of the Alliance.[4]

Teodoro Moscoso was pushed out of his position running the Alliance for Progress as Johnson appointed veteran diplomat Thomas Mann to simultaneously run the Alliance and the Latin America bureau at the State Department.

The Mann appointment sat poorly with Kennedy loyalists who viewed Mann as too pro-business. Arthur Schlesinger Jr. complained that the move amounted to "a declaration of independence, even perhaps a declaration of aggression against the Kennedys."[5] After Mann addressed a gathering of US ambassadors and AID mission directors, the *New York Times* blared a front-page headline, "US May Abandon Effort to Deter Latin American Dictators."[6] The "Mann doctrine," according to the *Times*, meant that Latin American leaders would not be held accountable for their internal actions as long as they defended Washington's interests, particularly its commercial ones.

In a phone call with Johnson the next day, Mann complained bitterly that the article was a "gross distortion."[7] Johnson joked that the real news would be when the reporter "writes a straight story." Humor aside, Johnson remained highly sensitive to any comparisons with Kennedy.

NEW PRESIDENT, SAME OLD OTTO

Johnson rapidly learned that his most pressing immediate issue with AID was battling Congress over its budget. In a discussion with Otto Passman and Congressman John McCormack on November 29, 1963, Johnson insisted that "in my relations with 110 other nations, about all I've got is the foreign aid bill."[8] He vowed to Passman that he would clean up AID so that it would "smell better" to the congressman.

Passman sounded agreeable. Although he complained that AID hadn't spent a sizable chunk of money which had already been appropriated, Passman pledged, "I will lean over backwards, Mr. President, to help you."

That sense of comity disappeared immediately after the call. The Louisiana congressman put out a statement suggesting that Johnson had tried to force his hand on foreign aid, but that he had stood tall and resisted. AID chief David Bell had warned Johnson that Passman was not to be trusted when it came to the budget, but the president had assumed that he could sway Passman by sheer force of will.[9]

About two weeks later, Passman's House committee voted to slash almost 30 percent from the foreign assistance budget. The *New York Times* called it a "personal defeat" for Johnson.[10] It was telling that cutting foreign aid was the first issue on which both Republicans and populist Democrats were comfortable openly opposing the new president.

Johnson was aware of public antipathy toward foreign aid. In a conversation with Under Secretary of State George Ball in the Oval Office, Johnson said he was worried that "we're going to get the stuffin' beat out of us" after he had seen poll results that indicated only one in ten Americans thought they were getting their money's worth out of foreign aid.[11]

Some of Johnson's closest advisers, including David Bell, were not sure the battle over the AID budget was winnable.[12] Aides kicked around the notion of asking former president Dwight Eisenhower to speak out in defense of the aid budget, a plan that was soon dropped.[13]

Johnson leaned into the fight. A White House press release skewered Congress for embracing "policies of weakness and retreat."[14] In phone calls and meetings at the White House, Johnson denigrated Passman as a "caveman" from the swamps of Louisiana and a "bandit wolf."[15] LBJ argued that aid opponents were "seriously endangering the future of their country," and added of Passman, "I think he's got a real mental problem."[16]

As a snowstorm blanketed Washington, journalist Max Frankel called the battle over foreign aid a "wild and largely partisan pre-Christmas tangle."[17] Johnson, worried that he might not prevail, delayed his departure for his Texas ranch.

Democratic leaders dragged House members back to the Capitol for a vote on the aid funding bill in the early-morning hours of Christmas Eve. The timing, bad weather, and the fact that many members had to return from their districts for the proceedings did little for the mood in the chamber.[18] With the desire to leave town reaching a fever pitch, Congress finally passed foreign aid funding. LBJ hosted a spontaneous Christmas Eve reception to thank supporters.

Many pointed to the passage of foreign aid funding as a significant early win for Johnson, but it was a triumph more of perception than reality. Johnson had expended considerable political capital to restore only a small portion of Passman's cuts. Johnson was more than willing to declare victory and head to his ranch at the end the turbulent year, but it was a sobering reminder that maintaining a strong foreign assistance program would not be easy.

JOHNSON IN THE SADDLE

Within weeks of taking power, Johnson talked to George Ball about cleaning out the "dead-wood" at AID.[19] LBJ's impatience with AID stemmed not from David Bell, but his deputy, Frank Coffin, and bad blood stemming from the interaction between Coffin and LBJ at a cocktail party in 1961.[20] At an event at the Mayflower Hotel in Washington, with a large number of members of Congress present, the conversation turned to foreign aid.[21] Johnson held forth in largely positive terms about the program to an informal gaggle. Without giving it much thought, Coffin corrected Johnson on what he viewed as a minor factual misstatement. Johnson was furious and turned on Coffin once the others were out of earshot, saying, "You have held me up to ridicule before my peers. I'll never forget this."

Fast-forward to November 1963. Coffin's nomination to move from AID to serve as ambassador to Panama was sitting on JFK's desk awaiting signature when the president traveled to Dallas. Coffin's ambassadorial appointment then became one of the first pieces of business Johnson had to consider as he assumed the presidency. Presented with Coffin's paperwork, LBJ was reported to have risen, torn the memo into pieces, and thrown it on the ground. "Frank Coffin will never be appointed to anything as long as I'm president."[22]

When Johnson cast aspersions on AID from the White House, they often seemed to reflect his dislike of Coffin. "Do you know any misfits in town that are not in AID?" Johnson asked one member of Congress.[23]

Johnson assembled a high-level panel chaired by Under Secretary of State George Ball to explore the possibility of breaking up AID.[24] The committee explored a wide variety of options, ranging from merging AID into the State Department to splitting its functions across half a dozen departments and agencies. These issues were debated only two years after JFK—and Congress—had merged the various agencies from the 1950s together into AID in the interest of greater coherence and effectiveness.

But President Johnson soon got bloodied in the press for considering reorganizing AID. A *New York Times* columnist claimed that AID was "fighting for its life" in the Johnson administration, and that highly placed figures in the State Department were eager to abolish the agency and take control of its funds.[25] A subsequent piece by the same author, also in January 1964, accused Johnson of a "retreat" from Kennedy's idealism and bending to the will of a "new Congressional 'know-nothing' bloc."[26]

All of these factors contributed to Johnson's decision to largely leave AID as it was. David Bell had carried the day, in no small part, by citing the work of the Senate Foreign Relations Committee, which had argued in October 1963, "The most crying need of the Agency is greater stability."[27]

President Johnson called together David Bell, Agriculture Secretary Orville Freeman, and budget officials at his Texas ranch for a series of key conversations in 1964. While it might sound hyperbolic, the decisions that emerged from those meetings on foreign assistance touched more lives in more-consequential ways than any other action taken by an American president short of world war.

Bell and Freeman had taken an early-morning flight on a small plane to Texas, and both were prepared to present their proposed budget for the coming year.[28] Johnson and the head of the budget office stressed the perpetual difficulty of getting AID's budget through Congress. Johnson had wondered earlier in the year when he could "get out of running this goddamn foreign aid lobbying," and LBJ and his budget chief had repeatedly pushed Bell on the overall amount he was requesting.[29] The wrangling was sometimes contentious.

Somewhat discordantly, the group then broke for a pleasant social lunch with the president and Lady Bird Johnson, making idle chitchat. The session resumed in the afternoon, finally arriving at a budget that Bell described as "significantly less than I had gone in with, but not so much less that I thought he was deeply damaging the program." But what puzzled Bell was the way Johnson had approached the process. With Kennedy, Bell had always felt that he and the president were tackling issues jointly and trying to determine the best course of action. With Johnson, Bell felt like he was constantly bargaining, "trying to win an argument."

In these conversations, Johnson repeatedly stressed the importance of AID being tougher on its recipients. Johnson felt strongly that too many countries were quick to take advantage of American largesse, and he wanted to see more emphasis on successful reforms.

As Secretary of Agriculture Orville Freeman maintained, Johnson was "a very frugal, practical, down-to-earth man," who continually asked him, "After you've given people food and they've had a meal, then so what? How is it going to help them to help themselves?"[30] Freeman also noted that Johnson frequently worried that "the State Department and the people around him in the White House were prepared to give the country away." As Barry Riley argued in his history of American food aid, LBJ's "instinctive tendency to want to help people in distress" was continually at war "with an almost overwhelming aversion to being viewed as a 'softie,' a push-over, a do-gooder, what he himself termed as 'a giveaway boy.'"[31]

The term of art at the time for assistance recipients taking greater responsibility was "self-help." When LBJ had visited India as vice president, he had returned and written a memo to President Kennedy arguing that the United States needed to be clearer about what it expected from assistance recipients. "Any help—economic as well as military—we give less developed nations to secure and maintain their freedom must be part of a mutual effort."[32]

As president, Johnson put those words into action. He urged that some sort of scorecard be developed to grade Latin American countries in meeting their Alliance for Progress obligations.[33] Johnson also made clear that he would be the final arbiter of whether or not countries were meeting their self-help obligations. He demanded personal approval of any AID project over $10 million—a level of micromanagement reminiscent of his insistence on personally signing off on individual bombing targets in Vietnam.[34]

"The basic idea is that our aid should be used as a sizeable carrot and a sizeable stick," argued the national security council staff at the time. "[A]id would be continued from year to year only if the receiving country lived up to its end of the bargain."[35]

The tenet of self-help is a critical one, and it is self-evident that aid dollars are more effective when governments are committed to sensible reforms and investing in their own people, and far less effective when such commitment is lacking.

The emphasis on self-help had begun under President Kennedy, but rapidly intensified under Johnson. With this emphasis came a greater focus on addressing the bottlenecks to broader growth rather than just standing up specific projects. As

Gordon Chase of AID noted at the time, "[V]irtually every significant loan we make involves protracted negotiations with the recipient government on the kind of self-help measures it is prepared to make."[36]

LBJ, while an outspoken proponent of self-help, applied it unevenly. In places like Vietnam, concerns about meeting agreed-upon benchmarks were set aside because of security concerns. Johnson also traveled widely as president, and he liked launching new AID projects during his foreign visits as a goodwill gesture.[37]

After his interrogations of Bell in Texas, Johnson eventually put forth what he called a "bare bones" budget request for aid, the smallest amount requested since the Marshall Plan had been established. Much to Johnson's relief, George Mahon had become chair of the appropriations committee. The Texas Democrat was a friend of the president and much more willing to rein in Otto Passman.[38]

It was at the second ranch meeting in December 1964 that LBJ, Bell, and Freeman set the course for Johnson's approach to aid. They met as Johnson was at the pinnacle of his power. In 1964, he had proposed the "great society" to eliminate poverty, signed the civil rights act outlawing segregation, and crushed Barry Goldwater in a successful election campaign.

Johnson, Bell, and Freeman had received alarming reports from their staffs and the scientific community that a global food crisis was imminent. The population of the developing world was expanding rapidly, US food surpluses were on a sharp downward trajectory, and there was a yawning gulf between the amount of food being produced in the developing world and the amount needed to feed hungry people.

At the time, about 60 percent of the world's population was chronically underfed, and more than half the deaths in the developing world were among children of pre-school age—a mortality rate more than sixty times higher than that in Europe and North America.[39]

Further heightening concern was emerging research that made clear the profound lasting impact of hunger on human development. As Alan Berg, a nutritionist at AID explained, "For years we had assumed that, given educational opportunities and other environmental advantages, children had every reason to be as bright, imaginative, and eventually productive as other children their age."[40] Yet the new research demonstrated that severe hunger, particularly among infants, had enduring and incredibly negative impacts on cognitive abilities and growth, a realization that hit Berg and others "like a ton of bricks." Hunger had the power to undermine a country's overall prospects for development to an alarming degree.

The crisis in nutrition was inextricably intertwined with rapid population growth at that moment in time. But the global population boom wasn't a factor of people, particularly poor people, suddenly having more babies. The boom was occurring, paradoxically, because more children than ever before were surviving through their first years of life. The post–World War II period marked a steep decline in infant mortality rates around the globe as sanitation improved, vaccination became more widespread, and important inroads were achieved against malaria and other tropical diseases.

But families in the developing world continued to have large numbers of children. In many cases it was a perfectly logical decision: Often only males could inherit land, so parents would have multiple children to ensure that a son would survive. There was usually limited or no access to contraception for financial or cultural reasons, and even though mortality rates had fallen, sickness and disease could still rapidly decimate families. Given the crushing burden of poverty, children continued to represent a valuable source of labor, and often the only social safety net for aging parents.

Johnson and others on his team recognized that they could not close the widening hunger gap entirely through food aid, and that the only viable alternative seemed to be to increase food production in poor countries while curbing population growth.[41] This led one commentator to describe the consensus that emerged from LBJ's ranch as a strategy to "promote more food and fewer babies."[42]

Promoting agriculture was the more-straightforward of the two propositions. Orville Freeman, the secretary of agriculture, had accepted his post in no small part because he wanted the Department of Agriculture to be more directly engaged in combating hunger at both home and abroad, and he provided AID with an important, and powerful, ally.[43] Walt Rostow and others had come around to the idea that agriculture could be an engine for growth. And certainly, Congress and the American people viewed America as the world's breadbasket and were comfortable sharing insights and technologies that would help battle hunger and boost markets for US exports in the process.

As a March 1965 statement issued by the White House Press Secretary argued: "The most grave health problem of the world remains hunger and malnutrition. Studies indicate that in some developing countries as high as 70 percent of pre-school children are undernourished or malnourished. Such malnutrition not only results in high child death rates and widespread disabling diseases but research has now established that it also produces permanent retardation of mental as well as physical development."[44]

The war on hunger was now front and center.

The issues of population growth and birth control were thornier issues for Johnson and AID. "Population control," as it was often heavy-handedly referred to—and sometimes practiced, at the time—had few advocates, much less professional practitioners. The Ford Foundation, the Swedish government, and the International Planned Parenthood Federation began providing modest funding toward this end in the late 1950s, and their often-delicate efforts reflected the considerable cultural and political sensitivities around the topic.[45] In contrast, the US government and the United Nations steered clear of family planning.[46]

A high-level commission chaired by General William Draper in 1959 had argued, "Problems connected with world population growth will be among the most serious to be faced by the younger generation of today," and recommended that the United States assist those countries that were asking for help in dealing with high birth rates.[47] President Eisenhower was unusually stern in his rebuke of the panel's proposal, saying at the time, "I cannot imagine anything more emphatically a subject that is not a proper political or governmental activity."[48]

The situation did not improve significantly under Kennedy. Kennedy approached the issue of birth control gingerly because it raised questions of his Catholicism and its acceptability to voters, an abiding concern at the time. Arthur Schlesinger maintained that as president Kennedy was "encouragingly ambivalent" about inter-national family planning, and advocated that the findings of birth control studies be made widely available, "so that everyone can make their own judgment."[49] There was no reference to family planning in the foundational documents of the Alliance for Progress because the issue was viewed as too controversial in the region—and in the United States.

Under Kennedy, David Bell had given Congress his assurance that AID would not consider the distribution of contraception in the developing world, which proved to be a major initial stumbling block to Johnson launching family planning programs.[50] Health programs (other than smallpox vaccination and very successful malaria eradication programs in Latin America and South Asia) were also a relative rarity at the agency at the time because, as Haven North of the agency explained, "The prevailing view of AID economists at the time was that public health programs did not contribute to economic growth."[51]

But the tide was shifting quickly. Part of the reason was the series of alarming reports of population increases such as those being shared with the president. Betty Friedan's *The Feminine Mystique*, which was published in 1963, helped advance the notion that women should have greater agency over all aspects of their life, at a time when women had all too often been treated as little more than baby factories. In 1965, in *Griswold v. Connecticut*, the Supreme Court struck down a state ban on married couples buying contraceptives, and more than twenty-five states operated family planning clinics with the support of federal funding.[52]

There was growing recognition within many developing countries that the rate of population growth was stretching their already shaky systems to the limit. Asoka Mehta of the Indian Planning Commission likened rapid population growth to "a thief in the night" that robbed countries of their economic gains.[53]

Officials at the White House recognized that a lack of access to contraception often manifested itself in high abortion rates. As a National Security Council memo argued: "twice the number of abortions as live births in some Latin American cities are cruel proof of the immediacy and tragedy of the problem in personal terms."[54]

Johnson pushed all his chips onto the table, and AID's support for agriculture, family planning, and health would increase every year during his tenure—despite continued downward pressure on the overall budget.[55] As Johnson declared in his 1965 State of the Union address, the world needed to "face forthrightly the multi-plying problems of our multiplying populations and seek the answers to this most profound challenge to the future of the world. Let us act on the fact that less than $5 invested in population control is worth $100 invested in economic growth."[56]

SHIFTING ALLIANCE

But if Johnson had decided to focus on a handful of big things, the Alliance for Progress was notable for its continued breadth of activities. Even while Thomas Mann had deemphasized the social reforms that had headlined the Alliance at its launch, the Alliance for Progress in the mid-1960s still employed a multifaceted approach.

While almost all countries in Latin America, except Cuba, received Alliance funding, Brazil, Chile, Colombia, Costa Rica, and the Dominican Republic received the lion's share. The investments were diverse but tied together by an overall strategy to achieve Walt Rostow's projected economic "take-off." Aid efforts ranged from the training of public administrators and urban housing programs to malaria eradication and establishing savings and loan associations to working with schools, labor unions, and farmers. Large loan programs were designed to both promote economic policy reform and tackle key gaps in infrastructure. With Mann in place, the private sector was an even more prominent focus, with a heavy nod toward import substitution and industrialization. AID missions also viewed strengthening the capacity of national planning agencies across the region as a key to long-term success.

In short, AID was trying to fulfill the lofty commitments made at Punta del Este which amounted to modernizing an entire region on an incredibly ambitious timetable. (Johnson over time expressed increasing irritation at the range of AID activities in the region, saying at one point, "[E]verything they do in Latin America, I want to relate to agriculture or education or health and I don't want any of this other crap."[57]

The United States and Brazil engaged in continual negotiations on policy reforms linked to lending, with emphasis on getting control of inflation and opening Brazil up to trade. Officials from the US Treasury Department were deeply engaged in these talks, and much of the AID program focused on northeast Brazil, the poorest region in that country. But a steady current of Brazilian political unrest blunted progress to an important degree. "Brazil was considered a country with a future as a great power, given its enormous resources," observed Herman Kleine, who served with AID in Brazil, "but it was a country whose future never seemed to come."[58]

The views among AID staffers who worked in Brazil were sharply split as to the efficacy of the program. Some highlighted the importance of AID in assisting four agricultural universities that ultimately helped fuel Brazil's rise as a food exporter. Marshall Brown, who was instrumental in lending programs to improve health and education in Brazil argued, "AID has contributed to strengthening Brazil's human resources, trained its leaders, [and] helped build many of its key institutions."[59]

This relatively rosy view is countered by Stuart Van Dyke who calculated that during his four years in Brazil the US government provided some $4 billion in grants, loans, and food assistance, but, "I am afraid that much of the money which our aid supplied was used as a crutch to justify postponing the basic reforms which were essential to rapid and orderly economic growth."[60]

The Alliance for Progress placed a great deal of emphasis on using multilateral mechanisms to promote regional integration, hoping that some of the same types of cross-border cooperation that made the Marshall Plan such a success could be replicated in Latin America. The Organization of American States was specifically given the lead in coordinating and supervising the Alliance, following the Marshall Plan model and trying to make the initiative less politicized, albeit with mixed results.

The newly established Inter-American Development Bank, the UN Economic Commission for Latin America, and the World Bank were also all deeply engaged, as were other US agencies like the Departments of Agriculture, Commerce, and Treasury, and the Export-Import Bank. The US business community was increasingly active across Latin America, as both a positive and negative force. While not fully appreciated at the time, that connective tissue of cooperation and integration promoted by the Alliance for Progress would profoundly shape the region over time—but not nearly as quickly as anyone would have hoped. Johnson himself would admit by 1965 that major assistance would be required in the region even after 1970—the original termination date for the Alliance.

National security concerns over the spread of communism continued to define Washington's dealings in Latin America. The Johnson administration, recognizing that its aid dollars were an increasingly scarce commodity, also pushed for greater self-help measures across the region—as long as they didn't interfere with the battle against Marxist insurgencies.

In 1965, a civil war erupted in the Dominican Republic, and President Johnson, fearing a replay of the Cuban Revolution, directly interceded in the conflict with US forces. The administration, eager to confine the unrest, dispatched teams drawn from AID, the State Department, and former Peace Corps volunteers to serve as a kind of shadow government in the provinces. AID staffer Lawrence Harrison recalls the experience: "We kept the government afloat. We paid salaries. We assured that the foreign exchange reserves did not drop below an acceptable level."[61]

After a 1966 election installed Joaquin Balaguer as president of the Dominican Republic, the United States was so deeply engaged that the US ambassador and senior AID officials took part in the Dominican Republic's weekly economic cabinet meetings. The US ambassador sat to one side of the Dominican president, the AID mission director to the other. AID staffers found the degree of US control unseemly. But even in such a curious and unsteady environment, US assistance continued to make long-term bets on the country, including through investments in establishing one of the Dominican Republic's best universities and sending more than one hundred young Dominicans to Texas A&M University to study agriculture.

Halfway into the Alliance for Progress's proposed ten-year existence, it was clear that aiding Latin America was more complicated than assisting post–World War II Europe, and that the tension between short- and long-term US imperatives in the region was shading the reputation of the program.

A 1965 AID internal memo, jointly authored by the Latin American bureau's chief economist and the director of the bureau's development planning office, contemplated the merits of a formal mid-decade review of the Alliance's progress, and put its complicated track record in a well-balanced light:

The great danger in such a review is that where accomplishment is tested against the highly unrealistic 10-year charter timetable, the Alliance can be construed as a dismal failure. With half the period consumed, the millennium is not yet in sight. Most of the problems to which the Charter was addressed in 1960 remain today in unattended, unsolved, and in some respects exacerbated form. Thus, although progress is discernible, and in some respects quite dramatic and real, it pales against the task defined in the Charter and the timetable which it provides.[62]

The degree to which anti-communism drove AID programs in the 1960s in both Latin America and Asia cannot be overemphasized. Some 80 percent of US assistance during this period was directed to countries that were seen on the front lines against potential communist expansion.[63] The overall size of the US assistance program tended to wax and wane with how Washington perceived the threat from Moscow and Peking.

Columnist Joseph Kraft, who supported LBJ's efforts to tackle global hunger in particular, had a refreshingly candid and sensible take on the foreign aid program. "The public reason for aid—the reason believed by most of the American people, by the bulk of the Congress, and by a large part of the not-very-bright majority of officials in the State Department—is that foreign aid stops communism and promotes governments friendly to the United States. The real reason for the aid program is to foster independent countries with growing economies."[64] This simple truth was always at the heart of the aid program and its merits, yet it was embraced surprisingly rarely.

And across the southern hemisphere, many Latin American leaders were reaching the conclusion that Washington was losing interest in the region because it was becoming preoccupied with the situation in Vietnam.[65] They were not wrong.

RAMP-UP

In Vietnam, President Johnson largely rejected Kennedy's earlier use of unconventional warfare and saw the challenge before him as one requiring the exercise of raw force. But the leaders who had overthrown Vietnamese president Ngo Dinh Diem proved largely incapable of effectively managing either domestic politics or prosecuting the war against the North.

For Johnson, this meant that US forces were going to have to do more of the heavy lifting. Johnson and Defense Secretary Robert McNamara used the August 1964 Gulf of Tonkin incident as pretext to greatly expand direct US involvement in the war. The United States had committed some 200 ground troops to Vietnam early in 1961. By the end of 1966, there were more than 385,000 American troops on the ground.[66]

Demanding better results in rural areas, Johnson also sharply increased the number of civilian advisers from 300 to 1,000 in just sixty days. AID's Rural Affairs staff in Vietnam, a group that probably knew Vietnam better at the ground level than any other Americans, saw only disaster. The AID mission director, Joseph Brent, and the head of the Rural Affairs program, Bert Fraleigh, complained that the rapid expansion of the US presence was "wholly counterproductive."[67] For Fraleigh the move was the beginning of the end of an effective civilian counterinsurgency response.

John O'Donnell, who worked for AID as a provincial representative in Kien Hoa, briefed Secretary of Defense Robert McNamara and General Maxwell Taylor, chair of the Joint Chiefs, in 1964. O'Donnell's assessment was every bit as bleak as Fraleigh's. "McNamara displayed absolutely no understanding of, or interest in" what needed to be done to win the rural population over to the side of the government.[68]

Johnson's new strategy wasn't just having major implications for AID's work in the countryside. With the Vietnamese government proving more venal than productive, Johnson felt that the best way to dampen potential protests against it would be for AID to supply a steady diet of consumer goods in Saigon and other major cities. AID was suddenly charged with the Sisyphean task of making sure that abundant commercial items were available in Vietnam at reasonable prices and that the country's war economy didn't suffer shortages and price spikes.

The public outcry in the United States over Vietnam was gaining momentum as more and more young people began to question the war in the jungles of Southeast Asia. More than 25,000 student protesters took to the streets in the first major antiwar demonstrations in Washington in April 1965—just a month after the start of Operation Rolling Thunder in Vietnam, the largest US bombing campaign since the end of World War II.

But for AID, the harsh reality of Vietnam was already coming home to roost. "Between my first visit to Vietnam in 1963 and my last visit in 1965," said development expert Vernon Ruttan, "I saw AID staff who had arrived in Vietnam with energy and enthusiasm leave with careers ground down as if by a meat grinder."[69]

Washington was slowly waking up to the fact that Johnson's initial instinct to ignore the civilian side of Vietnam was not working. "The situation in Vietnam is deteriorating, and without new US action defeat appears inevitable—probably not in a matter of weeks or perhaps even months, but within the next year or so," wrote National Security Adviser McGeorge Bundy in February of 1965, as troop levels rose sharply. "[T]he most urgent order of business will then be the improvement and broadening of the pacification program, especially in its non-military elements."[70]

David Bell's notes from a meeting at the National Security Council the next day reflect the same worries. "Number one problem is rural pacification," he wrote, observing that even when US troops recaptured areas, US forces were not effectively holding them or reassuring the local population.[71] There were increasing discussions at the senior-most levels of the US government of essentially putting the US military in charge of the aid programs, particularly in rural areas where security was poor.

But there was also a recognition, such as that voiced by Bob Komer, a senior official at the National Security Council, that most US soldiers didn't know much about "fertilizer, land reform, local education, public health, refugee care, [and] public safety."[72]

BIRTH OF A TIGER

About two thousand miles to the northeast of Vietnam, a very different story was playing out in South Korea. Korea too had suffered bitter war. The country had been under brutal Japanese dominion for about thirty-five years before being occupied by US and Soviet forces at the end of World War II. The country had been split in two after the subsequent Korean War, with a large contingent of US forces still stationed at the tense de facto border between North and South.

South Korea was left desperately poor as a result, with a per capita income in 1960 below that of both El Salvador and Liberia.[73]

"The country was devastated," Bradshaw Langmaid of AID observed, "the landscape outside of Seoul . . . almost barren." One of the few viable economic activities for many citizens was collecting and selling scrap metal from brass and copper shell casings left over from the war.[74]

However, South Korea's fate was seen as an important bellwether of US influence within the broader paradigm of the Cold War. As one White House staffer observed, "South Korea, by history and present condition, is a ward of the United States, and will be so judged around the world."[75]

As the United States pumped in reconstruction assistance, it found itself holding significant tracts of land in Korea that had been previously controlled by the Japanese and whose disposition was in question. Consequently, from 1948 to 1950 the United States, working with Korean officials, instituted an extensive program of land reform and redistribution.

Limits were placed on the maximum size of plot a farmer could hold, and many farmers were able to own land for the first time. The large landowners that would normally mobilize to oppose such redistributive measures largely kept silent because many of them had been closely tied to the occupying Japanese regime.[76] Less than half of Korean farmers in 1945 owned, or partially owned, the land they farmed. After land reform, that figure rose to over 90 percent. Not surprisingly, rural incomes, although still quite low, soon became much more equitable.

As Princeton Lyman argued, land reform had sweeping impact in that it "eliminated the last vestiges of a large land-owning class and eliminated in the process almost all the serious political divisiveness in the countryside."[77]

But beyond land reform, in the 1950s Korea was more a foreign aid cautionary tale than success story. The government of President Syngman Rhee largely resisted US recommendations for economic reform, growth was halting, and Korea appeared more interested in maximizing its assistance levels than taking steps toward self-help. It was clear that US economic and military assistance, absent genuine commitment from the government, would not be enough to drive change in Korea.[78]

Early in his administration, Kennedy had pushed a harder line in dealing with Korea. A memo was prepared for Walt Rostow that insisted the new US ambassador to Korea, Samuel Berger, and the new AID mission director, James Killen, "were selected for their jobs because they are very tough-minded gentlemen."[79] But this more hard-nosed approach was of no avail until the political landscape in Korea changed dramatically.

After Syngman Rhee was forced out of power by growing student protests, General Park Chung-hee came to power via a military coup in 1961. The coup initially brought a deep chill (although never a break) to the assistance relationship, but when Park won the 1963 election to become Korea's president, he made clear that he saw improving the economy as a central strategic and political priority.

Ambassador Berger delivered a blunt message to President Park: Because of the budget situation in Washington, the generous flow of aid to Seoul would not continue indefinitely.[80]

President Park approached the dilemma with determination. In a key step, Park appointed Chang Key-young as deputy prime minister and as chair of Korea's Economic Planning Board. The Economic Planning Board was responsible for directing the implementation of US assistance and managing the relationship with AID. One of Chang's first steps: to call a meeting of the planning board to listen to new AID director Joel Bernstein's advice on the economic policies he thought most vital to turn around Korea's economy.[81]

The partnership between Bernstein and Chang was essential. "He was a very strong figure," said Princeton Lyman of Bernstein. "Every Friday, the two would meet together for four or five hours."[82] The two negotiated tax rates, the Korean budget, interest rates, and plans for specific AID projects. The constructive pressure from the United States directly bolstered the standing of reformers in the Korean government and gave them additional ammunition in making their case for change.

"Every aspect of the Korean fiscal and economic picture for the year had to be approved by AID," said Eric Chetwynd, who worked in Korea at the time. "We came to the table with our model of what the situation should be; the Koreans came to the table with theirs and we would negotiate."[83] These talks also helped lay the groundwork for important initiatives such as establishing the Korean Institute for Science and Technology, which would help make Korea a tech leader for years to come.

One of the overarching agreements to emerge out of the new sense of collaboration was a focus on boosting Korea's exports.[84] The Economic Planning Committee set up a working group tasked with export promotion, and AID's deputy mission director Roger Ernst was named co-chairman of the export promotion group.

President Park demanded regular progress reports and made clear he would not brook failure. Deeply shaped by his military outlook, Park was decisive, and he consolidated his power to such a degree that few in government or the private sector challenged his decision-making. One historian described Park as instituting a "developmental dictatorship."[85]

Roger Ernst recalled when his team conducted a study of how many steps were required to get an export to market in Korea.[86] The findings: thirty-five government approvals were required before a product could be exported.

President Park was visibly angry when given the findings: "Cut it to seven, by Monday."

Park's staff produced a new plan requiring just seven steps, featuring a one-stop shopping center for would-be exporters to get a government sign-off. Ernst recalls that when Park's staff presented the new plan, two members of the cabinet objected. President Park dealt with them swiftly, saying, "I'll take your resignations."

Korea's model of development, particularly the commingling of US and Korean policy expertise, was similar to that successfully utilized in Taiwan and was not the traditional approach used by AID. US officials worked hand in glove with the Koreans on many of the vital but less-glamorous elements of governance: budgeting, revenue collection, allocations of foreign exchange, and statistical capacity.[87] The United States also continued to heavily underwrite the costs of the Korean military.

The agency launched a campaign to meet with individual businessmen and make the case for why they should concentrate on exports; instituted programs to promote quality-control measures in factories; and encouraged export promotion in regional centers away from the capital.[88] The bulk of AID's spending shifted to the big-ticket items that would help realize the export-driven vision of growth: manufacturing, energy, and transportation.[89]

In October 1965, Amicus Most of AID and the head of Korea's export promotion agency traveled to New York City where they met personally with potential buyers from Sears, Montgomery Ward, J. C. Penney, and other large chains.[90] A number of these companies soon established purchasing centers in Korea.

The Korea assistance effort brought together talented people on both sides of the equation. There were a large number of Americans who had forged close personal ties to the country during their service in the Korean War who returned as part of the assistance effort—ranging from semi-retired deans of American universities to the director of Texas's agricultural research system.[91]

The remarkable surge of reform in Korea was built on a solid foundation of investments in people, particularly in education and training. While some commentators from afar were quick to describe South Korea as a basket case in the 1950s and early 1960s, none of the AID staff who interacted with Koreans on a daily basis conveyed that impression in their contemporaneous observations.

"Their devotion to education was extraordinary," said Princeton Lyman.[92] Korea's literacy rate leapt from 20 percent in 1950 to 80 percent in 1965. This commitment to early education was supplemented by the three thousand Koreans who trained abroad, many sponsored by AID.[93] "We had these extensive training programs where we brought people to the States and put them through college and advanced-degree programs," explained Len Rogers of AID, "and we spent a lot of money on institutional development; spent a lot of money on bricks and mortar in universities and technical schools in developing countries."[94] Helping to develop those institutions was a crucial complement in that it allowed those well-educated Koreans to have an operational base and a means to amplify their voices in policy debates.

Before the Korean economy started to generate forward momentum, many well-trained Koreans had taken lower-level jobs in banks and factories. But when the opportunity arose, they seemingly came out of the woodwork. In essence, the large US investment in participant training and building up Korean universities had waited in dormancy until the moment when Korea finally made a broad national commitment to reform.

Those Koreans who studied economics and other disciplines in the United States became some of the most vocal and best-positioned advocates for advancing President Park's economic agenda, and in many cases AID officials ended up having extensive negotiations with the same people that the agency had helped train at American universities. "Practically all of Minister Chang's 15 to 20 bureau and section chiefs had benefited from overseas academic training," explained David Cole, "mainly in economics in the US and mainly sponsored by the various US aid programs."[95] US investments in long-term training increasingly meant that the heart of economic planning efforts was handed off from US officials to the Koreans themselves.

During this period in the 1960s, AID globally had a very large international training program, bringing some 6,500 foreign nationals to the United States for advanced education and training, and sending another 2,500 people to third countries for career advancement.[96] The average age of participants was twenty-nine, with the average length of stay in the United States being nine months. While certainly not the most headline-grabbing of AID's programs, participant training efforts were enormously influential in bending the arc of economic policy first in Asia, then later, in Latin America.

With this emphasis on learning, Korean planners displayed a willingness to be informed by their earlier mistakes. Princeton Lyman recalled the large fertilizer plant the United States had helped build in Korea in the 1950s. "It was an abject failure; we never succeeded in having the output it was supposed to have. We used to drive Congressmen miles and miles out of the way just so that we would not be anywhere near that plant."[97] Yet, hundreds of Korean engineers subsequently trained at the facility and, as Lyman adds, "They learned more about fertilizer and its production than any other country in the world."

American officials were deeply impressed by the work ethic of their counterparts. "If we sent a letter to the Planning Ministry on Friday requiring a quick, but complicated answer, they would work all weekend and more to meet the deadline," commented Vincent Brown of AID. "Sometimes they would rent a suite in a downtown hotel, so that their professional staff could work uninterrupted."[98]

The South Koreans devalued their currency; normalized relations with Japan; liberalized trade; and advanced a coherent economic strategy—all while mobilizing significant troops in Vietnam to assist the United States.[99] The government also agreed to raise electricity rates as part of a loan for a thermal plant in Seoul, making it possible for the facility to be self-sustaining without additional US assistance.[100] As David Bell wrote at that time, "Korea's self-help performance in economic stabilization and development has become one of the best of any aid recipient, thanks in large measure to the leadership of President Park and Deputy Prime Minister Chang Key Young, who have been willing to carry out politically difficult reforms."[101]

The results of Korea's experiment in reform: Korea's growth rates averaged almost 10 percent annually from 1963 forward for the next three decades.[102] Korea's exports climbed from $400 million in the early 1960s to over $150 billion less than twenty years later.[103] During that same period, average incomes in South Korea shot past every country in Latin America despite the fact that Latin America was well ahead of South Korea in 1960.[104] In the space of forty years, Korea went from being one of the poorest countries on the globe to its ninth-largest exporter.[105]

Political liberalization, in contrast, was much slower, and President Park became increasingly repressive until he was ultimately assassinated by the head of the Korean CIA in 1979.

US assistance to Korea was large—more than $12.7 billion in the thirty-year period between 1945 and 1975, with a rough split between economic and military support.[106] To put this in perspective, that is almost as much economic aid as the United States put into all of Africa for the same period.[107] There were intervals when US foreign aid made up more than 8 percent of Korea's entire GDP.

By almost any measure, it would have been impossible for South Korea to achieve what the World Bank now calls an economic miracle if not for the extensive infusion of reconstruction assistance after both World War II and the Korean War. And South Korea offers one of the relatively rare examples where the United States pushed hard on economic reforms in a country where it also had deep strategic interests, a striking contrast to the approach taking place at the same moment in Vietnam.

South Korea also demonstrates that meeting basic needs such as education and promoting macroeconomic reforms can be complementary. South Korea was an important wake-up call in illuminating the fact that investments in human capital through education and health are every bit as vital to the country's economic transformation as is building bridges, roads, and power plants.

Land reform efforts in particular deserve credit for not only shaping a more-just society but also ensuring that the impact of sensible economic reforms benefited a broader swathe of Korean society. This also underscores why the failure of Latin America to more broadly embrace land reform during the same period tended to calcify existing economic inequalities. US assistance played an important role in South Korea, but the drive and determination of the Korean people was paramount to its success.

There are reasons we should be circumspect in generalizing the lessons of South Korea. Korea after World War II was an unusually homogeneous society. Korea placed a very high value on education and was almost universally literate when the economy started to take off. The country had a strong strategic relationship with Washington and enjoyed high aid levels. The years of supplying US forces based in Korea had taught the Korean business community the importance of quality control and complying with contract specifications and standards.[108] The presence of some fifty thousand US troops in Korea on a semipermanent basis also provided an important, ongoing infusion of spending into the economy.

President Johnson traveled to Korea in October 1966 for a state visit. Madison Broadnax of AID helped plan one of LBJ's site visits to a place called Anyang Hill, perched above a farming center. "It was in the fall and the Koreans turned out every elementary school to come there to see and hear President Johnson."[109]

Secretary of State Dean Rusk kept nudging the president, saying, "You are over your time."

"We'll just cut out some other part of the program," responded Johnson as he relished the moment.

Johnson chatted with the head of the village, whom he later took for a helicopter ride, and the schoolchildren listened to the president raptly. "It was in October and the rice harvest and everything was a golden yellow," said Broadnax, "One of the most beautiful scenes you've ever seen."

Self-help had worked. Johnson was allowed a moment to savor an important triumph. Tougher tests lay ahead.

4

Crescendos

THE SHADOW OF FAMINE

With alarm growing in Washington about global hunger, it was inevitable that India would be a major focus. India was the largest recipient of American foreign assistance as Lyndon Johnson began his second term. Its population was greater than that of Africa and Latin America combined. Fears that communism could sweep across the continent remained acute as Moscow also continued to direct aid to New Delhi.

One history of US assistance to India notes that American officials still "looked in awe at the absorption of backward and undernourished China by communist forces" and feared a repeat in India.[1] "Vietnam is only an antechamber," Bob Komer wrote to LBJ in 1965. "[T]he Indian subcontinent is still the key area we, Moscow, and Peiping are all competing for."[2] US officials had taken to observing, "Where hunger goes, Communism follows."[3]

But the demands of feeding the world's largest free nation were immense. India had been the largest recipient of US food aid for more than a decade, and in 1964 an astounding 20 percent of America's entire wheat crop was delivered to India as food aid.[4] As food aid historian Barry Riley explained, US officials feared that "India's food import requirements might well prove insatiable, unaffordable, and eternal."[5]

A Senate report described the situation in India in harrowing, Malthusian tones:

Many of the people of India would like to enjoy a higher level of living than they now have. One has only to be in India during a famine to understand the hopelessness of the low-caste Indian. Hundreds of deaths from starvation occur during a single night. A higher level of living is so far beyond their reach that they can conceive of nothing better. Their numbers are determined, as in the case of the alley cats, by the bits of food that they can beg or steal.[6]

With an incendiary lack of common sense and cultural sensitivity, the report argued that "if just the excess of India's sacred cattle were used for food," India could solve its hunger problem.

India was not without blame for its shortcomings. The Indian government centrally managed many aspects of agriculture that made it difficult for farmers to make a living—keeping food prices artificially low, failing to allow greater private investment in fertilizer plants, and artificially inflating the exchange rate.

There was an emerging consensus in the Johnson administration to make a "big push" on Indian agriculture, a viewpoint shared by David Bell, Walt Rostow, Orville Freeman, Bob Komer, US Ambassador to India Chester Bowles, and AID Mission Director John Lewis.

But there were vivid differences among those advisers about how best to go about such a big push. Agriculture Secretary Orville Freeman and his young staffer Lester Brown advocated a hard line. They insisted that New Delhi would only reverse its counterproductive policies toward agriculture if the White House applied what John Lewis of AID called "extreme pressure."[7]

Orville Freeman saw the food aid program as the perfect point of leverage. Freeman argued that as the importance of food aid came into focus, "we began to realize that these countries were not using this food effectively" and were relying on the United States to bail them out when needed.[8] Freeman and Brown had pushed a relatively militant line on India without consulting the State Department or AID.

President Johnson sided with the hard-liners on his team and insisted that he personally approve every food aid shipment to India regardless of its size beginning in the spring of 1965.[9] It was a level of extraordinary presidential involvement in the aid program.

The impact of LBJ's decision was felt almost immediately. The India hands in the administration, or "India lovers" as LBJ sometimes derided them, were deeply uncomfortable with food being weaponized to advance a policy agenda. All of them knew that the Indian Agriculture Minister, Chidambaram Subramaniam, was supportive of the reforms which the White House was advocating. His chances of success seemed reasonable given that Indian prime minister Lal Bahadur Shastri, who had come to power in 1964, was seen as far more supportive of agriculture than his predecessors and had made Subramaniam his very first appointment.

In June 1965, Bob Komer sounded a nervous tone in a note to the president, arguing that further delays in food shipments "could cause speculation, hoarding, and price rises."[10] Komer appealed to National Security Adviser McGeorge Bundy. "Have we, in your judgement, gotten across fully to the President the risks as well as the benefits of the delaying tactics he's using on India?"[11] As LBJ continued to sit on the food shipments, Komer speculated that David Bell might quit because of the president's approach, noting, "I'm all for tough-minded use of aid, but we need to play a smart open-field running game—not use bulldozer tactics."[12]

Two events deeply complicated the already-complex situation. First, India's monsoon rains in 1965 were far lower than usual, causing the rice harvest to plummet almost a quarter from the year before.[13] The specter of a major famine occurring in the middle of the back-and-forth on food aid and agricultural reform was suddenly very real.

Then in September 1965, a seventeen-day war erupted between India and Pakistan over the disputed territory of Kashmir. Although fought to what amounted to a costly stalemate, the conflict was deeply unfortunate from Washington's view. Both India and Pakistan felt slighted when US aid was suspended (albeit briefly), and both argued that they deserved more support from Washington on the battlefield. For AID, having two large assistance recipients break into open warfare undercut the claims that US foreign aid was a force for peace and stability.

The dramatic developments did not alter Johnson's commitment to hold India's feet to the fire. In October 1965, Johnson dispatched Orville Freeman to hold secret talks with Agriculture Minister Subramaniam on the sidelines of a UN meeting in Rome. The agreement they struck, in writing, was seen as sufficiently sensitive that it was kept secret for decades. "It promised a 40 percent increase in agricultural investment in the coming year and further increases later," observed John Lewis, and included detailed commitments ranging from reforming pricing to the number of tons of fertilizer to be produced.[14]

In response, LBJ cracked open the food spigot, releasing half a million tons of wheat and a $50 million loan for fertilizer.[15]

The staff at the White House clearly hoped that the Rome deal could put an end to what they saw as increasingly perilous brinkmanship, and McGeorge Bundy and Bob Komer jointly wrote to the president in October 1965 positing that the time was ripe to "defuse the explosive issue of food as a political weapon."[16] During a review of the aid program the next month, they maintained that India was no less than "the make or break test case for the democratic approach to the harshest problems of poverty."[17]

Several days after Christmas in 1965, David Bell met quietly with the Indian ambassador to the United States, Braj Kumar Nehru. "What might the President's response be," Ambassador Nehru asked of Bell, if Prime Minister Shastri indicated that India would "adopt the policies the World Bank and the U.S. think are necessary, including liberalization, if we can be assured by the world community of the financing we will need over the next several years to carry through these policies."[18] Bell was restrained, but supportive, suggesting that this would be viewed as a very positive overture. For the first time in the modern era, India was emphasizing agriculture as much as industry in its national economic plans.

Then on January 11, 1966, the day after signing a declaration to formally end the war with Pakistan, while in the Soviet city of Tashkent, Prime Minister Shastri suffered a fatal heart attack. There was, and continues to be, considerable speculation that Shastri may have been poisoned given the timing of his death.

Indira Gandhi, daughter of India's first prime minister, was thrust onto the national stage as India's first woman leader with many even in her own party openly questioning her abilities.

Just weeks later, in February 1966, President Johnson delivered a major message to Congress. "Hunger poisons the mind. It saps the body. It destroys hope. It is the natural enemy of every man on earth," it said, "I propose that the United States lead the world in a war against hunger."[19]

But LBJ's commitment to lead a global war on hunger and the tumult in South Asia did little to change his belief that further pressure needed to be placed on India to ensure that it fulfilled the commitments made by its previous prime minister. Johnson continued to insist that a "short tether" be placed on all food deliveries to India until he saw New Delhi act. A beleaguered John Lewis observed, "It became evident that LBJ loved to make everyone, his own people and the Indians alike, sit up and beg."[20]

These same tensions cropped up as Indian ambassador Nehru met with LBJ in advance of a high-stakes visit by Indira Gandhi to Washington in March of 1966. When Nehru pointed out that the United States was the only major country with food to spare and maintained that it did not cost Washington anything to send it abroad, LBJ bridled, and pointed out that the US government had to pay "every nickel's worth" for the aid it shipped overseas.[21]

The White House and AID tried to use the planned meeting with Indira Gandhi to get Johnson to soften his position. "Thanks to Shastri's death, the over-all pause in our assistance has been stretched out longer than most of us expected," John Lewis plaintively wrote to Bob Komer. "Partly—only partly—because of this the Indian economy has been wrung out badly. It now faces deep short-term trouble on both the food and industrial fronts."[22] Lewis than rattled off the positive steps taken by the Indians on agriculture, family planning, economic liberalization, export promotion, and foreign private investment.

US Ambassador to India Chester Bowles reflected in his diary, "It is a cruel performance. The Indians must conform; they must be made to fawn; their pride must be cracked."[23]

Orville Freeman recalled Indira Gandhi's arrival at the White House at the end of March 1966. Her helicopter touched down on a pad just outside the diplomatic entrance, and a receiving line was formed with the president and Gandhi. As Freeman, who had met the prime minister a number of times before, shook hands with Gandhi, President Johnson quipped, "Madam Prime Minister, here's another one of your employees."[24]

The discussions between the two leaders, despite considerable apprehension among staffers on both sides, were genial, with Freeman saying the two got along "splendidly." Both leaders had come to power after the jarring death of their predecessor, and both faced elections and difficult internal issues almost immediately upon taking office.

That evening LBJ attended a reception at the Indian embassy, which he enjoyed so much that he stayed far longer than originally planned. Indira Gandhi seemed to have won over the American president and much of the press corps.

But the warm feelings of the visit to Washington were short-lived. Gandhi touched down in Moscow less than a month later. Upon the conclusion of her visit there, she and the Soviets issued a joint communiqué calling for a cessation of US bombing of North Vietnam. President Johnson's response to this move was described as alternating from "the violent to the obscene."[25] Johnson, a great nurturer of grudges, told confidants, "I'm not going to just underwrite the perpetuation of the government of India and the people of India to have them spend all of their goddam time dedicating themselves to the destruction of the United States."[26] Even David Bell, who was wholly supportive of the Indian reform effort, wondered why the Indians felt so compelled to "kick us in the shins about Vietnam."[27]

"LBJ had a very strong feeling about the Indians, because they were so critically independent," explained Maurice Williams of AID.[28] Johnson put his stance in Texas terms: "You sup at our table, you mind your manners." Williams argued that Johnson's position encouraged India to place the highest possible priority on raising agricultural production because they were "infuriated to be placed in the position of holding out a beggar bowl for American food aid."[29]

The short tether became even shorter, even as India's monsoon season faltered for the second year in a row. Gandhi's government faced the possibility of a terrible famine.

LBJ demanded that AID shave its shipping schedules to buy him more time. "There were periods when the timing of shipping the grain was worked out to the precise day on which the shipment of grain had to be on the boxcar to get to the port to get on the ship to reach India to keep the food supply flowing," explained David Bell. "I personally felt at the time—and still feel—that he carried this much too far."[30]

Some fifty to sixty million Indians were at risk of starvation.

Agriculture Minister Subramaniam, who was the most important advocate for these reforms, provided some context with a touch of understatement: "The United States always gives, but doesn't give graciously."[31] Johnson's hard line made it harder in many ways for Subramaniam because, as he said, "The speeches gave ammunition to those who were attacking me on the grounds that I was following American advice."[32]

As the food crisis with India had unfolded in 1966, David Bell decided to end his time at AID. Telling one interviewer that his time running AID had left him "bushed and broke," Bell shifted over to become a senior executive at the Ford Foundation—a role that allowed him to pursue many of the same goals with considerably fewer headaches.[33]

Bell deserves enormous credit for helping AID find its footing and for launching some of its most important work. There was almost universal agreement on who should succeed Bell when he left for a senior role with the Ford Foundation, and his deputy, William Gaud, was moved into the post in a smooth transition. In a conversation with powerful senator Richard Russell, Johnson described Gaud as "the best administrator in the government."[34]

Gaud was a decorated military officer who had served under General Joseph Stilwell in World War II and had been responsible for overseeing military assistance to India, China, and Burma.[35] Don Brown of AID described Gaud as being so fond of profanity that his language "often approached that of a master sergeant."[36] Highly industrious, Gaud's main form of recreation was to occasionally sneak off on his thirty-two-foot sailboat, the *Content*, on the Potomac.[37]

During his confirmation hearings, Gaud sounded a note of practicality, observing that "there is no such thing as the instant economic development" and that in all likelihood the United States would need a foreign assistance program for some time.[38] At Gaud's swearing-in, LBJ acknowledged that perhaps the supporters of the assistance program had been "too romantic and claimed too much," but that aid dollars ultimately produce greater "return than any other dollar we spend abroad."[39]

Back in India, Gandhi's Congress Party came under pressure because of the decision to devalue the rupee, a move championed by a consortium of foreign aid donors led by the United States and the World Bank. The move was felt acutely by consumers at a time when there was already a recession triggered by the back-to-back monsoon failures. "Foreign pressure came at a time when the new government of Mrs. Gandhi was less than six months old and was not yet firmly established," noted economists Anne Krueger and Vernon Ruttan, "the entire episode was seen as a disaster for the aid relationship."[40]

The State Department observed in an internal memo that there was a "prevailing ugly mood growing out of frustration, anger and annoyance both inside and outside the Congress Party" by August 1966 because, "It was alleged that Mrs. Gandhi was submitting to foreign pressure."[41]

Yet at virtually that same moment, LBJ scribbled on a memo regarding India, "We must hold onto all the wheat we can—send nothing unless we break an iron bound agreement by not sending."[42] The Department of Agriculture, which had advocated tough conditionality in the first place, was described by NSC staffers as "almost desperate" to keep wheat moving.[43]

Bill Gaud wrote to the NSC that India had already devalued the rupee by 57 percent, set aside thirty-two million acres of the most productive farmland for a crash production program, increased the number of students enrolled in schools, and devoted four times the investment in family planning than the three previous central economic plans combined.[44]

The tight leash was being felt in India. Prime Minister Gandhi made a national appeal in November of 1966 as larger portions of the country were placed under rationing and ration sizes were cut, and then cut again.[45] Some two hundred million Indians were receiving at least part of their food through the rationing system.

Food riots had broken out in several Indian states.[46] Walt Rostow warned that Gandhi might be forced from power because of the famine, adding that "peaceful change is most unlikely in a context of starvation."[47] Parliamentarians in New Delhi accused their own government of submitting to LBJ's "insult and national humiliation."[48]

Negative stories about Johnson's strategy, fueled by the Indian ambassador to Washington, were appearing in the *Washington Post* and elsewhere. (One aide recalled the president's response: "Goddamn it! Who leaked all this stuff about my holding up food aid in India? How in the hell did it get in the papers that I am playing dominoes with the starving millions of the Punjab?")[49]

Robert Komer cautioned Johnson that there were limits to forcing "the grain revolution down the throats of the Indian government."[50]

"You tell those guys that I'm tired of giving—of paying for their mistakes all the time," responded Johnson testily. "When they actually close the deal and sign the contract for these fertilizer plants, then I'm going to be more liberal, but they are not doing their job. They're leaving it all to us to do."

After further cautious appeals from his staff to release the food more quickly, Johnson snapped. He told his team that when there was a documented example of starvation because of the late arrival of American food, "You tell that Ambassador out there of mine, Chester Bowles—you tell that guy to go over there and when he's got a real authenticated case, pack up his bones and send them back here. Then I'll believe him."

His advisers were stunned into silence. Johnson was unbending.

As the drama surrounding food aid reached a breaking point, an equally important story was unfolding far from the headlines. In research labs and test fields in Mexico and the Philippines, crop scientists had been toiling in relative obscurity for years with the support of AID, the World Bank, and the Ford and Rockefeller Foundations.

The goal of these scientists: to help develop high-producing, disease-resistant strains of wheat and rice that would thrive in the often-harsh conditions of the developing world. These researchers included Norm Borlaug, supported by the Rockefeller Foundation, whose laboratory in Mexico was, according to one of his biographers, "a windowless tarpaper shack on 160 acres of dry, scrubby land" at "the ass-end of nowhere."[51]

Borlaug's story was improbable—he had never traveled out of the United States before his work in Mexico, could not speak Spanish, and had no experience breeding plants. But the struggle to produce more wheat became personal as he witnessed Mexico's poverty up close. As Borlaug wrote to his wife, "The earth is so lacking in life force; the plants just cling to existence. . . . Can you imagine a poor Mexican struggling to feed his family?"[52]

Yet through serendipity, backbreaking hard work, and sheer stubbornness, Borlaug cross-bred tens of thousands of varieties of wheat as he challenged almost every orthodoxy of plant science. Borlaug's results were inarguable. He produced short, hardy, high-producing varieties of wheat which increased yields by 600 percent and fended off the diseases that usually decimated crops.[53]

Similar breakthroughs, dubbed no less than a miracle by many observers, were achieved at the International Rice Research Institute in the Philippines where scientists produced dynamic gains in yields by cross-breeding long-stemmed rice from Indonesia and short-stemmed wild rice from China.

"These and other developments in the field of agriculture contain the makings of a new revolution," said Bill Gaud of AID in a speech at the Shoreham Hotel in Washington. "It is not a violent Red Revolution like that of the Soviets, nor is it a White Revolution like that of the Shah of Iran. I call it the Green Revolution." Gaud's words stuck, and the Green Revolution helped cement the notion that science and technology could help transform pressing global trends in food and population growth.[54]

AID played an important role in disseminating these new seed varieties in India and elsewhere with do-it-yourself kits that contained seeds, fertilizer, and basic information on how to use them.[55] AID also financed rural electrification, road building, and irrigation projects, and provided considerable technical expertise to farmers.[56]

AID invested heavily in building links between US and Indian educational and research institutions related to agriculture. AID brought more than two thousand Indian scientists to study agriculture and natural resource management in the United States, with more than one thousand Indian students obtaining advanced degrees from land-grant universities.[57] (There had been only about one hundred PhD students in agriculture in all of India at the time of independence.) AID also backed six American land-grant universities to help India develop its own network of agricultural universities. More than three hundred US professors and agronomists were posted in India.[58]

Today, more than 50 percent of Indian agricultural research staffers hold doctoral degrees, one of the highest rates in the developing world.[59] India went on to establish more than twenty-eight agricultural universities, a clear legacy of these investments.[60] In addition, Indian scientists have produced steady waves of their own technology, innovation, and insight. Similar AID investments in the Indian Institute of Technology in Kanpur—carried out in partnership with a coalition of nine major US universities, including MIT and Princeton—helped that facility become a leading breeding ground for Indian engineers and scientists.

In 1963, Norm Borlaug toured India with Indian agricultural scientist Mankombu Sambasivan Swaminathan, an important plant geneticist in his own right and an influential voice in adapting the Green Revolution breakthroughs to Indian conditions. During this trip, Borlaug encountered some of the social conditions—such as sharp caste divisions that often prevented land ownership—that stood in the way of greater uptake of the new wheat varieties. He also came away convinced that a major infusion of fertilizer would be key to the success of the program in India.

The advocacy of these two men, when coupled with that of Agriculture Minister Subramaniam, led Gandhi to take the risky move of buying 18,000 tons of the new hybrid seed from Mexico in 1966 just as the disputes with the Johnson administration were coming to a boil.[61] Minister Subramaniam dug up a cricket patch next to his home in New Delhi and planted it with the experimental wheat in an effort to build public demand for the product.

In January 1967, with local elections in India less than a month away, President Johnson was finally satisfied with India's progress, and approved the wholesale release of food stocks. Substantial amounts of food had gone through during even the toughest periods of the short-tether policy, but 1967 brought a gargantuan food relief effort. More than six hundred US ships, the largest maritime flotilla since D-Day, carried forty million tons of grain to stem the crisis.[62]

The combined impact of reforms pushed by the Indian agriculture minister and LBJ had an enormous impact. With fertilizer, irrigation, and greater use of pesticides, India's rice production jumped by more than 50 percent in twenty years, and its wheat output increased by more than 230 percent—all without a significant expansion of land under cultivation.[63] Subsequent droughts in the late 1970s in India did not require emergency food assistance, and India has become a food exporter.

Later, during the Nixon administration, AID and other donors formed the Consultative Group on International Agricultural Research, a collaboration of international research centers built upon the lessons in India and of Borlaug's work. Some estimate that the collective research breakthroughs of this network have increased food production in the developing world by 7 to 8 percent and cut malnutrition rates by more than ten million people.[64]

But the Green Revolution was not without its downsides. In India, as fields suddenly became more profitable, large landowners, usually upper caste, squeezed poor farmers off the land. Allison Butler Herrick of AID argued that it was often better-off farmers who benefited from the new varieties, because these varieties required the use of fertilizer, pesticides, and irrigation.[65] So, while the Green Revolution was a powerful force in staving off global hunger, it sometimes exacerbated rather than reduced income inequalities in developing countries.

In addition, the intensive use of pesticides, fertilizer, and water in Borlaug's approach raised significant environmental concerns. Some argued that making farmers more dependent on industrial inputs for their work only accelerated environmental degradation while pushing many poor farmers further into debt. Others noted that the emphasis on high-producing strains allowed global agribusinesses to play an increasingly dominant role.

In a balanced review of Borlaug's legacy, agricultural scientist Peter Hazell observed, "Fertilizers and pesticides were often used excessively or inappropriately, polluting waterways and killing beneficial insects and other wildlife. In some places, poor irrigation and drainage practices caused salt to build up in the soil to such an extent that farmers had to abandon some of their best farmland."[66] But, as Hazell also noted, "thanks to new seed varieties, Asia doubled its food production with only a 4 percent increase in land use," helping prevent widespread soil erosion and loss of biodiversity.

Borlaug was largely dismissive of environmental critics, accusing them of elitism, and insisting that, "If they lived just one month amid the misery of the developing world, as I have for fifty years, they'd be crying out for tractors and fertilizer."[67] Borlaug also argued bluntly when he won the Nobel Peace Prize in 1970 that the real problem was not farming techniques. "If the world population continues to increase at the same rate, we will destroy the species."[68]

While the environmental dimensions of the Green Revolution are vital to consider, it was a historic accomplishment that freed millions of the world's poor from the terrible oppression of constant hunger. The period between the end of World War II and the early 1970s saw agricultural yields around the globe increase by more than they had in the previous one thousand years.[69]

President Johnson saw the Green Revolution as a validation of his short-tether policy, which he acknowledged was "profoundly unpopular among India's leaders."[70] ("It was hardly more popular with those in our own government," added Johnson.) Johnson defended his approach with his trademark blend of grandiosity and self-pity. "I stood almost alone, with only a few concurring advisers, in this fight to slow the pace of US assistance, to persuade the Indians to do more for themselves, and to induce other nations to lend a helping hand. This was one of the most difficult and lonely struggles of my presidency."

An official NSC history of the episode declared that the Green Revolution "was probably as uniquely the president's personal achievement as any that emerged during his administration."[71]

Agriculture Minister Subramaniam, so pivotal to the success in India, lost his race for a parliamentary seat in the February 1967 election. He was awarded India's highest civilian honor, the Bharat Ratna, in 1998.

When AID mission director John Lewis later asked Indian Cabinet Secretary B. Sivaraman what he thought was the most important factor contributing to the Green Revolution, Sivaraman smiled and replied, "LBJ."[72] "I realized Sivaraman's meaning," said Lewis, "LBJ's behavior had been so abhorrent to Indian politicians and opinion leaders that it built a fire under them for agricultural expansion as nothing else could."[73] Indeed, subsequent Congress Party campaign posters often featured slogans calling on citizens to recall "the sour taste" of American food aid.[74]

The United States and India, working as partners, had staved off disaster. But that victory came at a cost, and the Green Revolution marked the beginning of a growing estrangement between New Delhi and Washington.

POPULATION CONTROL

"Population growth now consumes about two-thirds of economic growth in the less developed world," argued President Johnson in a 1966 message to Congress. "As death rates are steadily driven down the individual miracle of birth becomes a collective tragedy of want."[75] Given the political sensitivity of family planning—"a question for each family and each nation to decide"—Johnson also made clear that family planning assistance would only be proffered when explicitly requested.

Johnson gave some thirty speeches emphasizing the importance of addressing the population explosion, saying that it was "next to peace, the most important task."[76]

Perhaps no one followed these statements more closely than Dr. Reimert T. Ravenholt, who most commonly went by "Rei," a Seattle medical epidemiologist who was tapped to lead the population effort at AID.

"From Seattle, it seemed I would receive whatever I needed to run a program in Washington," recalled Ravenholt.[77] Yet, upon arriving in Washington, Ravenholt was given a fifteen-square-foot office, one secretary, and no funds specifically earmarked for his work. "With that," laughed Ravenholt, "I was supposed to drop the birthrate of the world."

Family planning programs were initially given a cold shoulder by much of the agency's staff who felt that it was a passing fad.[78] The fact that AID was overwhelmingly male likely also contributed to this attitude; many economists still viewed women as a marginal piece of the development puzzle.

David Bell, in one of his last appearances as the head of AID in 1966, told a congressional committee that AID did not plan on providing contraceptives in the developing world, and that it did not want funding earmarked for family planning purposes. Ravenholt started at the agency a week after Bell's testimony. "It looked hopeless. We didn't have money; we didn't have people. And I realized I'd made a huge mistake," said Ravenholt, "but my pride wouldn't let me just admit that."

In 1965, the program started with $2 million of discretionary funds, and Bill Gaud did considerable heavy lifting to help get the effort off the ground.[79] He stressed that such programs were voluntary. He carefully cultivated congressional support.[80] His cause was bolstered by strong backing from General William Draper who lobbied Congress to add an earmark for population programs and formed the Population Crisis Committee.

Senator Ernest Gruening of Alaska held multiple congressional hearings on population problems in 1966 and 1967 and made considerable progress in encouraging members to accept that there was an important role for AID in international family planning. The senator was also able to introduce a statement from former president Dwight Eisenhower, who acknowledged that his earlier disavowal of family planning efforts had been a mistake. "If we now ignore the plight of those unborn generations which, because of our unreadiness to take corrective action in controlling populations growth, will be denied any expectations beyond abject poverty and suffering," wrote Eisenhower, "then history will rightly condemn us."[81]

Early in his tenure, Ravenholt visited India, and the trip made a lasting impression.[82] Ravenholt left India convinced that millions of women in the developing world wanted to escape the cycle of repeated unplanned and unwanted pregnancies. His solution was simple and straightforward: provide women with contraceptive services. Yet the approach was not without controversy. As Steve Sinding, a family planning expert at AID, explained, "For the family planners, direct contraceptive services seemed the logical approach; for the social scientists, a more comprehensive assault on poverty, high mortality, and illiteracy seemed a much better way to go."[83]

Ravenholt was undeterred. He pointed to polling data indicating that many poor women wanted to stop having children but lacked both information and contraception. Boosted by congressional earmarks for the new program, Ravenholt set about recruiting personnel, often in conjunction with schools of public health, and he soon groomed an unusually dedicated cadre of highly loyal staff. But, according to a history of the family planning program by Phyllis Piotrow, Ravenholt's personal style and "insensitive and single-minded certitude" irritated many.[84]

International family planning took on a popular culture bent with the publication of *The Population Bomb* by Paul Ehrlich in 1968. The tract was breathless, with an opening sentence that declared "the battle to feed all of humanity is over." Ehrlich predicted that hundreds of millions around the globe would starve to death, and that "an utter breakdown of the capacity of the planet to support humanity" would occur within fifteen years, unleashing a cascade of famine, environmental ruin, and social collapse.

The book, rich in speculation and thin in science, became a bestseller. Ehrlich appeared on *The Tonight Show* with Johnny Carson more than twenty times to promote his work and he became something of a celebrity. Worrying demographic projections were not new, and more-measured findings in 1964 and 1965 had prompted President Johnson to make population control a key priority for AID in the first place, but *The Population Bomb* pushed the issue to the front of the national and international dialogue.

Ehrlich's argument found purchase with the rapidly growing environmental movement, and his message resonated amid the political turbulence of 1968—a time when it felt the political seams were pulling apart around the globe.

Many development experts were uneasy with the glibness of Ehrlich's message, pointing out that consumption by prosperous families in North America and Europe was placing far greater environmental strain on the planet than large populations of people in the developing world living in near-subsistence conditions.

Thanks to a rapidly expanding budget, Rei Ravenholt was in command of a small army of public health professionals and contractors.

The hyperbolic warnings of *The Population Bomb* were a double-edged sword. In one respect, they helped launch AID's family planning efforts, and make them one of AID's flagship programs over time. Family planning programs would ultimately give hundreds of millions of women the opportunity to have smaller, healthier, better cared for, and more prosperous families. The development of the Pill and the IUD seemed like the ideal technological breakthroughs to help transform the debate, and in many ways they were.

However, *The Population Bomb* also helped stoke concern about unchecked population growth among leaders in China and India that launched draconian measures to curb their birth rates. The actions by the Indians and Chinese in the following years were completely at odds with the voluntary nature of US assistance programs but also have to be considered when looking at the complex legacy of the world's awakening to the importance of family planning.

THE CHANGING FACE OF AID

As AID increasingly considered the role of women in development it slowly began to grapple with the issue of women in its own ranks. The agency first made a deliberate effort to recruit more women in 1966, bringing in a class of thirty women management interns. This came at a time when the initial graduates of the Peace Corps program were looking to AID as the natural continuation of their careers, and many of these Peace Corps vets were women.

These were not the first women at AID, but the conditions for the women who joined before 1966 were quite different. Many of the new women hires were shocked to see that the older women, who in some cases had been at AID for years, were working at about the same rank and pay as they were upon just entering. "You would see that these older women actually had academic backgrounds just as good as ours," explained Judy Bryson of the agency, but they "had come to the State Department or AID as secretaries"—the only position for which they could get hired at the time.[85]

These pioneers had to claw their way up from low-level clerical posts before reaching program jobs and leadership positions. Having to deal with an influx of young women in their mid-twenties who were suddenly coming in at a similar or higher level was uncomfortable all around. "They did not like us very much," said Bryson. "They really had a lot of scars of the battles they had come through."

It was not until 1971 that married women could join the Foreign Service. Previously, if a woman was single and in the Foreign Service, she was forced to resign if she married. (Single men in similar situations had been required to resign if they married a non-US citizen, subject to a review of the new spouse's background.)

America was experiencing rapid, turbulent social change, but both AID and the State Department remained relatively staid, white, and male. "If you went into the State Department cafeteria, which was a huge room, there were almost all men in sober suits," added Bryson. "The older women had survived by looking like the men by wearing very sober suits." In a similar vein, there were some minorities within the ranks at AID, but breaking into the system remained an uphill climb even for the well-qualified.

It took legal action to begin to more completely transform the workplace. Alison Palmer of the State Department filed the first equal employment opportunity complaint from within the ranks of the Foreign Service in 1968, ultimately winning her case three years later.[86] She subsequently launched a class action suit against the US Foreign Service in 1976, and her pursuit of greater equality in hiring and promotions played out over a difficult and contentious decades-long process.

A later survey of women staff at AID found that some 70 percent of them reported facing some type of sexual harassment in carrying out their work from supervisors, co-workers, people on the street, or government officials.[87] Although the findings were initially met with disbelief, it was only the hard push by a very determined group of women employees at AID that began to change the culture.

The role of women more broadly also became a focus with 1973 legislation by Senator Charles Percy of Illinois that mandated the agency pay particular attention to the role of women in development. The agency issued its first policy guidance on the topic a year later.[88]

Congress also pushed to make development itself more participatory, with congressmen Donald Fraser of Minnesota and Bradford Morse of Massachusetts arguing that democracy had too often taken a backseat in assistance programs.[89] The two members helped pass what came to be known as "Title IX" legislation in 1966, which called upon the agency to ensure broader participation in the development process by encouraging democracy.[90]

Although support for democracy had often been championed as an aim of foreign aid, particularly with regard to the Alliance for Progress, this was the first time AID was given a legislative mandate to pay attention to politics. One commentary at the time called the move a "classic example of a Congressional initiative thrust upon an unprepared and resistant Executive," although the legislation did allow the State Department to waive the conditions imposed by Title IX in countries it viewed as national security priorities, which it frequently did.[91]

AID's initial forays into democracy promotion were highly indirect, such as supporting farmers' cooperatives and training for community leaders. There was (and there still remains to an important degree) considerable resistance to the idea of mixing politics and development. Yet there is no escaping the fact that development is a deeply political endeavor. There really is no such thing as a truly neutral foreign aid program, even in cases where the intentions are purely humanitarian.

The initial Title IX efforts did not lead to wholesale changes in how AID practiced its work until many years later. As well-regarded democracy experts Tom Carothers and Dianne de Gramont observed of Title IX, "The US policy community had adjusted to living with undemocratic governments in developing countries"—particularly when the alternative was a potential takeover by communists.[92]

The fact that the United States was willing to dip its toes in the water of democracy promotion meant that other bilateral donors such as France and the United Kingdom did also. The World Bank and the regional development banks, in contrast, were much slower to support participatory governance as a core element of development.

The US role in encouraging other nations to develop foreign assistance programs and to build a community of practice among donor nations emerged as a quiet success story. From its beginnings in 1960, the US-chaired Development Assistance Committee of the OECD encouraged increased aid budgets, developed common standards for measuring development assistance, maintained authoritative statistics, conducted peer reviews of donor performance, and achieved consensus on good practice for development cooperation.

At this point, every formal Marshall Plan recipient was now a donor, a remarkable testament to the European recovery. Broadening the donor community had been one of the key objectives spelled out by Kennedy when he established AID, and this effort was by almost any measure very successful. If anything, European aid donors complained over time that they wished the United States was doing more.

The bottom line was striking: The United States provided close to 60 percent of all official development assistance in 1960; just a decade later, the US share had declined to about 45 percent. This dramatic shift came as a result of countries like France, West Germany, and Japan more than tripling their contributions between the 1960s and 1970s.[93]

AFRICA AND THE MOST DREADFUL SCOURGE

Africa was a relative afterthought for much of the 1960s, and despite the wave of independence movements and subsequent Cold War jockeying, most of America's assistance dollars flowed into Asia and Latin America.

During LBJ's second term, there was a simultaneous debate about putting more resources into Africa and significantly narrowing the focus of AID's programs on the continent.

The pressure to consolidate operations in Africa came in no small part from US ambassador to Ethiopia, Edward Korry. Korry argued to both the State Department and White House that assistance programs were spread too thin, leaving AID with a high administrative budget and misleading Africans and Congress about what could actually be achieved with those dollars.[94]

Korry urged that AID's operations be concentrated in no more than ten high-priority countries such as Nigeria, Ethiopia, and Ghana where the agency would maintain a country mission. Lower-priority issues and countries would be handled on a regional basis or through multilateral efforts of the World Bank or the UN. "The Korry Report received considerable acceptance within Congress," explained David Shear of AID, but also brought about a clear downside, "a fairly dramatic reduction in the overall budget for Africa."[95]

Congress set a worldwide ceiling on the number of countries allowed to receive assistance in 1966, forty each for economic and military aid, but the president was given wide authority to waive those restrictions, which he routinely did.[96]

At the same time, some of President Johnson's advisers were pushing him to come up with a sweeping plan for the continent; an "African Alliance for Progress."[97] Johnson was intrigued with the idea and charged AID and the State Department to explore plans along these lines.

On May 26, 1966, Johnson delivered a ringing endorsement of self-determination in Africa, stressed the importance of development, and spoke forcefully against racial discrimination in Southern Rhodesia (the white-ruled British colony that later became Zimbabwe.)[98] But ultimately Johnson was too distracted by Vietnam and his sagging popularity to mount a major assistance initiative in Africa. The abiding attitude toward the continent was encapsulated in a 1965 NSC memo: "In sum, we don't kid ourselves that Africa is vital, but neither can it be ignored."[99]

Yet Africa would become the crucible for one of foreign aid's most important and enduring triumphs against a killer that had stalked the globe for more than ten thousand years.

Edward Jenner, who pioneered the smallpox vaccine in 1796, called smallpox "the most dreadful scourge of the human species."[100] This was not hyperbole. Smallpox had claimed billions of lives over the centuries.[101] Although the disease had largely been curbed in Europe and the Americas, by 1966 there were still between ten and fifteen million cases annually in the developing world, claiming between one and a half to two million lives—a staggering death toll in its own right, all the more so when considered that it was almost entirely located in about thirty developing countries.[102]

The Soviet Union had first proposed a global effort to eradicate smallpox in 1958, but the international response had been halfhearted, with many countries, including the United States, preferring to focus on other diseases, such as malaria and measles.

D. A. Henderson, a thirty-five-year-old American physician who described himself as a "shoe leather epidemiologist" at the Centers for Disease Control, submitted a proposal to AID in 1965 for a joint, five-year effort by AID and the CDC to eradicate smallpox across eighteen countries in West Africa—the most important hub for the disease apart from India and China at the time.[103] "With the many nomads moving through West Africa, a region-wide program would be necessary for effective smallpox control," explained Henderson. "This would have to include Nigeria, which constituted 67 percent of the population of the whole area."

Much to Henderson's surprise, the proposal was accepted in full by President Johnson and AID. Because of the AID funding, the World Health Organization recommitted itself by a narrow two-vote margin to the goal of smallpox eradication within a decade. It was a rare moment when the United States and Soviet Union joined forces to advance an important global goal under a strategy set by the World Health Organization.

According to Henderson, he was chosen to lead the global effort because the head of the World Health Organization demanded an American be put in the position. He was sure it would fail—and wanted Washington to shoulder the blame.[104] Even Henderson admitted that the "ten-year plan was little more than a theoretical hope."[105]

The smallpox eradication effort began in earnest early in 1967. In many ways, smallpox appeared ideal for an eradication campaign. Jenner's vaccination was still highly effective 180 years after its invention. The disease only moved through human-to-human transmission, and new technologies were making vaccination efforts more effective. AID had partially funded the development of a new field vaccination method, building on methods pioneered by the US military, which used air pressure rather than a needle to administer the vaccine.[106] This method was further refined so that it did not require electricity, and could be run via a foot pump in even the most remote settings. In addition, the CDC had helped to develop a freeze-dried smallpox vaccine. (Keeping medicines cold in tropical settings that lack electricity has long been a major public health conundrum.)

The partnership between AID and the Centers for Disease Control was vital. AID provided funding, local expertise, connections to ministries, and help in addressing a series of inevitable logistical hurdles. The World Health Organization provided fuel and some measure of funding. The CDC brought its considerable medical expertise to the table.

However, the relationship between AID and the CDC often resembled that of an old married couple prone to constant bickering, already soured to a certain extent by an earlier and not very successful campaign against measles in West Africa. Henderson sniffed that AID was "difficult" and "unwilling," although he did allow that the agency was a significant contributor.[107] AID officials frequently found their CDC counterparts imperious and often ignorant of conditions on the ground.

As Henderson himself acknowledged, the "number of other imponderables—floods, wars and famines, hundreds of thousands of refugees, national bureaucracies and constraints that rivalled the U.S. in number and complexity" were obstacles he had never imagined. Dr. Bill Foege of the CDC, who led the program in West Africa, added, "It is clear, in retrospect, that we didn't know how to eradicate smallpox when the eradication effort began."

Because they were trying to eliminate continued transmission, it was essential that all eighteen countries in the region take part in the program, particularly Nigeria, given that it held the bulk of the population. But as Horace Ogden notes in a history of smallpox eradication, when a CDC representative arrived in Lagos, the government was resistant. Over six weeks, the US ambassador, the head of the World Health Organization office in Nigeria, and the AID mission all lobbied to get General Yakubu Gowon, the Nigerian military head of state, to sign off. Ultimately, a friend of a friend of the president's fiancée (who was a nurse) helped arrange a meeting. The eradication effort had its sign-off.[108]

The initial strategy to eliminate smallpox was built on what were then the best practices in public health: Teams would blanket West Africa with immunizations over a two- or three-year period, making sure to cover even remote villages. (And the campaign did achieve remarkable reach, delivering more than 150 million immunizations.) If small pockets of the disease remained after that, they would be wiped out, bit by bit.

But the situation turned desperate when logistical snarls prevented the delivery of the vaccines needed to cover a large part of Eastern Nigeria. Trying to contain the damage, Bill Foege of the CDC determined the best he could do was to set up a surveillance system to rapidly report areas facing smallpox outbreaks. Vaccinations would then be directed to those priority areas. "As each patient was detected," recalled D. A. Henderson, "he was isolated, all his contacts—and then the village where he lived—were vaccinated, and a search was begun to find the source of his infection so that other infected areas could be dealt with similarly."[109]

By the time sufficient supplies had arrived to finally allow the mass immunization campaign to begin in Eastern Nigeria, Foege couldn't find any smallpox in the region. His improvised containment strategy had proved more effective than the mass campaigns being undertaken elsewhere. "It became clear that under most circumstances, smallpox spread much more slowly than most had thought, much slower than measles or influenza, for example," explained Henderson. The disease also tended to be seasonal and cluster in a specific village or part of town, allowing resources to be closely focused.

The effectiveness of the surveillance-containment approach was rapidly replicated. Mobile teams were positioned to respond quickly, and the World Health Organization offered rewards to citizens reporting cases.[110] By focusing on a smaller caseload, medical teams were able to ensure that vaccines were properly administered, something that had not always been the case when vaccinations were being delivered in the millions. When applied in Sierra Leone, the surveillance-containment approach led to smallpox being eradicated in nine months. Surveillance containment became the driving strategy behind smallpox eradication not only in West Africa, but across the globe, and was crucial in helping tackle even larger caseloads in India and China.

The success was stunning, and even many of the skeptics of the smallpox eradication campaign began to think that it might be achievable on a global scale.

In October 1977, a Somali man was identified as the last natural victim to die of smallpox. On May 8, 1980, the World Health Organization declared the world smallpox-free. It was a remarkable triumph of science, international cooperation, and sheer will. The road had been anything but smooth, rife with bureaucratic sniping and clashing egos. But the willingness to cooperate across borders and to learn in the field resulted in something that was unprecedented in human history: the elimination of a naturally occurring disease. Perhaps even more remarkably, the smallpox eradication campaign was achieved only four months behind its self-imposed ten-year target.

The smallpox eradication campaign also provides one of the more-powerful examples of the return on investment from foreign assistance. Over ten years, the international community spent $98 million to eradicate smallpox, with developing countries providing slightly more than twice that amount. But as the Center for Global Development points out, because the United States no longer needs to vaccinate Americans or treat the disease, it saves an amount of money equal to its entire contributions toward eradicating smallpox every twenty-six days.[111]

VIETNAM

No issue dominated the Johnson years more than Vietnam. The United States dropped more tons of bombs on Vietnam than it unleashed throughout the entire duration of World War II. President Johnson saw the rapid expansion of AID programs in Vietnam as a crucial complement to military efforts.

Over the protests of the AID mission director in Vietnam, who argued that a lighter footprint made for more-effective counterinsurgency efforts, Johnson forward-deployed aid workers in a mammoth hearts-and-minds campaign.

In the United States, unrest flared across college campuses, and major protests filled the streets from Washington, DC, to Los Angeles. As Nicholas Katzenbach wrote to President Johnson in a confidential memo, "Hanoi's strategy is based on winning the war in the United States, not in Vietnam."[112]

The foreign assistance program became a convenient target for congressional ire with Vietnam, in part because about half of all US economic aid grants were being directed to that country.[113] Senator William Fulbright of Arkansas, chair of the Senate Foreign Relations Committee, pushed to have the entire aid program eliminated within twenty-four months, and he blamed assistance programs for pulling the American military into foreign entanglements like Vietnam.[114] AID's funding levels hit a new low point in 1967.[115] Lights in the hallways of the State Department were dimmed in order to save electricity, giving the building a half-dead feeling.[116]

As the rapid buildup of US military surge in the forces in Vietnam began in the summer of 1965, there was a concurrent surge in building of bases, airfields, and improvements at the ports to support this force. With a geyser of American money pouring into the country to erect the infrastructure of war, AID's leadership feared runaway inflation. Maintaining some sense of economic equilibrium became an imperative. "The only short answer," explained Bill Gaud, "was to import a great quantity of goods into Vietnam and sop up that money."[117]

Barry Zorthian, the chief spokesperson for the United States in Vietnam during the Johnson era, described the broad challenge facing AID: "Our task was to take the assignment we'd been given as Foreign Service officers and convert a mandarin, intrigue-filled society into a functioning, responsive government, pushing economic and political development for a largely rural population that was honeycombed with a very effective anti-government guerrilla force."[118]

Up until 1967, American political and military leadership continued to view security, politics, and development as distinct enterprises at the village level in Vietnam—much to the frustration of AID workers, who recognized that all three were interlocked. It was impossible to make lasting progress by providing villagers with healthier pigs if security was so poor that the Viet Cong entered villages every night. New rice varieties weren't going to buy loyalty if the Vietnamese government failed to provide a compelling political narrative to compete with that of the communists.

Part of the problem was that the relationship between economic development and communism was always poorly understood. "The simple assumption that communism results primarily from economic poverty is so widely accepted in the United States that it has become almost an article of faith," noted an unusually thoughtful Library of Congress report commissioned by the Senate Foreign Relations Committee in 1966.[119] "However, history seems to demonstrate that although there is a relationship between poverty and the growth of communism, it is a highly complex one." The report's coda: "Little is gained, indeed much is lost when, in our zeal in combating communism, we ignore the importance of good government, efficient administration, and the inculcation of justice in the aid-receiving countries."[120]

A precipitating moment came in March 1967 when President Johnson and his key military and civilian leaders gathered in Guam to discuss Vietnam. One of the key topics of the discussion was "pacification," the effort to win political and military support in the countryside. General William Westmoreland pushed for the military to take over pacification efforts.[121] But there remained real skepticism that the military would be up to managing the political and development aspects of pacification.

Recognizing that the existing approach wasn't working, the Pentagon, AID, and State Department embraced a new strategy in May 1967. The US government launched the clumsily named "Civil Operations and Revolutionary Development Support" program, most commonly referred to as CORDS. It was an integrated program under the military headed by a civilian, initially Bob Komer. For the first time, Washington's approach to counterinsurgency became, in the words of Rufus Phillips, "a fully integrated military and civilian effort."[122]

Large numbers of AID employees were suddenly serving in the military chain of command and operating significantly independently from both the embassy and AID mission. Clayton McManaway headed the plans and programs office for CORDS. "No one else wanted to do it," McManaway remembers, primarily because many staff feared it would harm their careers post-Vietnam, which it often did.[123]

Because CORDS was a presidential priority, resources flowed into the program, and some six thousand people were soon dedicated to the effort. For the first time, as Bob Komer related, LBJ now saw "the developmental war as equal in importance with the military war."

At Komer's urging, Bill Gaud established an entire bureau dedicated just to Vietnam. While it may seem odd in retrospect that a single country was being elevated to a level of importance usually assigned to entire continents, the Vietnam Bureau was soon AID's largest, and was directing more funding than dedicated to all of Africa. The AID mission in Vietnam quickly became the largest in the world, with the fastest expansion of AID staff working on any program in its history. AID personnel in Vietnam peaked at 2,300 in 1968, more than ten times the staff of the Africa Bureau.[124]

A center was created in Virginia for the sole purpose of giving AID staff headed to Vietnam language and security training. This training usually lasted six to nine months, with considerable emphasis on culture, language, and military readiness, "I was taught how to fire a weapon. I was taught survival techniques," said Julius Coles of the agency.[125]

Pacification placed considerable responsibility on the Vietnamese. "The Vietnamese ran every single operating program. Pacification was and is 99 percent pure Vietnamese in its staffing," explained Bob Komer, "We were the bankers. We provided the bulk of the logistics support. We were the shadow management."[126]

This emphasis on the Vietnamese role made AID's engagement pivotal, since they were the experts in coordination with the Vietnamese government. AID officers on the ground at the district and province levels had the lead on agriculture, economic

development, resettling displaced civilians, health care, and a range of other functions at the heart of the CORDS program.[127]

AID staff trained farmers, helped advance a land reform program, and tried to
encourage greater local participation in governance. The introduction of high-yield
rice varieties in the Mekong Delta was so successful that these grains were quickly
replicated by North Vietnamese soldiers to help increase their own rice production.[128]

Monthly progress reports from each of the provinces were delivered back to Saigon, an effort to quantify the success of CORDS.[129] Villages were deemed secure,
partly secure, or not secure, with rich layers of data entered into a computerized
system. The United States was deploying cutting-edge technology against an oppo-
nent mostly known for wearing rubber sandals through thick jungle cover. These
statistical compilations became infamous because they also measured "body counts"
of Viet Cong allegedly killed.

Although CORDS appeared to be making more progress than previous
approaches, it came with a cost. More than forty AID and State Department personnel lost their lives in Vietnam, Cambodia, and Laos between 1960 and 1975. Almost
three times as many diplomatic personnel were killed in the broader Vietnam theater
than in the rest of America's wars combined. Why? Vietnam was one of the largest-
ever deployments of civilian international affairs personnel, with officers from State
and AID used as the frontline implementers of the pacification program targeting
the South Vietnamese. Many of these officials were posted outside of Saigon in villages, and the Viet Cong viewed them as legitimate targets.[130]

Rufus Phillips put the situation in perspective. "The Americans had finally got
their pacification act together, by forming CORDS and putting Bob Komer in
charge. He was effective in a bureaucratic context as an organizer, coordinator, and
pusher for action on the American side. However, he was a hyperkinetic, too full of
bombast and arrogance to be successful with the Vietnamese."[131]

A certain aura of unreality continued to hang over the entire war. As Colonel
Edward Lansdale confided in Phillips as the two emerged from a discussion in Saigon, "I don't know what country they were talking about at that meeting, but it sure
as hell wasn't Vietnam."

The war was increasingly divisive within the ranks of AID. More and more AID
officers were facing the choice of serving in Vietnam or quitting the Foreign Service.
Morale ebbed. From college campuses to church pews to dining room tables to
the halls of Congress, the arguments about the merits of the long and increasingly
bloody war in Southeast Asia were personal, confrontational, and bitter.

"For almost twenty years I had trouble talking about Vietnam to anybody that
hadn't been there at the same time," Wade Lathram of AID observed. "These weren't
just another day at the office. We were civilians, but we were in a war. No place was
safe."[132]

In January 1968, the Viet Cong launched the Tet Offensive, a massive campaign
of surprise attacks across South Vietnam. Lathram remembers the frantic calls from

his staff reporting gunfire and explosions all over the capital. At four in the morning he got a call from the AID mission director.[133]

"I want to come over to your house," he said.

"Why?" asked Lathram.

"They've just blown in the back door with a rocket."

Lathram, who was scheduled to spend his twenty-fifth wedding anniversary with his wife in Hawaii, instead found himself "at my desk dictating a tape to my wife, with my helmet, my AK-40 and my M16 on my side."

The Tet Offensive sent shock waves across America, further undercutting already badly eroding public confidence in how the war was being prosecuted. Although the Viet Cong suffered devastating losses in the offensive, the attack was ultimately successful in achieving the communists' long-held goal of convincing the American public that Vietnam was a quagmire.

John Hummon remembers one of the agency's staffers briefing Bill Gaud shortly after Tet. The staffer insisted that the worst of the fighting had only lasted several days, but projects on the ground were continuing to move forward.

"Oh, for Christ's sake," responded Gaud. "We got the shit kicked out of us. Politically, let's face it, this is a disaster."[134]

Anger over Vietnam helped propel Senator Eugene McCarthy to a near upset of President Johnson in the New Hampshire Democratic presidential primary in March 1968. On March 31, President Johnson stunned the world when he announced that he was dropping out of the presidential race.

In early April, civil rights leader Dr. Martin Luther King Jr. was assassinated in Memphis, Tennessee. Riots erupted in Washington, Chicago, Baltimore, Kansas City, and elsewhere, sometimes with entire neighborhoods set aflame. Vietnam War protests continued to mount in their intensity.

On June 5, Bobby Kennedy was assassinated in Los Angeles hours after winning the California primary. Huge protests and bloody street fights marred the subsequent Democratic National Convention in Chicago.

With the election of Republican Richard Nixon in November 1968, the Johnson presidency ended in recriminations, doubt, and anger. Johnson had set the wheels in motion on some of the most momentous forward movements in the history of development: the Green Revolution; smallpox eradication; the rise of international family planning programs; and an enviable track record in participant training and improving the capacity of partner governments. But in development, as in the rest of his presidency, the legacy of Vietnam cast a long shadow. The historic failures of Vietnam would shade public perceptions of foreign aid and its effectiveness for years to come.

During LBJ's final days in office, some $300 million was approved by Congress for India. Maurice Williams of AID pushed the White House to release the funds. Johnson resisted, telling Williams, "Let Nixon worry about it when he becomes president. Let the Indians find out how he treats them."[135]

5

The Devil's Bargain

ENTER NIXON

With Richard Nixon's 1968 election victory, some feared that the Republican president would look to quickly minimize the nation's commitment to international development. This was far from the case, and Nixon defended foreign assistance as "essential to express and achieve our national goals in the international community."[1]

That said, Nixon—heavily influenced by his close confidant and National Security Adviser Henry Kissinger—wanted to fundamentally transform both the goals of the US assistance program and how it was delivered.

Kissinger, in particular, disagreed sharply with President Kennedy's view that foreign aid's long-term strategic aim was to build a broader community of free-market democracies. For Kissinger, aid was first and foremost a transactional tool. He saw aid primarily as a means to secure immediate diplomatic aims, influence great power relations, and pressure or reward developing countries.

Nixon's vision of development was shaped in part by some of his world travels before becoming president. He conducted a successful, low-key visit to Latin America in 1967. In Peru, where he had been greeted by angry mobs nine years earlier, "Nixon threw off his coat, undid his tie, drank local beer, ate Peruvian pastry, laid bricks on a school building under construction, and donated $15 to the same school." At a press conference in Argentina before returning stateside, he lauded Argentinian president Juan Carlos Ongania, who led that country's military government after taking power in a military coup, saying he was the "right man for Argentina at this moment," and adding, "United States–style democracy won't work here. I wish it would."[2]

After a trip to Africa that same year, Nixon wrote to former president Dwight Eisenhower, noting, "It's going to be two generations at best before there is anything we here in the United States would recognize as 'freedom' in Africa, and it's doubtful even then."[3] Nixon viewed pushing for Western-style democracy as a mistake. "With the election of President Nixon in 1968, the support for President Kennedy's program of development assistance had run out," observed Maurice Williams of AID.[4]

Nixon wanted to deliver aid based more on political fealty to Washington than progress toward economic reforms. A later congressional report complained that Kissinger viewed foreign assistance as simply "a bank balance upon which to draw when commitments were to be made."[5]

Nixon moved quickly to appoint a new head of AID. Bill Gaud was out after his long, stellar service at the agency, and John Hannah, the president of Michigan State University for twenty-seven years, was in. Hannah had strong party credentials from his involvement in Michigan Republican politics and had served as an assistant secretary at the Pentagon during the Eisenhower administration.[6]

Michigan State had been at the cutting edge of efforts to bring academic research to bear on development problems and had been the first major academic institution to collaborate with AID on the ground in South Vietnam before expanding its work to Nigeria and the Philippines. Hannah focused much of his efforts on agricultural production, education, and efforts to bring universities more fully into the development cause. A great believer in research and innovation, he quickly established a Technical Assistance Bureau at AID to assist in those efforts.

Reflecting White House priorities, Hannah paid relatively less attention to macroeconomic reforms and big infrastructure projects and was largely able to get along with Congress at a time when Vietnam and other frustrations continued to boil.

Hannah was conservative, exceedingly respectful of the military point of view, strongly anti-communist, and compassionate. He believed in a people-centric approach to development. But perhaps most importantly, given the rather jaundiced view of AID from the White House, Hannah was smart enough to see that the agency was in trouble.[7]

GRAND PLANS

In response to congressional calls for aid reform, Nixon and Kissinger formed a high-level task force on international development in 1969, chaired by Bank of America president Rudolph Peterson.[8] Members of the Peterson Commission served in a private capacity, but there was little mistaking the fact that its grand plans emanated from the White House.

In a series of memos, Kissinger was unusually candid regarding the poor standing of the foreign aid program. "Gone are the days when the program had such goals as restoring pre-war European production levels in four years, eradicating malaria from the face of the globe in five years," Kissinger bemoaned. "Instead, AID's congressional presentation has relied on such concepts today as: 'the smallest and tightest foreign aid program ever,' 'full repayment on loans with interest.' "[9]

For Kissinger, it was impossible to escape the conclusion that the aid program was in major crisis. "Public support has virtually disappeared, and President Johnson's last two budget requests were cut by 25 and 50 percent," he wrote to President Nixon. "We have fallen behind most other developed countries in the percentage of GNP provided in aid."[10]

Kissinger avoided the convenient excuse of blaming Vietnam and Congress for these woes. The national security adviser insisted that "our present program is not suited to the times."[11] He argued that since Nixon's overall approach to foreign policy was "to move the U.S. into a supporting rather than dominant role in world affairs," the same should be done with respect to foreign aid. (In 1970, Nixon would announce what he called the "Nixon Doctrine," which proclaimed that the United States would not "conceive all the plans, design all the programs, execute all the decisions and undertake all the defense of the free nations of the world.")[12]

In keeping with this more-circumscribed worldview, Kissinger pushed Nixon to move international economic development programs over to multilateral institutions like the World Bank, by 1975.[13] AID could then be abolished.[14] The United States had been the driving force in creating and shaping a whole series of multilateral development institutions, but up to that point had always viewed these multilateral approaches as a complement to its bilateral aid program rather than a substitute for it.

The Peterson Commission hewed a line almost identical to Kissinger's, arguing that the United States should "assume a supporting role and not become involved in the entire range of country development policies and programs."[15]

In AID's place, Kissinger and the commission proposed a new US International Development Corporation; a US International Development Institute to conduct research on development technology; and significant increases in World Bank funding.[16] Security assistance would be treated as a separate program.

Even while the Peterson Commission was early in its work, the president was already making the case for increasing the amount of aid funneled through the World Bank and the United Nations.[17] He also wrote in favor of preserving two key priorities of the Johnson administration: increasing food production and voluntary family planning programs.

Nixon's plan to abolish AID put John Hannah in a delicate position. In discussions with the White House, Hannah was largely supportive. Behind the scenes, he fought to keep the agency alive.

Maurice Williams, who was AID's deputy at the time, recalls Hannah bringing together his senior staff for an emergency retreat around a simple, dire question: "What are we going to do about this?"[18] What emerged was a proposal that had floated around for years: to organize AID around major functional activities such as education and health with more of a focus on meeting the immediate needs of the poorest.

Hannah's counterproposal landed with a thud at the White House, which pushed forward legislation along the lines of the Peterson Commission recommendations which had been delivered in March of 1970. However, Nixon's subsequent legislative package was dead upon arrival, except for Nixon's move to create the Overseas Private Investment Corporation as a separate agency to encourage greater lending to US firms operating in the developing world. Hannah quietly shared his idea for a revamped AID structured around efforts to address basic human needs with congressional Democrats.

Amid all the jockeying, discontent with AID was growing on all sides.

BIAFRA

The Nixon administration was confronted with a series of pressing humanitarian crises in Africa that seized national attention, the most urgent of which unfolded in Nigeria. Nigeria had been a major focus of AID's work in the region and, up until 1966, its prospects had seemed bright. As Sam Butterfield notes, Nigeria had achieved an annual growth rate of five percent, sharply increased domestic revenue, and nearly doubled the number of students in vocational and secondary schools within a five-year period.[19]

All of that changed after a May 1966 military coup plunged the country into separatist conflict as Eastern Nigeria declared itself the independent Republic of Biafra. Violence and displacement soon threatened mass starvation in Biafra as government forces mounted a punishing campaign against rebels and civilians alike. AID was called on to help provide relief.

Although AID's initial efforts in humanitarian relief in the early 1960s were relatively modest, with a single staffer and secretary, relief programs were becoming an increasingly important portfolio. In such situations, AID coordinated relief efforts and channeled resources through private relief organizations like the Red Cross, CARE, and Catholic Relief Services, as well as the United Nations. The agency's key role was to anticipate where needs were the greatest and direct supplies and money in that direction. Over time, AID would also play a substantial role in helping to build developing countries' own disaster early-warning and response systems, an important but often underappreciated effort.

Biafra provided a test of AID's humanitarian capabilities not only because of its immense scale, but because of its complicated politics.

"The Biafra civil war," recalled Jack Sullivan, who worked both at AID and on Capitol Hill, was "the first time that Americans sat down to eat their breakfasts, turned on the television set, and saw a little kid starving to death."[20] As the crisis had initially erupted, President Johnson made clear his approach to staffers in crude terms: "Just get those nigger babies off my TV set."[21]

Most of AID staff had been evacuated from the southeastern provinces of Nigeria, the heart of the ethnic Igbo separatist movement, in October 1967. The agency tried to push badly needed food into the region, but government forces blocked emergency assistance in an effort to starve out the Biafrans.

The eroding situation raised alarm bells at the Nixon White House. President Nixon attended a National Security Council discussion on Nigeria shortly after taking office in January 1969, with the key point of contention being whether the United States should recognize Biafra as an independent state. As Stephen Ambrose recounts in his biography of Nixon, the meeting began with the director of Central Intelligence, Richard Helms, listing the countries that had recognized Biafra up to that point. Nixon interrupted his spy chief: "Look, Dick, you've left out a couple of countries—Zambia and the Ivory Coast."[22] Helms, somewhat taken aback, pivoted to discussing the role of tribal rivalries in the war. Nixon again interjected, "Yes. And this is a problem which really goes back to the history of that country. The British colonial policy favored the Moslem Hausas in the north and that aggravated the tensions, and there's cultural as well as economic and political factors here. It's a very, very tragic problem." A Foreign Service officer who was in the meeting recalled being absolutely astonished by Nixon's command of the subject.

Even before the inauguration, First Lady Patricia Nixon had expressed concern that not enough was being done to staunch the suffering. "As the Federal troops advanced into the secessionist territory, the I[g]bos retreated," explained Henry Kissinger in a January 1969 memo to Mrs. Nixon. "Today approximately 7 million people are crammed into Biafra, which is only about one-quarter of what it was when the secession was declared. Starvation is a major problem and will probably get worse (some 3 to 4 million people could die within the next few months) unless more relief aid is sent."[23]

One of Kissinger's aides, Roger Morris, warned of "a protracted period of turmoil and potential savagery."[24] Kissinger and his aides argued that the State Department and AID tilted too heavily toward the government in Lagos, primarily out of the fear that the situation would encourage other secessionist movements across Africa. Morris argued that there was considerable evidence that AID chief John Hannah was pro-federalist because of the ties he had established with the Nigerian government during his days at Michigan State, and claimed that the State Department was telling AID to minimize reports of civilian casualties.[25] Kissinger himself complained, "State and AID have long discredited eyewitness accounts from Biafra on the grounds of pro-Biafra 'bias' among relief workers."[26]

Some in the Nigerian government spoke openly about using starvation as a weapon of war. President Nixon, for his part, sided with his National Security Adviser's view of events, writing in the margins of a Kissinger memo on Nigeria, "I have decided that our policy supporting the Feds is wrong. They can't make it—let's begin to get State off this kick."[27]

With conditions on the ground dire, a rising crescendo of voices across the political spectrum in the United States and Europe spoke up against the war. "By some strange political sociology, Biafran relief brings together the new left and the old right, Catholics and Jews, and a piece of almost every other branch of articulate opinion in the U.S.," wrote Roger Morris.[28] On July 10, 1969, Americans for Biafran Relief purchased a full-page ad in the *New York Times* pleading for action. "The Biafra war has claimed more children than soldiers. President Nixon is already trying to end one war. Asking that he do something about another may be asking the impossible. But he is the President of the most powerful country in the world and thus is the only man there is to turn to."[29] Seeing the ad in his daily press clippings, Nixon wrote to Kissinger, "Henry, I agree with this," and asked for an immediate plan to address the situation.

Nixon's proclamation sent AID into a mad scramble to mount a major airlift of relief supplies as officials on the ground tried to negotiate arrangements with both the rebels and the Nigerian government to allow access. The Nigerian government also pressured AID director Mike Adler to provide emergency and reconstruction assistance on its side of the front lines. Haven North of AID recalls the list of needs he received from the AID mission: "80 more five-ton trucks, 400 generators of all kinds, 10,000 blankets, 10,000 lanterns, nearly complete power stations."[30]

The White House immediately approved the request, and North and others at the agency were charged with turning those requests into a reality in ten days. UNICEF offered a dozen unassembled trucks, all delivered in pieces in boxes. Parts for smaller trucks were found in Texas. AID reached an arrangement with Chrysler which set up an assembly line in Pennsylvania.

The US Military Air Transport Service lent its logistical muscle, and AID had the equipment delivered to air force bases around the country, with all of the goods being funneled first through Charlottesville, Virginia, and then Cape Verde in Africa, where a different set of planes were positioned to carry the materials to Nigeria. "Within two weeks we delivered 63 trucks—17 more by sea—10,000 blankets, 10,000 lanterns, 400 generators," said Haven North, "from all over the country."

By January 1970, the separatist movement had collapsed, and the war ended. AID had done heroic work in delivering relief supplies, but the costs of the less-than-three-year conflict were appalling. More than a million people had died, with some estimates far higher than that. Deliberate starvation had killed far more people than guns, mortars, or tanks. Biafra remains an oft-forgotten genocide, and to this day the Nigerian government refuses to release an official death toll. For AID, it was a foretaste of the difficulties that come in trying to deliver humanitarian relief in active war zones.

SAHEL

By and large, AID had been relatively inactive in the former French colonies of Africa during its first decade, still viewing them as de facto French turf.[31]

But that all started to change with a desperate, slow-rolling crisis across the Sahel, the vast southern region of the Sahara that stretches across eight countries and more than three thousand miles. The emergency could not have been more different than that of Biafra. As Hariadene Johnson of AID observed, "It didn't have a starting date and a stopping date. It wasn't something that was geographically confined like a volcano or a hurricane. It was spread out over thousands of miles."[32]

The disaster was rooted in, of all things, an unusually good stretch of weather. A significant portion of the Sahel's twenty-seven million inhabitants were nomadic herders, and almost ten years' worth of abundant rains had encouraged them to move further and further north into the Sahara as grasses sprouted on once-barren lands. Herds prospered and family sizes shot upward—until the rains stopped.

"In 1970 the rains began to diminish, and by 1971 almost failed completely throughout the entire Sahelian zone," explained David Shear. Herders and their families were suddenly cut off. Some eight million people fled their homes. More than 100,000 perished. Shear remembers landing in Dakar, Senegal, during the peak of the crisis, where the first thing that hit him was a terrible smell. "We went directly to the port, where tens of thousands of tons of grain rotted in great heaps on the docks," said Shear. "The awful truth was that global assistance in the form of thousands of tons of grain had made it to the coast but was not getting into the interior."

AID was trying to push food aid into the Sahel countries in unprecedented magnitudes. Food was being sent via truck convoys starting in Algiers and crossing the Sahara to get into northern Mali. The US Air Force was conducting air drops of food into Chad, sometimes accompanied by spouses of AID employees who were fluent French speakers to ensure they could communicate with the air traffic controllers. "They were going in by boat, by plane, everything except camel," said Hariadene Johnson.[33]

Although the immediate priority was delivering lifesaving food, AID's leadership also recognized that they had a narrow but important window of opportunity to address some of the factors that made famines in the region a recurring phenomenon. The goal: to make the region food self-sufficient, and to convince Congress to make a long-term investment in dealing with the region's structural obstacles rather than just pouring in food aid.

AID, working closely with France and the governments of the region, established a coalition of twenty-five donors, the Club du Sahel, and established a commission of representatives from the Sahel states. The program promoted self-sufficiency and better environmental practices in agriculture, livestock, and fisheries. Congress endorsed the approach and provided substantial multiyear funding for the program in the hundreds of millions of dollars. Integral to this view was the notion that food production and sufficiency had to be viewed on a regional basis, and that more-open markets would lead to better prices for producers and more-lasting economic growth.

AID trained 150 Peace Corps volunteers to be food monitors; they began to unblock ports; and over a period of ten months moved close to a million tons of food and other relief supplies from docks to points as far as one thousand miles inland.[34] Much to the bewilderment of the French, livestock specialists were brought in from Idaho and Texas.[35] The agency engaged with governments in a multiyear process of dialogue on market reforms that opened up commodities to private traders. These reforms paved the way for the eventual devaluation of the Central West African franc, helping to fuel cross-border trade.

The Sahel marked one of the first times the development community deployed social marketing schemes to promote nutrition, and major US universities, such as

MIT, developed special degree programs on nutritional science in the wake of the Sahel crisis.[36] The emergency response and long-term development programs in the Sahel staved off an incredible amount of misery and set important economic reforms in motion. And in many ways, the Sahel effort was unusually sophisticated and well-designed: a regional approach involving multiple donors to harness long-term funding to address the structural causes of recurring famine, including through the use of innovative technology.

Yet the ultimate achievements of the effort in the Sahel also faced a hard ceiling, because the governments and institutions of so many of these countries—including Chad, the Central African Republic, Mauritania, and Sudan—remained riven by conflict, corruption, ethnic tensions, and maladministration. The French colonial system had left a dismal record of institutional weakness in its wake, and it was a price that the people who populated these former colonies would grapple with for years.

THE BLOOD TELEGRAM

On November 13, 1970, the enormously powerful Bhola cyclone swept through the Bay of Bengal with peak winds hitting 150 miles per hour. The storm surge was over twenty feet high, destroying the low-lying areas of what was then East Pakistan. It was the world's deadliest weather event, with some 230,000 to 500,000 people killed—many swept out to sea without a trace.

In many areas along the coast, some 85 percent of the houses were destroyed. But after the storm, the tragedy only accelerated.

Pakistan at that time was split between West Pakistan and East Pakistan, with India in between. Pakistan's capital and most administrative functions were in West Pakistan.

While the United States, the Soviet Union, Great Britain, and other donors rapidly mobilized to deliver assistance, the central government of Pakistan did almost nothing. "It was almost as if they just didn't care," said Archer Blood, the US consul general in Dacca, East Pakistan.[37] Making matters worse, Pakistani president Yahya Khan defended his government's limited response by saying that he had viewed the disaster area sufficiently when flying over it during a trip to China.

Amid growing anger among East Pakistanis against what they viewed as neglect from West Pakistan, the Awami League political party swept national elections in East Pakistan in December 1970 behind a pledge to achieve greater autonomy. As detailed in Gary Bass's fine book on the crisis, *The Blood Telegram*, some in West Pakistan saw the Awami League's push for greater local control as a bid for independence.

President Yahya refused to let the National Assembly be seated, further enraging East Pakistanis. White House staff warned Henry Kissinger that the likelihood of Yahya ordering a military crackdown in the East was escalating, and that the result would inevitably be a "bloodbath with no hope of West Pakistan re-establishing control over East Pakistan."[38] Kissinger, knowing well that President Nixon viewed President Yahya warmly, both diplomatically and personally, asked in response, "Why should we say anything?"

Nixon and Kissinger stuck with Yahya. Part of their justification for inaction was that President Yahya was serving as an informal conduit for Nixon and Kissinger to open up relations with China, and Yahya had passed a number of messages from Kissinger to the Chinese. Cold War politics were also at play. Pakistan allied more closely with the United States, while India engaged in extended flirtation with the Soviets. Kissinger was not going to let a potential military crackdown in East Pakistan derail his grand designs for geopolitical realignment.

On March 25, 1971, President Yahya unleashed General Tikka Khan and tens of thousands of East Pakistani forces in a brutal crackdown in the East. The scene in Dacca was horrifying. "Going into work, we would see dead bodies on the streets and in the park," recalled Terry Myers, who worked in the AID mission in East Pakistan. "We would pass by burnt out shanties by the railroad tracks. We could see the pockmarks and holes in the walls of the university dorms."[39] As Myers recalled, it was "not really development work. We were bearing witness." One of his Bengali project managers was hauled out of Myers's car despite his desperate pleas, taken around the corner, and shot.

A guerrilla force, the Mukti Bahini, quickly organized to resist the forces from West Pakistan in a growing civil conflict. "The reign of terror only served to fuel resistance," explained Maurice Williams of AID. "East Pakistan, with 75 million people existing on an average annual income of $55, most living on the edge of survival, was in imminent danger of mass famine."[40]

The Pakistani military targeted the large number of Bengalis who didn't speak Urdu with shocking atrocities. A wave of refugees headed toward northern India. Taken aback by what it called the "mediaeval barbarism" of the Pakistani military, the Indian government—which already saw itself as diametrically opposed to the government in West Pakistan—mobilized its intelligence services to covertly assist the insurgents in East Pakistan.[41] Nixon and Kissinger, who both disliked Indian prime minister Indira Gandhi, feared that New Delhi would use the crisis as a pretext for breaking Pakistan in two, but the actions by the Pakistani government were far more damaging to Pakistan's unity than any Indian plan.

Staff at the US consulate and AID mission in East Pakistan were revolted by what they were seeing: the conduct of a genocide by America's closest ally in South Asia often using US weapons. Hindu professors were singled out to be massacred and entire villages napalmed. Dr. Henry Mosley, a well-regarded American physician working on AID-funded cholera vaccine efforts, was so outraged that he concealed a hidden camera in his medical bag so that he could surreptitiously photograph the carnage. Terry Myers saw the military line up some six hundred people in a small town and mow them down with machine-gun fire. Receiving these reports from the field, White House staffers recommended that economic and military aid to Pakistan be suspended to pressure Yahya to halt his campaign. Kissinger demurred. He and Nixon did not want to take any action that would be seen as hurting President Yahya or helping Prime Minister Gandhi.

Those Americans working in East Pakistan were baffled and enraged by the inaction from Washington as the White House described the wholesale massacres as an internal problem best resolved by Pakistan.

"So, we sent a cable with a letter dissenting from US policy," explained Terry Myers.[42] "We could see the situation deteriorating. We became concerned about the possibility of hundreds of thousands of refugees fleeing to India and a possible war with India." Twenty-one staffers signed the document that was sent on April 6, 1971, about two weeks into the violence. It was the first dissent cable in the history of the State Department. The cable soon became known as "the Blood Telegram," since Archer Blood, the US consul general in Dacca, whose signature appeared at the end of the document, supported its key points.

The Blood Telegram was a blistering criticism of US policy: "Our government has failed to denounce the suppression of democracy. Our government has failed to denounce atrocities. Our government has failed to take forceful measures to protect its citizens while at the same time bending over backwards to placate the West Pak dominated government."[43] The cable lamented how quickly the United States had squandered its moral leadership of the free world.

Congress and the US media were becoming increasingly vocal in their complaints about Nixon's approach, and some of the key diplomatic communication on the crisis had been leaked to Democratic senator Ted Kennedy of Massachusetts.

The State Department renewed its internal appeals to halt aid to Pakistan and noted that the many refugees fleeing to India would need assistance. On April 29, 1971, Nixon commented with anger to Kissinger's deputy, Alexander Haig, "Someone is saying we are contemplating sending aid to help the Pakistani refugees. I hope to hell we're not."[44] And Nixon, who had been enraged by the Blood Telegram, wrote to his National Security Council staff on May 2 with regard to the idea of suspending aid to Pakistan: "To all hands. Don't squeeze Yahya at this time."[45]

Snippets from White House tapes make clear how much of US policy was being driven by Nixon and Kissinger's animus toward India. In May of 1971, Kissinger said of the Indians, "[T]hey're such bastards," while Nixon huffed that what the Indians really needed was "a mass famine."[46]

In July of 1971, Kissinger used a visit to Pakistan ostensibly to meet with President Yahya to feign illness for several days and secretly slip into China to discuss a possible presidential visit to Beijing. During these talks, Kissinger and the Chinese agreed there was no longer any need to use Pakistan as a conduit for communications, which could be managed through other means, such as the representatives from both countries at the United Nations in New York.[47]

That same month, Nixon ordered formal instructions that US policy should "tilt toward Pakistan." As Nixon biographer Stephen Ambrose observed, "By then there were ten million refugees. East Pakistan and India were becoming ever more desperate, world public opinion ever more outraged. But Nixon stuck with Yahya, among other reasons because Kissinger said Yahya provided the only link to China (which was not even remotely true)."[48]

The White House used foreign assistance as a blunt weapon throughout the crisis. Despite increasing clamor from State, AID, and Congress, Nixon at every turn tried to preserve assistance to the Pakistani government while severely limiting assistance to the almost biblical flood of refugees into India.

Maurice Williams estimated that only about $35 million of US food aid was directed to the refugees in India—while India spent some $830 million feeding them.[49] Nixon, bizarrely, continued to push brinkmanship in the region, searching for a pretext to start a war with India which he was eager to punish for its overtures to the Soviet Union. Gandhi and India were being pushed to a breaking point, and they ramped up their assistance to the resistance movement in East Pakistan.

By December 1971, the Indian military was openly supporting Bengalis in fighting against the troops from West Pakistan, and President Yahya declared war on India. The Nixon administration quickly suspended all assistance to New Delhi.[50] Pakistani forces in East Pakistan were rapidly routed by the combined Indian and resistance fighters, and Pakistani forces surrendered in Dacca on December 16, 1971. The new nation of Bangladesh had been born.

President Nixon became the first US president to visit the People's Republic of China in February 1972. His trip was widely hailed as a diplomatic triumph. Many of those brave dissenters in the US consulate in Dacca who had signed the Blood Telegram were essentially blackballed from further professional advancement, with Terry Myers being a surprising exception. Kissinger's lengthy autobiographies attempted to gloss over his terrible role in condoning a genocide in which hundreds of thousands of people, perhaps millions of people, were killed and more than ten million people driven from their homes. This period remains one of the darkest stains on American foreign policy in its history.

THE THINGS WE CARRIED

In early November 1969, President Nixon spelled out his new approach to Vietnam: "Vietnamization." Vietnamization, in short, meant turning more and more of the war fighting to Vietnamese government forces to allow American troops to draw down. The United States accelerated arming, equipping, and training Vietnamese forces toward that end. Not long after, Nixon announced the withdrawal of 50,000 American troops, and US force levels in Vietnam crested at just over 540,000. On the pacification side, the United States would expand the civilian protection approach taken by CORDS late in the Johnson administration.

On November 15, 1969, the Moratorium to End the War in Vietnam brought more than half a million peaceful protesters to the streets of Washington, DC, in what was the largest antiwar demonstration in American history.

"I had five children at that time, most of them teenagers, who were all actively against the war, as were most of my friends," recalled Robert Nooter of AID, "so, it was an extremely difficult period on a personal level."[51] Nooter opposed the war, "even though my job caused me to do certain things in connection with it, which I hope I did in a responsible way." When close family friends came to Washington to join the protests, the Nooter family was more than happy to have a crowd of people camped out with sleeping bags in their basement. But Nooter drew at least one red line for his visitors: They could not "put a Viet Cong flag in the front yard."

Disquiet with the war was growing at AID and the State Department, in part because both institutions were opaque about the burgeoning death rates within their own ranks. It wasn't until 1972 that the State Department acknowledged to its own staff how many people had been killed in the field.[52] Foreign Service officers became increasingly vocal with their concerns about Vietnam, and junior officers quit the service at record rates. Some fifty Foreign Service officers wrote to Secretary of State William Rogers condemning Nixon's 1970 decision to invade Cambodia, the largest ever such protest. When the contents of the letter leaked to the press, President Nixon placed a 2 a.m., profanity-laced call demanding that all the offending staffers be fired. To Rogers's credit, they were not.

When an article on the massacre of civilians by US forces in the village of My Lai included a passage by the reporter noting that US civilian forces in Vietnam had long argued against such "tough tactics," President Nixon complained that AID and State Department "PR types" never missed "a chance to cut the war effort."[53]

While Nixon stressed Vietnamization and "peace with dignity," some of the tactics on the ground were designed to intensify the conflict, from the secret bombing of Cambodia and Laos to some deeply troubling activities under the CORDS program. Late in Johnson's term, CORDS launched an accelerated pacification program, designed to push out from hamlets and bring ever greater areas under government control. In places like the Mekong Delta, this strategy, coupled with greater rural assistance, seemed to deliver real gains. Controversially, this program accelerated under President Nixon, and CORDS became closely involved in supporting armed actions against the Viet Cong as part of Operation Phoenix.

With US involvement directed by the CIA, Operation Phoenix sought to ruthlessly uproot undercover Viet Cong operating in the South. The CIA station chief in Vietnam, William Colby, later testified that Operation Phoenix killed 20,587 Vietnamese, although some others place that number higher.[54]

Although Operation Phoenix was primarily managed by the Vietnamese, some of those Americans familiar with the program on the ground complained that it was little more than a broad assassination campaign, and that abuses, including the systemic use of torture, were widespread. Others claimed that while there were excesses in Operation Phoenix, they were sensationalized. The program became one of the most disputed elements of an already deeply controversial war.

Not only were considerable numbers of AID staff serving in the CORDS program, but AID-funded public safety programs had trained many of the Vietnamese involved in Operation Phoenix. Appearing on *Meet the Press*, John Hannah admitted that his agency was being used as cover for CIA agents in Southeast Asia, which led to a storm of congressional complaints and the practice (largely) being discontinued.

Operation Phoenix inflicted real pain on the Viet Cong, but it also fueled the growing sense in the United States that America had become hopelessly entangled in a dirty war on behalf of a corrupt, undemocratic Vietnamese government. When four students protesting the US invasion of Cambodia were shot and killed by members of the National Guard at Kent State University in Ohio in May 1970, it seemed more than apparent that the American public would never fully support the war.

In Saigon, AID churned on despite the shifting winds in the United States. "The program was huge capital projects, major road construction; we established the first traffic light system in Saigon, major commodity import programs, huge, huge things," related Bob Lester of AID, who was sent to Vietnam on his first tour.[55] "The corruption was unbelievable, but no one really cared." Lester noted that he was later told by an AID mission director that he wouldn't hire anyone who had served for more than six months in Vietnam, "because there were no rules."

The war ground on into Nixon's second term. "People who were influential in State, and particularly on the National Security Council staff, and the Ambassador in Saigon, still thought it was a war to be won," explained Miles Wedeman of AID.[56] "It was clear this was not going to happen."

On January 23, 1973, the parties to the conflict signed the Paris Peace Accords, ending the United States' direct involvement in the Vietnam War. Maurice Williams recalls being briefed by Henry Kissinger in March 1973 about his desire for AID to prepare plans to assist North Vietnam as part of a potential peace package. Kissinger indicated that Williams should envision an AID program for North Vietnam of up to $4.75 billion over five years as part of an effort to sweeten a potential deal.[57]

Williams could not envision Congress or the public ever supporting a program of such magnitude for a government it had been fighting for a decade. Kissinger arranged for Nixon to hold a private meeting with Williams, where the president told him that US assistance would be essential to heal the wounds of war and "obtain agreement for disengagement of American forces and release of American prisoners of war held in Hanoi."

But the promise of massive assistance to the North never gained traction, and neither did peace itself. With the end of US combat operations, and the South Vietnamese government struggling to get its own house in order, Saigon fell to the Viet Cong on April 30, 1975, with the South surrendering. AID and State Department personnel were hurriedly evacuated, with the chaotic scenes of helicopters departing from the roof of the US embassy offering enduring images of imperial overreach. (As they prepared to evacuate, some AID personnel were shocked to see a number of their former South Vietnamese employees wearing North Vietnamese military uniforms.)

The legacy of Vietnam was a bitter one for America, and particularly for AID. Bob Komer, who had played such an outsized role in designing US assistance to Vietnam during the war, called the conflict "a strategic disaster which cost us 57,000 lives and a half trillion dollars."[58] Using the high range of estimates for the total costs of the war, it was calculated that the United States could have paid off the mortgage on every home in the nation with what it spent in Southeast Asia. More than $28.5 billion of economic and security assistance poured into Saigon, and at one point, more than 25 percent of AID's entire global staff had been located in Vietnam.[59]

While it is easy for development experts to look back at the 1960s and early 1970s and celebrate flagship accomplishments such as the Green Revolution and the eradication of smallpox, these victories were obscured in public opinion by the specter of Vietnam. The number of Americans thinking the United States spent too much on foreign assistance rocketed from 33 percent in February 1965 to 75 percent by the Fall of Saigon in 1975.

While it is common to observe that Vietnam created a crisis in the public's view of the US military, it arguably hit assistance programs harder and in a more lasting fashion. For many Americans the line between foreign aid and military entanglements had become hopelessly blurred.

THE SMELL OF BURNING RUBBER

Although Nixon and Kissinger felt strongly that most foreign aid should be shifted over to multilateral institutions, they strongly supported the bilateral family planning program. As adviser Daniel Patrick Moynihan said of Nixon, he made clear that he saw "little progress for the world if we do not seriously attend to this issue."[60] Moynihan and Kissinger noted to Nixon that family planning efforts were "very small compared to the magnitude of the problem," but urged the United States to "avoid playing too dominant a role in international population problems."[61]

Eventually, John Hannah placed family planning and humanitarian programs in a single bureau, arguing, "[T]he major persistent disasters today are hunger—half the world's children go to bed hungry—and the pressure of population on limited environment and resources."[62]

Family planning efforts were now centrally managed, with Rei Ravenholt given unusual latitude and authority over personnel, spending, and the direction of the program. Steve Sinding, who later ran population programs at AID, explained the significance. "It was the only example in my experience with AID going over thirty years of a true unified global program in which the regional bureaus were secondary to a global strategy run out of the central office," he said.[63]

Ravenholt finally had the resources and control that he had dreamed of when he moved from Seattle, and he continued to believe that the best way to bend the curve of population growth was to make contraception widely available in the developing world. In this respect, Sinding argued that Ravenholt was shaped by his training as an epidemiologist: "Rei saw high fertility as a communicable disease basically."

With bipartisan congressional support, family planning funding went from $5 million in 1967 to $125 million by 1974.[64] The rush of funding allowed the agency to support research on ways to improve contraceptive technologies, strengthen supply chains, and work with a growing cohort of NGOs to deliver family planning services. The agency later boasted that it "has been involved in the development or enhancement of every modern contraceptive that is currently widely available in the world."[65]

AID, recognizing that attitudes toward family planning were as important to address as the supply of contraceptives, also began to experiment with social marketing campaigns. Its first major effort took place in Jamaica in 1974, where AID developed contraception specifically designed to appeal to men ("Panther" brand condoms) and women ("Perle" birth control pills). Both products were sold commercially, supported by ads on television, radio, and in print. Social marketing campaigns but also would prove increasingly important, and effective, not only in family planning but in public health campaigns more broadly.[66]

Ravenholt's supply-side-driven approach to family planning achieved some important early successes. In Bangladesh, the government adopted a community-centered system in which contraceptives were distributed to women by women from the same locality.[67] The average number of children for a woman in Bangladesh peaked at close to seven in 1970, sharply dropping after that point.

Using a community-based approach to distributing family planning, usually relying on women, became a staple of international practice. These community workers were also able to refer local women to health-care workers when it was appropriate. Women, not surprisingly, had far greater trust in other women.

Countries like Indonesia, which developed a strong family planning program with AID's help, also saw dramatic declines not only in fertility rates, but in maternal mortality as well. But the impact of family planning programs would still take a number of years to be fully evident in most locations; demographic shifts are far from instantaneous.

While there were some major successes with the family planning program during this pioneering period, and many more to come later, the limits of flooding developing countries with contraceptives were becoming apparent—and institutional resentment toward Ravenholt and his often-imperious style was rising.

Because Ravenholt enjoyed a veto over projects and the assignment of population staff, some came to see him as "largely unsupervised and unsupervisable."[68] When Ravenholt's team grossly overstocked contraceptives in Asia hoping that they would be redirected to India, where AID's program was growing smaller, his critics pounced. Sam Butterfield, who was AID mission director in Nepal at the time, complained that pills and condoms were piled up in storage and near the end of their shelf life.[69] "We assessed our options, and none were good," he said. "The least bad one appeared to be to destroy the old stock as discreetly as possible by setting it on fire in a safe, remote location."

Butterfield, reluctantly, asked for funds from the Asia bureau to carry out "this embarrassing task." The head of the Asia bureau, Jack Sullivan, took the opportunity to skewer Ravenholt. He sent the AID administrator a memo entitled "The Smell of Burning Rubber," in which he argued against the extensive authorities which had been granted to Ravenholt, and insisted the current problems had been entirely predictable.

"His idea was to send helicopters over the jungles and drop condoms," said Richard Benedick of AID, caricaturing Ravenholt's position.[70] And while Benedick notes that Ravenholt achieved a great deal, he felt that Ravenholt was so focused on family planning that he excluded "every other shred of common sense."

The 1973 *Roe v. Wade* Supreme Court decision had a seismic impact on international family planning. Where international family planning had found supporters and opponents in both parties before *Roe*, moving forward it became a partisan flashpoint. Family planning practitioners were just beginning to understand the rich and complex interaction of family planning, health, education, and nutrition. It was those nascent efforts that would lead Steve Sinding to argue, "I think that along with the Green Revolution, population assistance has been the greatest success that AID has had over the last thirty or forty years."[71]

BACKLASH

The attitude toward AID and foreign assistance in general was increasingly sour. The backlash was fueled in large part by Vietnam, but also by a raft of books that came out that were deeply critical of AID, the World Bank, the United Nations, and assistance in general—a number of them written by veterans of AID.

Samuel Huntington, a Harvard political scientist, argued in 1968, in *Political Order in Changing Societies*, that while development was leading to economic growth and greater social participation, it was also driving chaos, instability, and the growth of authoritarian regimes—arguments not dissimilar to those voiced by Senator William Fulbright earlier in the decade when he insisted that foreign aid led the United States into the Vietnam War. Gunnar Myrdal published a blistering critique of foreign aid in Asia, *The Asian Drama*, which argued that economic assistance was doing little to make a dent in poverty.

Development Reconsidered, by Edgar Owens, an experienced AID program officer, maintained that too much aid flowed to governments while ignoring the needs of villagers in the countryside. "As our foreign aid programs have become identified with elitist governments and programs that favor the rich," complained the book's foreword, written by two members of Congress, "they only widen the gap and deepen the discontent with the people we want most to help."[72]

Books like *Small Is Beautiful: Economics as if People Mattered*, by E. F. Schumacher, although less specifically about AID or international development, made the case that large-scale infrastructure projects, such as dams, were destructive while small irrigation projects were far more effective.

In an era of polarized politics, critics on both the left and the right found lots to dislike about the aid program. On the left, foreign assistance was derided as a tool of capitalist imperialism, a kindhearted face masking aggressive efforts to trap developing country labor within a system that inherently favored industrial nations. The economic theories of Walt Rostow, which had been so influential in AID's early days, were seen as making the rich richer and the poor poorer. These complaints were added to well-warranted concerns about the environmental impact of big infrastructure projects and the ease with which assistance poured into repressive countries.

Criticisms from the American right were also vocal, particularly under Democratic presidents. At their heart, many of these concerns boiled down to a belief that aid was interfering with markets and served as a subsidy to inefficient, bloated developing country governments.

Within the ranks of AID there was a great deal of disillusionment by the early 1970s. There was anger and frustration with the bloody futility of Vietnam, fatigue from the constant reorganizations, and impatience born of the realization that development was a much more difficult endeavor than most had predicted. Many women were angered by the continued discrimination in the ranks.

And other than Vietnam, no area of AID's work had become more disputatious than Latin America. Teddy Moscoso, the original coordinator of the Alliance for Progress, blasted the program's approach, arguing that the United States was "naive and arrogant in assuming that Latin America's problems were principally the consequence of neglect by the United States."[73]

Tensions within the Alliance were a two-way street. At a 1967 meeting of presidents from the region, held again at Punta del Este, a number of countries denounced the Alliance, including Ecuadorian president Otto Arosemena, giving additional ammunition to US congressional critics. A number of Latin American leaders also felt, not without cause, that the United States was too distracted by Vietnam to fulfill its commitments in the region.

These concerns were captured in the 1971 book *The Alliance That Lost Its Way* by a former senior staff member of AID, Jerome Levinson, and the journalist Juan de Onis. The book, still one of the better histories of the Alliance, painted a highly mixed picture. One of its key messages: Political turmoil across the region, including the rise of a number of authoritarian regimes, had made the extensive ambitions of the original Alliance goals almost impossible to achieve.

While the sweeping goals set by Alliance participants as it was established were compelling and helped to galvanize public support, they also made for a convenient cudgel when they were not fully realized. A 1969 review by AID of the Alliance conducted for the House of Representatives acknowledged that fully accomplishing the goals was impossible.[74] Interestingly, the report noted that one of the prime impediments to realizing those goals had been the failure of Alliance leadership to recognize the importance of family planning in its original conception, as "staggeringly high" birth rates across the region were largely canceling out gains in education, economic growth, and food production.[75]

Where the Alliance had targeted 2.5 percent annual increase in per capita GDP, the actual average across its eighteen countries stood at 1.5 percent growth when the report was released. The Alliance had called for six years of universal primary education across the hemisphere. Enrollment of school-age children increased by 50 percent in seven years, yet over twenty-seven million children in the region still weren't in school—three-quarters of a million children more than in 1960 because of population growth.[76]

AID argued that its accomplishments in the region were substantial and, in many ways, they were. But AID's sixty-page report to Congress had very little to say about democratization, land reform, or justice systems, the social reforms that were a key part of JFK's original vision. In fact, even some aid proponents worried that assistance dollars were reinforcing the systems they hoped to change, and some thirteen constitutional governments were replaced by military dictatorships in the region during the Alliance's life span.

While AID prided itself as an innovator in looking at countries holistically in its programming, there were clearly limits as to how that was applied in Latin America. "The strict macro-economic approach to development that we tried in Latin America for years and years and years worked in terms of accelerating development and getting some infrastructure built," observed David Lazar of AID, "but it wasn't as effective as that same amount of money could have been had there been greater sensitivity to how those countries worked as countries."[77] The essence of the Alliance's aspirations—fundamentally reforming an entire region—was an aim to which neither the United States nor its aid recipients were ever fully committed.

Many veterans of the agency argued that the greatest accomplishments of the Alliance were not easily measured. "Governments in Latin America had always been the tool of the elite, of the rich, or of the military. What the Alliance did, among other things, was to make development a priority," argued Donor Lion of AID.[78] Those sentiments were echoed by Nicolas Ardito Barletta, the former president of Panama, who insisted that the most enduring legacy of the Alliance was to make it so that development issues "became one of the key items on the political agenda."

Some of AID's most important investments were in building the intellectual and managerial capacity of its counterparts. Between 1963 and 1973, AID funded hundreds of Brazilians studying agriculture in both Brazil and the United States, and Brazil emerged as a major agricultural research hub and a food exporter. An AID evaluation notes that Brazil now funds about half of all the agricultural research in Latin America, and that almost all of the postgraduate programs AID helped initiate in Brazil continued after assistance ended.[79]

The situation in Chile illustrates the deeply anachronistic legacy of the Alliance for Progress and US involvement in Latin America. After Salvador Allende became the first democratically elected Marxist leader in Latin America in 1970, the Nixon administration made it clear that they supported removing Allende by any means possible. The CIA encouraged a coup, backed targeted assassinations, blackmailed politicians, and poured bribes into anti-Allende militia groups.

When the Chilean armed forces staged a coup in September 1973, with the air force strafing the presidential palace and Allende killing himself as troops advanced,

General Augusto Pinochet grabbed power. Pinochet's reign was brutal, and thousands of his political opponents were tortured and assassinated, or "disappeared." A number of protesters were burned alive by Pinochet's security forces, and his regime became synonymous with the worst excesses of Latin American strongmen.

Allende's earlier efforts to nationalize much of Chilean industry had left the economy in shambles. "At the time of the coup, inflation was running at 1,000 percent annually, and GNP was down 25 percent," recalled Stuart Van Dyke of AID.[80] Pinochet, with little background in economics, turned to a small cadre of Chilean economists trained through US assistance efforts, both from the US government and the Rockefeller and Ford Foundations. Dubbed the "Chicago boys" because they had been educated at the University of Chicago before the Allende presidency, these Chileans were adherents of economists Milton Friedman, Theodore Schultz, and George Stigler (all eventual Nobel winners).

Almost by accident, these Chilean economists—including Jorge Cauas, Sergio de Castro, Jose Pinera, Miguel Kast, and others—gravitated toward positions of power. "They began to return after the coup, and found places in the central bank, the Ministry of Finance, and the Ministry of Planning," explained Van Dyke. Friedman himself traveled to Chile to conduct a series of seminars for military leaders, some of which Van Dyke attended. "I have never seen one man make so profound an impression on such an influential group in so short a time. He spoke of limited government, privatization, deregulation, and using the forces of the market to allocate capital and labor. They loved it."

The Chicago boys were given relatively free rein, and they pushed forth classic conservative economic policies. They privatized state-held corporations, encouraged foreign investment, privatized the pension system, and opened up the economy. The United States offered substantial technical assistance and support through AID, which operated a large mission in Santiago, and the country received considerable support from international financial institutions. The results were described by some as the "Chilean miracle," and the Chilean economy boomed. But Chile's economy, despite its impressive growth, retained stark gaps between the country's wealthy and its poor.

So how does one grade US foreign assistance in a country like Chile? It was US assistance that helped to train and educate the Chicago boys, dramatically reduce poverty rates, and put Chile on a path toward rapid agricultural export-growth. It was also US foreign policy, directed by Richard Nixon and Henry Kissinger, that funneled US taxpayer dollars through the CIA to abet extralegal killings and human rights abuses.

NEW FACES—AND AN OLD ONE

President Nixon cruised to a landslide victory in his 1972 reelection campaign with the nascent Watergate scandal barely making a dent in the public consciousness. With his reelection, Nixon engaged in some changes of personnel at both State and AID.

"The Nixon White House consolidated its control of the bureaucracy by removal of senior officials believed to be too independent or too liberal. John Hannah, as Administrator of AID, was both," explained Maurice Williams.[81] Hannah was summarily dismissed by phone while vacationing in his home state of Michigan.

Henry Kissinger became the first person to concurrently serve as the national security adviser and the secretary of state, giving him remarkable powers within the foreign policy team. Kissinger evinced very little interest in the foreign aid program beyond providing "deliverables" to generate positive press coverage, although he did seek to punish countries that voted against US proposals at the United Nations by reducing their aid programs.

Nixon did direct Kissinger to make sure that Hannah came in for a personal farewell, noting, "He's done a superb job against great odds."[82] Hannah had done a steadfast job leading AID, and the trio of Hannah, Bill Gaud, and David Bell, three strong chiefs who led the agency for more than a decade, deserve enormous credit.

Hannah's replacement, Daniel Parker, was the most political choice to head the agency to that date. An active Republican, Parker was the CEO of the Parker Pen Co., founded by his grandfather in 1888. One droll newspaper profile described him as being "born with a silver pen in his hand."[83]

A successful businessman and a former marine lieutenant, there was little in Parker's résumé to suggest that he had given much thought to international development. A helicopter pilot, he also dabbled in photography and ceramics. Although a competent manager, Parker's appointment marked the beginning of a downward slide for the agency. Parker was perhaps the least visible of all the AID administrators, both inside headquarters and out, with some describing his behavior as almost reclusive.

Coming from a manufacturing background, Parker approached the position of AID chief as a matter of management technique. He pushed the agency to use computers and satellite photography and was consistently focused on how innovation and new technologies could speed private sector investment. Unfortunately, many of his staff saw this as little more than a focus on gadgetry. As Lloyd Jonnes of AID said of Parker, "He had little or no exposure to the principal problems that he was being asked to deal with."[84] Jonnes added, "I had the impression that he was not particularly optimistic about what we were doing."[85]

NEW DIRECTIONS

The situation with Congress was coming to a head even before Parker's appointment. President Nixon submitted new foreign assistance legislation in 1971, built upon his vision of largely turning over US foreign aid to multilateral institutions.[86] The congressional response was swift: killing Nixon's proposed aid overhaul and sharply cutting funding for the program as a whole. Anger united the disaffected elements on the right and left, with liberals fed up with Vietnam and conservatives stewing that a number of aid recipients had voted to grant China (rather than Taiwan) a seat at the United Nations. As Kissinger complained to President Nixon in the Oval Office, "[T]he same group that has blocked the reorganization of the foreign aid program has now killed it."[87]

The Senate refused to pass authorization bills for either economic or military assistance, and the foreign assistance program operated on a continuing resolution for the entire year—a practice which was unprecedented at the time.[88] The defeat sent shock waves through Washington. "A group of Republicans led by Paul Findley of Illinois wrote a letter to Nixon," recalled Jack Sullivan, "saying 'Unless you change foreign assistance, it's dead.'"[89]

As a result of the drawdown in Vietnam and the budget cuts, AID hit a new low in its total overseas staff, at just over 3,800 personnel—an almost 30 percent decline from the end of the Johnson presidency.[90] AID and the entire foreign assistance program were on life support. Defenders of the program realized that foreign aid would have to be reshaped to make it more palatable.

One particularly influential individual in that regard was Jim Grant. Grant had worked at AID, first in the Middle East bureau and then later as a mission director in Turkey. At the start of the Nixon administration, Grant had become the head of the Overseas Development Council, an organization dedicated to studying development and mobilizing support for it.

Grant was convinced that foreign aid had to be presented in more human terms. Voters didn't care about macroeconomic reform; they could be convinced to care about educating kids, feeding the hungry, and sheltering the poor.

Public polling underscored Grant's position. Asking about specific topics within assistance—such as providing humanitarian relief or education—almost always produced far more positive poll responses than asking about the development program as a whole. Jim Kunder, a former deputy administrator at AID, captures the paradox: "Americans have a distaste for foreign aid in the abstract and are supportive of its real-world components."[91]

Grant felt that AID needed to make poverty eradication its headline goal rather than economic reform.

The House Foreign Affairs Committee took the lead on a major overhaul of the foreign aid program that Congress passed in 1973.[92] "The bill just took off like wildfire, because nobody liked the way foreign aid had been done," said Jack Sullivan. "We were going to get aid more directly to the people."[93]

This legislation, widely known as "New Directions," fundamentally reshaped AID and America's approach to the world in ways that still reverberate to this day. The core of the new approach: a focus on helping the poorest meet their basic human needs.

AID, and its funding, would be primarily organized around sectors, such as education, family planning, health, and nutrition. Congress enumerated a lengthy list of priorities: eradicating poverty, increasing the productivity of small farms, boosting literacy, making taxation more progressive, combating corruption, creating jobs, slowing population growth, reducing infant mortality, and more.[94]

Congress added significant new restrictions and directives that required Congress to be notified for even relatively minor shifts in spending at the agency. For their part, many developing country governments were less than thrilled with the focus on basic human needs, worrying that it would balloon social spending at the expense of other national priorities.[95]

There were clear winners and losers as AID came to focus on the poor majority rather than national economic reform and country-level economic strategies—or on broader institutional development.

AID would soon evolve into a public health behemoth, arguably one of the most important institutional players in affecting the health and well-being of the poor in human history. Health programs, particularly those for women and children, have always been some of the easiest for members of Congress to justify. The combination of significantly increased health spending, and a focus on health interventions at the community level, led to a boom in efforts to establish rural health-care facilities, social marketing efforts on good health practices, and the training and deployment of armies of public health workers in locations where basic health care had often been unattainable.[96]

Agriculture was the other big winner. The legislation's focus on the rural poor invariably meant a greater emphasis on farming and nutrition. Agriculture and nutrition leapt from about a quarter of the agency's budget in 1973 to over 60 percent of the budget by 1976.[97] The agency had a hard time hiring agricultural officers fast enough.[98]

But perhaps the biggest winners of the New Directions legislation were those that AID increasingly relied on to carry out its work: contractors, NGOs, universities, and others. The combination of continued downward pressure on overall staffing levels, and the congressional push to carry out smaller and more-complex projects at a village level, meant that AID was forced to shift from being an operational agency to a contracting institution. AID would design, approve, and pay for the programs while others would implement them.

The reliance on implementing partners allowed the agency (and supportive members of Congress) to make the case that foreign aid wasn't really foreign. AID could point to major American universities, land grant colleges, trusted NGOs like Save the Children and CARE, as well as a growing cadre of for-profit contractors and argue that its programs were creating American jobs and promoting a vital new form of international collaboration.

However, this process made AID significantly more bureaucratic over time. Instead of hiring engineers and economists, the agency suddenly needed staff that could better understand the arcana of contracting and federal compliance laws. And as AID became a more-cumbersome bureaucracy, it lost its grip on what had been its overriding mandate during its more than a decade of operations: structural economic reform.

Part of the rationale for New Directions was that the World Bank would lead economic reform efforts; however, the Bank also embraced a basic human needs approach around this time. This is not to say that policymakers at AID no longer cared about economics, but their approach to economics had altered fundamentally. After New Directions, AID and the Bank were trying to transform countries from the bottom up rather than the top down. This led Frederick Gilbert of AID to wonder: "How can you operate an agency devoted to international economic development without giving prominence to the discipline of development economics?"[99]

New Directions legislation pushed the agency into more-localized, people-oriented programs—some done via NGO grants, and some through massive, complex, and not always very effective integrated rural development programs. By 1977 the Congressional Budget Office noted, "Large-scale, capital-intensive projects considered less likely to benefit the poor directly have been all but discontinued."[100] The only major exception to this was large aid recipients receiving aid primarily for security or strategic purposes, such as Egypt.[101]

The move away from large infrastructure projects was understandable given the mixed track record of AID and the World Bank in this arena during the 1960s. But it also ruled out some efforts that had been a success. For example, Ray Love of AID argues that rural electrification efforts in the Philippines and Bangladesh were of tremendous value to rural populations. "It was creating employment for them and it was improving the quality of their lives."[102]

One of the other significant losers in New Directions was the participant training programs that had played such a critical role in the breakthroughs in Korea, Taiwan, Indonesia, Chile, and elsewhere. US foreign aid programs, including those preceding AID, funded participant training for some 350,000 people from the developing world.[103] One study of Thailand found that nearly 40 percent of senior Thai officials had been trained under AID funding.

But after New Directions, as Samuel Butterfield wrote, "Country missions were pressed not to provide assistance for education above high school, since higher education would not directly help the poor."[104] Efforts to stand up teacher-training colleges, send promising graduate students abroad to study, establish research institutions, and fund public administration and "institution building" programs all suffered a steep decline.

"Human resource development is the most important thing in any country," argued Donor Lion. "I think it's even more important than, and in fact contributes to, appropriate policy."[105] Participant training and international education efforts were not without flaws. Some students failed to return home or went into the private sector. The impact of participant training—while obvious from the long view of history—was not always easy to measure, making it an easy target.

"From my view, I've always felt that this was the *sine qua non* of international development," said AID's William White of participant training. "The legacy is the trained people who run these projects and continue to administer them, who continue to govern long after AID has gone."[106] The agency started to move away from that approach in the 1970s.

In response to New Directions, AID developed a conceptual framework to tackle basic human needs. Many within the agency worried that an effort focused solely on the "poorest of the poor" risked completely abandoning core elements of economic growth, and eventually landed on a formulation directed more at "poor majorities" and producing growth with equity.[107]

AID's policy shop developed a series of benchmarks for measuring an individual's relative poverty: a per capita income of less than $150 annually; less than fifty-five years of life expectancy; and a daily diet of less than 2,160 calories.[108] These benchmarks were an important first step in the more metrics-driven approach to poverty that has since become the norm.

"New Directions rescued AID," insists Jack Sullivan. "We saved a program we all believed was extraordinarily important."[109] But in many ways, New Directions was a devil's bargain. AID met genuine needs by increasing spending on health services, education, and literacy. However, lifting entire countries up by focusing on small, largely rural projects carried out by intermediaries was enormously difficult. "We launched many integrated rural development projects," argued Frederick Gilbert, but many "were discovered to be unsustainable and mostly collapsed of their own weight."[110]

James Kunder, a longtime AID hand, argued that attacking development on a sectoral basis often ended up treating symptoms rather than core maladies. "The real way to ensure that children in developing countries will not suffer from malnutrition or preventable childhood diseases, over time, is to strengthen programs that support free market economic growth, and programs that spur democratic, participatory political systems."[111] Yet Congress and the administration largely dismantled the agency's apparatus for engaging in high-level dialogue on economic reform.

AID's strategy became much more trees and much less forest. When decisions became driven by an overall disease burden in a country, its raw numbers of poor people, or an average daily calories count, discussions of whether a country was a good partner willing to embrace reforms tended to get squeezed out. Growth and income generation, while not panaceas, often became an afterthought.

With less of an emphasis on economic reform, some countries seemed content to subcontract the care and feeding of their poor populations to aid agencies.

Ironically, the core impetus for New Directions—the charge that development programs had largely failed during the 1960s—appears to simply have been wrong when it came to economic growth. There was dynamic, almost unprecedented, growth in per capita GNP among the least-developed countries between 1950 and 1975.[112] As Theodor Galdi of the Congressional Research Service wrote, the average growth rate of 3.4 percent was "faster than today's developed countries grew during their development, faster than the LDCs had ever grown before, and faster than anyone expected them to grow."[113] Literacy climbed from 40 percent to 50 percent during the 1960s, and enrollment in secondary and tertiary schools had increased by more than 600 percent during the same period.

The New Directions legislation remains the broad organizing principle of AID to this day.

THE MIDDLE EAST

As the Nixon administration sank deeper into crisis in its second term, with the resignation of Vice President Spiro Agnew and the unfolding Watergate scandal, a series of events unfolded in both the Middle East and the United States with considerable implications for the future of foreign aid and the prospects for development around the globe.

Egypt launched a surprise attack on Israel on October 6, 1973. The eventual outcome was largely a stalemate, but the Arab forces fared far better than in early conflicts, and both Israelis and Egyptians began to question whether their tensions could be resolved successfully purely on the battlefield.

Nixon and Kissinger saw an opening to improve relations with Egypt as it moved away from the Soviet Union, and aggressively pursued a regional peace accord. The fabric that would weave together much of the US diplomatic strategy in the region would be a massive infusion of US assistance to Egypt and Israel.

When key oil-producing nations imposed an oil embargo on the United States in 1973 because of US support for Israel in the Yom Kippur War, oil prices quadrupled over a three-month period.[114] Beyond the obvious discomfort for consumers at the gas pump and mounting pressure on industry and agriculture, Middle Eastern oil producers saw a major influx of wealth. As economist Edward Schuh explains, considerable pressure was applied to commercial banks to encourage them to turn around and lend the petroleum dollars they held in their coffers.[115]

Developing countries, feeling the squeeze from rising oil prices, often faced a choice between devaluing their currencies (triggering sharp rises in the cost of consumer goods) or taking loans out on the international market.

With loans easily available and interest rates low, taking on more debt became the easy alternative for many developing countries. "The problem was," according to Schuh, "that the commercial banks in their rush to keep the money moving did very little by way of sound appraisal and analysis to determine whether the developing countries would be able to service and eventually repay their loans." This influx of cash at low interest rates helped fuel the longest sustained expansion in the global economy since World War II. Only later did the downside of easy, undisciplined borrowing become apparent.

On June 30, 1974, the House Judiciary Committee voted to impeach President Nixon due to the Watergate cover-up, and Nixon became the first, and only, US president to resign from office in August of that year. Gerald Ford was the new US president. Ford's pardon of Nixon ensured that his tenure in office was a brief one. AID had survived the nadir of its standing with Congress and the US public, but it had emerged as a very different institution.

6

The Carter Years

OUTSIDERS

On November 2, 1976, Jimmy Carter defeated Gerald Ford in the presidential election, and he vowed to take a decidedly different approach to America's place in the world. Carter emphasized the importance of human rights and moral leadership in foreign policy, and he and his team embraced the emphasis on basic human needs at the core of New Directions. More than three-quarters of AID's assistance was flowing to nations with a per capita income below $300, and the focus of programs was directly on the poor majority in these countries.[1] Consequently, the 1970s also marked a much stronger push by AID into Africa. In 1973, there were only eight AID missions on the continent; by the end of the decade there would be twenty-eight.[2]

Carter and his secretary of state, Cyrus Vance, recognized that the links between the United States and the developing world were increasingly complex and interdependent. "In general, our ability to trade effectively with developing states will increasingly depend on our willingness to respond wisely to their interests and concerns," wrote Vance. "We also share an interest with developing countries in narrowing the combustible disparity between wealth and poverty. We share an interest in striking an even balance between the burgeoning demands of more people for a better life and the immutable reality of limited resources."[3]

In March of 1977, President Carter appointed John Gilligan to run AID, introducing him in the Rose Garden as someone with superb management capabilities who was gifted with a "sensitivity about the needs of human beings."[4] Carter was personally committed to the aims of the foreign assistance program, and he hoped to double aid spending during his time in office.[5]

In his early appearances before Congress, Gilligan stressed that the developing world represented an increasingly important market for the United States. More than 11 percent of US GDP was coming from exports—roughly quadruple the figure from when AID was established—and almost 30 percent of export trade was with developing countries.[6] Some four out of five new manufacturing jobs in the late 1970s were driven by US exports, and the United States was exporting more to the developing world than Europe.[7]

The United States had put in place some trade preferences for goods from developing countries in 1975 that allowed many of them to enter into the country duty-free, a practice which many other industrialized countries adopted in different variations.[8] However, these duty-free preferences were not applied in key areas where US industries might suffer, most particularly in textile and footwear manufacturing—the exact markets that were often most promising for developing countries. The tendency to practice protectionism in areas like textiles, and an unwillingness to eliminate agriculture subsidies, meant that the US market wasn't fully open to developing countries who could offer these products on a competitive basis—if given the chance.

The US share of global GNP fell from about 40 percent in 1955 to about 25 percent in 1980, more a reflection of growing global prosperity than a decline in US economic fortunes. The World Bank and others started labeling countries as least-developed, low-income, lower-middle-income, and upper-middle-income to better capture the differentiation of the developing world.

Accelerating economic growth in the developing world also meant that foreign aid dollars were no longer the dominant form of finance for many countries. By the end of Carter's term, development assistance would make up about 35 percent of the total flows to the developing world, with private investment and remittances playing an increasingly important role.[9]

As a congressman and then governor of Ohio, John Gilligan was notable for enacting a state income tax and substantially increasing investments in basic social services, particularly education. However, Gilligan did himself no favors when he announced at the Ohio State Fair, "I shear taxpayers, not sheep." He lost his 1974 reelection bid.[10]

In many ways, Gilligan's career at AID came to mirror his gubernatorial term. Gilligan recognized that as a result of the dramatic drawdown from Vietnam, AID had become headquarters-heavy. Part of this dynamic was also budget-driven: It cost three to four times as much to maintain staff in the field than it did stateside. By 1976, twice as many people worked in Washington, DC, than abroad at a time when the agency was trying to implement smaller and more locally driven projects.

"President Carter was particularly interested in foreign aid," said Gilligan. "First, he wanted AID to be more effective, to deliver assistance to foreign nations in a more timely way, and at the same time build their capacity to effectively use the assistance."[11] Carter pushed Gilligan to get projects and programs approved more rapidly, and to minimize the frequent delays in project implementation due to congressional reviews and revisions that had become commonplace in the wake of New Directions.

Gilligan was adamant that the lengthy "back-to-the-field and back-to-Washington reviews" for projects had to be streamlined. Gilligan wanted to give missions more authority and send more officers to the field.[12] Gilligan told an important congressional oversight chair, "[I]f the Navy were run the way AID is run we would have the whole fleet on the beach before we got permission from Washington for a change of course."[13] Gilligan went on, "I thought I knew a little about the operation of a civil-service bureaucracy, but I've never seen anything like this."[14]

Unfortunately, Gilligan's description of his own staff to a reporter—"Over age, over rank, overpaid and over here"—was all too quotable, and badly alienated the workforce he was charged with leading. It wasn't surprising that AID professionals, "most of whom were serious people trying to do a good job," explained Robert Nooter, "had trouble looking kindly" at Gilligan.[15]

Gilligan was taken aback to learn his approach was poorly received. "It was so shocking to him," said Nooter. "He simply couldn't grasp the fact that what he'd been doing had been perceived by the staff as an absolutely terrible job."[16]

In a visit to Mali, Gilligan remarked without irony, "This doesn't look anything like Ohio."[17] Career staff accompanying him were taken aback by his negativity during his field visit. Even after being presented with evidence of effective programs, Gilligan privately accused his team in Mali of perpetrating "an enormous hoax on the US taxpayer." With no understanding of what the situation in the Sahel had been like only several years before, Gilligan could only see despair on an alien landscape.

Gilligan's rhetoric, combined with a number of news stories that claimed some AID staff were enjoying lavish lifestyles abroad—with one mission director spending $1,700 on silverware, and another leasing a house for $38,000 a year—made it easy for critics to paint a picture of an agency badly out of touch with its new directive to address basic human needs.

In many ways, Gilligan never recovered from his early gaffes. By the time he got up to speed on how development works, he had lost a great deal of confidence among staff. He does, however, deserve credit for shifting personnel patterns at AID back toward the field.

"The late 1970s was a period when we had gone beyond infrastructure development and big development projects; now we were looking at basic human needs, trying to meet the needs of the poor in rural areas," Parker Borg of the State Department notes. "The AID missions seemed to lack a clear understanding about what they might attempt and how they might achieve success."[18]

Part of the real challenge during this period was the fundamental paradox of New Directions: It was an approach to foreign assistance predicated on the idea that the United States could focus on the essential needs of the poor. However, truly addressing the conditions that kept many poor and marginalized inherently meant addressing a complex stew of social, political, and economic factors—often at a national level.

THE LEAKY UMBRELLA

More and more parts of the US government had come to engage in providing foreign assistance. AID maintained the bulk of programs and control over the budget, but the number of players on the ground was proliferating. The State Department provided assistance for refugees; the Department of Agriculture had an important role in food programs; the Treasury Department controlled flows to the multilateral banks; the Peace Corps carried out grassroots programs in scores of countries; the Overseas Private Investment Corporation financed investment in the developing world; the US Forest Service was involved in forestry programs—and the list continued to grow.

Senator Hubert Humphrey, a Minnesota Democrat and the former vice president under LBJ, wanted to see management of all US assistance programs coordinated under a single broad umbrella of an International Development Cooperation Agency. Although President Carter had a notoriously leaden touch in dealing with Congress and was often estranged from congressional Democrats and Republicans alike, Humphrey's support for establishing a coordinating body over these disparate agencies helped legislators to generally embrace the concept. President Carter's executive order creating the International Development Cooperation Agency did not encounter strong resistance. However, the challenges of coordinating the foreign assistance program across multiple and strong-willed agencies immediately became apparent.

Tom Ehrlich, a former State Department attorney, was put in place to head the International Development Cooperation Agency, with most of his staff drawn from AID. While agency heads supported the concept of coordination in the abstract, they were instinctively resistant to taking marching orders from anywhere but the White House. AID had always been seen within the federal government as a weak sister compared to more-powerful and high-profile bureaucracies at the Departments of State, Agriculture, and Treasury, and these larger departments viewed the International Development Cooperation Agency as tilting too heavily toward AID.

"To be charitable," an AID-sponsored history acknowledged, the International Development Cooperation Agency "was not the coordinating mechanism envisaged either by Senator Humphrey or, in all likelihood, by President Carter. The only entity it coordinated was AID, and since it was staffed with fewer than 75 people, [it] could make only a marginal impact on overall bilateral and multilateral assistance policy."[19]

Not only did other agencies not really take part in the coordination efforts, but AID had another layer of bureaucracy added over its own operations in what the head of AID's policy shop, Alex Shakow, called "a time-consuming and enervating process."[20]

The International Development Cooperation Agency eventually withered on the vine, as the subsequent Reagan administration let it fade into obscurity.

GOING GREENER

Other areas of emphasis during the Carter years yielded more-enduring results. Carter was the leading proponent of AID taking a larger role in environmental programs, and these efforts became an important part of its portfolio over time (with more emphasis under Democratic than Republican presidents).

Domestically, Carter set aside more public lands than any president since FDR. He established cap-and-trade standards for industrial emissions, an approach that would become a cornerstone of subsequent efforts to combat global climate change. Carter was also "the first US president to put conservation of the environment on the global agenda," argued his adviser Stu Eizenstat, including by commissioning the "Global 2000 Report," which "called attention to global environmental trends in population growth, water, agriculture, and forests."[21]

The move to give environmental issues more prominence was a positive outgrowth of the foreign aid criticisms that had dominated the early 1970s. AID had been reluctant to view development through an environmental lens, and the agency had been sued by a consortium of environmental groups after five people died in Pakistan as the result of overexposure to insecticides. Jane Stanley, one of AID's early environmental officers, observed, "I got the feeling when I first got this assignment that many in the mission viewed this as a new fad that would go away after a while."[22]

Forest management was a large part of the focus that emerged at AID. This not only included efforts to conserve existing forests and create national preserves, but to reforest lands that had become barren with overuse. Carter issued a directive in 1979 that AID was to place highest priority on environmental problems, including deforestation, and this push set the stage for the United Nations and the World Bank to become more active in these areas as well.

AID's approach to forestry and parklands wasn't based on telling the poor to preserve lands purely for preservation's sake. Instead, AID made the case that sound environmental management offered lasting economic and social benefits. For example, reforestation programs could lead to sustainable harvests of lumber that would provide steady income over multiple years rather than a one-time windfall from clear-cutting. It also meant less erosion, which allowed for better management of nearby crops.

In Nepal, local committees were created to discuss how forests were being used, and to what end. According to AID, some 14,000 community forestry user groups were ultimately established, which included about one-third of Nepal's entire population in some form.[23] Revenues from more-sustainable forestry were pumped back into local priorities, such as building schools, providing clean drinking water, and offering vocational training. More democratic management of these resources had clear benefits: Nepal's total forest cover is now more than 40 percent higher than when it hit its low point—a remarkable achievement considering the steady growth in population over the last fifty years.

Similarly, establishing nature preserves and national parks helped create opportunities for tourism, and a boom of hospitality industries surrounding such parks. The enduring popularity of—and revenue from—ecotourism in places like Costa Rica was a direct outgrowth of some of AID's early investments in community-driven natural resource management.

Understanding the link between environmental protection and livelihoods was vital and helped dispel the notion that environmentalism had to be pitted against prosperity.

RAVENHOLT NEVERMORE

By 1977, the United States was far and away the most important global player in family planning, providing more than 90 percent of funding for family planning assistance in developing countries.[24]

But senior officials in the Carter administration took office with a clear desire to strip Rei Ravenholt of the special powers he enjoyed and remove him from his post.[25] Ravenholt's personal style was obviously partially to blame, as was the mounting evidence of the limits of his strategy to flood countries with contraceptives.

Congress was pushing AID to explore integrated strategies for family planning, with an emphasis on both supply of contraceptives and efforts to invest in basic education for girls.[26]

Ravenholt blamed Jack Sullivan and Sander Levin, both political appointees at the agency, for targeting him, accusing Sullivan of being "an anti–birth control Catholic zealot."[27] Ravenholt, later in his life, spun elaborate conspiracy theories about his ouster, going so far as to suggest that Pope John Paul I was assassinated because he was set to embrace international family planning.[28] It was an unfortunate end for Ravenholt.

"Both sides of the issue made tremendous mistakes," said Duff Gillespie, a longtime hand in the agency's family planning programs. "What Rei should have done was look at the writing on the wall, gracefully leave, and his life would have been different."[29] Gillespie argued that Ravenholt's legacy remains significant, and important innovations from the Ravenholt era included the greater reliance on demographic analysis and data, price savings by buying contraceptives in bulk, and the development of sophisticated social marketing campaigns.[30]

Ravenholt argued that the efforts which he directed can be credited with "at least a quarter billion births prevented," and that they helped to shape a world where "women and couples of the world are able to just have the children they want and can care for."[31]

Ravenholt's boldness helped to quickly ramp up family planning programs. The less dramatic and better integrated approaches of his successors paved the way for more powerful impact. By appreciating the fact that family planning decisions weren't made in a vacuum and were indeed deeply tied to issues such as basic education, economic opportunity, social norms, and better information, the program became steadily more effective.

Indonesia and Kenya both serve as good examples of the achievements of US family planning efforts. Indonesia's fertility rate dropped from 5.6 to 3 births per woman from 1970 to 1991. The net impact of that on a macro level: 12 million fewer people in a country that is already Asia's third most populous.[32]

Understanding the local context was a big part of the success in Indonesia. Women were visited after giving birth by community health workers to inquire if they were interested in contraception. Family planning programs used social marketing, grounded in Islamic teaching, to promote happy, small, and prosperous families. Everything from puppet shows to radio commercials was used to reach people who couldn't read.

The Kenya experience was somewhat similar, with the average Kenyan woman giving birth to eight children in the 1970s decreasing to less than half that today. In 1978, only 6 percent of Kenyan women used contraception, and that figure climbed to more than 60 percent today. The Kenyan success was driven in no small part by a willingness to work with health clinics that were either run by local governments or the private sector, both of which often provided family planning services free of cost. The innovative approach to service delivery, and moving services closer to where people needed them, not only slowed fertility rates but significantly improved health in general, including vaccination rates. And, unsurprisingly, greater access to contraception led to fewer abortions in Kenya.

CAMP DAVID

By the Carter era, a major new strategic priority was already starting to consume a lion's share of the aid budget: the Middle East.

Assistance levels escalated quickly in the wake of the Yom Kippur War in 1973, and then on September 17, 1978, Egyptian president Anwar Sadat and Israeli prime minister Menachem Begin signed the Camp David Accords, a historic breakthrough only achieved after arduous negotiations facilitated by Carter and his team. "Israel and Egypt were promised very large, and equal, amounts of United States aid, most of which came from the AID budget," explained Allison Herrick of AID.[33] For Israel it was the $1.25 billion annual cash transfer in addition to military aid.

The large annual cash transfer to Israel had very little to do with the need for traditional economic development. As Walt Rostow noted twelve years before the Camp David Accords, "The policy problem we have to work around is that Israel's outstanding economic performance raises it far above the level where AID normally pulls out. For instance, its per capita GNP of $1,250 is 70 percent of the UK's, 90 percent of Holland's, equal to Austria's, 130 percent of Italy's and 200 percent of Greece's."[34]

The inclusion of funding for Israel made it harder for many members of Congress to vote against other foreign aid spending, and the powerful Israeli lobby on Capitol Hill in turn supported aid programs in general.

In Egypt, in addition to military aid, the economic aid was equivalent, but it was divided between cash, project aid, commodities, and food. The amount of assistance for both countries could not be changed without changing the other.

Egypt wanted its assistance on an all-cash basis, but as Bradshaw Langmaid of AID observed, trust in the Egyptians to do the right thing with such a large infusion of cash was limited. "Those who made the original decision knew full well that the Egyptians were going to do enough stupid things with their economy that they couldn't sustain the program politically in the US context if there wasn't a development component to it."[35]

John Gilligan often sounded less than entirely enthusiastic about AID's substantial push into the Middle East, and the blurring of the lines between economic and security assistance.[36] Gilligan was probably the only AID chief to be so publicly critical of the large amount of security assistance directed toward both Israel and Egypt.[37]

The Egyptians repeatedly grumbled about the assistance being turned into AID projects and pointed to the large amounts of regional trade that it had lost because of the peace deal with Israel. But Egypt's economy was still riven by heavy subsidies and sweetheart deals for those in positions of power in Cairo. Because Egypt was receiving such high levels of aid, with much of it driven through projects, Cairo soon hosted the largest AID budget and mission since Vietnam.[38]

AID's focus on small, local projects as a result of New Directions simply would not work in Egypt. "You had to obligate $1 billion a year," explained Owen Cylke of AID. "It took a lot of those to add up to a big number."[39]

Efforts to engage the government in discussions of meaningful economic reform were largely stillborn. "The Egyptians would engage you in endless hours of discussion," said Cylke, "but had no intention of changing the price of bread or the price of power or the price of anything." The Egyptians were unwilling to move off certain positions: Bread was free; power was free; connected elites had to be given a piece of any deal. During one of Cylke's long discussions at the Egyptian Ministry of Industry, one of his colleagues leaned over and whispered, "This looks like the Politburo from Bulgaria."

The program in Egypt made some inroads during this period, engaging the government on the value of family planning programs, standing up health clinics in rural areas, and introducing new farming methods, but it was clear that expectations on all sides were not being met.

Egypt, as had Vietnam before it, raised the vital question of how exactly development programs should work when driven primarily by security concerns. The issue came to the fore during the Carter administration when Congress decided that security assistance that was also designed to promote economic and development goals should have its own distinct account, the Economic Support Fund, largely controlled by the Department of State.[40]

In many cases, the objectives of security and development moved easily together. For example, reducing infant mortality, promoting basic education, and combating disease could help make a partner country more stable and a more reliable ally. But receiving large amounts of security-driven assistance could also be counterproductive, convincing some partner governments that the status quo did not need to be altered. In Egypt, there was no incentive for the government to embrace fundamental economic reform when it knew that US funds would keep flowing regardless.

Even the strongest AID administrators have limited ability to push back against the State Department, White House, and Pentagon when development programs take on a strategic security imperative. Yet, the White House and State and Defense Departments have repeatedly gotten the connection between aid programs and security wrong. Foreign assistance is best at promoting the slow, long-term structural changes required to modernize political and economic systems; it is of limited utility in reshaping the political or military environment of a country in the short term.

The State Department was always an enthusiastic supporter of the Economic Support Fund, over which it often exercised greater policy direction, because it was highly flexible and not confined to specific purposes the way most development accounts were. In some cases, it was used to support economic reforms. But in other cases, it was distributed more for political purposes than developmental ones, leading it to be sometimes viewed as "walking around money" for diplomats. And flexible money has its uses in diplomacy, as the Egypt case makes clear—where the promise of aid helped secure the peace deal. The Economic Support Fund account rose steadily as a proportion of the overall assistance budget from the mid-1970s onward.[41]

LOOSE LIPS SINK GILLIGAN'S SHIP

Between New Directions easing congressional concerns and the Camp David Accords leading to a spike in funding for the Middle East, AID's budget had climbed back to a record high by 1979.[42] But John Gilligan was unhappy with the surge in assistance designed to support security aims, and at a press briefing in January 1979 he complained that the level of aid which Israel and Egypt received was equal to that of sixty-three other aid recipients combined.

"The Secretary of State promptly went to the White House and said, 'Please remove this fellow, he's making intemperate remarks about things that affect our foreign policy,'" recalled Robert Nooter.[43]

Gilligan was summoned to meet with Secretary of State Cyrus Vance the Saturday morning after his comments had appeared in the press. It was his first major meeting with the secretary of state—two years into his tenure. Vance fired him on the spot.[44]

When news hit the press about his dismissal, Gilligan sheepishly insisted that the secretary of state had simply talked to him about "other assignments." His resignation letter noted with some pride that under his watch AID had been scandal-free and now had "more people in the field than at any [other] time in the recent history of the agency."

Carter tapped Doug Bennet to replace Gilligan. Before joining AID, Bennet had been a staffer to Ed Muskie in the US Senate, and when Cyrus Vance became Carter's secretary of state, he brought Bennet in to serve as assistant secretary of state for congressional relations. In the 1960s, Bennet briefly worked at AID and then served as an assistant to Chester Bowles when he had been the ambassador to India.

Bennet continued Gilligan's emphasis on decentralization and encouraged greater collaboration with the Peace Corps in the field. Not surprisingly, he also looked to repair congressional relations. Bennet was one of the most intellectual AID administrators, and he boosted the agency's evaluation efforts. Bennet put great stock in impact evaluations and was more than willing to share the results with the Hill in a transparent manner. He did not expect every program to deliver miraculous results; he expected the agency to be honest about its successes and failures and to learn from them.

THE OTHER GROUND WAR IN ASIA

In November 1979, Iranian students seized the US Embassy in Tehran, triggering an extended hostage crisis. In December 1979, the Soviet Union invaded Afghanistan, adding to the aura of crisis. Jimmy Carter looked increasingly ineffectual on the world stage. Republicans ridiculed Carter's early emphasis on a human rights–driven foreign policy as naive.

Interestingly, although Carter is often noted for his emphasis on human rights in his approach to foreign policy, there was no major shift in the patterns of how the United States distributed assistance during his presidency. To his credit, Carter did establish an interagency group on human rights and foreign assistance, chaired by Deputy Secretary of State Warren Christopher, which tried to resolve thorny questions about when aid should be suspended because of rights abuses.[45] There was a genuine dialogue, but as author David McLellan argued, Secretary of State Cyrus Vance weighed human rights abuses on a case-by-case basis, and he "drew the line at human rights sanctions against countries essential to American security."[46]

For AID, the Soviet push into Afghanistan meant once again ramping up assistance to Pakistan, which had been almost completely suspended earlier because of its nuclear weapons program. The Afghanistan–Pakistan border quickly became the new front line of the Cold War.

However, the revived partnership with Pakistan got off to a rocky start. When the United States offered $300 million in assistance to Pakistan, Pakistani president Zia complained, "That's peanuts."[47]

At the White House, Carter convened a national security meeting to deal with the issue. As Jack Sullivan of AID recalled, "Carter did not like that one bit. He was angry."[48] After extensive back-and-forth—trying to balance anger over the slight with the important security concerns in play—it was decided to reduce the overall package of assistance by $46 million of food aid. (While the Carter team put substantial assistance into Pakistan, it would be dwarfed by the package that was put together under the subsequent Reagan administration, which committed more than $3.25 billion in military and economic aid to Pakistan over a five-year period.)[49]

CARTER CONCLUSION

While geopolitics played an outsize role in the tail end of the Carter administration, and ultimately Carter's electoral demise, it was the global economic climate that was having a more-powerful ripple effect across the developing world. Toward the end of 1979, oil-producing countries again engineered a sharp price spike, and the United States started borrowing to finance its deficit spending.

This quickly had a cascade effect across the developing world. Interest rates shot up. Many countries were forced to refinance loans at higher rates than they had anticipated, and debt obligations soared. Capital flows started to shift away from developing countries. The decisions to loan great volumes of money to the developing world earlier in the 1970s suddenly looked dubious. The days of cheap and easy finance for developing countries had ended.

Edward Schuh described the impact: "Many countries, especially those in Latin America, have experienced sustained and significant declines in per capita incomes. These problems have been exacerbated by their unwillingness, or political inability, to undertake the economic reforms needed to get their economies back on a sound path to economic recovery."[50] The issue of debt and structural economic reform would linger as a central question for years to come.

The late stages of the Carter administration also saw a renewed focus on economic growth and economic policy in development. "There is a tendency to think that the shift toward renewed concern with economic growth and economic policy frameworks came with the Reagan administration," commented Frederick Gilbert, "but I like to remind people that it really started towards the end of the Carter administration."[51] These questions only took on more urgency with the debt crisis.

At AID, Doug Bennet had done a solid job of keeping the agency out of the headlines and avoided any major scandals, but he did not have sufficient time to really bring his own imprint to the agency. After AID, Bennet went on to serve as president of National Public Radio and then as president of Wesleyan University. When his staff at NPR bemoaned the difficulties of dealing with Congress and raising money, Bennet told them, "If you think this has a limited constituency, you should see AID's."[52]

On November 4, 1980, California governor Ronald Reagan crushed Jimmy Carter at the ballot box in a landslide.

7

The Reagan Years

SECURITY FIRST, ECONOMICS SECOND

President Ronald Reagan took office with a burst of enthusiasm after a sweeping electoral victory and the release of the fifty-two American hostages held in Tehran on the day of his inauguration. Unfortunately for AID, the agency was initially one of the prime targets for the president's team of smaller-government, conservative Republicans. A sense of unease pervaded AID when Ed Feulner Jr., the president of the Heritage Foundation—a conservative think tank long opposed to aid—was appointed to run the transition team for the agency.

David Stockman, head of the Office of Management and the Budget, had become a mini-celebrity as he advocated a combination of deep government spending cuts and supply-side economics. Stockman pushed for a $2.6 billion cut in the foreign assistance request President Carter had sent to Congress, and a $791 million reduction in funding already authorized.[1]

Stockman excoriated the foreign assistance program. He said that deep cuts were warranted because AID and other implementing organizations were "infested with socialist error" responsible for "turning Third World countries into quagmires of self-imposed inefficiency."[2] There were informal discussions within the agency about whether it should entirely eliminate its health or education portfolios.[3]

The task of trying to blunt Stockman fell to the new head of AID, Peter McPherson. McPherson, who would go on to become the agency's longest-serving chief and one of its best regarded, had gained his exposure to development early as a Peace Corps volunteer in Peru in the mid-1960s. In a slum built atop a landfill, he had worked on school feeding and credit union programs with local Roman Catholic priests.[4]

After a stint at the IRS, McPherson rose quickly within Republican ranks, serving as a special assistant to President Gerald Ford and general counsel to the Reagan transition team.

The stars aligned well for McPherson as AID administrator. He was well liked within the White House, including by highly influential chief of staff James Baker. Democrats in Congress remained supportive of efforts to combat extreme poverty, and most AID staff soon came to feel that McPherson was their best buffer against the administration's more-intemperate factions.

The effort to slash the assistance budget soon became a test of wills pitting Stockman against both McPherson and the new secretary of state, Alexander Haig. Haig made his case shrewdly, arguing that deep cuts to the aid program would make countering Soviet moves in the developing world more difficult.

Stockman pushed McPherson to accept an automatic 8 percent cut in AID's total staff. McPherson countered that this goal could be achieved equally effectively through attrition, with none of the disruption. Both men took their case directly to Reagan, and McPherson ultimately prevailed in an Oval Office debate that played out before a bemused president.

The appeal to a muscular US foreign policy vision prevailed, and Reagan came to see US foreign assistance as an essential element of projecting America's influence. He significantly expanded aid budgets and shifted their priorities toward security aims. He reduced US commitments to multilateral organizations and put a higher percentage of funding into a smaller cluster of strategically important countries, including Pakistan, Egypt, Turkey, and later, Central America.

The total development aid budget jumped sharply from $7 billion in 1980 to $12 billion in 1985, very much in line with Reagan's priority of fighting the Cold War.[5] Economic Support Funds climbed from 50 percent of the budget to over 65 percent in the same time frame. Secretary of State Haig (who was to be replaced by George Shultz in mid-1982) had argued that aid recipients should be graded not by their human rights record but by their loyalty as allies in the struggle against communism.[6]

On the Hill, some conservative Republicans were taken aback to find that their votes were now required for passage of the assistance bills they had always resisted. As Republican congressman Jack Kemp (referring to himself in the third person) bemoaned, "Yes, Jack Kemp is going to vote for his first foreign aid bill."[7]

At the United Nations, the new deputy US ambassador, Ken Adelman, appeared shocked that providing foreign aid to developing countries did not automatically secure compliant votes for Washington's preferred resolutions. He published an article in *Foreign Policy* magazine, wondering: "Did all that money buy America any love?"[8]

Peter McPherson gained considerable goodwill from President Reagan when he took part in a White House ceremony where the president announced the administration was pulling $28 million in foreign aid from twelve countries.[9] Reagan, Haig, and McPherson posed with a large cardboard check made out to the "US taxpayers, c/o President Ronald Reagan." The cuts were largely symbolic, but the president delighted in the theater and repeatedly asked Stockman why other agencies couldn't do the same thing.

The effort to push back Soviet expansionism in the developing world played out across the globe. Elisabeth Kvitashvili of AID remembers counting Tennessee mules as they were offloaded from C-130s in Pakistan to be used by the CIA to push supplies to resistance fighters in Afghanistan.[10] Kvitashvili, who had grown up in a family that had suffered a great deal as a result of Soviet aggression, viewed the aid flowing into the Afghan Mujahedin resistance as "god's work" at the time. She does recall being somewhat uncomfortable that some of the groups they were working with embraced more-extreme Islamic views and were also receiving funding and support from Saudi Arabia. As Kvitashvili reflects, "Looking back now, and in hindsight, I wince."

But if security was the overriding imperative of the Reagan administration approach, it was also underpinned by a clear economic philosophy. In 1981 at a summit on aid issues in Mexico, Reagan declared, "The rationale for aid to countries whose low economic performance results more from inappropriate domestic policies than from external factors needs to be re-examined."[11] This meeting in Cancun, attended by twenty-two nations, was seen as a key barometer of Reagan's approach, and as Reagan biographer Lou Cannon notes, "The meeting was one of the few of Reagan's presidency where he was exposed to pleas for help from such impoverished nations as Bangladesh."[12]

The meeting was less controversial than most expected, and other countries were pleased that Reagan seemed sincere in listening to their point of view. Reagan, however, was somewhat surprised when, in the middle of trumpeting the achievements of free-market farming in the United States, President Julius Nyerere of Tanzania pointed out, "US agriculture is the most heavily subsidized in the world."

Peter McPherson explained the Reagan administration's decision to transition away from a basic human needs approach.[13] "Unfortunately, the burden of meeting those needs grew each year," he argued, and countries were not taking "full responsibility for their future." Although committing to retain the more-popular elements of the basic human needs approach, McPherson argued that what developing countries needed most was the political courage to "lay off superfluous government employees" and reduce subsidies.[14] Added McPherson, "We are not an international welfare agency."[15]

McPherson advanced a "four pillars" strategy that stressed policy reform, building institutions, technological innovation, and private sector growth.[16] He created a new Bureau of Private Enterprise. Many at AID felt that McPherson's emphasis on economic progress and institutional reform was a welcome course correction after New Directions.

What seems to have most elevated McPherson were his interpersonal skills that helped him manage the diverse constituencies with a stake in the assistance program. He was one of the rare administrators able to balance his approach between economic reforms traditionally favored by Republicans and the basic human needs strategy favored by Democrats. He met daily with his congressional relations and public relations staffs.[17] He also valued the agency's career staff, establishing the office of the counselor in his executive suite as the highest-ranking career post at AID when the White House put a political appointee into the deputy administrator position (which had traditionally been held by a senior career officer).

McPherson significantly revived the participant training programs that had fallen out of favor in the 1970s. More than 17,000 scholarships were provided in the 1980s, mainly targeted at institution building and strengthening human capital. "I thought long-term participant training was critical," said McPherson. "We pushed it hard."[18] McPherson mandated that all projects over a certain threshold had to include a participant training component or explicitly explain why they did not. Andrew Natsios, who would later run the agency, argued, "Universally, AID officers have repeatedly said that this was the most successful category of program the agency ran."[19]

Privatization was also a consistent theme out of the Reagan administration. In many cases, privatization of state enterprises made sense, and the private sector could deliver goods more efficiently. However, privatization could also be a big step backward for countries if public assets were sold off below market value, especially when sold to political insiders, or if such privatization caused large numbers of people to lose access to services. Each case presented complex issues requiring careful economic and political analysis.

Economists Anne Krueger and Vernon Ruttan framed the emerging consensus around economic policy and development at the time:

> Indeed, one of the major lessons of experience with the development process is that the primary determinant of a country's growth rate, and probably also of the economic return on many individual projects, is its own economic policies. Countries that have experienced above-average rates of growth have generally managed their governmental budgets fairly well, have maintained realistic exchange rates, have avoided high and uneven rates of protection, and have usually let their labor and commodity markets function without undue restrictions. These policies alone do not guarantee high rates of growth. But serious departure from such policies for a sustained period of time has generally led to difficulties in the growth process.[20]

In many ways, this view was not particularly different than what US policymakers had advocated in early cases such as Taiwan and South Korea.

Reagan put together a high-level commission, chaired by Deputy Secretary of Defense Frank Carlucci, to make the case for his approach to aid. "The keystone to our recommendations is the conclusion that economic and military assistance must be closely integrated," stated the group's findings. "On a global level, threats to security and prosperity are increasing. The military power of the Soviet Union and its surrogates has been expanding rapidly."[21]

The calls for economic reforms were made more urgent by the global economic climate and the toll of the debt crisis in the developing world. A UN report argued,

"For the vast majority of developing countries, the first half of the 1980s has been the most difficult period since the Depression years of the 1930s."[22]

Commodity prices tumbled sharply, leaving countries with less money at the moment they needed it most. Copper prices plunged from $1.30 in 1980 to half that several years later, with similar declines in commodities like cocoa and phosphates that were big money earners. Many developing countries sharply curtailed imports in an effort to get their debt under control.

Most African countries were seeing substantially more money flow out than in, with some commentators suggesting that developing countries were stuck in a trap reminiscent of the debtors' prisons of days of old.[23]

BABY FORMULA

There were times when the Reagan administration's predilection for free-market solutions was costly. One such example cropped up very early in the first term, surrounding the issue of the use of baby formula in the developing world.

At the time, about eleven million infants died in the developing world every year before their first birthday. The biggest killer of these children was simple diarrheal diseases—the kinds of illnesses that breastfeeding can help to prevent. Two articles in the *Journal of Pediatrics* had presented findings that showed illness occurred at rates sixteen times higher among babies that were not breastfed in their first two months of life. The head of the World Health Organization, Halfdan Mahler, maintained, "Evidence from developing countries indicates that infants breast-fed less than six months, or not at all, have a mortality rate 5 to 10 times higher in the second six months of life."[24]

There was growing evidence at the time that the effort to aggressively advertise and market baby formula in the developing world was a public health disaster. In cases where a mother was unable to breastfeed, formula obviously could be a lifesaver. But breast milk was far richer with natural nutrients that help strengthen a baby's immune system. Formula was frequently used improperly, mixed with dirty drinking water. It was also prohibitively expensive, and parents often ended up skipping needed feedings because of the cost. AID health programs generally did not promote formula, and strongly encouraged breastfeeding.

However, formula sales in poor countries had become big business, with the Swiss firm Nestle S.A. and a handful of American companies dominating the $2 billion a year market.[25] "Until a few years ago, when they ended the practice in response to widespread protest, Nestle and the American formula companies advertised heavily in the print and broadcast media of developing countries," the *New York Times* noted. "In Brazil, where infant formula was the most advertised product after cigarettes and soap, the advertisements usually promised, if only subtly, that formula was the modern method of infant feeding, associated with upward mobility."[26]

Based on a growing body of medical research and the hue and cry of the advocacy community, the World Health Organization proposed a code that would restrict some of the marketing practices for baby formula.

The Carter administration had supported the proposed World Health Organization code. Peter McPherson had a career staffer, Bob Berg, reexamine the issue. For Berg, the issue was clear: "Fifty thousand infants a year were dying around the world according to the best estimates because of the mis-marketing of this infant formula."[27] He knew the administration would not vote in favor of the code, but reasoned that the least it could do was take the "not very brave" position of abstaining on the vote, as many Europeans countries planned to do.

Berg was able to quickly convince the State Department to accept a US abstention.

Not long after, Berg recalls young conservative firebrand, John Bolton—a political appointee at the agency who started out as AID's general counsel, then shifted to run its policy office—triumphantly entering the senior staff meeting. Bolton declared, "This is a great day for America. The United States has just voted no on the infant formula code. We have shown to the world what we stand for."

Berg stood up and responded, "I'm sorry, John. This is a day of shame for the United States." He walked out of the meeting.

Bolton had maneuvered behind the scenes to galvanize White House opposition to the code, alleging that the code would hamper free trade and run counter to US law. The United States was the only country to vote against the code.

In response, two senior health and nutrition staffers at AID, Eugene Babb and Stephen Joseph, announced they would resign in protest, which they did, as the new administration remained unyielding. Peter McPherson told reporters that the integrity of the policy process required "adherence by all senior officials once decisions have been made."[28]

A HUNGRY CHILD KNOWS NO POLITICS

Toward the end of the Ford administration, AID's Office of Foreign Disaster Assistance was granted special authority to largely skip the lengthy bureaucratic requirements the rest of the agency usually faced. When lives were in imminent danger, the Office of Foreign Disaster Assistance could buy relief supplies at a moment's notice and contract the services of whichever NGOs were best positioned to deliver that assistance.[29]

Notably, lifesaving aid was meant to be delivered on the basis of need rather than on political considerations.[30]

In 1983, initial reports from charities working in Ethiopia indicated that an increasingly serious famine was gripping that country. However, Ethiopia's hard-line Marxist-Leninist government restricted travel on the ground, making it very difficult to verify the situation. But by any measure, it was increasingly clear that a combination of drought, conflict, misguided government policies, and environmental degradation were translating into wholesale suffering in a situation that would ulti-mately claim between 400,000 and 1 million Ethiopian lives.[31]

As food aid historian Barry Riley observed of the Ethiopian government policies that were driving the crisis, "In effect, they replaced a system that operated poorly to improve the lot of the average Ethiopian with one that did not work at all."[32]

Much blame lay with the Marxist Ethiopian government. As economist Amartya Sen observed, "No famine has ever taken place in the history of the world in a func-tioning democracy."[33] In an increasingly global economy, famines have largely been relegated to situations where governments hide the suffering of their own people or block relief efforts.

The Reagan administration initially balked at providing aid. An initial AID assessment maintained that no additional food should be provided because the Ethiopian government could not, or would not, distribute it.[34] There were also significant concerns that the Ethiopian government would simply divert food aid to its own military forces. "Thousands of Ethiopians were undeniably starving to death," commented Riley. "Top lieutenants in the Reagan administration wanted to know—using the language reminiscent of Lyndon Johnson's displeasure with India two decades earlier—why on earth should the United States provide help to a country whose government had so willingly delivered itself into the Soviet orbit."[35]

"The government of Ethiopia tried to keep the disaster news from getting out and tried to slow down the delivery," argued Peter McPherson. "[T]he Soviet ties and distrust of the Ethiopian government made it harder in Washington."[36]

McPherson was originally disinclined to have the agency ramp up food deliveries. Hariadene Johnson of AID recalls a weekend discussion in the Office of Foreign Disaster Assistance with McPherson, where staff of the office tried to explain that "when disasters happened, AID helped, that we didn't really draw a line between the Cold War boundaries."[37]

"That's before we were here," McPherson replied.

But despite McPherson's initial reluctance, considerable debate continued within AID about the merits of providing food. "It didn't look like a disaster. It looked like a development problem that the Africa Bureau should handle," observed a staffer who wished to remain anonymous. "And it looked political."[38] The staff also worried that there would be no clear exit if it got involved in a messy, protracted situation like Ethiopia. This same commentator added, "How will we know when we're done, and if we don't know, how will we ever get out?"

That said, key members of the agency's staff, including Ray Love, a senior official on the Africa team, and Julia Chang Bloch, who was in charge of food programs, felt that food aid needed to be delivered despite the many glaring shortcomings of the Ethiopian government. However, one of those most opposed to the move was once again John Bolton, who found key allies outside the agency intent on punish-ing Ethiopia.

Hearing the various arguments, McPherson consented to increase supplies in 1984, but not substantially so. The administration's reluctance to provide much more than token levels of assistance soon bubbled over into a dispute with Congress. Democratic representative Howard Wolpe, who chaired the Africa Subcommittee of the Committee on Foreign Affairs, accused the administration of cherry-picking hunger estimates to make it look like the fewest possible number of Ethiopians were in need.[39]

Several events forced the administration's hand. News coverage of Ethiopia was increasingly harrowing. "I came home one night. I remember sitting on a couch. I turned on the TV evening news," recalled Ray Love. "Then the TV camera started moving toward the village. It got closer and closer, and then you could see the village and a group of people. Eventually, we were looking at this kid, an emaciated little baby standing there with his mother."[40] Love turned to his wife and said, "Tomorrow morning we're going to have no trouble getting that food aid through."

Republican senator John Danforth toured Africa to get a firsthand look at the famine, and although he did not go to Ethiopia, he traveled to neighboring Somalia, also facing very difficult conditions. Upon his return, he arranged a hurried meeting with President Reagan, showing the president visceral photographs of the conditions.[41]

Peter McPherson traveled to Ethiopia shortly after, in November 1984. When he returned, he met with President Reagan, also sharing his photographs and impressions. Vice President Bush, White House Chief of Staff James Baker, and National Security Adviser Robert McFarland also attended the session. McPherson had been quietly trying to build support in the administration for expanded assistance, and he sensed that he had his moment. McPherson was blunt with the president, arguing that a huge response was needed.[42]

Reagan was swayed, and he famously declared after the meeting, "A hungry child knows no politics."

AID estimated that more than a million tons of grain would be required to stanch the crisis, and McPherson made sure to get in a dig at the Soviet Union for providing "very little" aid to help Ethiopia in its hour of need. Bags of wheat emblazoned with the AID logo were loaded onto Soviet Mi-8 helicopters and carried to the countryside.[43]

In March 1985, musician Bob Geldof released a star-studded song, "We Are the World," to raise millions for famine relief. And although the money raised was not a large percentage of what was ultimately spent on the famine, "We Are the World" further mobilized the public worldwide, and governments allocated more money to the famine because of it.

The United States mounted one of its largest-ever relief efforts in response to the African famine. AID negotiated an agreement with the Ethiopian government that AID would deliver most US food through private charities in return for a small portion going through the government. As McPherson explained, "I saw that food as the price we had to pay to move the famine food."

AID, wary of relying on the Ethiopian government to distribute aid, bought and rented trucks outside of Ethiopia and brought them into the country. In contrast, other donors who were relying on the government to distribute aid soon found their shipments of food rotting on the docks in the Ethiopian ports of Massawa and Assab. AID essentially shamed other donor countries into pressuring the Ethiopian government to distribute food more quickly by pointing out that it would be highly embarrassing if the press saw the stacks of food being wasted as people starved to death.

And while the United States ultimately delivered enormous amounts of food under very difficult conditions, accounting for about half of the total famine relief the region received during this period, the cost of initial inaction and delays in response were high. "Conflicts between AID, State, and the National Security Council usually are not over denying aid," wrote Andrew Natsios, who would later go on to become head of the Office of Foreign Disaster Assistance under George H. W. Bush and the AID administrator under George W. Bush. Natsios noted that the "notorious instance" of the Ethiopia case likely contributed to a much higher loss of life. "NSC policymakers in the Reagan administration, intent on punishing the brutal Mengistu regime, stone-walled the AID response until President Reagan intervened," continued Natsios, who made his observations with the benefit of a number of years passing.[44]

"Overall, the U.S. probably should have done more, earlier, and in hindsight, I wish we had," reflected Peter McPherson, while still arguing that US efforts to make a brutal communist government more accountable to its people had considerable merit.[45]

The Office of Foreign Disaster Assistance would increasingly become entangled in situations that were a combination of wars, humanitarian emergencies, and sometimes famines—so-called "complex emergencies." As one Office of Foreign Disaster Assistance staff member commented of Ethiopia, "With that, everything changed. We were never the same again."[46]

Several years after the Ethiopia famine, AID, the United Nations, and an umbrella grouping of thirty-five NGOs launched a major effort, Operation Lifeline Sudan, that would create humanitarian corridors and transport systems for beleaguered parts of that authoritarian country. This aid would eventually support over seven million people, and its operation would stretch over more than sixteen years.[47] Long-duration emergencies had become a new normal.

The famines in Africa during this period spurred AID and a series of partners to develop the Famine Early Warning System, or FEWS. The warning system ties together satellite imagery from NASA, information from local markets of food prices, rainfall estimates, and crop conditions to provide an ongoing barometer of emerging food scarcities.[48] Knowing when and where famines were likely to occur helped everyone get out ahead of them by pre-positioning relief supplies and addressing key obstacles to food distribution on the ground.

Keeping an eye on local markets and food prices remains a key element of this system. Better understanding the choices that poor families face as food prices fluctuate often provides a sensitive indicator of trouble on the horizon.

Starting out as a relatively simple system focused on fourteen African countries in 1985, the Famine Early Warning System is now a sophisticated surveillance network that covers some forty countries in Africa, Central America and the Caribbean, and Central Asia.

Ironically, just as the agency was launching major efforts to better identify famines, it was beginning what would become a steady erosion over time in its emphasis on agriculture—in part because world food prices were so low at the time. The constituency for agriculture programs had shrunk, and many developing countries had become more focused on their urban, rather than their rural, populations.[49]

CHILD SURVIVAL

One of the greatest breakthroughs in saving the lives of children around the world came through something known as oral rehydration therapy. Simplicity itself, this basic mixture of sugar and salts fits in a packet not much bigger than a tea bag. Mixed with water, it stems dehydration and diarrheal disease far more cheaply than administering fluids intravenously, which is often too expensive and impractical in the developing world.

Perfecting oral rehydration therapy took more than two decades of research and testing, growing out of failed efforts to develop a more-effective cholera vaccine, with AID playing an important role in its development.

The initial large-scale testing of oral rehydration therapy was carried out by a group of young National Institutes of Health and Centers for Disease Control medical researchers working at the International Centre for Diarrhoeal Disease Research in Bangladesh and its predecessor institution, the SEATO Cholera Research Laboratory in East Pakistan, for which AID provided sustained funding.

There was widespread initial skepticism toward oral rehydration therapy from both health professionals and patients, many of whom were doubtful that a simple mix of sugar, water, and salt could prove as effective as an IV or antibiotics. Yet, oral rehydration therapy was tested effectively at scale during cholera outbreaks in crowded camps for the displaced in Bangladesh in the 1970s. AID, the World Health Organization, and others further refined the treatment, and the World Health Organization and UNICEF agreed on a standard formula for rehydration packets to be distributed around the world.[50]

Fast-forward to the early 1980s. Peter McPherson wanted to focus on a few highly visible and popular elements of public health. Child survival programs were obvious candidates. AID and its partners launched a massive campaign of vaccination and oral rehydration therapy distribution, dubbing these two approaches as the "twin engines" of child survival. McPherson had been deeply influenced in this strategy by former AID staffer Jim Grant, who had become the head of UNICEF. Grant had, in turn, been deeply influenced by Jon Rohde, one of the former AID-financed medical researchers.

AID launched a series of health policy papers emphasizing a selective primary health-care approach which focused on immunizations, nutrition, family planning, and especially oral rehydration therapy. UNICEF set a target of an 80 percent immunization rate by 1990—an ambitious aspiration given that the figure was well below 40 percent when the initiative was launched. At the conclusion of a major conference on child survival, Grant, McPherson, and others agreed to set a target of two million lives saved by the end of the third year of the program. As McPherson put it, "I've learned you need big ideas and big goals."[51]

Jim Grant and Peter McPherson relentlessly stumped for their approach. Any time McPherson made remarks, regardless of the issue, he almost invariably finished his comments with a reference to immunization and diarrheal diseases. Jim Grant carried an oral rehydration packet with him wherever he went.

It was a heady time for AID's health programs. Instead of petitioning Congress for additional resources, Congress was consistently providing funding higher than the administration had requested. A large and effective coalition of NGOs, the National Council for International Health, and UNICEF all helped mobilize support. In just six years, AID's health budget leapt by 500 percent. AID's development of the demographic health survey helped it become one of the leading public health information systems in the world. AID had been transformed into a public health juggernaut, and health and disaster relief programs would remain the largest part of its portfolio going forward.

This focus on child survival, coupled with increased funding, contributed to important advances in nutrition. And once again some of the simplest and cheapest interventions proved the most effective. Research funded in part by AID helped lead to the realization that giving a child two cents' worth of vitamin A every six months could help to sharply curtail child mortality.[52] This also led to fortifying foods such as flour, cooking oils, and sugar on a large scale.

While the exact health interventions obviously varied significantly country by country, vaccinations and oral rehydration therapy were indeed the twin engines across the board. AID and UNICEF hit their mutual target, and immunization rates in the developing world leapt from 37 percent in 1984 to over 80 percent by the early 1990s.[53] Oral rehydration therapy became one of the most important lifesaving interventions around the globe, reaching almost three-quarters of the world's children by the mid-1990s. AID, UNICEF, and others argue that oral rehydration efforts save over a million lives every year.

THE FAMILY PLANNING WARS

Although family planning was an integral part of effective child survival programs, it became an unprecedented political football during the Reagan administration. McPherson's role in the entire situation was complex, as he both defended the program from its most conservative critics and supported new restrictions that made family planning less available for hundreds of thousands of women.

Immediately after coming into office, the Reagan administration signaled its desire to completely discontinue the family planning program. One of the champions of abandoning international family planning efforts was John Bolton. In Reagan's first budget, the president asked for zero family planning funds.[54] Bolton further irritated congressional Democrats by exploring ways he could transfer funds out of existing family planning accounts and put them into economic growth programs. (Congressional Democrats were so enraged that funding levels for family planning programs consistently went up during the Reagan era.)

Many Reagan appointees sought to apply the president's sunny, supply-side approach to economics to family planning. One such appointee, Frank Ruddy, who headed the Africa Bureau, said that concerns about rapid population growth were little more than "pessimism and defeatism," and "the exact opposite of what President Reagan stood for: people are not the problem; inefficient, oppressive governments are."[55] In Ruddy's view, human ingenuity and growth would naturally counterbalance population growth, and governments simply needed to get out of the way. The administration also promoted the views of economist Julian Simon, who argued that rapid population growth meant more chances for new Beethovens, Einsteins, and Mozarts.[56]

In the spring of 1983, it came to light that Joe Speidel, the head of the population office, had published an article which discussed abortion. Peter McPherson came under tremendous pressure to fire Speidel, which he did. Steve Sinding was appointed to succeed Speidel, and he saw educating McPherson about family planning as crucial.[57]

"I had to get myself through the issue and think about it carefully in very concrete terms," said McPherson.[58] He was swayed in part by a study from Chile that had shown there were fewer abortions when family planning was available. McPherson embraced the family planning program as he better understood its import and impact, to the point where Sinding declared, "Peter proved, in my view, to be a hero in protecting the population program from the real wishes of many of the political people around Reagan."

But McPherson had to make significant concessions to keep the program afloat. One of them was directing funding to what is known as natural family planning, or the rhythm method. The data had made clear that such approaches were consistently ineffective. Yet McPherson eventually directed Sinding to fund some of the adherents of natural family planning. Most family planning professionals thought it was a terrible idea, but it felt like the price of doing business.

The family planning issue became even more controversial with a major once-in-a-decade International Conference on Population that took place in Mexico City in the summer of 1984. AID received a draft paper from the White House on what came to be known as "the Mexico City policy" (or the "global gag rule," in family planning circles), shortly before the conference. Steve Sinding recalls, "The statement began by saying that population was neither a positive nor negative factor but was neutral; that abortion was an abomination, and the U.S. will not support any organization that is engaged in abortion, and that we will defund all governments, NGOs, foreign and domestic, that engaged in abortion."[59]

In short, the White House was declaring its intent to defund any NGO or foreign government that advocated for legalizing abortion or carrying out any kind of abortion services—including in instances where the life of a mother was clearly at risk or a baby was clearly not viable.

Sinding told McPherson that he thought the White House proposal was both unconstitutional and a violation of the sovereignty of countries receiving US assistance. McPherson enlisted the legal teams at State and AID, who also noted that such restrictions would likely be unconstitutional if fully applied to US NGOs. The language was then changed to target foreign NGOs, who didn't enjoy US constitutional protections.

Stories about the intense internal infighting over the proposed Mexico City policy spilled into the press. The *New York Times* wrote that the situation had "sharply divided" the Reagan team, with White House chief of staff James Baker trying to resolve the disputes, and adding, "Mr. Reagan's conservative supporters believe they are entitled to some substantive victories, and they think they may have one in the administration's emerging position on world population control."[60] Alabama Republican senator Jeremiah Denton, a strong proponent of the Mexico City policy, assailed AID staff for calling the policy "extremely and unnecessarily controversial" in leaked internal documents. The *Times* also noted that the draft of the Mexico City paper called rapid population growth a "localized" problem that was "evidence of too much government control and planning rather than too little."

The family planning community pushed back against the notion that economic growth was an easy answer to population growth. "The argument about market forces is extraordinarily naive," argued Dr. Fernando Tamayo, the president of the family planning NGO Profamilia. "Perhaps in a century or two it might be true, but the world doesn't have time to wait. Take Colombia. We have had slower economic growth than, say, Mexico and Brazil, but we have reduced birth rates faster than either, thanks to our program."[61]

The public debate became heated. As pro-life economist Julian Simon continued to argue that in free-market economies, "free people create additional resources," Sharon Camp of the Population Crisis Center retorted, "The right-to-life movement does not want to see reform of family planning programs, they want to see them burn in hell."[62]

The US delegation to Mexico City was all male, and the Mexico City policy would remain in place for nine years—until a Democratic president was elected. "We tried in a variety of ways to ameliorate the effect of the policy," recalled Steve Sinding, "but it had an unmistakably chilling effect."[63] The Democratically controlled Congress, disturbed by the events of Mexico City, gave the agency one of its largest single increases in family planning funding between 1984 and 1985.

Not long after the Mexico City conference, a hard-hitting two-part series appeared in the *Washington Post* on China's one-child policy and the horrific human rights abuses that had accompanied it. China's approach was diametrically opposed to that supported by AID, but the harrowing stories of forced abortions and women having their houses knocked down for having a second child mobilized action on the Hill. The foreign assistance act was amended to ensure that the United States would automatically defund any organization taking part in a coerced sterilization or coerced abortion program. The immediate result was to defund US contributions from the UN family planning program, given its modest but continuing involvement in China.

The stretch of turmoil around international family planning left Peter McPherson taking flak from all sides. Mother Teresa spoke with him about her views on US family planning efforts. The Planned Parenthood Federation took out ads on buses in the DC metro area showing a woman from the developing world holding an emaciated infant and proclaiming, "The right-wing fanatics have picked their next target."[64] A number of the ads singled out McPherson by name.

Some thirty conservative groups called for McPherson's removal. McPherson, as was his style, met with the groups to hear them out. The groups complained that McPherson and AID were subverting the anti-abortion regulations, and one attendee, Paul Weyrich, ranted that McPherson was "unfit to hold office."[65]

The fallout from the abortion debate was far-reaching, and the effort to curb abortion by attacking family planning services was profoundly counterproductive. The war against women's access to contraceptives, public health services, and sex education invariably led to more abortions—legal or not. This also meant increased maternal and infant mortality at a time when AID and other organizations were making a Herculean effort to curb such deaths.

The fractious debate over abortion was all the more unfortunate because it came at a time when AID and others were beginning to get much smarter about the role of women in development. As Samuel Butterfield notes, more and more countries were accepting the broad rationale for promoting family planning, recognizing that providing girls with basic education, contraception, and expanded economic opportunities had a powerful, positive impact on family size and well-being.[66] Instead of seeing economic growth as a panacea and all government interventions as a curse, a sensible mix of government services and good policies were usually more effective.

There was also long-overdue recognition that women were a major economic force unto themselves, and that too much planning had simply involved men talking to men. A major 1982 study on the status of women in Nepal found that in rural areas women contributed twice as much labor as men, and were primarily responsible for farming.[67] This was not news to anyone who had ever spent time in a village in Nepal, but it was a major shift in thinking for many policymakers in Washington. Even the agency itself recognized that misunderstanding the role of gender can lead to serious flaws in project design and diminish the returns on investments in general.[68]

It was all the more baffling, then, to make an assault on reproductive health a centerpiece of the administration's approach as it simultaneously argued for the importance of women in development and tried to reduce infant and maternal mortality.

AID staff, by and large, gave McPherson high marks for his willingness to defend the agency's programs, even if he was not always successful in doing so. "Many people were unaware of how much he had accomplished," said Allison Herrick of McPherson, "because they didn't know how stringent the position was before it was softened."[69]

Paradoxically, the Mexico City policy reinforced the commitment of many developing countries to embrace family planning programs, hardly the intent of its advocates, and pushed the international family planning community to approach its work with greater solidarity.

THE KILLER IN THE WINGS

Even as the world was making historic advances in reducing infant mortality, a monstrous new killer was lurking in the wings: HIV/AIDS. Few development professionals appreciated the terrible toll this pandemic was poised to inflict, and the obdurate resistance of President Reagan to treat a public health crisis transmitted largely by sexual behavior the same as he would treat other public health crises further fueled suffering both domestically and internationally.

The early reporting on the emerging pandemic feels dated beyond its years. Under a headline of "New Homosexual Disorder Worries Health Officials," the *New York Times* wrote in May 1982 that the "serious disorder of the immune system that has been known to doctors for less than a year—a disorder that appears to affect primarily male homosexuals—has now afflicted at least 335 people, of whom it has killed 136."[70]

In 1984, researchers discovered the virus that caused AIDS, but it would be another two years before AID implemented its first HIV/AIDS programs.[71]

Duff Gillespie of the agency recalls Peter McPherson, whom he regarded as an effective administrator, saying, "You know, we're not going to get involved in this. This is something that's just not going to be worth our while."[72] With no small amount of rue, Gillespie adds, "We really just didn't have any idea." Someone was brought in from the Centers for Disease Control to help start a program, but initially it was only given token funding. A great deal of time and effort was spent trying to build support for a UN agency dedicated to dealing with HIV/AIDS. Many developing countries were also reluctant to accept funding and programs in this area, worried about the stigma associated with a disease that some referred to as the "gay plague."

"I recall the transition from viewing it as an obscure epidemic about which the World Health Organization was overly exercised," said Ann Van Dusen, "to the realization that this was a pandemic that would change everything."[73] Unfortunately, the tendency of President Reagan and many of his key advisers to view AIDS as a question of morality rather than public health meant that the pandemic would continue to gather terrible momentum.

Brigadier General John Hutton, the White House physician, said that President Reagan had a tendency to think of AIDS like it was measles and "would go away."[74] Reagan's opinion started to shift with the death of his friend and fellow actor Rock Hudson late in 1985. After Hudson's death, Reagan sought out Hutton to discuss the disease at some length. After learning more about the pandemic, Reagan replied, "I always thought the world would end in a flash, but this sounds like it's worse."

THE AFRICAN CHESSBOARD

Large parts of Africa continued to reel as a result of the debt crunch. The General Accounting Office noted that during the 1980s, "thirteen of the region's countries— representing one-third of its population—had lower per capita incomes in 1989 than they had at independence in the 1960s."[75] Africa's debt was at 100 percent of GDP and more than three times that of total export earnings.

While emphasizing the importance of AID as a tool in the Cold War helped secure congressional support for the agency, the reality of Cold War politics played out harshly on the ground in Africa. In countries that weren't Cold War hot spots, AID had a commendable record in promoting economic reform and child survival. When geopolitics intervened, it was often a different story.

Zaire, today's Democratic Republic of Congo, offered a prime example. Led by Mobutu Sese Seko, Congo was the poster child of a modern kleptocracy. Mobuto looted billions from his desperately poor, mineral-rich country, stashing his lucre in Swiss banks. President Mobuto lived with the excess of a cartoon villain, building a lavish palace deep in the jungle with a nearby runway large enough to land a Concorde jet, which he sometimes rented to fly to Europe. He owned yachts and a fleet of Mercedes that bounced across the country's crumbling roads.

During the Carter years, US–Zaire relations had dipped, largely because of Mobutu's scandalous human rights record. However, the civil war in neighboring Angola, steeped in Cold War tensions, soon meant that Zaire was back in favor with the Reagan administration. Vice President Bush visited the country, as did a series of other US dignitaries. Mobuto in turn visited Reagan in the White House in 1986, with the president praising Mobutu for his "heroic economic reforms" and his "good sense and good will."

One AID officer recalled that when Japan donated twenty-five tractors for village agriculture, every single one ended up on the personal farms of the ruling elite.[76]

"For the U.S. and Russia, it was a marginal involvement, but for the Africans, it cost a lot," Philip Birnbaum of AID said.[77] "We convinced ourselves that, somehow, he was going to contain the Cubans in Angola, and in some other places in Africa. So, we tolerated his corruption, and now the country is in shambles." While AID worked through local and international partners to a great extent to prevent US funds from being siphoned off, it was still a remarkably poor investment.

A similar dynamic played out in Liberia, where the administration backed military strongman Samuel Doe. Like Mobutu, Doe was also notoriously corrupt, but generous US military and economic assistance continued. Part of the reason the aid continued to flow: The United States maintained a Voice of America transmitter just outside Liberia's capital, and the government allowed the United States to refuel military planes there on short notice when needed.

"Liberia is corrupt from stem to stern," an unusually candid late-1970s cable from the AID mission observed. "There are no rewards for faithful work nor sanctions for mal- and misfeasances."[78]

"It is nothing short of tragic that the U.S. failed to use its influence and the millions of aid dollars to move the country toward a more open political system," said Harvey Gutman of the agency.

US relations with South Africa also became increasingly controversial during the Reagan era. A broad anti-apartheid campaign gained steam across the United States amid mounting repugnance with South Africa's system of legally sanctioned racial discrimination. Increasing numbers of US banks, pension funds, and companies were pressured into refusing to do business with the white minority South African government, even as the Reagan administration made the case that the country remained a key strategic partner.

The mounting pressure eventually pushed Reagan, who had strenuously resisted sanctions, to sign an executive order prohibiting most new loans to South Africa in hopes that such a move would ward off even stiffer restrictions by Congress.[79]

In 1986, Congress mandated that AID target programs specifically at the Black majority population in its anti-apartheid legislation that also called for sanctions against South Africa. This led to administration objections, but AID moved to put in place a "foundation-like" program that gave small grants to a variety of local anti-apartheid organizations. This included legal defense support for anti-apartheid leaders arrested by the government. It was a program that even the most hardened of protesters back in the United States would likely have supported.

But more broadly, as economist Vernon Ruttan complained, "The Reagan administration's foreign assistance objectives in Africa were remarkable for their lack of clarity."[80]

Peter McPherson and his Africa team launched an innovative effort, the Development Fund for Africa, relatively late in the Reagan years, to change how aid could be delivered on the continent. In many ways, the effort probably would never have made it through Congress without the considerable trust and goodwill that McPherson had generated on both sides of the aisle, and with the president himself.

The Congressional Research Service notes that the Development Fund for Africa was driven in large part by mounting frustration with congressional directives telling the agency exactly how it should spend its money in specific sectors—giving AID very little program flexibility.[81] Trying a different approach, Congress appropriated the entire budget for Africa through a single account in 1987, the Development Fund for Africa.

The rationale for creating the fund was to free underfunded Africa programs from the straitjacket of allocating money strictly by sector—with a clear understanding from Peter McPherson that AID would allocate the funds for development purposes according to country needs and its professional judgment—relatively free of State Department or other pressures.

Longtime AID Africa hand, Carol Peasley, called the Development Fund for Africa, "the best legislative framework within which I worked over my 35-year career with AID."[82] She argued that the legislation allowed for a focus on countries that were committed to development and policy reforms and encouraged better strategic planning. The legislation also waived the "Buy American" provisions, which usually required the agency to purchase American vehicles and supplies even when they were much more expensive than other alternatives.

The Fund offered governments direct budget support in cases where they were willing to embrace policy reforms—less on the macro-economic front, and more within specific areas such as agriculture, basic education, health, and the environment. This sense of partnership required intense collaboration and translated into some real successes in areas such as expanding access to basic education for girls.

In its assessment of the Development Fund for Africa, the General Accounting Office was quite positive, saying that it had provided a stable source of funding; it had been implemented in keeping with congressional guidelines; it gave AID greater flexibility; and it improved project planning and implementation.

Yet, for all of its originality and solid record of success, the Development Fund for Africa had a relatively brief life span, lasting only about a decade. Mounting budget pressures eventually pitted the Development Fund for Africa against priorities in other regions. And after McPherson's departure from AID, there was less trust on the Hill that the agency would put such flexibility to good ends. "[While] it enabled the Africa Bureau to do some of its most creative programming," recalled Peasley of the Development Fund for Africa, "its life was too short."

THE MIDDLE EAST

In Egypt, the Reagan administration faced the same challenge that had beset the Carter administration: an abundance of money to spend and an Egyptian government unwilling to reform. Marshall Brown of AID joked that the government's ideal use of aid dollars would have been to "build a large monument for each minister."[83]

AID had launched an extensive series of programs in family planning, health, agriculture, and education (with an emphasis on basic education for girls). Most of these programs were relatively decentralized in an effort to bring benefits closer to the people who needed them the most. Health and education indicators showed broad improvement, as one would expect with the large amount of money being put into these areas.

But the Egyptian government's heavy involvement in the economy, including a complex web of counterproductive subsidies, went largely untouched. Some calculated that it would have been cheaper to buy imported fertilizer and distribute it for free than to keep the heavily subsidized Egyptian fertilizer plants open.[84] AID was consistently given the message by the State Department that it was allowed to promote reform—but not to the point of antagonizing the Egyptian government.[85] There was a collective failure in the US foreign policy establishment to fully appreciate that this unwillingness to demand accountability from the Egyptian government would come with its own long-term strategic costs.

For Peter McPherson and AID, there was still the imperative to make sure the Egypt money got spent—and spent well, if possible. Worse still, on the eve of a visit by Egyptian president Hosni Mubarak to Washington, the State Department was pushing to increase the cash portion of aid to Cairo by $200 million. Peter McPherson explained, "I was likely to lose on the question with Secretary Shultz because of Middle East political issues unless AID had a better idea."[86]

Of the many areas where Egyptian government subsidies were problematic, the water supply stood out among them. Those who benefited the most from the water subsidies were those with piped water and sewer service to their homes; poorer families had to buy water off the back of mules and often paid ten times the price of families with plumbing.

After McPherson had heard all the alternatives for the Egypt program he said, "Let's spend a billion dollars on water." After considerable internal lobbying within the administration, McPherson secured broad support for his plan. He made the pledge to invest a billion dollars in Egypt's water and sanitation systems to Mubarak, and AID launched an extensive effort to repair and expand the water and sewage systems for Cairo, Alexandria, and other major Egyptian cities.

In 1986, the *New York Times* put some AID investments in perspective. "The program became staggering in its scope. From 1975 to 1985, more than $968 million was allocated just to overhaul Egypt's water and sewage systems. Nearly $816 million went to create more electricity; two large thermal-power plants cost more than $250 million apiece. More than $2.5 billion was provided in low-interest credits with which Egypt could buy American grain."[87] The *Times* noted that more than a third of Egyptian power was generated by US plants. A US-backed microwave system was the backbone of the telephone network. But as one Egyptian official bemoaned, "We are becoming more dependent when we were supposed to become more self-reliant."

Despite the many people who benefited from clean water and better health care, Michael Pillsbury argued, as have many others, that Egypt—across both Democratic and Republican presidents—was one of AID's most notable failures. By 1985, Egypt had been given more than $10 billion of assistance, and the AID mission in that country was the largest in the world, "[y]et Egyptian economic socialism was largely unchanged"—even in the avidly pro-free-market orientation of the Reagan years.[88]

James Fox of the agency also maintained that despite improvement in some key indicators, such as life expectancy, aid to Egypt "is typically regarded within the institution as AID's most conspicuous failure."[89] He points out that AID evaluations show "the usual mix of success and failure, but those dealing with policy issues are almost uniformly negative until the early 1990s."

The Congressional Budget Office noted that Egypt's GNP grew at an average annual rate of 5.6 percent between 1974 and 1993, but unemployment continued to rise, and per capita GNP actually fell an average of 0.2 percent a year between 1988 and 1993—primarily because of government control of large enterprises.[90] The failure to pursue reform in Egypt would leave the core problems for a later and more-painful reckoning.

US engagement in the Middle East, while driven more by strategic considerations than development ones, clearly had important implications for AID as an institution and the way it went about its work. In August of 1982, President Reagan deployed eight hundred marines to Lebanon as part of a multinational force overseeing the Palestine Liberation Organization's withdrawal in the wake of the civil war in Lebanon.

On April 18, 1983, the US Embassy in Beirut was hit by a massive car bomb that tore away most of the front of the building in the middle of a workday.

Anne Dammarell was sitting in the embassy cafeteria at that moment:

> I thought it was a clap of thunder because the day was overcast. And at the same time that happened, everything went black, and silent. I felt a shock go through my whole body. If you ever put your finger in a plug when you were a kid—you know how the electricity goes through your finger like a zigzag? [T]hat's what happened throughout my whole body . . . When I woke up I thought there was something on my face—and I thought it was the wall of the building. And I thought I was trapped. I tried, I said to myself, "Well, just test it to see if you can push that wall away," because I thought it was a concrete wall. I couldn't get my hands to move. I didn't realize both my arms were broken.[91]

Dammarell and her colleague Bob Pearson were the only two people in the cafeteria to survive the blast. The attack killed sixty-three people, including seventeen Americans. President Reagan called the bombing a "cowardly act" and insisted that "the vicious terrorist bombing" of the Beirut embassy would not deter US efforts to find peace in the Middle East.[92]

But then on October 23, 1983, a suicide bombing of the US Marines barracks in Beirut killed 241 American troops, hastening the withdrawal of US forces from the region. Reagan called the bombing of the marine barracks the "saddest day of my presidency, perhaps the saddest day of my life."[93]

In many ways, the multiple suicide bombings in Lebanon marked a new and troubling period for those carrying out America's development and diplomatic work abroad: They were now seen as targets in ways that they hadn't been since the days when they were forward-deployed in Vietnam. Security concerns would make it continually harder for AID staff to conduct field work, and AID and State staffers increasingly remained behind the walls of their embassies and missions.

EYES TURNED SOUTH

Latin America became a major focus for President Reagan and AID over the course of his two terms in office. The record of the administration and AID in Latin America sparked heated debates about anti-communism, support for repressive regimes, human rights, and the relative efficacy of the large volumes of aid that were pumped into Central America.

The administration's major initial thrust in the region was the Caribbean Basin Initiative which was formed amid rising concerns about the regional economic situation and communist inroads in the region.

The program focused particularly on the smaller states in the Eastern Caribbean, many of which were economically and politically unstable, although it also included the larger Caribbean countries, as well as Central America. The administration wanted to spur greater investment in the region, in part by giving select countries privileged access to the US market and boosting the private sector. AID's role was to help develop local capacity to engage in international markets and improve the investment climate, and the agency ultimately received several hundred million dollars in a supplemental appropriation for its work in the Caribbean Basin.[94]

Although he had long been dismissive of development's relative strategic importance, Henry Kissinger chaired the National Bipartisan Commission on Central America which made long-term recommendations on objectives and funding for assistance in the region. Central America had taken on new strategic importance in Kissinger's eyes as the result of the Marxist Sandinista overthrow of the authoritarian government in Nicaragua in 1979 and then the subsequent Sandinista victory in a democratic election in 1984.

Marshall Brown of AID recalled that he and Peter McPherson met with Kissinger in a small conference room on the west side of the State Department in one of several discussions about Latin America assistance.

"What do we need?" asked Kissinger in his gravelly, thickly accented voice.

"Well, we need a ten-year program supported by ten billion dollars," said Brown.

"Too long," growled Kissinger. He insisted that Congress would never tolerate a ten-year plan and would become disinterested well before that.

"Three years," he counteroffered.

McPherson and Brown suggested that three years was too short a time frame to achieve much development. The group jousted back and forth, finally settling on five years.

The Kissinger Commission delivered its final report in January 1984 and flagged poverty as the overriding issue facing the region. It noted that growth had been remarkable during the 1960s and 1970s, but that insufficient progress had been made in dealing with inequality. It also observed that the rising energy costs of the 1970s, coupled with falling commodity prices and high debt, triggered recessions across the region. According to the report, "The consequence has been that standards of living, already low in comparison to the developed world and badly skewed, have been cut back across the board."[95] Kissinger's remedy followed exactly what he had hashed out in a conference room with McPherson: a proposed $8 billion in assistance in the region over a five-year period beginning in 1985.

The approach articulated by the Kissinger Commission was designed to promote democracy, make societies more equitable, and stabilize economies.[96] But many were unwilling to take the commission's recommendations at face value despite its bipartisan makeup of senior foreign policy voices, given Kissinger's track record in places like Vietnam, Cambodia, and East Pakistan.

"Their program is in no way neutral," an American volunteer working on relief projects in El Salvador complained to the *New York Times*. "It has a very clear political purpose."[97] El Salvador was a particularly controversial situation given the country's civil war and its history of brutal human rights abuses. Jorge Sol, El Salvador's former economy minister, argued that US assistance had been "very successful in economic terms, but a disaster in social terms," bolstering the country's economic and political elite while making little difference in the lives of the poor.

There were growing complaints that the United States was pouring more money into Central American countries than they knew how to use, and internal audits and a congressional study detailed poor accounting procedures, programs that didn't reach intended beneficiaries, and some skimming of funds.[98] "They haven't shown they know how to spend the money they have," griped Congressman Clarence Long, Democratic chair of the appropriations subcommittee, as Reagan looked to quickly ramp up funds even higher.

Perhaps the most striking early success of the big push in Central America was Costa Rica. In the early 1980s, Costa Rica was in a full-blown financial crisis. Per capita GNP declined 22 percent between 1981 and 1985, inflation hit 90 percent in 1982, and the price for key exports like bananas and coffee slumped.[99] Costa Rica was viewed as strategically significant, but far less so than Honduras, which served as a launching pad for efforts to undermine the Sandinista regime and funnel support to Contra rebels.

Costa Rica had always been a fascinating anomaly in a region where military juntas and civil wars were all too common, enjoying unusual political stability. The oldest continuously functioning democracy in Latin America, Costa Rica disbanded its military in 1948 and emphasized peaceful resolution of conflicts in the hemisphere.

The United States put over a billion dollars of assistance into Costa Rica during the 1980s, making its support contingent upon major economic reforms. James Fox of AID commented that the agency diagnosed Costa Rica's economic problems as stemming from three primary problems: an overreliance on commodity earnings; a government that was too large; and an anemic financial sector.[100]

The Costa Rican government moved with genuine urgency, devaluing its currency and making important moves to reduce its deficit in 1982.[101] As a result, inflation started to quickly fall. The growing emphasis on an export-driven economy helped create significant numbers of jobs for unskilled workers, including those in rural areas. Importantly, the reforms enjoyed the support of successive governments, in no small part because the growing earnings from exports were politically popular.

More than a decade later, the Congressional Budget Office reflected: "The result was that Costa Rica returned to a path of rapid economic growth and continuing improvement. Unemployment fell dramatically after 1983. Nontraditional exports to countries outside Central America more than doubled, and foreign direct investment in Costa Rica reached new highs in the 1990s."[102]

The situation in El Salvador, a country roughly the size of Massachusetts, was a stark contrast. A civil war erupted in 1979 between leftist forces and the country's ruling military junta. Notoriously, Archbishop Oscar Romero was killed by a government death squad just days after he publicly called on the United States to suspend assistance to his country because of abuses by the Salvadoran armed forces in 1980. Eight months later, Salvadoran National Guard forces beat, raped, and murdered three American nuns and a missionary. The Carter administration suspended the flow of aid after the attack on the American nuns.

In 1981, government troops massacred more than two hundred men, women, and children in the village of El Mozote, and as journalist Ray Bonner noted in 1981, "[M]ore than 40 percent of the people were landless peasants and fewer than 2 percent of the population controlled more than half the good agricultural land."[103] Despite the abuses, the Reagan administration greatly expanded the program in El Salvador as a pillar of its Central America strategy, making the Reagan administration's approach to Latin America a lightning rod.

AID made a major push on land reform efforts in El Salvador, including programs that gave land to tenant farmers and helped convert large estates into cooperatives. After some major progress, the program was sidetracked by broader social unrest.

By 1987, a *New York Times* reporter in El Salvador painted a grim picture of the continuing conflict in El Salvador and the US role in it:

> The country's continuing crisis, after the expenditure of more than $2.5 billion of United States aid and seven years of intense attention from Washington, also raises fundamental questions about the direction of American policy. . . . While peasants make up the majority of the population, political power remains in the hands of the urban elite. Most Salvadorans are afraid of policemen and soldiers, and few of the poor would dream of seeking legal redress against a landlord because virtually no judge would favor a poor man. . . . The rich, on the other hand, appear to have barely felt the weight of the war and the bankrupt economy. The sons of the rich are safe because there is no draft and the army press gangs do not pick up young men in affluent neighborhoods.[104]

And it was a botched assistance effort—one that had nothing to do with AID—that almost brought down the entire Reagan administration when it came to light that the National Security Council had been illegally selling weapons to Iran in an effort to fund the Contras after further direct military support had been prohibited by a frustrated Congress.

Huge volumes of assistance were poured into countries such as Honduras, Costa Rica, and El Salvador by AID during this period. In some cases, like Costa Rica, the economic results were both fairly immediate and lasting. El Salvador finally forged a peace agreement in 1992 and has seen economic progress since that time, although it is still plagued by historic inequality and violence resulting from the drug trade.

Defenders of AID's record point to real accomplishments in Central America during this era. Critics point to the human costs of a strategy that placed human rights and the rule of law as subsidiary to the goal of containing a Nicaraguan threat that was gravely exaggerated.

"If it weren't for Nicaragua you wouldn't have had the Central America Initiative," reflected Marshall Brown. "Similarly, I think it's fair to say that without the threat of Fidel Castro, 20 years earlier, you wouldn't have had the Alliance for Progress."

WOODS APPOINTMENT

In 1987, Peter McPherson announced that he had accepted the post of deputy secretary of the treasury under Jim Baker. Following the tenure of McPherson was never going to be easy, but his successor, Alan Woods was not lacking in confidence.

Woods had previously served as the deputy US trade representative, and he was convinced that the path to successful development ran almost exclusively through macroeconomic reform and openness to trade. Woods had also served as an assistant secretary of defense and on President Nixon's press staff, along with a stint in the private sector.[105]

Woods lacked McPherson's finesse in managing the competing constituencies for foreign assistance programs. His chief of staff derided public spending in developing countries on education and health as "consumption" activities that were to be discouraged.[106]

Woods wanted to shake up AID's bureaucracy and adapt a free-market credo—something that he would get a chance to do, as he was kept on in the position as Vice President George Bush swept to a comfortable win in the 1988 presidential election. But Woods also closely guarded a secret that would make his tenure as AID administrator a short one.

The Reagan years offered striking dichotomies. Peter McPherson's tenure as one of the most effective AID administrators sat alongside a number of badly flawed and ideologically driven polices. A president who ran twice successfully as a small-government conservative considerably expanded the overall foreign aid program. A team that placed economic policy at the center of its development philosophy set in motion changes that helped make health and humanitarian assistance the agency's two largest portfolios. And for many of the agency's staff, the Reagan era was an unexpected respite from constant budget pressures and reorganizational battles.

But still, as President Reagan and Soviet premier Mikhail Gorbachev met in a series of historic summits in 1986 and 1987, foreign assistance levels began to slide downward.

Vice President Richard Nixon's motorcade is assaulted by protestors in downtown Caracas, Venezuela in 1958. Fears of a communist takeover of Latin America drove much of the support for creating a new foreign aid agency. RICHARD NIXON LIBRARY AND BIRTHPLACE

JFK meeting with the President of the Republic of Ghana, Kwame Nkrumah, in March 1961 at the White House. Amid Cold War jockeying, Kennedy wooed Nkrumah with a large aid package despite the fears of his advisors. ABBIE ROWE.
WHITE HOUSE PHOTOGRAPHS. JOHN F. KENNEDY PRESIDENTIAL LIBRARY AND MUSEUM, BOSTON

President Kennedy delivers remarks to a group of AID mission directors in the Rose Garden shortly after the agency was established, telling them, "There will not be farewell parades to you as you leave or parades when you come back."
ROBERT KNUDSEN. WHITE HOUSE PHOTOGRAPHS. JOHN F. KENNEDY PRESIDENTIAL LIBRARY AND MUSEUM, BOSTON

From right to left, President Kennedy, General Lucius Clay, and David Bell discuss the foreign aid program in the Oval Office. Bell, who Kennedy named to lead AID as its second administrator, was in many ways the father of the modern aid program.
ABBIE ROWE. WHITE HOUSE PHOTOGRAPHS. JOHN F. KENNEDY PRESIDENTIAL LIBRARY AND MUSEUM, BOSTON

Much of AID's early work centered on Latin America through the Alliance for Progress. Here, a farm worker stacks Pangola grass at a farm research station in Matao, Brazil. AID HISTORICAL ARCHIVE

Walt Rostow, pictured at a national security council meeting in 1966, was uniquely influential in shaping development policy under both President Kennedy and Johnson—as well in setting a hawkish approach to Vietnam. LBJ LIBRARY PHOTO BY YOICHI OKAMOTO

President Johnson and AID chief Bill Gaud at the White House. Johnson had outsized impact through foreign aid in launching the Green Revolution and international family planning programs—even as the situation in Vietnam increasingly consumed his administration. WHITE HOUSE PHOTO WITH THANKS TO THE GAUD FAMILY

South Korean investments in education, supported by substantial U.S. assistance, were critical in that country's impressive economic gains. AID NARA

Delivering a smallpox vaccine in Niger in February 1969. The effort to eradicate smallpox was driven by an unusual alliance between the United States and Soviet Union with the Centers for Disease Control, AID, and the World Health Organization joining forces to eliminate a disease that killed more than 300 million people in the 20th century alone. DR. J.D. MILLER, CDC VIA CREATIVE COMMONS

Rufus Phillips, pictured in the Mekong Delta, directed AID's Rural Affairs office in Vietnam, an effort to use foreign aid as a strategic counter-insurgency tool. The Vietnam program eventually dwarfed the agency's work in other regions, with the staff dedicated to Vietnam being ten times greater than for the whole Africa bureau by 1968. FROM THE RUFUS PHILLIPS COLLECTION VIA CREATIVE COMMONS

President Nixon meeting with Indian Prime Minister Indira Gandhi (directly facing Nixon) in Delhi in 1969. Nixon's intense dislike of Gandhi led him to tilt heavily toward the government of Pakistan when a civil war erupted in that country and millions of refugees poured into India. U.S. EMBASSY NEW DELHI

JOINT STATE/AID/USIS MESSAGE:

1. AWARE OF THE TASK FORCE PROPOSALS ON "OPENESS" IN THE FOREIGN SERVICE, AND WITH THE CONVICTION THAT U.S. POLICY RELATED TO RECENT DEVELOPMENTS IN EAST PAKISTAN SERVES NEITHER OUR MORAL INTERESTS BROADLY DEFINED NOR OUR NATIONAL INTERESTS NARROWLY DEFINED, NUMEROUS OFFICERS OF AMCONGEN DACCA, USAID DACCA AND USIS DACCA CONSIDER IT THEIR DUTY TO REGISTER STRONG DISSENT WITH FUNDAMENTAL ASPECTS OF THIS POLICY. OUR GOVERNMENT HAS FAILED TO DENOUNCE THE SUPPRESSION OF DEMOCRACY. OUR GOVERNMENT HAS FAILED TO DENOUNCE ATROCITIES. OUR GOVERNMENT HAS FAILED TO TAKE FORCEFUL MEASURES TO PROTECT ITS CITIZENS WHILE AT THE SAME TIME BENDING OVER BACKWARDS TO PLACATE THE WEST PAK DOMINATED GOVERNMENT AND TO LESSEN LIKELY AND DERBERVEDLY NEGATIVE INTERNATIONAL PUBLIC RELATIONS IMPACT AGAINST THEM. OUR GOVERNMENT HAS EVIDENCED WHAT MANY WILL CONSIDER MORAL BANKRUPTCY, IRONICALLY AT A TIME WHEN THE USSR SENT PRESIDENT YAHYA A MESSAGE DEFEND- ING DEMOCRACY, CONDEMNING ARREST OF LEADER OF DEMOCRATI- CALLY ELECTED MAJORITY PARTY (INCIDENTALLY PRO-WEST) AND CALLING FOR END TO REPRESSIVE MEASURES AND BLOODSHED. IN OUR MOST RECENT POLICY PAPER FOR PAKISTAN, OUR IN- TERESTS IN PAKISTAN WERE DEFINED AS PRIMARILY HUMANI.

A copy of the famous "Blood Telegram" sent back to Washington in 1971 by State and AID staffers in East Pakistan, at considerable risk to their careers, objecting to the Nixon Administration's willingness to turn a blind eye to atrocities taking place on the ground. ADAM JONES, GLOBAL PHOTO ARCHIVE, VIA CREATIVE COMMONS

Women working over a map at the family planning seminar held at a maternal health center. Family planning programs at AID grew exponentially under Presidents Johnson and Nixon and stand out as one of the agency's most important successes over the last half century despite becoming an increasing flashpoint in U.S. domestic politics. AID HISTORICAL ARCHIVE

The head of AID under President Carter, John Gilligan, meets with Emperor Haile Selassie of Ethiopia. As repeated droughts gripped the Sahel region of Africa, AID and other donors grappled with how best to break an increasingly deadly cycle of famine. AID HISTORICAL ARCHIVE

Peter McPherson, pictured here with President Ronald Reagan and Secretary of State Alexander Haig, gained considerable good will from Reagan when, as the incoming head of AID in the 1980s, he took part in a White House ceremony with the president announcing that they were pulling $28 million in foreign aid from 12 countries. McPherson posed with a large cardboard check made out to the "U.S. taxpayers, c/o President Ronald Reagan." AID HISTORICAL ARCHIVE

Peter Mcpherson presents information on the Ethiopian famine to President Reagan in the Oval Office during a pivotal meeting on the emergency after which Reagan rapidly ramped up long-delayed humanitarian relief and declared "a hungry child knows no politics." Also pictured, Vice President Bush, Chief of Staff James Baker, Counselor Ed Meese, and NSC Director Bud McFarland. WHITE HOUSE PHOTO

Alan Woods, pictured at right in Egypt, argued strongly as the AID administrator under the first President Bush that U.S. assistance programs should be more directly wed to U.S. economic interests—before cancer cut his term short. AID HISTORICAL ARCHIVE

As change swept across Eastern Europe after the fall of the Berlin Wall in 1989, Ron Roskens—pictured here with seamstresses in Albania—oversaw an agency that was increasingly scandal-plagued and adrift under his watch. AID HISTORICAL ARCHIVE

Brian Atwood, pictured here with South African Archbishop and human rights champion Desmond Tutu, led AID at an unusually tumultuous time, and much of his tenure was spent fighting off a hostile attempt by Senator Jesse Helms of North Carolina to eliminate the agency and dramatically reduce foreign aid. The effor to eliminate AID and fold its remnants into the State Department was a battle which stretched over several years and in which Atwood and the agency ultimately prevailed. CAROL PEASLEY, AID

President Bill Clinton and First Lady Hillary Clinton during a 1998 visit to Africa. President Clinton was particularly focused on aid efforts in Eastern Europe and the former Soviet Union. Hillary Clinton was an outspoken voice on the role of women in development and a regular visitor to AID projects in the field. She and Vice President Al Gore became important allies in discussions about AID's potential reorganization. CAROL PEASLEY, AID

AID was increasingly called upon to deliver relief into active war zones in the messy aftermath of the Cold War in the first half of the 1990s. The Clinton Administration faced sharp questions about its early handling of complex crises in Bosnia, Haiti, Somalia, and Rwanda, with its track record improving substantially over time. Pictured is the sprawling refugee camp in Goma, Zaire in 1994.
J. ISSAC, UNITED NATIONS ASSISTANCE MISSION FOR RWANDA PHOTO VIA CREATIVE COMMONS

Although George W. Bush evinced little interest in international development before becoming president, after the terror attacks of September 11 he launched major initiatives to combat HIV/AIDS and promote economic growth while simultaneously trying to guide large-scale reconstruction efforts in both Iraq and Afghanistan. Here Bush is pictured at the Kasisi Children's Home in Zambia. SHEALAH CRAIGHEAD / THE BUSH CENTER

Andrew Natsios, the first AID Administrator under President Bush, is pictured here with the president discussing the situation in Sudan at the White House. KIMBERLEE HEWITT, WHITE HOUSE PHOTO

In both Afghanistan and Iraq, AID staff were frequently deployed alongside the military as part of Provincial Reconstruction Teams in a fashion that harkened back to the Vietnam era. Here a team inspects an industrial park in Kandahar, Afgahnistan. CHIEF MASTER SGT. RICHARD SIMOSEN U.S. ARMY VIA CREATIVE COMMONS

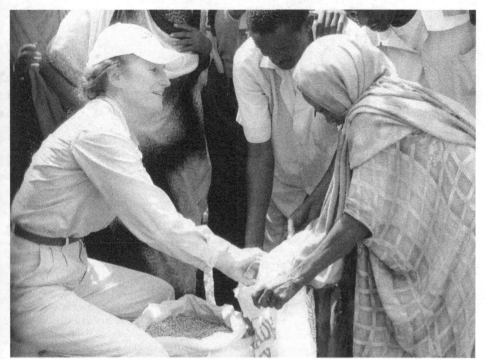

Henrietta Fore, the first woman to lead AID, at a food distribution center in Ethiopia in 2007. She focused heavily on efforts to rebuild the agency's staff. AID

Democracy promotion became an increasingly important priority for the agency over the years, albiet a priority that was often unevenly advanced. Here a voter in the Anbar province of Iraq displays her ink-dipped finger indicating that she had cast her ballot. JIM HUYLEBROEK FOR CREATIVE ASSOCIATES INTERNATIONAL

Although AID and other donors played a key role in the Green Revolution, agriculture programs were increasingly marginalized in the 1980s and 1990s. In response to a global food crisis, President Obama sought to reverse that trend by launching the Feed the Future innitiative early in his presidency. Here, Kenyan smallholder farmers display some of the sweet potatoes grown as part of his program. AID

An earthquake registering 7.0 on the Richter Scale hit Haiti just days after Rajiv Shah (pictured at far right) became head of AID. Here Secretary of State Hillary Clinton, Shah, and U.S. General P.K. Keen meet with Haitian President Rene Preval in a tent at the Port-au-Prince airport shortly after the quake hit. U.S. STATE DEPARTMENT

Some of the damage inflicted by the Haitian earthquake. International relief efforts were massive and often controversial. ERIC QUINTERO, INTERNATIONAL FEDERATION OF THE RED CROSS VIA CREATIVE COMMONS

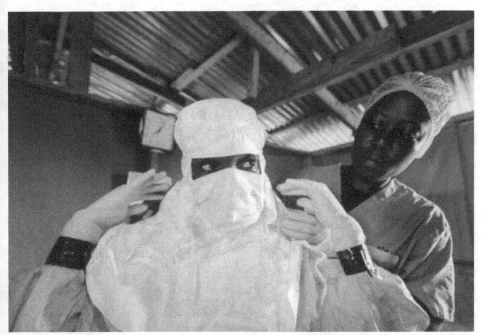

The United States deployed more than 2,700 government personnel and spent more than $2.5 billion to combat the Ebola outbreak in West Africa in 2014 with AID playing a vital role. Despite repeated warnings from epidemiologists, few imagined that the United States would be in the throes of a pandemic by 2020. MORGANA WINGARD, AID

President Barack Obama with the two AID administrators during his eight years in office, Gayle Smith and Rajiv Shah, both standing. Also pictured, U.S. Trade Representative Mike Froman (left), Senior Director for African Affairs Grant Harris (center) and Deputy National Security Advisor for Strategic Communications Ben Rhodes. PETE SOUZA / THE WHITE HOUSE

AID Administrator Mark Green and first daughter Ivanka Trump meet with women coffee entrepeneurs in Ethiopia in April 2019. Green faced the unenviable task of managing AID while reporting to a president who frequently denigrated foreign aid, multilateral cooperation, and the developing world itself. U.S. STATE DEPARTMENT

8

Uneasy Victories

BACK TO THE USSR

President George Herbert Walker Bush had a sterling set of foreign policy credentials for a modern president, having served as an ambassador to China and the United Nations, having run the CIA, and having spent eight years as vice president. James Baker, his secretary of state, and Brent Scowcroft, his national security adviser, were both well-regarded internationalists.

On December 7, 1988—roughly a month after George H. W. Bush's election victory and a month before his formal swearing-in—a major earthquake struck Armenia in the Soviet Union. Between 25,000 and 50,000 people were estimated to have been killed in the quake, with more than twice that number injured.

Soviet leader Mikhail Gorbachev was in the middle of a visit to New York City to meet with both Reagan and Bush when the quake struck. Gorbachev had been greeted by excited crowds, intrigued by his push for openness and engagement with the West. He immediately cut his trip short because of the quake, and he also did something unexpected: He asked for help in coping with the disaster, a remarkable shift from Moscow's long-standing insistence that it was entirely self-sufficient.

Although the US decision to offer assistance was technically made by President Reagan, it had the direct support of the president-elect. Less than a decade before, the United States had delayed lifesaving aid to Ethiopia because of concerns about the revolutionary government's close ties with Moscow. Now, the United States and a whole range of European governments were providing humanitarian assistance directly to the Soviet Union.

It was the first large package of foreign assistance to Moscow since the 1940s, with the United States shipping food and blankets and dispatching physicians and highly trained search-and-rescue teams to comb the wreckage for survivors.[1]

The Armenia quake also marked an important inflection point for AID's Office of Foreign Disaster Assistance. Unhappiness with the quality of the Armenia response led to the creation of Disaster Assistance Response Teams, or DARTs. These small, flexible field teams, based on models the US Forest Service used in fighting forest fires, were designed to be largely independent and to guide relief efforts. As Richard Olson noted in a history of the office, these teams were self-sufficient and modular, and could easily expand when crises grew severe.[2] New technologies like satellite phones and the fax machine gave the office the ability to respond in real time from on the ground in even the worst of disasters, and it would revolutionize emergency response.

AID was being called on more and more frequently to provide relief. Julia Taft recalls that during her three and a half years running the office, it responded to some 260 disasters—ranging from mudslides and cyclones to civil wars and famines. The easing of Cold War tensions was not translating into a quieter world.

THE WOODS REPORT

At AID, Alan Woods was pouring considerable energy and attention into a major report, "Development and the National Interest: US Economic Assistance into the 21st Century," which was quickly dubbed "The Woods Report."

The preparation of the report had involved a large team at the agency, but career staffers felt that the content was taking on much more of a political bent as the draft neared finalization. As a result, the career staffers asked to have their names taken off the report.[3]

Very few people at the agency realized what was driving Woods's urgency to release the report: He had been diagnosed with cancer and had only a few months left to live. The report was Woods's capstone and his parting shot. Even these many years later, the report is compelling, but not always in ways the authors had hoped. Given his illness, Woods did not care about being impolitic, and many parts of the report discuss the most serious issues facing the aid program with refreshing candor. Other sections of the report read more as a polemic, and on balance, the analysis was much stronger in diagnosing challenges than in identifying practical recommendations to address them.

Compounding matters, Woods launched a press campaign around the report's release that leaned into its most hyperbolic conclusions. The report dropped a hand grenade into the foreign aid debate, with some observers reading its harsh analysis of aid shortcomings as fundamentally anti-development.[4]

Woods was fond of noting that the *Washington Post* ran a four-column story on the study titled, "Foreign Aid Largely a Failure."[5] The report argued that "only a handful of countries that started receiving US assistance in the 1950s and 1960s has ever graduated from dependent status," and that US foreign aid had not "always succeeded in fostering growth-oriented policies."[6]

The report highlighted Japan, Taiwan, and South Korea as "proof positive that the right donor program and guidance, when matched by the right recipient policies, can result in a smoothly phased transition from dependency to self-sufficiency."[7] But it also argued that these were exceptions rather than the rule, and that the shortcomings of the aid program were "political, and may be intractable."[8]

The villains in the Woods Report were clear: protectionist US trade policies; a lack of free-market zeal in aid programs; and a tendency to favor security interests over economic reform.

Looking at cases ranging from Egypt to Vietnam to El Salvador, the report called excessive amounts of security assistance "counterproductive," because it alleviated the consequences of bad policy choices.[9]

The report noted that Bangladesh had made great progress in textile exports based on sound economic policies, but that pressure from US domestic textile producers meant that Washington was now curbing the future export growth of these textiles.[10] The bottom line: The United States "will have penalized a developing country that was making a good faith effort to produce, export, and earn hard currency."

The report identified AID's field presence as its core strength, but decried the fact that the agency was increasingly yielding its technical expertise to contractors, with staff "weak in the very areas that can be most important: political development analysis and economic policy."[11] The Woods Report joined many others in complaining about congressional earmarks and reporting requirements, citing an estimate that it would take a single person 140 years of labor to complete all of the annual reports required by legislators. The report also noted that individual giving to charitable causes overseas by Americans was on about the same scale as the entire foreign economic aid program of the US government—some $6 billion in aid through church groups, donations to NGOs like the Red Cross and CARE, and direct cash payments.[12]

The bottom line for the Woods Report: US "economic and trade policies, the dynamic growth of the American economy, and the foreign investment decisions of our vast private sector" were greater determinants of growth in the developing world than aid. Given the sheer size and influence of the US economy, this conclusion was not controversial. "The most important contribution the U.S. makes to economic progress in developing countries is its own growth," the report maintained.[13]

The report followed a curious logic: Since US growth had a significant influence on developing countries, aid programs should be reoriented to benefit the US economy. Woods advocated a return to big infrastructure projects carried out by US firms that prioritized American goods and services, believing that US growth would trickle down to the developing world.

Instead of truly free markets, Woods had embraced mercantilism. Woods's preference for what is often called "tied" aid—assistance that requires purchasing goods and services from the country providing it—would find some ardent supporters on Capitol Hill among members who had never much liked foreign aid in the first place. A cable was sent to all AID missions encouraging them to have "met with, entertained and written to at least as many if not more businessmen/women than government bureaucrats."[14]

A subsequent report by Michael Crosswell, an AID economist, argued that the Woods Report's view that foreign aid had not promoted developing country economic growth was flawed. Crosswell's calculations indicated that among AID recipients:

> From 1965 to 1990, 41 countries, inhabited by more than 2.1 billion people, achieved significantly positive average annual rates of economic growth in per capita income, ranging from 1.3 to 8.4 percent. The average growth rate for these countries was 3.3 percent. Of the remaining countries, some have realized greater success more recently. If we look at the period 1985–1995, an additional 16 countries (280 million people) achieved significantly positive growth. Combining the two groups, 57 out of 90 countries, embracing nearly 2.4 billion people (80 percent of the total population of 3 billion), have been able to sustain economic growth at meaningful rates for a reasonably long period of time.[15]

Economist Edward Schuh complained that AID's leadership under Woods "made a grievous error in failing to understand the difference between bloated parastatal institutions that displace activities more properly located in the private sector, and those public-sector institutions needed to provide support for the private sector by developing new knowledge, developing new technology, providing for the schooling and education of the population, and improving health and nutrition."[16]

The role of education in development deserves special mention, and it has been an area of remarkable progress where foreign aid played an important role. Lawrence Summers, who was chief economist for the World Bank and later the US Treasury Secretary, argued that "investment in girls' education may well be the highest return investment available in the developing world."[17] Summers maintained that education for girls was particularly powerful because of its impact on so many other facets of life: "When girls are educated, they have economic opportunities. Their families have more of a stake in their survival and their success. They marry later and are able to take part in household decisions. They choose to have fewer children and can invest more in the health and development of each child. Their daughters and sons have expanded horizons, and often they escape from poverty."

Around the globe, access to a basic education has been revolutionized. Consider Nepal. As Samuel Butterfield observed, in 1950 only about 1 percent of Nepal's children were in school. "By 1979, with help from foreign aid," Butterfield writes, "Nepal had increased attendance to 77 percent of the elementary school-age population."[18] AID built schools and provided technical advice through NGOs and schools like the University of Oregon and Southern Illinois University, and exerted consistent moral pressure on developing country governments to take education for girls as seriously as for boys.

In developing countries the total number of enrolled students rose from about 100 million in 1950 to 738 million in 1990.[19] This was not just a function of population growth. In 1950, 38 percent of the primary school–age population was enrolled.

That figure would grow to 78 percent by 1970 and to 99 percent by 1995. Adult literacy climbed from 56 percent globally in 1950 to 77 percent by 1995.[20]

Economists and development experts were slow off the mark in recognizing that investments in education could help drive growth. As Vernon Ruttan argued, removing distortions in monetary, fiscal, and trade policies did not produce development, because "the real sources of economic growth are investments in human and physical capital" that made societies and institutions more productive.[21] You couldn't simply ask government to get out of the way and let markets work if the public was poor, uneducated, and in ill health.

While Woods remained on the job after the release of his signature report, and many at the agency were unaware of his sickness, his health rapidly deteriorated. The agency's management began to drift, marking a period when AID's regional bureaus began to accumulate more and more power. Woods died in June 1989.

RON ROSKENS

The death of Alan Woods, and the fallout from the Woods Report, were dispiriting for many at AID. Unfortunately, the agency's new head would prove to be one of its worst.

Part of the problem stemmed from the otherwise quite capable Secretary of State Jim Baker. "James A. Baker III had little interest in development, had few thoughts about it, but was quite certain that it had a very limited role in US foreign policy per se," wrote Gerald Hyman of AID. "He did not much want to be bothered by it himself, nor did he want the State Department to be bothered by it very much."[22] Given his worldview, a relatively weak and compliant AID administrator was ideal.

His choice, after some delays: Dr. Ronald Roskens.

Well-established in Nebraskan Republican political circles, Roskens had just been fired as president of the University of Nebraska, the reasons for which were somewhat controversially never made public.[23] Roskens had held various positions at Iowa State and Kent State universities, including serving as dean of students at Kent State during the notorious National Guard shootings on that campus. He had no development experience at the time of his appointment.

At Roskens's swearing-in ceremony, James Baker articulated five key foreign policy challenges which he hoped AID would address: consolidating progress toward democracy around the globe; strengthening international ties; pushing for vibrant, free-market economies; assisting regional peacemakers; and addressing transitional threats such as drug trafficking, terrorism, and environmental damage.[24] Within AID, this mandate became known as "Baker's Charge."

An article in the *Foreign Service Journal* observed that a committee of senior staff was tasked with turning Baker's vision into a practical implementation plan, but "many development professionals were dismayed to learn that the early drafts omitted any mention of development itself."[25]

At a time when the Woods Report had highlighted the importance of economic policy reform, Roskens eliminated AID's chief economist position and its Office of Economic Analysis.[26] Even when the Senate Foreign Relations Committee twice requested a survey of how AID recipients were performing in the area of economic policy reform—an inquiry at which most AID administrators would leap to respond—Roskens rebuffed the efforts.

Roskens spent a great deal of time and energy focused on the perks of his office. One of his first acts on the job was to demand a more luxurious car to transport him to the office, the costs of which angry congressional appropriators subtracted from the agency's operating budget. He spent a considerable sum renovating his office, and paid particular attention to being photographed with heads of state during his trips abroad.

THE WALL COMES DOWN

The appointment of Ronald Roskens to run the agency coincided with sweeping change on the geopolitical landscape. In June of 1989, the labor union–driven Solidarity party triumphed in Poland's elections. Just a month earlier, Hungary began to open its borders to the West. Across Eastern Europe, revolutionary fervor against the communist order was in the air.

In a July 1989 visit to the region, where he was greeted by almost rapturous crowds, President Bush called for the United States to support all those striving for free markets, free governments, and reintegration with the West. The "Velvet Revolution" swept Czechoslovakia. In November 1989, East Germany allowed free passage to West Germany as ebullient crowds dismantled the Berlin Wall.

President Bush and Secretary of State Baker seized the opportunity to push for a fundamentally reenvisioned Europe. Baker developed, and Congress soon approved, a huge new assistance program, the Support for East European Democracy, or SEED, Act, which initially focused on Poland, Hungary, and Czechoslovakia, but would expand across the region in the months and years that followed.

Baker adopted a radically different approach with the Central European effort. As an official AID history notes, the program would be designed and managed in Washington. "There would be no long studies and no complicated strategies, structures, or processes. Unlike developing countries, whose political elite often had little real interest in economic or political reforms, Central European reformers demanded them, so there was no need to agonize about political will or sequencing or trade-offs; the problem was simply to get the assistance to them as quickly and efficiently as possible."[27] The coordinator for the programs in Eastern Europe reported directly to the secretary of state, but AID and other agencies involved still controlled appropriations for projects. In Eastern Europe, AID deployed smaller, leaner presences than its traditional missions.

The development challenge in Eastern Europe, and subsequently the former Soviet Union, was strikingly different than the ones to which AID was accustomed. The populations across the regions were by and large well-educated, reasonably healthy, and had achieved a socioeconomic status that would normally merit graduating from assistance. Many of these countries were eager to reintegrate with European economic and political institutions. It was easy to see why Baker and others in the halls of the State Department saw the task before them as substantially different from—and easier than—traditional development.

But there were some important caveats. Eastern Europe was *terra incognita* for AID staff. No one had worked as a junior officer in Poland or Hungary, much less Russia, Armenia, or Bulgaria. There were no templates for rapidly converting economies and political systems from closed, communist systems to free-market democracies. In the most-repressive countries, entire generations of the best and brightest talents had been lost. As AID would later acknowledge, "there was an under-appreciation of the immense complexities of the transition process. Initially AID launched projects of a pilot or demonstration nature, but these were fragmented, disconnected, and insufficient to address the enormity of the need."[28]

A whole array of US government agencies was eager to be involved in the work in Eastern Europe and the former Soviet Union. The Departments of Energy, Defense, Justice, Agriculture, Labor, Health and Human Services, Commerce, Treasury, and others all wanted a piece of the action, and AID had weak leadership and limited leverage to influence these players. There was also a considerable diaspora from Eastern Europe in the United States and a large number of professional organizations eager to engage in Eastern Europe: lawyers, bankers, stockbrokers, unions, and chambers of commerce that were enthusiastic to offer expertise in modernizing the region. AID was a key actor, but at times it was just one of many voices around the table at State Department coordination meetings.

In December 1989, President Bush and Soviet premier Mikhail Gorbachev met for a summit in Malta shortly after the fall of the Berlin Wall, and they all but declared the Cold War over. Almost exactly two years later, in December 1991, the Soviet Union dissolved, leaving twelve new countries in its wake—all drawn along the lines of the former Soviet Republics.

For AID, the rapidly moving events meant an enormous and complicated new caseload: twelve new countries formed out of the Soviet Union, seven out of the former Yugoslavia, and added to this were the Baltics, the Caucuses—almost all of Eastern Europe. There had not been such a significant shift in the US foreign aid portfolio since the fast-moving days of independence movements in Africa and Asia in the early 1960s.

AID programs in the region initially focused on stabilizing post-communist economies and encouraging privatization as Eastern Europe went through what would become a predictable pattern of challenges. First, production plummeted as state-owned enterprises stopped operating. Second, government revenues contracted sharply with the loss of income from these state-owned enterprises. Then, a wave of hyperinflation hit.

Some of the agency's initial efforts were quite successful. For example, Poland's inflation rate hit 600 percent in 1989, but the country's leadership, with Western help, introduced sweeping reforms and quickly brought inflation under relative control.[29] The approach, dubbed "shock therapy," was effective in the Polish context, despite triggering substantial short-term hardship. In a number of cases, the United States provided emergency food assistance to blunt the impact of the economic upheaval.

AID dedicated substantial attention to the energy sector in the region, working to help manage the breakup of state-run utilities, establishing modern regulatory and legal frameworks for power producers, and trying to wean Eastern European states off of an overreliance on Russia as their sole energy provider.

AID, with prodding from Congress, also utilized new mechanisms for assistance, particularly through the creation of Enterprise Funds for ten different countries in the region. The Enterprise Funds, each with its own independent board, functioned as venture capital funds to invest in these countries. While the track record of the different funds varied, the use of public funds to help spark investment set an important precedent, and AID would increasingly adapt and employ this model which had long been utilized by its sister agency, the Overseas Private Investment Corporation. (AID inaugurated its Development Credit Authority guarantee program in 1999 and its Global Development Alliance partnerships with the private sector in 2001.)[30]

But what went unnoticed all too often in coordination meetings in Washington were the strikingly different conditions across the countries of Eastern Europe and the former Soviet Union. Shock therapy and rapid privatization made a good deal of sense in some settings, far less in others.

Countries with the closest links to the rest of Europe had an easier road. Nations like Estonia, Latvia, Slovenia, and Hungary saw their future in the European Union and moved fairly adroitly in that direction, with significant European and US assistance. From economic policy to rebuilding university systems and modernizing farming techniques, assistance and direct person-to-person and organization-to-organization links were invaluable in a series of relatively smooth transitions. (An eventual pushback from communist forces would come later in some of these settings.) The attraction of potential European Union membership was a powerful magnet and roadmap for reform in Eastern Europe, yet at the same time it aroused fears in Moscow that the West was intent on further encircling its already-weakened position.

Other countries began from a very different position. Carol Adelman of AID recalls reports from the first team to visit Albania, one of the most repressive countries in all of Eastern Europe, in 1991. "Ether was still used in hospitals, there were just two hundred cars in the entire country, and the infrastructure was dilapidated," she said.[31] "The fanciest hotel in the capital city of Tirana offered its premier guests hot water for one hour each evening." Jails had long been filled with political prisoners and their children.

The issue of privatization was a sensitive one, and not always well handled. In some countries, governments initiated the privatization of state-held assets rapidly and without excessive missteps. In other cases, and sometimes at the urging of AID and international financial institutions, countries pushed through on selling valuable government assets without a sound plan.

"Economies are very delicate instruments, resembling a machine with thousands and thousands of interconnected wires," commented former AID staffer Jacob Kaplan.[32] "What was done in Eastern Europe was to pull out all the wires at once and hope new market economies would emerge in full bloom." Even in the best cases, privatization usually produced significant unemployment, since so many state payrolls had been padded with redundant employees.

As the situation in the former Soviet Union unfolded, initial US overtures to Russia were largely limited to humanitarian relief. Washington hoped that limited technical assistance would bolster Russian reformers and ease some of the pains of transition. Both the White House and Congress were nervous about assisting a country that had long been its ideological opposite.

In August of 1990, President Saddam Hussein of Iraq invaded Kuwait with 140,000 troops. More than half a million US troops, bolstered by an unusually broad alliance, in turn expelled Iraqi forces from Kuwait. By February 1991, President Bush announced Kuwait liberated and the Iraqi army defeated—although Bush decided to leave Hussein as president of Iraq. President Bush's approval hit an astronomical 89 percent in the wake of the successful military campaign. (Meanwhile, AID found itself mounting a difficult relief effort to assist Kurdish Iraqis who had understandably, but mistakenly, thought they had a green light from Washington to break away from Iraq.) All of this accumulated to pull significant attention away from Russia, although it obviously remained a strategic priority.

It was only after an attempted Russian coup in August of 1991 that Congress and the administration began to seriously discuss more-substantial levels of assistance designed to drive a broader societal transformation.

As the Congressional Research Service noted, more and more people in Washington were coming to view "this period as a rare and perhaps fleeting window of opportunity to affect a successful transition to democracy and free market economies."[33] Aid volumes were moving up sharply, but a deep and mutual wariness remained.

AID staff in Russia and the former Soviet Union were often taken aback by their new working environment. "Many people in the embassy told me they had never left the embassy during their tour," recalled Barbara Turner of AID.[34] "They read the newspapers, met with Russian officials, attended conferences," she said, "but they lived in a compound and they really did not go and meet with the Russian population." The US intelligence community and the State Department knew a great deal about Russia's nuclear weapons and senior political leaders, but very little about the lives of average people and the actual functioning of the economy. In Moscow, AID was initially prohibited from hiring any Russian staff, a significant impediment.

Turner recalled an early meeting with the US ambassador to Russia, Robert Strauss. When she told him that AID was eager to move beyond providing humanitarian assistance and set up a stock market, reform the health-care system, and bring private innovation to Russian farming, he replied, "Hot damn, this is exactly what we need."

"I think the embassy people were ready to fall off their chairs," Turner observed. Cold War perceptions died hard, and many in the Foreign Service opposed establishing an AID mission in Moscow. Turner recalled guidance from Washington that no program was to be authorized to last for more than a year—an extraordinary limitation given the immensity and complexity of Russia's challenges.

POWER TO THE PEOPLE?

Although AID had long encouraged popular participation in development, active democracy promotion by AID was relatively recent.

In the 1950s and 1960s, public administration had been a major push for US assistance programs, particularly in Latin America. However, this focus on the relative competence of government was often democracy-neutral. Indeed, many of these programs took place in conjunction with military governments. There were some pilot efforts to foster "democratic private and local governmental institutions," but democracy strengthening was not a major emphasis for AID.

President Carter sparked interest in democracy programs, particularly in Latin America, with his emphasis on human rights, aided by legislation enacted in 1976 that called on the State Department to produce annual human rights reviews of countries receiving US assistance. The legislation included up to $3 million annually for programs to "encourage or promote increased adherence to civil and political rights."[35] In March of 1977, Carter declared during a speech at the United Nations that he would be critical of governments that employed repressive tactics—even if they were anti-communist.

In a speech before the British Parliament in June 1982, President Reagan proposed an effort "to foster the infrastructure of democracy, the system of a free press, unions, political parties, universities, which allows a people to choose their own way to develop their own culture, to reconcile their own differences through peaceful means."[36]

Congress, with strong leadership from Congressman Dante Fascell of Florida, subsequently established the National Endowment for Democracy, along with the four pillars through which it directed its activities: the National Democratic Institute, the International Republican Institute, the American Center for Labor Solidarity, and the Center for International Private Enterprise.[37] The National Endowment for Democracy would "foster the infrastructure of democracy" around the globe.

In 1984, AID created an office dedicated to democracy assistance in its Latin America bureau, building on the legacy of human rights initiatives begun in the

Carter administration and pulling together something of a hodgepodge of programs on elections, human rights, civic engagement, anti-corruption activities, and rule of law reforms.

Then, the collapse of the Soviet Union and the opening of Eastern Europe turned what had been a relatively niche part of the agency's activities into a major focus. In November 1991, AID issued a global policy on democracy, emphasizing governance, human rights, representative democracy, and capacity building.[38]

AID helped train ministers to manage budgets and parliamentarians to draft legislation and conduct oversight. The agency worked with political parties and provided local NGOs with guidance on how to operate a nonprofit. The agency supported election monitoring and the establishment of fair election systems. (In some places, such as the former Soviet Union, the concept of local NGOs that routinely disagreed with the government was a relatively alien concept.)

Democracy promotion, while perhaps excessively focused on the conduct of elections in its early days, made important contributions in helping to undergird the essential functions of more-open societies. Notably, democracy promotion centered on the idea of government accountability to its own citizens in everything from policy to budgets to access to justice.

A substantial number of those engaged in democracy-promotion activities in Eastern Europe and the former Soviet Union had cut their teeth on this politically sensitive work in Latin America. There were certainly weaknesses in design and execution with AID's early democracy work, but the United States led the way in what became an important arena for international development cooperation.

"When we tried to interest other donors in democratic governance as a part of development, we encountered a lot of timidity in the 1980s, but by the 1990s that changed," observed Jim Michel of AID.[39] By the early 1990s, AID and other donors increasingly, albeit selectively, began to link assistance levels to human rights and government performance. The United States was a leader in this effort, freezing aid to both Kenya and Malawi for a period of time because of governance concerns, and also building and sharing with other donors its expertise in programs to promote both popular understanding and institutional capacity for democratic governance.

Noted democracy expert Thomas Carothers observed that many market reform enthusiasts were increasingly willing (the Woods Report aside) to recognize that governance issues lay at the root of many development problems.[40] Even the World Bank, traditionally loath to address governance issues and risk offending its members, argued in *Sub-Saharan Africa: From Crisis to Sustainable Growth* in 1989 that "underlying the litany of Africa's development problems is a crisis of governance."[41]

The push for democracy promotion very much reflected the moment: The West had triumphed in the Cold War, and liberal democracy felt like a prerequisite for a modern, economically prosperous state.

But shaping enduring democratic change was more difficult than many realized in the giddy years after the fall of the Berlin Wall. It is worth noting that Latin America, where AID had worked on democracy the longest, is the most democratic bloc of developing countries, and the Organization for American States has made defense of democracy by its member states a key organizing tenet. The military coups that plagued the region have become much rarer, and most governments are democratic in nature. The embrace of democracy in the Americas has yielded lasting benefit, although historic concentrations of political and economic power with enduring patterns of privilege and corruption continue to impede more rapid progress in the region.

AID WITHOUT THE COLD WAR

Anti-communism had long been the lodestar for justifying the foreign assistance program, and the fear of Soviet and Chinese influence in the developing world had often been the only thing to convince recalcitrant members of Congress to support AID. Assistance for education, child survival, and maternal health essentially piggybacked on security. It was no coincidence that AID's budget went up around moments of great tension in the Cold War—from the Cuba crisis onwards—and that it tended to trend downwards as those anxieties cooled.

The emerging challenges that AID faced were disparate: the environment, democracy, HIV/AIDS, the fallout from regional conflicts, and concerns about the narcotics trade and terrorism. These were not activities that fit neatly under the same umbrella.

Much of the debate around AID suggested that even while geostrategic rivalries were easing, economic ones were not, and the Congressional Research Service raised concerns in 1991 "over our declining industries, our share of world trade, our ability to compete regionally and internationally."[42] The European common market was starting to emerge as a potential competitor. The impact of globalization on economies was only beginning to be understood, and both developed and developing nations were coming to grips with the fact that international trade agreements were remaking the economic landscape.

While part of the rationale for foreign aid had always been growing foreign markets for US exports, the Woods Report created a climate where increasing numbers were advocating that assistance programs more clearly benefit US firms.

Four Democratic senators—David Boren of Oklahoma, Robert Byrd of West Virginia, Lloyd Bentsen of Texas, and Max Baucus of Montana (dubbed the "Killer Bs")—introduced "Aid for Trade" legislation in 1991.[43] The law would have required AID to invest more in big infrastructure projects built by US firms. The bill breezed through passage in the Senate by a vote of 99–0 but was heavily watered down after strenuous objections from the State Department.

The bill was emblematic of growing insecurity about the domestic economy. While the United States had long enjoyed significant benefits from the international trading system which it had done so much to design and establish, concerns about the impact on the domestic workforce, and a general unease with the accelerated pace of change, would not ease anytime soon.

Foreign aid was a natural target in such a climate, and funding became more difficult to pass. The Bush administration tried to align itself with the prevailing mood. A former AID staffer, David Steinberg, told the *Christian Science Monitor* that containment of the Soviet threat would now be replaced by "an effort to assist directly American businesses that compete in certain world markets."[44]

There was also a sense of fatigue. Talks of a "peace dividend" after the Cold War had proven largely illusory. With the US domestic economy slumping and budget deficits rising, a significant number of Americans wondered when they simply could stop spending time and money dealing with the rest of the world.

A conservative Republican primary challenger to President Bush, Patrick Buchanan, complained, "We cannot afford to continue sending out $300 million every single week in foreign aid to socialist and Third World regimes, not one of which has gotten off Uncle Sam's welfare rolls in 20 years."[45] Even foreign assistance defenders recognized that change was needed. "Over the past several years, a broad consensus emerged that the existing rationale, purpose, and strategy of the foreign aid program were outdated," argued Larry Nowels, an analyst at the Congressional Research Service.[46]

ONE OF MANY

Congress remained eager to micromanage the foreign aid portfolio. More and more earmarks were attached to AID's budget, along with a variety of directives, most of which the agency felt it had to honor to stay on the good side of Congress. As the *New York Times* noted, it was not unusual for "dozens of clauses, conditions, and constraints" to be added to the annual aid bill, with detailed guidance often buried in House and Senate Committee reports.[47] AID funding often included highly specific directives, such as $100,000 for a research station in the Galapagos Islands, half a million dollars to study tropical bird migratory patterns, and scores of grants to specific departments at specific universities—invariably in the home state of the senator or member of Congress who added the provision.[48]

Earmarks were relatively rare for development assistance in the first two decades of AID's operations, but by the 1990s they had become pervasive. Over 90 percent of Economic Support Funds were earmarked.[49] Earmarks made it harder to program funds flexibly, and money earmarked for specific countries often sent a message that they would receive funding whether they pursued reforms or not. NGOs and contractors often lobbied for earmarks that would underwrite their areas of expertise.

Policy direction from the White House and AID's leadership was becoming less important because the agency was already being told how and where to spend its money. The Foreign Assistance Act had swollen to five times its original length.[50] One congressional task force during this period described AID as being "hamstrung by too many conflicting objectives, legislative conditions, earmarks, and bureaucratic red tape."[51]

The number of players in the US government engaged in foreign assistance continued to grow. In 1989, the Congressional Research Service reported that seventy-eight different US government entities, in one form or another, were engaged in activities that provided some form of benefit to foreign governments.[52]

Issues regarding developing country economic policies were now heavily influenced not just by AID, but by the Departments of Treasury, Agriculture, and Commerce, the US Trade Representative, and others.[53]

AID had more demands upon it than ever before, the foreign assistance landscape was increasingly crowded and poorly coordinated, and no obvious solution was in sight.

GENERAL MAYHEM

Much of the friction during the Roskens era centered around findings by AID's inspector general at the time, Lieutenant General Herbert Beckington. (Inspectors general are largely independent internal watchdogs in federal agencies.) Beckington had served in the US Marine Corps for over three decades, commanded the 7th Marine Regiment in Vietnam, and had served as a military aide to Vice President Hubert Humphrey (not an easy cultural fit with an agency that was full of former Peace Corps volunteers).[54]

Beckington and his staff were eager to shine light on what they viewed as a culture of malfeasance at the agency. Beckington approached his work with an assumption of guilt: Every recipient country was corrupt, and every official on both sides of the assistance equation, deeply suspect.

Unfortunately for the agency, the Roskens era gave Beckington plenty of ammunition with which to work. A former head of the Africa Bureau, Charles Gladson, pleaded guilty to falsifying $15,000 in travel reimbursement claims.[55] William John Burns, a financial supervisor at AID, pleaded guilty to embezzling more than a million dollars. Tara Gloria Lewis pleaded guilty to embezzling more than $300,000 of AID grant money from an educational NGO. James Erickson, who had run AID's malaria research program, pleaded guilty to receiving illegal gratuities and making false statements.[56] Donald Enos of the agency pleaded guilty to accepting more than $90,000 in bribes.

Roskens himself was soon in the investigatory crosshairs. Beckington accused Roskens and his wife of accepting more than $7,000 in compensation from outside groups for their travel expenses.[57] (Beckington's report went so far as to take Roskens to task for accepting a pair of University of Nebraska football tickets worth $40, despite the fact that Roskens had been the former president of the university.) The White House would later clear Roskens of these ethics charges.[58] However, the aura of scandal only added to the impression that the agency was rudderless.

Beckington and his staff pointed out that AID had the highest percentage of senior officials under indictment in the entire US government, with a crime rate "higher than that of downtown Detroit."[59] Beckington's deputy told a group of senior agency staff, "[W]e know you are all crooks. We want you to know we are going to expose you."[60] AID staff started to refer to Beckington as their own J. Edgar Hoover.[61]

The relations between Beckington and the agency grew so fractious that investigations of both AID and the inspector general's office were launched by the General Accounting Office, the Senate Committee on Governmental Affairs, the Office of Management and Budget, and a presidential ethics office.[62] Beckington raised, and then dropped, a plan to force AID staff to submit to polygraph tests. And while these investigations and counter-investigations raised increasing concerns about Beckington's methods, they were also forthright in expressing concern about AID's management and accountability.[63]

The gloomy prognosis from the American Foreign Service Association newsletter in 1991: "Doubts regarding the agency's continued effectiveness and relevance are multiplying, budgets are diminishing, morale is slumping."[64]

The steady churn of allegations led to an increasing focus on the agency by major media outlets, another bout of damaging new stories, and considerable rehashing of existing scandals. CNN devoted an entire special to AID mishaps. In one of the most damaging parts of the special, CNN highlighted how a tainted batch of oral rehydration therapy provided by a contractor who later pleaded guilty to fraud led to the deaths of four infants.[65] A food aid program for Sudan delivered animal feed instead of powdered milk, and toxic waste was sent to Zimbabwe.[66]

With the spate of damaging stories, it was perhaps inevitable that AID would soon find itself in the last place it wanted to be: as a topic in the 1992 presidential election between George Bush and Bill Clinton.

A lengthy undercover investigation exposed AID financing for efforts to entice US companies to move manufacturing from the United States to Latin America. Both *60 Minutes* and *Nightline* ran major features on the practice, making AID a part of the national conversation.[67] While AID and the Bush White House argued that the program strengthened trade and investment capacities in Latin America, the evidence was politically damning.

An AID grantee had published ads in the United States encouraging US companies to move to Central America to take advantage of the cheap wages. "Rosa Martinez produces apparel for US markets on her sewing machine in El Salvador," the text of one ad in in a trade journal read. "You can hire her for 33 cents an hour."[68] This aggressive effort to encourage firms to invest overseas in an industry where the United States had already suffered major job losses did not sit well with lawmakers or the public.[69] Apparel workers in the developing world were willing to work for much lower rates than in the United States, a reality of globalization that went far beyond AID, but the agency made a major misstep in being associated with trumpeting that fact.

Senator Al Gore, running for vice president, accused Vice President Dan Quayle of using "our tax dollars to subsidize the recruitment of US companies to move overseas and throw Americans out of work," and subsequently got into a shouting match with Labor Secretary Lynn Martin on the subject.[70] Congress added restrictions to the foreign aid bill prohibiting AID from financing projects that would result in US job losses.[71] Some members of Congress wanted to go much further and cut off all of AID's operating expenses until a more-complete investigation could be conducted.

AID had plunged into a valley of despair.

FERRIS COMMISSION

Amid all of the confusion, scandal, and efforts to carry out its work despite the distractions, AID underwent yet another review by a high-level presidential commission. The effort, launched by President Bush, was chaired by George W. Ferris. With only five members, it was one of the more-streamlined commissions to examine AID. Ron Roskens, inexplicably for the head of AID, didn't participate in the commission's work for its first year, saying, "I have no desire to engage in turf battles."[72]

The commission released its report in September of 1992—the fall of the presidential election year.

The report was unusually direct in its findings: "There is a widespread perception, whether justified or not, that AID programs are riddled with waste, fraud and abuse." The report identified many of the usual suspects that made AID less effective, particularly the kudzu-like growth of congressional earmarks and directives, along with the failure to rewrite the Foreign Assistance Act.[73] (The Foreign Assistance Act was first passed in 1961 and has been almost countlessly amended over the years but never fully rewritten. As a result, new responsibilities have continually been added while old ones haven't fallen away.)

"AID doesn't have any mandate," the chair of the commission, George Ferris, argued. "It doesn't have any clout."[74] In the report's view, AID was isolated from the fast-moving political events of the 1990s at a time when "maximum flexibility is required."[75] In a note of frustration, Ferris also complained that the commission had not even been able to schedule a meeting with Secretary of State James Baker to discuss its findings.

The report observed that AID had more than 4,200 direct-hire employees, and more than 7,450 foreign nationals and contractors, in its employ across some 90 countries. The commission advocated deep cuts in staff, projects, and the number of countries in which the agency worked, likening it to the need to cauterize a wound.[76]

Because it viewed foreign assistance's ultimate purpose as advancing US foreign policy goals rather than promoting development, the commission recommended that AID be merged into the State Department.[77]

The commission incorrectly argued that AID's independent status was a "historical" accident" rather than a matter of deliberate design. President Kennedy, following a tradition set in the creation of the Marshall Plan, had been quite deliberate in separating long-term development efforts from direct State Department control.[78]

Shockingly for AID staff, Roskens and his senior management team acquiesced to virtually all of the commission's twenty-five major recommendations, including the proposed merger with the State Department. However, implementation bogged down. Although the report recommended cutting programs in as many as thirty countries, there was pressure to add at least fifteen new countries to the assistance program because of the transition in Eastern Europe and the former Soviet Union. Numerous agencies—including the State Department—objected to withdrawing assistance from existing recipients.[79] It was agreed that further action would be delayed until after the election.

BITTER FRUIT

The fallout from the Roskens era would be considerable and lasting. As a former AID employee recalled, Roskens was "a perfect example of how a well-connected political hack could wreak enormous damage on a small agency."

AID was emerging from the Bush years battered and grappling with important and challenging work across Eastern Europe and the former Soviet Union—not to mention complex emergencies in Somalia and the former Yugoslavia.

The foreign policy events of the four-year Bush presidency have filled tomes. President Bush and his team deserve enormous credit for managing the collapse of the Soviet Union adroitly. President Bush's coalition building and use of force to eject Iraq's forces from Kuwait was rightly heralded as a major success, even if his handling of postwar Iraq was not. The United States and the European Union deserve substantial credit for presenting a positive vision around which reformers in much of Central Europe could drive their countries toward.

But for AID, the end result of the Roskens era was a diminished agency that appeared ripe for dissolution. Staff members were increasingly cautious and understandably worried that any misstep would be used against them. AID was increasingly becoming an institution that would spend a hundred dollars to make sure that it did not waste a penny.

AID's relative weakness had been closely watched on Capitol Hill—particularly by a number of politicians eager to end foreign aid. Ron Roskens had done what few others had managed: He created a bipartisan consensus on foreign aid. Unfortunately, the consensus—even among supporters—was that foreign assistance was broken.

9

On the Precipice

On November 3, 1992, Arkansas governor Bill Clinton was elected president, defeating incumbent George H. W. Bush and Texas businessman Ross Perot, who ran as an Independent. For Bush, it was a striking reversal given his approval ratings after the Gulf War.

Clinton assumed office acutely aware that the American public had denied George H. W. Bush a second term in no small part because they felt he was excessively focused on international affairs. Accordingly, investing in the budget of AID was never President Clinton's highest priority, as he focused on reviving the domestic economy. Senator Patrick Leahy, who oversaw the AID budget on the appropriations committee, told colleagues that he had been informed by the president that all cuts to foreign assistance were fair game—as long as funding for support to the former Soviet Union wasn't touched.[1]

Newly appointed Secretary of State Warren Christopher told a group of international businessmen that his signal priority was "American jobs" and that he saw himself as head of the "America desk" at the State Department.[2] With jobs the administration mantra, and expectations for a peace dividend still high, both State and AID were prime targets for cuts.

"At the beginning of 1993," observed the usually quite low-key Congressional Research Service, "the US Agency for International Development was demoralized and, for all practical purposes, leaderless."[3]

ATWOOD APPOINTMENT

After a stalemate of several months as a result of multiple politically well-connected individuals competing to head the agency, Brian Atwood was nominated by President Clinton to run AID in May of 1993.

Atwood had a good international pedigree. He had served in Spain and the Ivory Coast as a Foreign Service officer. He had been dean of the Foreign Service Institute, which trains Foreign Service officers. He had also served as president of the National Democratic Institute which promoted open governments around the globe. "Unlike some other AID administrators, Atwood was himself a practiced political operator," one profile observed. "He had spent five years on the staff of Senator Thomas Eagleton. He served as assistant secretary of state for legislative affairs in the Carter administration, and as noted, he was recruited to AID from an already confirmed position as undersecretary of state for management. He would take the political openings afforded him."[4]

Atwood would need every bit of his political acumen. He knew that he had inherited a disheartened agency that had been mired in repeated scandals, acknowledging early in his term, "[W]e are in deep trouble."[5] The most immediate problem took the form of potential budget cuts, with some projects targeted for 60 percent reductions. Atwood wasted no time in making his case with Congress, the American public, and the White House, saying, "There has to be a greater appreciation of the relationship of our spending overseas to our domestic well-being."[6]

Pointing to conflicts in Somalia, Haiti, and Bosnia, Atwood argued that preventing crises through smart foreign assistance programs was easier and cheaper than waiting until such situations were out of control. But Atwood and his team recognized that the agency would need to do more than marshal a strong argument. Early in 1993, even before Atwood's appointment, President Clinton launched the National Performance Review led by Vice President Al Gore to "reinvent government" by streamlining operations and improving efficiency across a range of agencies.

Atwood volunteered AID as one of the three major "reinvention laboratories" for the National Performance Review as soon as he took office.[7] Volunteering to be part of the National Performance Review made clear that Atwood recognized the agency had significant problems while investing senior White House officials in a joint reform effort. By embracing change, he not only helped to dampen criticism, he also won important allies in Vice President Gore's office.

The initial National Performance Review assessment of AID included thirty-eight substantial recommendations.[8] Parallel to the National Performance Review process, President Clinton named Deputy Secretary of State Clifford Wharton to conduct a review of the foreign aid program. (Wharton's tenure was brief, and he resigned under somewhat murky circumstances before his report was released.) Both the National Performance Review and the Wharton report agreed on some important points, particularly that AID was diluting its impact by having too many projects spread across too many countries.[9] With a field presence in ninety-nine countries, and more than 2,200 active projects—each governed by a thicket of federal rules and regulations—the Wharton report argued that AID was "consumed by process."[10]

Atwood took dramatic action, announcing plans for the closure of twenty-one AID missions around the world. Some, such as Zaire, were shuttered because they were viewed as bad partners. The largest numbers designated for closure were in countries such as Costa Rica that were deemed ready to graduate from assistance programs. Other missions were closed because they were too small, too expensive to operate, or, in some cases, unsafe.[11] It was the first major reduction in the number of countries receiving US assistance since the Marshall Plan.[12] AID also made clear that it was discussing further closures with the State Department.[13]

AID, in conjunction with the National Performance Review, also announced that it would organize its work around strategic objectives rather than projects and measure its results with quantifiable indicators.[14] Some of these new measures built on best practices of the earlier Development Fund for Africa legislation.

Atwood's very public embrace of reform paid dividends. The *New York Times* declared in 1993, "The long-troubled Agency for International Development, which administers most of America's direct foreign aid, is showing signs of revival under its new administrator."[15] The *Times* credited Atwood for tightening lax management, eliminating programs that had outlived their usefulness, changing the way assistance was distributed, and closing missions.

THE COMING ANARCHY

Expectations for a peace dividend were dashed on the harsh rocks of reality as a messy series of conflicts erupted around the globe. Absent the Cold War, long-suppressed ethnic and sectarian fissures erupted in Africa and Europe. Making matters worse, President Clinton's shaky handling of these crises early in his term projected a sense of uncertainty that added further fuel to the fire.

The situation in Somalia, which had begun as a humanitarian operation, morphed into a hunt for a notorious warlord, Mohamed Farrah Aidid. Few at the senior levels of the US government had fully thought through the implications of this shift. The notorious Black Hawk Down incident in October 1993—when eighteen US service members were killed after a daylong firefight in Mogadishu—set the tone. Widely portrayed as a debacle by the US media, few reporters pointed out the other side of the ledger: The US forces killed more than five hundred Somali militia in the firefight as they held off ten to twenty times the number of their own forces.

"The losses shocked America," recalled Clinton years later, adding, "I thought I knew how President Kennedy felt after the Bay of Pigs."[16] Clinton declined to pursue further military options in Somalia, recognizing that there was little support for continued engagement there and having very little interest in making the case why there should be.

In Bosnia, Europe seemed equally reluctant to take a leadership role in resolving a conflict that was accompanied by widespread ethnic cleansing. A series of peace talks collapsed, and a UN protection force was so ineffectual that some of its members were taken hostage and chained to bridges to prevent NATO bombing.

In Haiti, a US military show of force against the armed forces that had ousted the democratically elected government was aborted at the first sign of resistance. This led to further complaints about Clinton having an unsteady hand when it came to international affairs. Clinton's national security adviser Anthony Lake joked darkly to the president, "Sometimes, I really miss the Cold War."

There was a growing debate about the phenomenon of "failed states"—that is, countries that had completely ceased to function. Decades of development were suddenly being swallowed by armed conflict. And the post–Cold War conflicts had a very different feel to them. Almost all of them were wars within states rather than between states. This was a crucial distinction because most international peacemaking mechanisms were set up to resolve disputes between countries rather than within them. There was no clear roadmap as to how, when—or even if—the UN or other bodies should intervene in a civil war. Most of the victims in these new wars were not soldiers or police, they were innocent civilians. About 90 percent of those killed were noncombatants. The violence was clearly accelerated by the availability of cheap weapons, with land mines available for as little as $3 apiece, and even AK-47 machine guns for only $6 each in some settings.[17] "Policymakers of good will and human decency were confounded and often paralyzed by the rush of murderous events in the 1990s," observed the Carnegie Commission on Preventing Deadly Violence.[18]

Nowhere were the shortcomings of the international community more obvious than in Rwanda, where such hesitancy led to appalling inaction. In a short period of several months, well more than half a million people were slaughtered in a genocide led by the country's Hutu-dominated government as it tried to permanently eliminate its Tutsi minority. Tutsi-led exile forces in neighboring Uganda led a swift counterattack, overthrowing the government and forcing millions of Hutu refugees into the lawless expanse of Eastern Zaire.

The reaction from the West: It pulled out a lightly armed UN peacekeeping force as the carnage began. "Like others, I had become both defensive and cautious about UN peacekeeping in general and didn't see any practical way for the UN to restore order in Rwanda at this point," said Madeleine Albright, who was US ambassador to the UN at the time.[19] "Mindful of my conversations with the parents of Americans killed in Somalia, I worried that more of the lightly armed UN peacekeepers might be victimized."

Both President Clinton and Albright would later admit that failure to take more vigorous and timely action in Rwanda was a profound moral and strategic failure. However, Clinton attributed his reluctance to take decisive action on a lack of knowledge about what was taking place on the ground at the time, which the subsequent release of declassified documents from this period make clear was simply not the case.[20] As Lieutenant General Romeo Dallaire, the head of the UN peacekeeping force that was withdrawn as the genocide commenced, said of Clinton, "He can excuse himself as much as he wants to the Rwandans, but he established a policy that he did not want to know."

"The circumstances that led to the 1994 Rwandan genocide provide an extraordinary and tragic example of the failure of the world community to take effective preventive action in a deadly situation," observed the Carnegie Commission, adding, "This has been one of the most horrifying chapters in human history."[21]

For each of these complex emergencies—in Somalia, Bosnia, Rwanda, Haiti, and beyond—AID was being called on to deliver humanitarian assistance and stanch the bleeding as best it could. As Atwood put it, AID was being confronted by "countries without leadership, without order, without governance itself."[22] When the choice of the State Department, White House, and Pentagon was inaction, it almost invariably meant a greater burden for AID. Disaster Assistance Response Teams from AID were active on the ground in Bosnia and Rwanda even as the United States and Europe dithered over any potential diplomatic or military response.

As public horror over Rwanda and the condition of the refugee camps in Zaire grew with harrowing morning-news broadcasts from the camps, AID and its international partners mounted a massive relief effort. After a tour of the huge refugee camp in Goma, Zaire, Brian Atwood held a series of interviews with the major US news networks. The White House had pushed him to do the interviews to highlight its response to the crisis. However, Atwood infuriated some at the Pentagon by arguing that without the direct engagement of the US military in the relief effort, the loss of life in the camps would be catastrophic.[23] Shortly after his return to Washington and meeting with Clinton in the Oval Office, Atwood joined President Clinton in the Rose Garden as the president announced that he was deploying the US military to support the humanitarian effort, the decision having been made as Atwood was returning to the capital.

It was an astounding paradox: The US government had done almost nothing as hundreds of thousands of Tutsis had been slaughtered in Rwanda but was now mounting an enormous relief operation to assist the Hutus, who had been forced out of the country—some of whom had perpetrated the killings in the first place. Hutu military and militia forces were openly commingled with the huge refugee populations in the camps, and only a gargantuan humanitarian relief effort by AID, the US military, the UN, and a range of European partners prevented the death toll from spiraling even further out of control.

AID was being called upon to navigate warring parties on the ground as it delivered assistance, leading to sharp questions about whether such humanitarian assistance was being delivered on a neutral basis. Humanitarian workers were also increasingly seen as targets by forces on the ground. Sometimes these relief workers were targeted to slow the supply of food, water, and shelter to opposing forces. Sometimes they were targeted for ransom. In some cases, they were killed to silence the voices that were speaking out about atrocities on the ground. A particularly disturbing case occurred when six Red Cross nurses were murdered in their beds in Chechnya in 1996. The international relief community largely vacated Chechnya after the killings, and the Russian government was left free to prosecute the war against the Chechen rebels with maximum brutality and no international oversight.

In the mid-1990s, North Korea, long an international pariah, faced crippling famines with millions of people at risk as a result of its Stalinist economic system. Reports of poor peasants being reduced to eating bark dribbled out of the secretive country. Concurrently, the North Korean government continued to pursue an ambitious nuclear weapons program.

In response, the Clinton administration engaged in extended negotiations with the North Korean government, hoping to get it to abandon the nuclear program in exchange for assistance with energy programs and the provision of substantial amounts of food aid.

The conditioning of humanitarian relief on unrelated policy issues harkened back to the previous times this debate had played out over AID's history: with President Johnson during India's famines during the 1960s; President Nixon, with relief for refugees from East Pakistan in the 1970s; and President Reagan during the Ethiopian drought during the 1980s. In all cases, this cut against the humanitarian principle that assistance should be delivered purely on the basis of need, and obviously the need in North Korea was considerable.

Assistance to North Korea was highly contentious. Humanitarians argued that far more needed to be done because millions were at risk of starvation, and that assistance might encourage North Korea to end its long isolation. Others argued that food aid was helping to prop up a brutal authoritarian regime directly responsible for the famine at a time when it wasn't serious about abandoning its nuclear program or protecting its own people. Further complicating matters, the North Korean government continued to place tight restrictions on those delivering food aid, with US food aid being delivered through a skeleton crew of World Food Program officials operating out of the North Korean capital, and diverting food aid from the hardest-hit parts of the country to protect its political support in the areas around the capital.

Equally clearly, the Clinton administration used food as a bargaining chip in negotiations, and Brian Atwood spent considerable time battling the State Department on the issue. Food deliveries were ultimately substantial, amounting to hundreds of millions of dollars. Yet Andrew Natsios, who would later become AID administrator under President George W. Bush, contends that an earlier and less-politicized humanitarian response could have prevented many of the more than two million deaths that resulted from a famine hidden from the media and the world.[24]

The Clinton administration and the world showed significant improvement in dealing with the spate of complex emergencies and civil conflicts as time passed. After a shocking massacre at Srebrenica and the continued shelling of Sarajevo in Bosnia, pressure grew on the United States and the European Union to act more forcefully. After seeing a picture of a young woman who had hanged herself after fleeing a Bosnian enclave, Vice President Al Gore discussed the situation with President

Clinton. "My twenty-one-year-old daughter asked about that picture," said the vice president. "What am I supposed to tell her? Why is this happening, and we're not doing anything?"[25]

Clinton responded with a combination of intensive US diplomacy and NATO air strikes against Serb positions which helped drive movement toward the Dayton Peace Accords and an end to the war. The international community also helped stage imperfect, but largely effective, interventions that stabilized the situations in Sierra Leone, Kosovo, and the breakaway Indonesian province of Timor Leste. The notion that sovereign governments had a fundamental responsibility to protect their own citizens gained currency, and international tribunals—first, the International Criminal Tribunals for Rwanda and for the former Yugoslavia, and later, the International Criminal Court—were established to bring accountability for war crimes and crimes against humanity.

There was renewed emphasis on conflict prevention as a clearer picture of the combination of factors that contributed to civil conflict and mass violence emerged. Rapid population growth; high infant mortality; large, restless youth populations; economic distress; a history of ethnic or sectarian cleavages; and democracies with shallow roots all made for explosive combinations of shared grievance and potential mass violence.[26]

As AID continued to deliver humanitarian assistance, it was also increasingly being given an important role in trying to help societies reconstruct themselves in the wake of damaging conflicts or transitions from autocracy to democracy. In a place like Bosnia, not only had hundreds of thousands been killed and driven from their homes, but large portions of the country's infrastructure had been destroyed, and animosity within and between communities ran deep. In addition, the former Yugoslav republics, including Bosnia, still required fundamental economic reform to transform from the earlier socialist era.

Work on such transitions fell into an odd nether space in the US assistance program, neither humanitarian relief nor long-term development. Transition work had to be rapid, sensitive to a highly charged political environment, and designed to not only help reconstruct infrastructure but also mend a deeply torn social fabric. Almost no one in the agency was trained to be specifically expert in nurturing a fragile peace.

In response, Brian Atwood established the Office of Transition Initiatives. The new office often focused on restoring an independent local media, since such voices were often sidelined as countries slipped into war. The office also promoted local reconciliation efforts and, in places like Bosnia, helped communities begin rebuilding houses—if such communities were willing to welcome back ethnic minorities.

The model of the Office of Transition Initiatives was soon adopted by a number of other donors, and its creation was just one of the many specialized instruments that popped up to address post–Cold War conflicts. Over time, AID would develop sophisticated methods and dedicated staff to track early warning signs of conflict.

It is difficult to adequately describe how quickly not just AID, but the international community as a whole, evolved to deal with the messy reality of civil conflicts in the 1990s. The international community deserves every bit of scorn and oppro-brium it received for its missteps in Somalia, Rwanda, Bosnia, and beyond. But equally true, an entire community of people who treat peacebuilding and conflict prevention as a vocation emerged during this period, and their approaches rapidly became increasingly sophisticated. Work in conflict zones and fragile states became a principal focus of development agencies and organizations. This work remains com-plex and often involves hard moral and strategic trade-offs, but enormous progress was made during this period—even as immense humanitarian needs were consum-ing larger and larger portions of budgets.

Atwood launched another signature program in an effort to stem the cycle of crisis in Africa: the Greater Horn of Africa Initiative. Atwood often noted that the United States was putting twice as many relief dollars into East Africa as development dol-lars. Similar in many respects to the goals of the Sahel program decades earlier, the Greater Horn of Africa Initiative tried to ease vulnerability to famine and conflict by addressing their root causes.

"When I first came into the office, there was a lot of skepticism in the Bureau about this new effort," said Glenn Slocum of AID. "My predecessor told me it would pass in a few months, and we would be back to doing business as usual."[27] Slocum also recalls that the State Department was quite nervous about the effort, skeptical as to why AID should have a role in analyzing political tensions—long the analytical purview of the CIA and State Department. This reluctance to better marry political economy analysis and development policy had long been an Achilles' heel in the US government's approach to foreign assistance.

BORIS AND BILL

In Russia, it looked like the narrow, historic window for lasting reform was closing quickly, and the country faced increasingly dire straits as Clinton came into office. As the Congressional Research Service noted, Russia's inflation rate hit 2,000 percent in 1992, with that country $6 billion behind on debt payments.[28] Concerns about potential domestic Russian unrest and perhaps even mass starvation began to rise. A range of observers, including former president Richard Nixon, argued that sub-stantially more US assistance would be required to address a situation that clearly touched a broad range of key US strategic interests.

Hard-liners in the Russian Duma attempted to circumscribe the powers of Presi-dent Boris Yeltsin, and Yeltsin pushed for a national referendum to assert his authori-ties. "My entire foreign policy team and I had a vigorous debate about how I should respond," recalled Bill Clinton.[29] Some of Clinton's aides advised caution, fearing that Yeltsin might lose the referendum or that he was stretching his power too far. Clinton, who would develop a real affinity for Yeltsin over time, went with what he called his "gut instincts" and decided to place his bets on the Russian president as the best vehicle for reform.

Russia was the area where Clinton was consistently most engaged in the foreign aid program. "A public poll said that 75 percent of the American people were opposed to giving Russia more money," noted Clinton, but he felt "we had no choice but to press ahead. America had spent trillions of dollars in defense to win the Cold War; we couldn't risk reversal over less than $2 billion and a bad poll."

Clinton expressed considerable surprise that Republican congressional leaders, including Republican senator Bob Dole and congressman Newt Gingrich, largely agreed with him. Gingrich said that US support for Russia's transformation was a "great defining moment" for the United States, and Dole worried that a failure to assist Russia could replay the same harsh treatment of Germany after World War I that culminated in the events that led to World War II.

The overall assistance package for Russia soon expanded to four times the level under the Bush administration. Collectively, the former states of the Soviet Union went from receiving almost no aid to becoming the second-largest recipient of foreign aid from all US sources by 1994. Growing pains were inevitable.[30] Another sign of the high priority placed on the region: Brian Atwood's first trip as the head of AID was to the former Soviet Union.

Like the earlier work in Eastern Europe, assistance for the former Soviet Union was directed by a central State Department coordinator. This meant that most of the initial designs for programs were drawn up in Washington. Squabbling between the different agencies was a recurring problem, and the number of players involved in the process proliferated further after Vice President Gore launched a commission with his Russian counterpart, Viktor Chernomyrdin, to look at US–Russian cooperation across a range of issues. Some sixteen different US agencies had a hand in implanting US assistance programs in the region.[31] There were programs to provide housing for decommissioned Russian military officers and to assist unemployed nuclear scientists, along with a panoply of economic and social reform programs similar to those in Eastern Europe. Efforts to strengthen the media, NGOs, and basic democratic governance were woven throughout.

Jim Norris, the first AID mission director in Moscow, recalled the environment at the time. "Some senior government officials had an attitude of 'Don't just stand there. Do something!'"[32] Terry Myers of the agency added, "It was mind-boggling, the changes taking place at that moment. And how little we knew or understood."[33] At one moment AID staff thought the entire former communist leadership would be tried and convicted; the next, they were being pardoned and reemerging on the national stage. Staff members were being pulled rapidly from Africa and Asia to serve in the region, and many found themselves applying for a cold-weather allowance for the first time in their careers. Many shared Myers's assessment that Moscow "was dark, cold, and mysterious," as AID employees tried to get used to near-constant Russian surveillance.

The rush to effect change in such a complicated landscape, deeply distorted by years of communist rule, produced uneven results. "In 1992 and 1993, some of the early AID projects provided funding to encourage US businesses to invest in Russia,

although neither the legal framework nor the supportive institutions that such investments required to be viable existed," explained Jim Norris, who had been trained as
an economist at MIT. "Not surprisingly, nearly all of these projects failed." There was
no viable commercial or tax law; the private sector was virtually nonexistent; and the
concept of civil society as a check on a democratic government was foreign.

Other efforts, Norris noted, had considerably more success because they were
targeted to establish viable frameworks, such as programs to create private control
of housing. Stephen Giddings, who worked on housing reform for AID, noted that
during the Soviet era, a family's home was likely to be "a cramped room or two in an
apartment in a crumbling, dimly lit, government-owned high-rise with a leaky roof
and nonworking elevators."[34] Rents for these communal apartments were highly subsidized, as were utilities, but the overall quality was quite low. AID worked to help
draft laws and regulations that would allow for a market-based approach to housing,
and introduced means testing to make sure that subsidies were directed toward those
who needed them. Initial progress was significant, with some 40 percent of housing
stock privatized, and some thirty different banks having taken up mortgage lending.

During 1993, there was considerable criticism in the United States that assistance
wasn't doing enough to reach average Russian citizens.[35] In response, the Clinton
administration announced in April 1993 that it would push its programs to a more
grassroots level, with three-quarters of new aid to be disbursed outside of Moscow.
In many ways, the decision harkened back to the New Directions debate of the early
1970s. In the Russian context it perhaps made even less sense, as the core problems
facing Russia were deeply structural. People-to-people activities and support for
Russian NGOs were welcome, but fixing Russia's economic and political system
remained the core challenge.

Congress and the White House wanted programs to move fast—and understandably so. But this also led to many avoidable mistakes. Curt Tarnoff of the Congressional Research Service characterized these early efforts as pushing "out all kinds of
assistance at once, without a coherent strategy to guide the timing—training bankers
when there [was] no banking system, sending Peace Corps business advisors to assist
new entrepreneurs when no credit programs were yet available."[36]

Russia, in many ways, was an example of both the successes and failures of privatization. The early privatization of small businesses in Russia was largely effective,
with individuals being issued stock certificates to buy a piece of stock in a local shop
or business. Many of the shopkeepers and employees banded together to purchase
the stores they were already operating. Even Charles Flickner, a longtime Republican Hill staffer most well-known as a frequent critic of AID, praised the agency for
privatization efforts that "put about 80,000 small enterprises and 14,000 medium
and large industrial enterprises in private hands."[37]

However, the privatization plans for large companies were problematic. Vouch-
ers were distributed to the public to buy shares in privatizing companies, but they
were not indexed to inflation, and many citizens ended up selling them for a pit-
tance. Terry Myers recalls, "I was able to pay $10 in the subway for a 'privatization'

certificate entitling the bearer to 10,000 rubles' worth of stock."[38] A powerful oligarchy of private businessmen close to the Kremlin swept up enormous wealth and control.

This fueled mounting public dissatisfaction with a system of capitalism that felt as predatory as the Soviet propaganda had warned. The honeymoon was painfully short in both Washington and Moscow. The Aldrich Ames spy scandal in February 1994—which revealed that Russia was still actively collecting intelligence on the United States—led to questions about Russia's ultimate motives. And Russian hardliners were proving more durable, and adept at winning parliamentary elections, than most had imagined.

In June 1995, two of the most senior members of the House of Representatives, Democratic congressman Dick Gephardt and Republican Robert Michel, wrote a highly critical memo to the Clinton administration, which called the Russia aid program "simply inadequate in its strategy, its intensity, and its implementation." The memo quickly became public.[39] The collective disquiet with the aid program and the situation in Russia, combined with concerns about the US budget deficit, quickly translated into pressure to cut the program. From 1995 onward, the budget levels for aid to the region bounced up and down, even as the domestic US debate about who was to blame for the unsatisfying state of affairs in Moscow periodically flared up.

The Clinton administration deeply engaged Russia throughout its two terms, but Russia's transformation to democracy and free markets was fractured and incomplete. The window of opportunity that opened with the fall of the Berlin Wall effectively closed in Russia with the rise of Vladimir Putin to Russia's presidency in May 2000. Putin, a career KGB officer, longed to return Russia to its great power status of the Cold War and firmly rejected the democratic norms which Boris Yeltsin had risked so much to advance. Although US assistance programs in Russia were maintained after the Clinton administration, the chance for more-fundamental reforms had evaporated.

The shared failure to capture the moment in Russia was an enormous lost opportunity. Both the United States and Russia had too much difficulty overcoming the deep well of enmity and distrust that had built up during the Cold War, and both were unwilling to mobilize the level of resources and dedication required to effectively reenvision the Russian state.

But while the stalled transition in Russia would remain a growing source of problems over time, the US and European assistance efforts in Eastern Europe and across some of the former Soviet republics had more-lasting results.

Across Eastern Europe and the former Soviet Union, the United States assisted more than thirty countries. An entire swath of countries that had been dominated by the Soviets after the end of World War II moved quickly toward European integration and modern, functioning democracies. More than a dozen countries rapidly graduated from the need for substantial assistance.[40]

AID argues with merit that millions of people benefited from the transition to market economies, tens of thousands of new businesses and enterprises sprang up, and living standards—despite a sharp initial dip during the transition period—sharply rebounded across the reform-minded states in the region. In other countries the overall record has been more mixed, and the former Soviet republics in Central Asia were obviously starting from a position far behind that of their Eastern European counterparts.[41]

Like anywhere else, aid played an important contributing role in assisting transitions and blunting the human costs of the political and economic disruption across the region, but the greatest factor in shaping the relative successes and failures of the countries of Eastern Europe and the former Soviet Union were the decisions and actions of the people and governments of those countries. This period presented countries across the region with a stark fork in the road between modernization and integration with Europe or clinging uneasily to the remnants of socialism and authoritarianism.

SUSTAINABLE DEVELOPMENT

As part of the effort to further distance itself from the Roskens era, and as the first Democratic administration in over a decade, Atwood and his team were eager to articulate their own development vision. They felt there was no longer any real overriding strategy to the agency's work, and that it was imperative to make a much stronger link between strategy and results.

In March 1994, AID released its policy priorities under the broad banner of "Sustainable Development." This new strategy focused on five priority areas: promoting economic growth; advancing democracy; strengthening public health and family planning; protecting the environment; and providing humanitarian relief.[42]

The US focus on democracy promotion, women and family planning, and the environment all had significant influence on the world's approach to development. Environmental issues were on the agenda of the World Bank and others in no small part because of US efforts to put them there. The Clinton administration, and particularly Vice President Gore, also deserve credit for making climate change part of its agenda and a much larger part of the global dialogue. Unfortunately, it did not take long for the issue of climate change to become increasingly politicized.

AID was able to bring a more-sophisticated approach to environmental issues and the tricky nexus of the environment, politics, and growth during this period. Philip-Michael Gary of the agency talked about how AID approached the role of the large multinational corporation, Freeport Mining, and its operations in Indonesia. "In earlier administrations, that was sort of a hands-off problem," he said. "It was far too political and delicate."[43] Yet, with the shift toward more international focus on the impact of environmental issues, the AID mission in Jakarta was encouraged to engage in addressing such concerns and exploring how they could best be mitigated at a local and national level. "I think that kind of shift benefited everybody," observed Gary, "the willingness to engage on sensitive issues and having the confidence in the

AID missions, certainly in the larger countries, to have the in-house skills to be able to engage."

And while it is important to focus on those areas where AID's emphasis was escalated by the new Sustainable Development strategy, it is also useful to note one sector where AID's influence was waning: agriculture. The decline in agriculture could be traced back to the Reagan administration, but the trend only accelerated as AID was being asked both to take on new responsibilities and to streamline its portfolio during the 1990s. Caught in an accelerating budget squeeze over the course of Clinton's two terms, and with the lack of vocal support on the Hill, AID's spending on agriculture projects declined about 60 percent.[44]

AID's work in agriculture was not being curtailed because the agency regarded it as ineffective. "A single finding from the literature overwhelms all others," argued Jim Fox of the agency. "Investments in agricultural research have generated high economic rates of return, indicating that the social benefits of the investments justify the costs in virtually all countries."[45]

DEMOCRACY PROMOTION

With Brian Atwood's background running a democracy promotion institution, it was no surprise that the Sustainable Development strategy included a strong emphasis on helping to build free governments. But this was not just personal preference on Atwood's part; with the enormous upheaval across Eastern Europe and the former Soviet Union, governance obviously had to be front and center. Outside of those regions as well, there was increasing recognition that more effective governance and institutions were a key part of the development puzzle.

Most democracy experts would agree that initially too much emphasis was placed on holding democratic elections without commensurate planning for power-sharing, governance, and the ability for a country to develop robust, capable institutions.

Democracy expert Tom Carothers, who has written extensively on the topic, notes that the enabling environment for democracy—not unlike economic reform efforts—played a considerable role in their likelihood of success.[46] And perhaps even more than economics, the underlying dynamics of power and class, concentrations of wealth, existing social cleavages, and political traditions played an enormous role in governance.

The experience in Eastern Europe had sharpened AID's approach to democracy building, and the agency had expanded its capacity to offer technical assistance in this area. AID's work in democracy, much like its efforts to develop better conflict-prevention mechanisms, often necessitated close collaboration between AID and the State Department because of the highly political nature of the work.

Trying to inject considerations of democratic governance into programming in the wake of the Cold War often involved difficult trade-offs. Philip-Michael Gary of AID recalled being in Washington to discuss the situation with President Yoweri

Museveni in Uganda. The democracy program in that country generated considerable internal debate at AID. The head of AID's democracy office at the time, Jennifer Windsor, pushed Museveni directly, saying that Uganda needed to get away from its strongman model.[47]

Museveni's countered, "We come out of a history of Milton Obote and Idi Amin," said the Ugandan, citing the country's former authoritarian leaders. "Winner take all; losers die. The only basis for political party here would be tribe. If you have tribes, nobody's prepared to lose. If I set up political parties, I am just organizing a civil war."

Ultimately, Museveni, with tacit support from Washington, embraced a one-party democracy with democratic procedures and transparency within the single-party system. The hope was that this would allow for a steady evolution toward a multiparty democracy. "Obviously, since he's still there it didn't really work," said Gary, adding that the agency was ill-equipped at the time to address some of these very thorny issues at play in a place like Uganda, including how best to address the widespread trauma from earlier conflicts and abuses.

Late in the Clinton administration, the State Department tried to organize a "community of democracies" to help struggling, nascent democracies and encourage more well-established democracies to band together in that effort. The enterprise had mixed success but was a forward-looking recognition of the considerable pressures that income inequality, nationalism, and nostalgia for earlier authoritarian systems would place on free governments.

There was growing appreciation that elections and political parties were vital, but so too is actual governance and the durability and quality of public institutions. That said, how exactly to strengthen institutions and make them more effective is no simple task, usually requiring far longer investment horizons. Long-term investments in participant training in the 1960s, and to a lesser extent in the 1980s, had obviously delivered considerable returns in building far more capable governments, but there seemed to be little appetite either in the administration or Congress to revive them.

A WOMAN'S WORLD

During Atwood's tenure as administrator, AID enjoyed a frequent, high-level visitor to its programs in the field: First Lady Hillary Clinton. During almost every one of her trips to the developing world, of which there were many, Clinton saw AID's work up close.

"She was particularly taken with the programs for the poor, of which naturally AID had many, and especially when they involved economic or health projects for women and when she could meet the ultimate recipients directly and hear their stories," wrote Gerald Hyman.[48] After meeting Muhammad Yunus of Bangladesh, and seeing his work with the Grameen Bank offering small community-based loans for poor entrepreneurs, Clinton became an avid supporter of micro-enterprise programs.

Barbara Turner of AID notes that Clinton always insisted on meeting with women's groups and organizations that worked with children, and when she did so she was often accompanied by a country's foreign minister or even president.[49] "Often the local officials didn't even know those groups existed," added Turner. "Her visit and attention to these groups made a huge difference."

President Clinton once half-jokingly told Brian Atwood, "Every time Hillary travels to the developing world, she asks for more money for AID." It wasn't surprising then that AID followed the administration's natural inclinations and leaned heavily into an emphasis on women and girls in its programming. This was, of course, not the first time AID had focused on women and girls, but it reached a new prominence during this period.

Nobel Prize–winning economist Arthur Lewis of St. Lucia observed:

> In most underdeveloped countries woman is a drudge, doing the household tasks which in more advanced societies are done by mechanical power—grinding grain for hours, walking miles to fetch pails of water . . . It is open to men to debate whether economic progress is good for men or not, but for women to debate the desirability of economic growth is to debate whether women should have the chance to cease to be beasts of burden and to join the human race.[50]

One of the key areas for emphasis during this period was a push by AID, and subsequently large multilateral organizations, to keep larger numbers of girls in school in Asia, Africa, and Latin America. AID, as part of its already impressive body of work on child survival, also promoted the importance of breastfeeding globally after a 1995 study indicated that more than half of the deaths of preschool children in the developing world were caused by factors related to malnutrition.[51]

AID sponsored research on breastfeeding, engaged in intensive social marketing campaigns promoting the practice, and provided extensive training for clinic workers on breastfeeding and nutrition for mothers and children. This was a remarkable historical evolution for the agency, which had gone from a formal position of defending the baby formula industry in the Reagan years to becoming a champion of breastfeeding less than a decade later.

Of course, any serious discussion of the role of women and children in development also entailed considerations of international family planning. The Clinton administration abolished the Mexico City restrictions on organizations receiving US family planning funds almost immediately upon entering office—delighting family planning organizations and infuriating conservative members of Congress. By the mid-1990s, AID was operating family planning programs in close to eighty countries around the globe.[52] When AID began its family planning work in the mid-1960s, only seven countries had official policies supporting family planning; by the mid-1990s, this figure was ten times that number.

Family planning programs in places like Thailand achieved remarkable progress. With a mix of AID and Thai government funding, and a combination of smart policies and a willingness to work with the private sector, Thailand went from women averaging 6 children to around 2.3 in about a dozen years.[53] The need for AID funding evaporated as the Thai government fully managed the program.

Similarly, an AID program in Ecuador, carried out in conjunction with the Medical Center for Family Planning Orientation and Services, helped operate more than twenty clinics, almost all run entirely by women. AID provided training and some equipment. The majority of the clinics became self-sufficient, including in indigenous communities where previous family planning efforts had largely stalled.[54]

The issue of foreign aid, family planning, women's rights, and Hillary Clinton came into the limelight with her participation in the 1995 UN women's conference in Beijing. The question of whether or not Clinton should attend became a political lightning rod. Madeleine Albright recalled, "Conservative activists argued that US participation would constitute an endorsement of China's human rights policies. Columnists suggested that the US delegation was intent on redefining motherhood, fatherhood, family, and gender. Talk show hosts claimed that Hillary Clinton sought absolute statistical parity between men and women in every workplace."[55]

Ultimately, Clinton chose to attend, and she rose to the occasion. She rebuked China for its failure to allow free speech, spoke eloquently in support of families, and articulated the formulation that became famous: "Human rights are women's rights, and women's rights are human rights." "When she finished," Albright observed, "the applause came in waves." AID issued its Gender Plan of Action not long after, with Brian Atwood noting upon its release, "[P]erhaps the greatest accomplishment is the increasing realization that for development to be effective, programs must pay attention to the central role of women."[56]

But AID's emphasis on women and promoting family planning was not without significant blowback, and anti-abortion groups were increasingly galvanized, advocating steep funding cuts and trying to resurrect Mexico City restrictions legislatively.

UNEASY SIBLINGS

To fully understand the central drama of the Atwood years—the agency's survival—it is useful to step back and examine the long and sometimes uneasy relationship between AID and the State Department.

The State Department, all the way back to AID's creation, disliked the idea of the agency being granted independence. Having lost that battle when AID was established, the State Department fought periodic rearguard efforts to have AID folded into the State Department. "The aid program is too intimately involved in our foreign relations to allow for the fiction that it is a technical operation which State can delegate to an operating agency," wrote a State Department official in 1962.[57]

It would be easy to assume that State–AID tensions were merely a battle over turf and money, and there was no small measure of that involved, but the institutions were also driven by very different cultures, missions, and ways of viewing the world.

First and foremost, diplomacy and development have different imperatives and time frames. The State Department looks to contemporary diplomatic issues and relationships and how they can be leveraged to support US strategic interests. Ambassadors are held to account, above all else, for the events that happen on their watch—even when they sometimes have limited control over how those events unfold. Development, in contrast is a long-term endeavor where lasting change even in the best of cases takes years and decades.

For a great majority of the time, State and AID sort out mutual accommodations. "They work together, they clear cables together," commented Bill Gaud, who had run AID in the 1960s, "and all of our program decisions are made with the knowledge of the State Department people who are interested."[58] AID proposes country allocations and the State Department reviews them; for economic support funds, State proposes country spending levels after consultations with AID.

However, State and AID are organized quite differently. AID was fairly decentralized, driven by country missions, while State tended to be more top-down in orientation. Ambassadors varied widely in how closely they engaged with the assistance programs in their countries.

There were persistent and growing sources of tensions. AID frequently advocated fundamental economic or social reforms, but those reforms often carried significant political implications. The State Department tended to be more comfortable with the status quo, having created an important web of existing relationships.

State Department officials have no shortage of complaints about their AID colleagues, often feeling that they are not attuned to sensitive issues of diplomacy, that they are slow and overly deliberative, and resentful that the agency has a wealth of program funds while the State Department is comparatively bereft. As Owen Cylke of AID observed of the relationship, "They didn't like the arrogance of AID. They didn't like the fact that we had a billion dollars. They didn't like the fact that they didn't control it."[59]

The post–Cold War period only exacerbated the tensions. A deputy assistant secretary for Africa at the State Department joked to an AID colleague around this time that the "world had turned upside down. AID is suddenly working on political development, democracy, and governance," while the State Department was being asked to track HIV/AIDS and other health issues.[60] Everyone seemed to be on everyone else's territory. The creation of a new under secretary of state for global affairs to look at environmental and population issues, with former senator Tim Wirth appointed as the first incumbent, only added to the confusion.

At one point, when an AID staffer reported hearing a fair amount of animosity from State Department colleagues toward the agency during an Africa trip, Brian Atwood smiled ruefully and responded, "Well, that's probably my fault. Many of them think that I'm trying to be the secretary of state for AID, that I'm too vocal on issues that I shouldn't be vocal on."[61] Atwood's tendency to speak out on issues like democracy and crisis prevention contrasted with Secretary of State Warren Christopher's almost painfully subdued public presence.

Most importantly, the State Department and AID have always had a fundamentally different view of why the United States promotes development. For the State Department, foreign aid has always been viewed as an instrument to achieve broader foreign policy objectives. For those at AID, development was an important strategic and foreign policy objective in its own right. While that may seem like a minor difference, it leads to very different worldviews and program objectives and raises fundamental questions about how you measure effectiveness.

These long, lingering tensions were about to explode.

THE END OF AID?

Driven by resentment with President Clinton's initial health-care plans and early stumbles on the international stage, the Republican Party stormed into House and Senate majorities on November 8, 1994—one of the largest shifts in congressional power in US history.

In January 1995, Vice President Gore solicited ideas on how to streamline the foreign affairs bureaucracy. It was against this backdrop that Secretary of State Christopher, hoping both to achieve the goals of directly controlling more foreign aid and appeasing the new Republican majority, floated a dramatic reorganization proposal: consolidating AID within the State Department. Christopher's staff tried to use the National Performance Review process to make their case, writing to Vice President Gore's staff that AID was a "rogue elephant" that ignored the State Department in the budget process.[62]

The State Department's proposals to eliminate AID—previously floated in the Bush administration by Secretary of State James Baker—also raised the idea of folding the US Information Agency and the Arms Control and Disarmament Agency into the State Department. State argued that their plan would save money, reduce staff, and eliminate the "turf consciousness of the other foreign aid agencies."[63]

However, Atwood, unlike Ron Roskens before him, pushed back against his own secretary of state. He began frenetically lobbying internally against the plan, meeting with both Vice President Gore and Secretary Christopher to make his case. Gore urged Atwood not to overreact or to threaten to resign, suggesting that it would compromise his ultimate decision. Atwood concurred, and argued that AID continued to play a unique and important role and that it made little sense to abolish the agency while it was in the middle of a White House–led reform effort. Some at AID also noted, quietly, that the State Department had been reluctant to embrace managerial reforms and appeared more interested in gobbling up AID's resources.

Ultimately, the National Performance Review team was unimpressed with the State Department plan. "It didn't make any sense," said Elaine Kamarck of the National Performance Review of the idea of merging AID under the State Department. "They have totally different missions."[64] Kamarck's opinion would be far from the last word on the subject.

In January 1995 it became public that the administration had rejected the State Department plan. In comments to the *New York Times* an administration official, speaking on background, noted that these other agencies were already cutting costs and personnel, adding, "It's important to finish the restructuring task inside each agency."[65] AID had won a reprieve—albeit, a brief one.

Congressional Republicans saw a golden opportunity, none more so than Senator Jesse Helms of North Carolina. Helms had long been known for his isolationist views and extreme dislike of foreign aid. Helms was not just bellicose; he and his staff were knowledgeable about parliamentary procedure, and Helms regularly held up ambassadorial nominations to win concessions on policy issues.

Helms, in a nightmare scenario for those who cared about US foreign policy, had ascended to the chair of the Senate Foreign Relations Committee and made clear to his staff that eliminating AID was his top priority. His call was supported by Senate Majority Leader Bob Dole, Speaker of the House Newt Gingrich, and Senator Mitch McConnell of Kentucky, who oversaw the agency's budget, and declared, "AID is a dinosaur. It's time to put it to rest." Former secretary of state James Baker—under whose direct watch the most damaging of AID's scandals and mismanagement had occurred—joined in, testifying to the House of Representatives, "AID's only useful purpose is to serve as a standard for inefficiency for other agencies to avoid."[66]

In March of 1995, Helms announced his plan to abolish AID, the US Information Agency, and the Arms Control and Disarmament Agency.

"AID now faced the bureaucratic equivalent of a two-front war," observed Neil Levine, who was a legislative affairs officer at AID during this period.[67] "Its authorizing committee sought its elimination through consolidation into the State Department, along with a drastic reduction in its budget. Its bureaucratic superiors at the State Department not only agreed with the consolidation—they had actively advocated it." Senator Helms tried to force the administration to yield by grinding all the other actions of the Senate Foreign Relations Committee to a halt, refusing to act on ambassadorial nominations or treaty ratifications, while bombarding AID with information requests.

It was hard to imagine a more difficult spot for AID: The Cold War rationale for its operations had dissipated; it was emerging from a series of deeply damaging scandals; the State Department was eager to absorb it; and the new Republican majorities in the Senate and House were dedicated to eliminating the agency. This was a multifront war that AID should not win. Congressional Republicans moved forward with legislation to abolish the agency.

Conservative think tanks also amplified their criticisms of the aid program and how funding was allocated. The Heritage Foundation hyperbolically claimed, "Not one country receiving foreign aid has succeeded in developing sustained economic growth."[68] The Heritage Foundation also made the case that "economic freedom" should be the overriding imperative in distributing funding. As one Heritage scholar put it, "Once countries follow economic freedom, it will naturally lead to political freedoms."[69] The Heritage approach did introduce a welcome measure of analytics into the debate, but the initial version of the foundation's "Index of Economic Freedom" bluntly assumed that adopting *laissez-faire* economic policies would drive successful development.

Yet, neither AID nor Atwood were willing to go quietly.

A *New York Times* profile of Atwood in April 1995 noted that most Americans viewed foreign aid with even greater disdain than welfare, and that both the secretary of state and congressional majorities were aligned against the agency. "But after a passionate round of lobbying, speech-making, letter-writing, log-rolling, string-pulling and plain old pleading that could serve as a model of how such behind-the-scenes battles are fought, Mr. Atwood persuaded Vice President Al Gore to reject Mr. Christopher's proposal, and he and his agency are still standing. At least for now."[70]

Atwood pointed to his record of closing missions and better managing the budget while making the case that in a world full of crises, it was shortsighted to eliminate an agency that was on the front lines of crisis prevention. The *Times* also noted that "the strains on Mr. Atwood are starting to show" as he decried the fact that "it has been possible for demagogues, isolationists, and populists" to exploit people's fears in an effort to disband AID. No easy resolution to the fight over AID was on the horizon, which led the *Times* to comment:

> For Mr. Atwood, this new threat means remounting his lobbying bicycle. It will mean more speeches to foreign policy groups to rally support. It will mean many more one-on-one meetings on Capitol Hill to defend programs like assistance for Africa and population stabilization. It will also mean more get-togethers with editorial writers and appeals to relief groups to urge Congress to preserve the $13.7 billion foreign aid program. It will require more broadcasts of the agency's public service ads, which describe the agency's efforts to help eradicate smallpox, fight famine, protect rain forests and increase literacy rates—all while creating hundreds of thousands of American jobs.

With backing from the White House, Senate Democrats were able to stall debate on the initial Helms legislation.[71] The fight over AID's future fell into an extended period of trench warfare, with tempers running high, particularly between AID and Helms and AID and the State Department. Helms and other Republicans attempted to gut AID's budget as a precursor to eliminating it.

AID pulled out all the stops in mobilizing support. Because the budget cuts proposed by Helms and others were so large—about 30 percent of the agency's total budget—AID felt empowered to mount a classic "Washington Monument" defense and point out what would happen to its most important programs if they were cut by a third. (The term comes from the hypothetical example of the National Park Service saying the first thing it would close if its budget was cut would be public access to the Washington Monument because it is a beloved tourist site.)

The *Washington Post* highlighted the potential impact of the budget cuts at AID: "Four million children would not be vaccinated against such preventable diseases as measles, whooping cough and diphtheria. Cuts in family planning services, under attack from religious lobbies in Congress as well as from budget cutters, would result in 600,000 more unintended pregnancies a year, which would lead to 420,000 additional births, 180,000 more unsafe abortions and 4,000 maternal deaths."[72]

Agency staffers detailed how much of AID's budget was spent on contractors, educational institutions, and nonprofits in each congressional district, noting that 80 percent of its total funds were spent in the United States (a point that many aid reformers saw more as a problem than a point of pride). AID was able to get supportive op-ed pieces in newspapers in forty-six states, including Alabama and Mississippi, in part by emphasizing the importance of American jobs linked to emerging markets. AID pointed out that between 1990 and 1993, forty-three of the top fifty consumer nations of American agricultural products were once US foreign aid recipients.[73] AID noted that 40 percent of all US exports went to the developing world, accounting for over $180 billion of American goods and some 3.6 million US jobs.[74]

Behind the scenes, AID also drew attention to the State Department's management struggles, asking conservative lawmakers and pundits if they were comfortable creating a "mega-State Department."

The *New York Times* reported that a number of Republicans were "infuriated" with the intensity of AID's campaign, and they were further angered after an internal memo leaked indicating that the agency's legislative strategy was to "delay, postpone, obfuscate, and derail" the Republican plan.[75]

AID noted that the cost of US assistance to Africa cost the average American family about $3 a year—about the same as a "single meal at a fast-food restaurant."[76] The agency pointed out that in poll after poll most Americans thought that foreign aid consumed about 20 percent of the federal budget—a larger portion of federal spending than the Pentagon or social security—when in fact only about 1 percent of the federal budget was dedicated to foreign assistance.

Perhaps more than anything, the agency tried to marshal as much evidence as possible that Senator Helms's oft-repeated claim that foreign aid was flushing money down a rathole was simply wrong. Economist Jim Fox of AID argued, "There has been a steady and dramatic improvement in indicators of the quality of life for ordinary people in developing countries. Throughout the developing world, people are living longer lives, they are eating better, and they are far more likely to be literate than ever before in history."[77]

While there is obviously room for debate about the relative effectiveness of AID programs, conditions on the ground in much of the developing world were evolving incredibly quickly due to a combination of forces: an increasingly global economy; important advances in lifesaving, scalable technologies; the concerted development effort by a host of multilateral and bilateral donors; and the perseverance and vision of the people of the developing world. None of this is to claim any part of this process were perfect, or that many had not been left behind, but a largely virtuous circle was profoundly bending the arc of human development.

Some of these advancements either would not have happened, or would have happened more slowly, without the benefit of foreign assistance—including the elimination of smallpox, the Green Revolution, the sharp rise in literacy among girls, slowing birth rates, and the millions of lives saved through basic interventions like oral rehydration therapy.

And even as the debate about the US foreign aid program raged, there was a growing recognition among voices from the developing world that development was about more than just statistics or economic returns. Amartya Sen, the Nobel Prize–winning economist, argued that development was fundamentally about "enlarging people's choices, capabilities and freedoms, so that they can live a long and healthy life, have access to knowledge, a decent standard of living, and participate in the life of their community."[78]

Jesse Helms was unmoved. Although he still needed votes to eliminate AID, he was already inflicting considerable pain on the agency. As Hattie Babbitt, the deputy administrator at the time, explains, the deep cuts in AID's operating expenses—which covered staff costs—were strategic. "If they could just starve AID to death, he could kill it."[79]

Helms's strategy was compounded by one of the agency's self-inflicted wounds. AID's management bureau during this period was run by Larry Byrne. As Hariadene Johnson of AID said of Byrne, "He quickly worked himself into the most hated man at AID."[80] Byrne had gotten his position largely because his wife was a Democratic congresswoman from Northern Virginia, and he pitched himself as a management guru.

The cornerstone of his plan to overhaul the agency's management, and a key commitment within the National Performance Review, was to install an advanced computer network, dubbed the New Management System, which would include detailed data on budget, country indicators, and program performance to allow for better budget decisions. The broad concept had merit: The computer systems at both AID and the State Department were antiquated, and this type of data-informed decision-making would gain considerable traction in later years.

But if the concept was sound, its implementation was not. The New Management System was expensive and beset by constant delays and glitches—at a time when operating expenses for the agency were already on life support. The Helms-engineered cuts to operating expenses made it so that AID's leadership felt it had to lay off staff. Whether or not there was a viable alternative to cutting personnel was hotly debated. "It was unnecessary," argued Bob Lester of the agency, who was closely involved in many of the senior management decisions at the agency during this period. "It was just wrong."[81]

Having to go through the wrenching process of firing staff members in the middle of a battle over the agency's existence only added to the atmosphere of deep uncertainty, aggravation, and fear.

One AID staffer anonymously called Brian Atwood's reluctance to dismiss Byrne "a fatal flaw" in his tenure.[82] Atwood, for his part, found it very difficult to get rid of Byrne because of his wife's political influence and her willingness to push the White House to keep him at the agency.

The drama then took another turn as Helms introduced what a number of staffers soon dubbed the "Sophie's Choice" amendment, in reference to the William Styron novel and subsequent movie about a mother forced to decide which child would be spared during the Holocaust.[83] The Helms legislation would require that the administration eliminate at least one foreign affairs agency, and achieve $1.7 billion in savings in programs and operating expenses—but left the decision as to which agency would be eliminated and how exactly budgets were to be cut to the White House.

Helms's pressure tactics were becoming harder and harder for the State Department and White House to bear. Helms only agreed to release the nominations of nineteen ambassadors and allow consideration of a major arms reduction treaty in exchange for Democrats allowing a vote on his proposal. Behind the scenes, the politics were raw, as Neil Levine described:

> The deal—the so-called "unanimous consent agreement"—featured a bazaar of legislative factors, feints, and counter-feints, involving high stakes pressure on both sides. Senate Majority Leader Bob Dole warned the administration that failure to compromise could jeopardize a vote on Bosnia troop deployment and Democratic Senator Jeff Bingaman threatened to hold up action on flag desecration legislation, a Republican priority.

Atwood's team took its already intensive lobbying efforts to a whole new level, simultaneously courting the White House, Congress, the media, and the NGO community. The relationship with the State Department, while still functioning largely normally in the field, had been reduced to internecine conflict in Washington. Atwood leaned heavily into the relationships he had cultivated with Vice President Gore and First Lady Hillary Clinton.

To the agency's dismay, the legislation passed both the House and the Senate, although it was widely assumed that the Arms Control and Disarmament Agency would be eliminated rather than AID. Then, in April 1996, after titanic internal struggles, President Clinton vetoed the legislation, calling it an "improvident" measure that should not be imposed on any president.[84]

ALBRIGHT AND A DEAL

Against this stormy backdrop, Secretary of State Warren Christopher announced his departure. After considerable jockeying among several contenders, Madeleine Albright was sworn in as the first woman secretary of state in January 1997. Albright was more interested in development than Christopher and had served on the board of the National Democratic Institute when Brian Atwood had been its president.

But Albright was also eager to break a logjam of issues which Helms had paralyzed, including payment of US dues to the United Nations, a host of ambassadorial nominations, and further progress on the Chemical Weapons Convention treaty.

During her confirmation hearings, Albright, who had been serving as the US ambassador to the United Nations, told Helms that she approached the idea of consolidating the foreign affairs agencies with an open mind—despite the presidential veto of the Helms legislation the year before.

Albright's efforts to woo Helms in ways large and small stretched well beyond a willingness to reexamine the idea of eliminating AID, as *Time* magazine described:

Secretary of State Madeleine Albright has made it her business to charm the courtly porcupine who chairs the Senate Foreign Relations Committee . . . interrupting her global travels to tour his home state, where she gave the Jesse Helms Lecture at Wingate University, Helms' alma mater. . . . Afterward, she gave him a T-shirt inscribed SOMEBODY AT THE STATE DEPARTMENT LOVES ME. Two weeks ago, when he showed up at a Washington softball game between her staff and his, he was wearing it. . . . This would all be a postfeminist embarrassment if Albright's wiles hadn't been so successful. Bitterly opposed to the worldwide chemical-weapons ban, Helms relented during Albright's pilgrimage to Wingate and let the treaty proceed to a Senate vote, where it was ratified. Although Helms feels toward the United Nations about as warmly as he does toward gays and lesbians, at Albright's behest he is working on a bill to pay $819 million in back dues that the US owes.[85]

Albright had reached the conclusion that the cost of an indefinite standoff with Helms was too steep. Albright also seemed to have little personal objection to having AID more closely under State Department control. She exerted steady pressure on Atwood to give into a deal that Helms would support. It made for many uneasy moments between Albright and Atwood, although their relationship never seemed to be marred by the same acrimony of the Christopher era.

In an uneasy reminder of the world's turbulence beyond the beltway, US embassies in Kenya and Tanzania were bombed by al-Qaeda terrorists in August 1998, killing 224. For employees of AID and the State Department it was another devastating blow after years of being denigrated in Washington.

In 1999, a compromise was finally reached that ended what had been a four-year battle over AID's future—even as the scandal over President Clinton's affair with intern Monica Lewinsky dominated headlines around the globe. The US Information Agency and the Arms Control and Disarmament Agency were both eliminated and folded into the State Department. AID remained independent, but it would no longer report directly to the president and would instead report to the secretary of state. The dotted line between AID and State had been made solid after more than thirty-five years. Movement on the Chemical Weapons Convention treaty began almost immediately after the vice president's office announced the restructuring, and some modest budget relief for both State and AID followed not long after. Albright's approach had paid immediate dividends.

In a final dig, Helms also secured a concession to have AID's press office, which had been a constant thorn in his side, moved over to the State Department. (This change would later be reversed.)

What to make of the protracted battle? As the Congressional Research Service wrote not long after the reorganization was announced, "With AID remaining an independent agency but placed under the direct authority of the Secretary of State, it is anticipated that initially there will be very little change in the way the agency operates and how it implements US development assistance policy."[86]

But there was lasting fallout. "AID lost its direct, legal, line to the President," observed Bob Lester. "It also meant that State had the authority, although it didn't exercise it at this time, to take direct control over AID's budget. These two events were the slippery slope of State control over AID."[87] AID's influence over policy issues was eroding, and many of the details of its relationship with the State Department remained somewhat ambiguous despite all the wrangling.

Enormous amounts of time, energy, and resources had gone into the battle, diverting considerable attention at the senior-most levels of State and AID.

This was all the more unfortunate because there was growing unity of vision about the approaches that made for effective development. The long debate over economic growth versus basic human needs had been largely resolved. Sound economic policies had to be coupled with effective social policies and investments in key elements like education and health care. Poverty alleviation and sound macroeconomic reform could coexist. Equally significant, competent governance that enabled people to participate in decisions about economic and social investments helped to make those decisions sustainable.

The effort to eliminate AID stalled partly because the agency's leadership waged a very effective counterinsurgency effort, and partly because congressional Republicans misread the state of public opinion on foreign assistance and America's place in the world at the time. America was simply not more isolationist after the Cold War. As Stephen Kull, a researcher at the University of Maryland who has extensively polled on assistance, observed in 1995, "A majority of Americans would like to see a revival of the postwar universalist vision that prompted the U.N. Charter," with a collective approach to security and shared development burdens. Most recognized a true retreat from the world as impractical.

AID emerged from the reorganization battle bloodied. In the 1990s, total AID direct-hire staff dropped from over 3,000 to close to 2,000.[88] By the turn of the century, AID's direct-hire staff was about half the size it had been two decades earlier.[89] In 1995, the agency's total number of direct hires was fewer than had worked in the Vietnam mission alone in the early 1970s.[90] The agency was also left with a graying workforce, with more than one-third of its Foreign Service employees nearing retirement age.

Once famous for its ability to directly implement development programs, AID had shed its expertise in core competencies such as agriculture, engineering, and monitoring and evaluation. With fewer and fewer staff, AID had no choice but to let contractors do the work that had traditionally been done in-house. As former AID deputy administrator Carol Lancaster explained, "AID has left the retail game and become a wholesaler. In fact, it's become a wholesaler to wholesalers."

The combination of hostile congressional oversight, budget cuts, and expanding regulations bogged the agency down in ways both large and small. At one point in 1998, AID gave its program managers a checklist of congressional requirements and prohibitions: it was twenty-five pages long.[91] Parker Borg of the State Department described what he saw as a result:

> AID had moved from being an organization which planned and implemented projects to an organization which solicited bids from outside organizations and oversaw contractors who implemented the projects. The process for each project took several years. After selecting the initial contractor, the study would begin, but this required the assembly of all of the experts on every facet of the project, including sometimes the environmental impact statement. Various modifications would be necessary along the way to meet changing AID priorities or changing circumstances on the ground. Once the project was approved, the contract went out for another round of bids for its implementation. At about the time AID might be ready to launch the new project, changes of administrations in Washington, the AID leadership in the country, or the Mission's internal priorities could send the whole effort back to square one.[92]

ATWOOD OUT AND ANDERSON IN

With reorganization settled, Brian Atwood announced his departure from the agency in July 1999. He had served six years, the second-longest tenure of any AID administrator. He had been nominated as ambassador to Brazil as a graceful way to extricate him from Washington. Senator Helms, predictably, blocked the nomination until it was eventually withdrawn. Atwood remained active in foreign affairs and development, including service as chair of the OECD Development Assistance Committee.

Atwood was outspoken as he headed for the door, telling the *New York Times* that the administration was allowing itself to be "pushed around," and that cuts in foreign assistance would create major problems.[93]

"We have a crisis," said Atwood. "[Y]ou'll see democracies being defeated and radical leaders coming into office." Atwood praised President Clinton and Secretary Albright, but also made clear that he felt the administration had been too reluctant to expend political capital in fighting back against what he called "backdoor isolationism." "I believe we've become complacent," Atwood added, "and I believe a large part of it is because of a failure of American leadership."[94]

While his tenure had its flaws, it is not an overstatement to say that AID would no longer exist if it was not for Atwood standing up to two secretaries of state and the chairman of the Senate Foreign Relations Committee.

It is also useful to note that one of Atwood's most important accomplishments had largely flown under the radar during his tenure. He had long advocated for a policy focus on ambitious, clearly measurable development targets. When the Development Assistance Committee of the OECD (the DAC) was asked by its members to undertake a "reflection" on development policy, it was Atwood, with the support of the Japanese, Dutch, and British development ministers, who pressed for an outcome that would endorse such targets. His leadership helped to assure their adoption by the OECD in 1996 and their endorsement at the G8 Summit in 1998. He was thus instrumental in enabling those international development goals to be transformed into the universal United Nations Millennium Development Goals in 2000. The Millennium Development Goals, with their central aim of reducing extreme poverty by half by 2015, were transformative, and significantly shifted how both wealthy and poor countries thought about development.

Atwood was succeeded by J. Brady Anderson, who served out the balance of the administration's second term. A former assistant attorney general of Arkansas and a friend of the Clinton family, Anderson earned generally positive marks for his five-year service as US ambassador to Tanzania. While younger, Anderson had learned Swahili during his work in Africa with Wycliffe Bible Translators.

Anderson's tenure brought a respite from the bruising battles of the Atwood years. He saw some marginal improvements in the budget and operating expenses, while emphasizing the importance of women in development. His time was absent major scandals or major breakthroughs.

Anderson was fond of telling staff that he viewed himself as a caretaker, and it is difficult to disagree with his own assessment.

AID had survived a sustained congressional assault on its existence, barely. It was poorly positioned for what would follow.

10

After the Towers

After the closest, and one of the most drawn-out, presidential contests in US history, George W. Bush prevailed over Vice President Al Gore in the 2000 presidential election.

For most supporters of development, the end of the Clinton administration and beginning of the George W. Bush term felt like a further valley. AID had been battered by the protracted turf and budget battles of the 1990s, forcing the agency to make deep staff cuts and leaving it a shell of its former self. While Bush had campaigned on a platform of "compassionate conservatism," few expected global development to be a high priority for the incoming administration—particularly since during the campaign Bush had spoken out forcefully against what he derided as "nation building," arguing that the United States was right to stay out of the genocide in Rwanda as it unfolded.

The Bush administration tapped Andrew Natsios to lead AID, and for many at the agency he was a reassuringly familiar face. He had run the Office of Foreign Disaster Assistance and then run the bureau in charge of food and humanitarian assistance in the elder Bush's administration, and he was well-steeped in development and humanitarian policy.

A former lawmaker from Massachusetts, conservative by that state's standards, he had also been vice president of a large private charity, World Vision. Just prior to his appointment, he had been brought in as a troubleshooter to help get the "Big Dig" project, which buried a major highway under downtown Boston, back on track. Natsios had also served for over two decades in the US Army Reserve, achieving the rank of lieutenant colonel, and had served in the Gulf War—experience that would prove useful during his tenure.

Natsios spoke movingly of his personal experience with US foreign assistance, saying that he went to see the village in Greece from which his grandfather had emigrated where incomes and livelihoods had been totally transformed by the Marshall Plan.[1]

Natsios, and many others, recognized that the role of foreign assistance was evolving in a globalized economy. In 1969, some 70 percent of all the money that flowed from the United States to the developing world was in the form of foreign aid. When Natsios took office, only about 20 percent of the capital flowing from the United States to the developing world was in the form of foreign aid, with the balance coming from the private sector, remittances, NGOs, and private philanthropy. Private capital flows to developing countries had leapt from $30 billion in 1990 to $188 billion in 1999, and the emerging economies, those that had achieved middle-income status, were financing more of their development with their own domestic resources.[2] Recognizing this, one of Natsios's first actions as administrator was to initiate the Global Development Alliance, a new approach to encourage increased AID investment in public–private partnerships. Globalization had become one of the most powerful forces in development, but was not without significant complexities.

However, Natsios did not see AID's work purely through a prism of market solutions, noting, "Broad and deep development happens when a government that is held accountable for its actions energetically takes up the task of investing in collective goods like health, education, and the rule of law."[3] During his first meeting with the entire agency staff, Natsios declared, "There will be no famine on my watch," and he made considerable efforts to focus the agency's relief work on man-made rather than natural disasters.[4]

Natsios had a savvy understanding of the administrative and political hurdles to development, and his essay, "The Clash of Counter-Bureaucracy and Development," published in 2010, is a sobering must-read for anyone trying to understand the institutional complexities faced by any AID administrator.[5]

Natsios was known for a forceful personality, with one former AID employee saying that he "cared desperately about development."[6] Natsios realized that a big part of his job would be regaining lost ground. He viewed the loss of staff in the 1990s as particularly damaging. "It is said in the US military that it takes 20 years to train a battalion commander, which is roughly the time needed to train an AID mission director," Natsios said.[7] The personnel cuts and freeze on hiring at AID had resulted in very thin ranks of senior career officers at the agency.

After the Sturm und Drang of the Clinton years, there was little debate around Bush's initial aid budget. "Hardly a word has been spoken about an item that once received fierce annual scrutiny—foreign aid," a column in the *Philadelphia Inquirer* observed in April 2001.[8] "One reason may be that in an era of budget surpluses, Congress feels less urgency to find spending cuts. Another may come as a surprise to many Americans: The United States gives so little foreign aid that it's hardly worth fighting about."

At last, it appeared that the agency might be able to settle into a period of relative calm.

SEPTEMBER 11

On a bright blue brilliant September morning in 2001, nineteen al-Qaeda terrorists hijacked four American planes, crashing them into both towers of the World Trade Center, the Pentagon, and an open field in Pennsylvania, killing almost three thousand people and wounding twice that number.

Andrew Natsios was traveling in Eastern Europe and watched on television as events unfolded. He called Janet Ballantyne, who was serving as his deputy at the time.[9]

"Janet, this is not an accident," said Natsios.

"No, it's not," she replied.

"You need to get everyone out of the building," insisted Natsios.

Ballantyne said that they weren't supposed to move anyone until they heard from the Office of Personnel Management.

"Forget them," responded Natsios. "You get everyone out of the building." There were false reports around this time that a car bomb had detonated at the State Department. Because there was no intercom system at AID's headquarters in the Reagan Building, Ballantyne had to literally go from floor to floor telling managers to evacuate staff.

It took Natsios a week before he could return to Washington from Bulgaria because flights remained grounded. Natsios insisted that a speaker system be installed in the building almost immediately. At AID, and all over Washington, cement blast barriers, shatterproof windows, and long security lines were the new normal.

Natsios was called to the White House three weeks after the attacks by National Security Adviser Condoleezza Rice, with clear instructions not to put the meeting on his schedule.[10]

Natsios asked, "Why?"

"Just come to the meeting," was the response. In the waiting area, Natsios turned to Peter Pace, the vice chairman of the Joint Chiefs of Staff, and Richard Haass, who ran the policy planning staff at the State Department, and asked, "Why are we here?"

"I have no idea, Andrew," responded Haass.

As soon as the meeting began, it was obvious that President Bush was about to launch an invasion of Afghanistan, which commenced in early October 2001. Condi Rice told Natsios that she wanted a heavy AID presence on the ground, because "The president is very concerned that this intervention in Afghanistan not look like a Russian invasion, so you, Andrew, are going to be out in front for this. You are leaving next week with the presidential plane to go to all of the countries north of Afghanistan."

The Afghanistan operation would require overflight and logistical cooperation from a number of Central Asian countries. Uzbekistan, Tajikistan, Kyrgyzstan, and Turkmenistan offered support, and all had only received relatively modest US assistance after the collapse of the Soviet Union. New aid packages were announced for these countries, even as some members of Congress expressed quiet concerns that their authoritarian tendencies had made them poor partners in the past.[11]

As the first troops hit the ground, Natsios was the first senior US civilian official on the ground in Afghanistan in over a decade. He traveled under heavy guard, assuring leaders in the north of the country, who had long led the resistance to the Taliban, that substantial assistance would be forthcoming.

For a president who had run on a platform opposing nation building, Bush was about to launch into not one, but two, massive exercises in rebuilding entire states after war.

Just as much of American political life was profoundly upended by the terror attacks of September 11, so was the situation at AID. Leaders of both parties mobilized around the concept that development was an important and undermaintained part of the US international posture, ushering in a period of dramatically increased budgets for development. It was, paradoxically, a period that brought about some of the best-conceived US foreign assistance programs and some of the worst. There was a huge rush of new recruits to the Foreign Service and to the US military.

Congress and the American public were exceedingly willing to give Bush what he wanted when it came to international affairs, whether it related to military commitments or long-term development efforts. The rally-around-the-flag sentiment was overwhelming. In the Senate, a bipartisan resolution was introduced that called for tripling foreign assistance levels within five years. As *USA Today* observed, "It took nearly 4,000 American deaths, the destruction of the World Trade Center and a war in Afghanistan to make it happen, but key members of Congress now want to share more of America's wealth with other nations."[12]

The Pentagon, eager to stabilize the situation on the ground in Afghanistan, and then later Iraq, became an active booster for reinvigorated development programs, providing lawmakers important cover to boost aid budgets.

The Bush administration's post–September 11 National Security Strategy formulated defense, diplomacy, and development as an interdependent troika, often referred to in shorthand as the "three Ds," significantly elevating the importance of development. "So development would be seen through the lens, not primarily of some humanitarian commitment to poverty reduction or disease eradication or economic growth," Gerald Hyman observed, "but as an intimate part of national security."[13]

AID issued a major policy paper in 2002, "Foreign Aid in the National Interest," to cement its place in this new ecosystem. On balance, it was a thoughtful piece of work, perhaps even more so for the moment when it was written. The report argued:

> Unless a country's leaders make smart choices for national priorities and show their political will to work with outside donors, development—and development assistance—cannot succeed. Unless sensible policies are put in place, with the rule of law to promote good governance and individual freedom, development cannot be sustained, particularly for agriculture, the engine of growth for most poor countries. Unless countries invest

in health and education, people cannot take on the demands of today's competitive workplace, and development cannot even start.[14]

The report had remarkably little in the way of references to terrorism or extremist Islam, although it did make a link between failed development efforts and a range of transnational threats ranging from disease and terrorism to crime and environmental degradation.[15]

The report argued that promoting democracy and good governance helped to create a virtuous circle where resources were used to advance the public good, decisions were made by consensus, disputes were resolved peacefully, and countries became more attractive to private investment.[16] The report pointed to research suggesting that in reform-minded policy environments, every dollar of aid attracted two dollars in private capital—whereas, in poor policy environments, such assistance tended to drive out private capital and calcify failed policies.[17]

To its credit, the report followed this overall outlook to its logical conclusion, arguing that assistance levels should be more closely tied to government performance and a willingness to reform: "If there is no political commitment to democratic and governance reforms, the United States should suspend government assistance and work only with non-governmental actors."[18]

But if "Foreign Aid in the National Interest" was a sound narrative, AID's operating environment had changed so significantly as a result of September 11 that its commonsense precepts were under continual siege. AID and the development community may have yearned for a co-equal seat at the table with the State Department and the Department of Defense, but they would also quickly find this new interrelationship was rich with moral hazard.

Country after country was being offered expanded assistance not because they were committed to development or their own people, but because they were partners in the war on terror. The military government of Pakistan, which had been cut off from US aid because of its nuclear program, saw US economic and military assistance renewed. The floodgates of US assistance were often opened to exactly those countries which "Foreign Aid in the National Interest" argued so persuasively were the worst places to invest.

"During the Cold War, if somebody said they were anti-communist, the attitude was, give them money no matter how terrible they are," commented Senator Patrick Leahy of Vermont, who argued that those same mistakes were repeated in the aftermath of 9/11.[19]

There was also a misperception in some quarters that terrorism was driven by poverty and underdevelopment. "Any connection between education, poverty and terrorism is indirect, complicated and probably weak," argued Princeton economist Alan Krueger. "Terrorism is not a response to economic conditions. It's a violent political act."[20] The September 11 hijackers had hailed primarily from middle-class Saudi families.

With the shift to an anti-terror paradigm, the emphasis on democracy promotion of the Atwood years sometimes took a backseat to an operating principle that supported stability and strategic alignment with Washington. AID created a new Office of Military Affairs to help liaison with the Department of Defense. The agency also established the Office of Conflict Mitigation and Management, an important source of quality analysis on conflict and development.

While many in Washington got the nexus between development and terrorism wrong in the wake of September 11, it was clear that many of the most important development challenges lay in "fragile states"—countries where weak institutions and a variety of other factors left societies vulnerable to violence.

On the ground in Afghanistan, the US military recaptured Kabul and much of the Afghan countryside. AID staff worked out of the US embassy—which had sat essentially abandoned for years. The cafeteria was still littered with newspapers and magazines from when the embassy had been hastily evacuated more than fifteen years earlier.

The living conditions were rudimentary. Elizabeth Kvitashvili slept in an underground bunker with four other women, without heating, for the first couple of months. "There were two usable bathrooms and one shower for about forty civilians," Kvitashvili said of the living arrangements; it "was dank, cold and just plain horrible."[21] Kvitashvili recalled traveling the country by road, assessing conditions, making recommendations, monitoring progress, "and everywhere I went I was welcomed, America was welcomed, by the Afghans."

That blush of optimism would prove to be short-lived.

A NEW WAY OF DOING BUSINESS

In his memoir, George W. Bush recalls how his view of Africa, and international development, was shaped by a trip to The Gambia in 1990.[22] His father, the president at the time, had asked him to attend a celebration of the country's twenty-fifth independence anniversary. After arriving, Bush decided that The Gambia looked like it had not developed a great deal since the 1700s. "Laura and I were driven around the capital, Banjul, in an old Chevrolet provided by the embassy. The main road was paved. The rest were dirt." The independence ceremony was held in the national stadium. "The paint was peeling, and concrete was chipped away," wrote Bush. "I remember thinking that high school stadiums in West Texas were a lot more modern."

Bush said he also held long discussions on Africa with Condi Rice. "Condi had strong feelings on the subject. She felt Africa had great potential but had too often been neglected," recalled Bush. Cutting against expectations, Bush wanted to make Africa a priority. Bush argued that US "foreign assistance programs in Africa had a lousy track record," mainly because they were designed to support anti-communist governments. Bush wanted to take a new approach: "We would trust developing countries to design their own strategies for using American taxpayer dollars. In return, they would measure their performance and be held accountable."

Behind the scenes, an interagency group hashed out exactly how such a process might work. They coalesced around a view of a major fund that would work in low- and lower-middle-income countries that scored well on a strictly applied set of indicators that included ruling justly, investing in people, and pursuing sound economic policies. It would be a data-driven approach to development. If a country met agreed-upon benchmarks, they would be given significant flexibility with the funds they were granted, an approach that had been attempted with the earlier Development Fund for Africa. It was in many respects the way staff at AID had always felt that a significant proportion of foreign assistance should work.

As Gerald Hyman explains, the idea was to "provide substantial funds to those countries that had already made the 'right choices' and were already implementing the 'right policies' but whose governments were probably paying a political price for having done so."[23] This was different than traditional conditionality, where donors provided money and recipients pledged to institute reforms—a process that often fell apart at the implementation stage. Countries would qualify for funding by their existing performance, rather than promises, and the United States and the recipient would engage in a dialogue about how an infusion of funding could best be used. Then a mutual "compact" for development would be launched.

There were significant divisions within the administration about who should manage this new creation. Andrew Natsios, whose staff had done considerable work on its design, obviously wanted it housed within AID. For Natsios, this was a chance to get AID back to the original business model developed by President Kennedy for AID in 1961.[24]

Natsios was a close friend of White House chief of staff Andrew Card, and both hailed from Massachusetts. Natsios had been assured by Card that the president had repeatedly expressed his desire for AID to run the initiative.[25]

Gary Edson, a deputy on the National Security Council and a key player in the process, had a divergent view. Natsios characterized Edson's opinion: "AID can't run this. They are incompetent. We don't think Andrew can save it." Natsios, in turn, expressed little patience for Edson.

In a March 14, 2002, speech at the Inter-American Development Bank, days before a major international conference on development finance in Monterey, Mexico, President Bush unveiled his new plan for what would become the Millennium Challenge Corporation. Bush committed to back his plan with major resources, saying that the Millennium Challenge Corporation would be funded $5 billion annually within three years.

In Monterey, Bush expounded further on the concept behind the Millennium Challenge Corporation. "Pouring money into a failed status quo does little to help the poor, and can actually delay the progress of reform," he said.[26] "We must accept a higher, more difficult, more promising call."

The Millennium Challenge Corporation would be independent. Natsios had lost his battle to have it housed within AID. Part of the reason the Millennium Challenge Corporation was ultimately designed as independent was because of fears that it would be too encumbered by existing regulations if housed within the agency.

There is now near universal appreciation regarding the degree to which the Millennium Challenge Corporation strategy, with its heavy reliance on analytics, has changed development. The appeal of clear and measurable benchmarks is considerable, and the willingness to use data to inform decision-making has brought an important rigor to development practice, as has the use of positive pressure to improve key benchmarks. As David Ray of CARE argued, the Millennium Challenge Corporation represents, "in the broadest sense, a success for the reform principles of transparency and accountability, and to some degree, local ownership."[27]

While AID remains a far larger development entity, it increasingly adopted the Millennium Challenge Corporation model where it could—not surprising, given that many within the agency had championed the idea in the first place. By almost any measure, the Millennium Challenge Corporation stands out as one of the most important development initiatives of the last fifteen years, its strong bipartisan backing ensuring its continuation through subsequent administrations.

The launch of the Millennium Challenge Corporation was not without difficulties, and it underestimated the hurdles of getting its first country agreements in place, a process which often took two years. That slow start dampened congressional enthusiasm for larger Millennium Challenge Corporation budgets.

Creating an entirely new foreign assistance instrument would be an incredibly important part of President Bush's development legacy, but the Millennium Challenge Corporation would be dwarfed by Bush's next move on foreign aid.

PANDEMIC

"One problem in Africa stood out above all others," recalled Bush, and that was "the humanitarian crisis of HIV/AIDS."[28] Although the United States was spending about half a billion dollars annually to fight the crisis when Bush took office, it was fighting a losing battle. "I decided to make confronting the scourge of AIDS in Africa a key element of my foreign policy," said Bush.

More than ten million people in sub-Saharan Africa had died as a result of the pandemic, and in some countries up to a quarter of the entire population carried HIV. Experts delivered disturbing projections, suggesting that AIDS would be the worst public health crisis since the bubonic plague, with total infections on a trajectory to surpass 150 million by 2010. Nearly three-quarters of the total global infections were in Africa, and many governments were moving painfully slowly to respond. The unchecked advancement of the disease was undoing years of development progress.

Bush tasked his White House staff to come up with a plan. Author Peter Baker offers a good account of the deliberations that followed.[29] Several key players were involved: speechwriter Michael Gerson, who some viewed as "the custodian of compassionate conservatism in the White House"; Josh Bolten, the White House deputy chief of staff for policy; Gary Edson; and a handful of others—with both the Department of Health and Human Services and AID being consulted periodically.

Bolten brought the key White House players together, along with one notable outsider: Anthony Fauci, the director of the National Institute of Allergy and Infectious Diseases, a well-regarded researcher on the disease.

Bolten asked Fauci how he would combat the pandemic in a query rarely heard in the halls of government: "What if money were no object?"

"I'd love to have a few billion more dollars for vaccine research," Fauci replied, "but we're putting a lot of money into it, and I could not give you any assurance that another single dollar spent on vaccine research is going to get us to a vaccine any faster than we are now," adding, "The thing you can do now is treatment."

Those at the White House were surprised, primarily because Fauci's answer ran counter to what the Centers for Disease Control and AID had been advocating. Traditional public health doctrine stresses focusing on preventive rather than curative health. AID and the Centers for Disease Control argued that massive education programs in sub-Saharan Africa, coupled with blanket distribution of condoms, were the best ways to stop the epidemic from spreading. Both of those agencies argued that treatment for HIV/AIDS with antiretrovirals was too expensive to be taken to scale. They didn't think there was a great deal to be done for those who had already contracted the disease. "We thought antiretrovirals were a bad idea," said Natsios, "and didn't support it. CDC said the same thing to the White House."[30]

But at the White House Fauci said that the development of lower-cost antiretrovirals could avert the disease from being an almost immediate death sentence for millions. "They need the money now," he argued. "They don't need a vaccine ten years from now."[31]

As Peter Baker notes, the sensitivity of the plan was such that the White House kept its initial formulation secret from Secretary of State Colin Powell, Health and Human Services Secretary Tommy Thompson, and Andrew Natsios at AID. This was even more extraordinary given that the planning was unfolding at the same time as the administration was gearing up to invade Iraq and enter its second major theater of war.

Just before his aides presented their final vision of a plan to Bush, the president attended a meeting with Jewish leaders in town for the White House Hanukkah celebration. One of the attendees recounted how his father had tried to get President Franklin Roosevelt to act sooner to end the Holocaust. One Bush staffer was convinced that the "sense of moral imperative" carried through from the meeting with Jewish leaders to the White House deliberations on a plan for AIDS.

White House aides were advocating a five-year $15 billion effort. Budget officials in the meeting "were kind of gasping" at the price tag, according to one participant, a huge expenditure with spending for Afghanistan, and soon Iraq, mounting.

Bush pointedly called on those who he knew favored the program, including Michael Gerson.

"If we can do this and we don't, it will be a source of shame," responded Gerson.

After the meeting, Bush would tell an aide, "Look, this is one of those moments when we can actually change the lives of millions of people, a whole continent. How can we not take this step?"

Over the days that followed, a number of Bush's political advisers tried to discourage him from announcing the plan during his State of the Union speech, concerned that the public would think the president cared more about international issues than domestic ones. There was also considerable debate within the White House about where this new initiative should be housed: within AID, the Centers for Disease Control, or as an independent body. Gary Edson, again, did not want this major new initiative centered at AID. And Andrew Natsios had done neither AID nor his own standing any favors when he had landed in hot water in June 2001 after saying that many Africans couldn't handle the regime required to take antiretroviral drugs because they "don't know what Western time is."[32] Following outrage from AIDS activists and others, Natsios apologized.

Shortly before the State of the Union, the president assembled Vice President Richard Cheney; Secretary of State Powell; Secretary Thompson of Health and Human Services; Condi Rice; the White House chief of staff; and Andrew Natsios.[33]

Bush and his advisers spelled out the plan to the assembled group. Bush was sticking with the aim of spending $15 billion in five years. In terms of bureaucratic structure, the White House had landed on something of a strategic fudge. The head of the program, the global AIDS coordinator, would be an ambassador sitting in the US State Department reporting directly to the secretary of state and charged with coordinating programs carried out by AID and the Centers for Disease Control. (Over time, AID has managed about 65 percent of these program funds; the CDC, about 35 percent.)

As the details were presented to the senior administration officials, Bush turned to Natsios.

"Andrew, I presume you have reviewed this, and you helped negotiate this structure that we have created, and you're fine with it."

"Well, Mr. President," responded Natsios, "I found out about this about two hours ago."

"What did you say?" asked a visibly irritated Bush.

"I found out about this two hours ago," repeated Natsios.

"Don't come in here and tell me that AID has agreed to this when they haven't," barked the president at his aides. "This meeting is adjourned."

The president left the office in a fury. Natsios would later note that Gary Edson bore much of the brunt of the president's anger for freezing AID out of the discussions.

But while Edson might have been stung by the rebuke, the organizational structure of the plan was not revisited. Patrick Cronin of AID argued that the clashes over the response to HIV/AIDS and the Millennium Challenge Corporation damaged Natsios's stock within the administration, "You have to make trade-offs and compromises, and Andrew often refused to do that."

"I propose the Emergency Plan for AIDS Relief, a work of mercy beyond all current international efforts to help the people of Africa," President Bush declared in his January 2003 State of the Union address.[34] "This comprehensive plan will prevent 7 million new AIDS infections, treat at least 2 million people with life-extending drugs, and provide humane care for millions of people suffering from AIDS." For most, the President's Emergency Plan for AIDS Relief came to be known by its acronym, PEPFAR.

Citing the dramatically falling prices of antiretroviral drugs, Bush argued, "Seldom has history offered a greater opportunity to do so much for so many." Bush asked Congress to commit $15 billion over the coming five years, including close to $10 billion in new money, to tackle AIDS in the hardest-hit countries in Africa and the Caribbean.

A biography of Bush by Jean Smith declared the announcement by Bush "in many ways the high-water mark of his eight years in the White House."[35] Smith continued: "Americans across the political spectrum were captivated by the president's determination to take on a pressing humanitarian task of such magnitude. World opinion responded in a similar fashion, and the affected countries of sub-Saharan Africa and the Caribbean were deeply appreciative." Before the Iraq War had begun, Smith saw it as a moment of "universal respect" for Bush.

While there was some initial skepticism that Congress would support such high levels of spending on HIV/AIDS, those concerns were soon dispelled. The House supported PEPFAR's initial approval by a vote of 375–41, with all but one of the no votes being Republicans. Given lingering resistance in some Republican quarters to acknowledge the severity of the pandemic, this was a move that would have been impossible for a Democrat to pull off with the same level of support. As one Hill insider who wished to remain anonymous observed, "This was an extraordinary crisis, and the president's response showed American leadership. The money and follow-up were unprecedented. It almost became a competition between Congress and the executive branch to see who could spend more on PEPFAR."[36]

Bush, eager to have the profile of a successful businessman affiliated with the new program, tapped Randall Tobias, the former CEO of pharmaceutical giant Eli Lilly, to run PEPFAR. Tobias brought an almost obsessive dedication to measuring results and impact to his work, and it had paid off at Eli Lilly, as revenues rose from $14 billion to $90 billion under his watch.[37]

Tobias suggests that the decision to have PEPFAR outside of AID was more of a foregone conclusion than many at the agency had presumed. He said that when he was considering accepting the position, President Bush told him directly that PEPFAR would be overseen by the secretary of state but would be separate from State, AID, and the Department of Health and Human Services, "because that was the whole point—to take a totally fresh approach outside existing bureaucracies."[38]

Immediately after President Bush announced his appointment at a White House ceremony in July 2003, he convened a meeting in the Oval Office with Tobias, Condi Rice, Colin Powell, Andrew Natsios, and other senior officials. "The president proceeded to tell the room, in a friendly but firm way," recalled Tobias, that a number of people in the room felt that PEPFAR was best placed in their own organizations, but that Tobias had a direct mandate from Bush, and everyone's people "were to get on board."[39]

Under Tobias, PEPFAR's emphasis on numbers and impact was key, and the Bush administration established numeric targets for care, treatment, and prevention from the onset. The broader international health community was organized and forceful in its support, and the sheer number of lives saved by PEPFAR provided powerful fodder to make their case. Perhaps most importantly, the gamble on Anthony Fauci's strategy of treatment worked. Antiretrovirals proved surprisingly effective in stopping the pandemic from spreading, because they suppressed viral presence to such a degree that it made HIV transmission significantly less likely.

Jean Smith argues that the commitment to fight HIV/AIDS was deeply personal for the entire Bush family:

> Bush visited sub-Saharan Africa twice to monitor the workings of PEPFAR, and Laura went five times. Their twin daughters were also strongly committed. Barbara, after graduating from Yale in 2004, abandoned her plans to become an architect and went to work for an AIDS clinic at the Red Cross Children's Hospital in Cape Town, South Africa, and then in Botswana and Tanzania. Jenna, after finishing her studies at the University of Texas, worked as an intern for UNICEF in Paraguay and Panama.[40]

In 2003 George and Laura Bush met Mohamad Kalyesubula, a PEPFAR patient in an AIDS clinic in Uganda.[41] As Bush recollected, Kalyesubula was wasting away, barely nourished, battling constant fevers. Having been confined to bed for a year, death looked imminent. A sign over the clinic door read: "Living Positively with HIV/AIDS," and the president and Mrs. Bush were serenaded by a chorus of children, many orphans who had lost parents to the disease.

"I have a dream," Kalyesubula told Bush. "One day, I will come to the United States." Several months later, Kalyesubula received his first antiretroviral drugs. Steadily gaining strength over time, he took a job at the same clinic where he had been treated. In 2008, Bush invited Kalyesubula to a White House ceremony for the signing of a bill more than doubling the US commitment to fight HIV/AIDS. Bush could hardly recognize Kalyesubula, saying that more than anything his transformation reminded him of Lazarus rising from the dead. "He was not the only one," said

Bush. "In five years, the number of Africans receiving AIDS medicine had risen from fifty thousand to nearly three million—more than two million of them supported by PEPFAR."

This is not to say that PEPFAR was without controversy or its missteps. Development experts tended to view some of its initial—and more-ideological—components as what one senior NGO official called, "the price of admission for conservative support."[42] This included requirements that a third of funding for programs under PEPFAR that focused on prevention to be dedicated to abstinence-until-marriage efforts, and an insistence that NGOs working through PEPFAR sign an "anti-prostitution" pledge—which was later struck down as unconstitutional.

Because of its strong congressional support, generous funding, and the seriousness of the pandemic, PEPFAR soon became something of an elephant in the room with regard to US development programs—effectively dwarfing many other parts of the agenda. (Cumulative spending on PEPFAR passed $65 billion by 2015, the largest-ever contribution by any donor to combating a single disease.) A former AID staffer noted that there has always been "a lot of negativity about PEPFAR at AID," in part because PEPFAR ended up being such a large portion of the development budget in many developing countries.[43] Getting the overall approach to development right was very difficult when 70 percent of the US assistance for a country such as Nigeria or Ethiopia was going into a single health program.

Many development experts, while lauding the number of lives saved by PEPFAR, had a sometimes-cool view of the program during the Bush years as an overall approach to development. (Most of these concerns were expressed discretely, as few wanted to risk being perceived as opposed to the plan.)

For many observers, PEPFAR was emblematic of a disease-specific approach disconnected from consideration of broader health systems. Barbara Turner of AID makes the case that PEPFAR in its early days replicated some of the mistakes of 1970s-style development.[44] Rather than building up a government's ability to deliver health care, PEPFAR sometimes served as a parallel system. For example, she recalls in Tanzania, "PEPFAR built a new building for the HIV/AIDS staff separate from the ministry of health, not even on the same compound." At a maternity ward not far from the capital, the Centers for Disease Control constructed a new, air-conditioned wing intended for HIV/AIDS patients as pregnant women sat outside, baking in the intense heat. Doctors had reserved space in the new wing for their private offices and conference rooms.

Laurie Garrett, a public health expert, argued that PEPFAR quickly became "a $20 billion annual charity program," and that without greater efforts to establish workable local health institutions, "little will remain to show for all of the current frenzied activity."[45]

Andrew Natsios has been open in acknowledging some of these early challenges. "As I look back at the PEPFAR program, I now realize that it is not a development program at all, but an emergency humanitarian program (indeed, it was called the President's Emergency Plan): centrally managed, standardized across all countries, with little long-term institution or capacity building, and aimed at the one simple purpose of saving lives," he concluded.[46] An NGO official also added a similar observation: "This was a humanitarian response that hung around to become a development program—even though it was very ill-suited for it."[47]

Yet PEPFAR's accomplishments remain prodigious. A PEPFAR report to Congress notes: "As of September 2014, 7.7 million people have received lifesaving ART [antiretroviral therapy] due to PEPFAR support. Over 1 million babies have been born HIV-free to HIV-positive mothers." As Democratic congresswoman Karen Bass observed, "Every place I have traveled in Africa, President Bush is an absolute hero and is credited with saving millions of people's lives." That is no small thing. "Bush did more to stop AIDS and more to help Africa than any president before or since," argued Peter Baker. "He took on one of the world's biggest problems in a big, bold way and it changed the course of a continent."

The bottom line: PEPFAR was grandiose, not without its flaws, and it has saved the equivalent of a large city of human lives. Bush and his advisers shrewdly realized they had a unique "Nixon to China" moment when it came to development, and they were able to expand the foreign assistance program in a way that would have been impossible for a Democratic administration.

The many lifesaving successes of PEPFAR would not have occurred without AID doing so much to manage the bulk of the program on the ground. AID was able to leverage its field presence and strong relationship with partner countries to effectively deploy epidemiological data that allowed governments and NGOs to better target their efforts.[48] The social marketing practices it had refined in dealing with family planning and other health issues paid considerable dividends in educating developing country publics about HIV/AIDS. Without near-constant cajoling by AID, many governments would have ignored the ravages of the disease among commercial sex workers, injecting drug users, homosexuals, and the transgender community. By the end of the Bush administration, AID would have almost one thousand staffers working on HIV and AIDS issues, with four out of five of those staffers based in the field.[49]

"AID may be viewed as the neglected stepchild in DC," argued a Senate Foreign Relations Committee report in 2007, "but in the field it is clear that AID plays either the designated hitter or the indispensable utility infielder for almost all foreign assistance launched from post."[50] This report noted that in addition to its core caseload, AID was often the one doing the heavy lifting for the new programs designed outside the agency. "In Ghana, the Millennium Challenge Corporation is building on an AID project as one of the major components of its compact," the report observed. "In Ethiopia, Tanzania, Rwanda, South Africa, Mozambique and Zambia, AID is either the main or supporting implementer of PEPFAR program funds."

It was a deeply complicated moment for AID. "Whatever the reasons," argued Gerald Hyman, "the simple fact is that the presumptive development agency had lost the two new, very major assistance programs—a loss that was felt almost like an amputation even though they had not been appendages in the first place."[51] The idea that it was easier to work outside AID rather than inside it had gained considerable purchase.

THE MOSQUITO'S DEADLY BITE

The work on HIV/AIDS, massive in its own right, also led to other notable disease campaigns. In 2000, all UN member states agreed to the Millennium Development Goals, a series of measurable targets in health, education, and poverty reduction to be met by 2015. While the Bush administration had offered only minimal support for the concept of such global goals, it did use the moment to help galvanize further support for fighting both tuberculosis and malaria. In 2002, the Global Fund to Fight AIDS, Tuberculosis, and Malaria was established, with broad support from a range of donor governments, private philanthropy, and the business community. In particular, the Bill & Melinda Gates Foundation became a major contributor to this effort, its resources and influence in many ways rivaling that of many governments.

AID's ramped-up role in fighting malaria deserves special mention. The President's Malaria Initiative was launched in 2005. It is far less well-known than PEPFAR, but it has consistently received good grades from those familiar with its operations, particularly for its general management. The malaria initiative took the opposite approach of PEPFAR and was embedded in country health systems from its onset, its coordinator located within AID. US bilateral support for combating malaria has grown steadily over time, becoming almost as large as the Millennium Challenge Corporation's entire annual budget, with far fewer headlines.

The US government has a long history with malaria eradication efforts, helping first eliminate malaria domestically in 1951.[52] Initially, US efforts abroad focused largely, but not exclusively, on Latin America. In the 1940s and 1950s, the United States relied heavily on the newly discovered chemical DDT, which had been developed in 1939 by Swiss chemist Paul Hermann Müller. Müller received a Nobel Prize for his work in 1948. DDT proved highly effective at killing mosquitoes and it appeared to have no immediate effects on mammals. It was widely used as part of Allied war efforts, particularly in jungle regions where malaria was endemic.

The United States was eager to share this technology with developing countries, but many lacked the institutional and technical capacity to deploy it on a national basis. US projects in the 1940s and 1950s largely focused on providing technical assistance to build host-country capacity to use DDT in anti-malaria campaigns. In the 1950s, the World Health Organization proposed a worldwide campaign to eradicate malaria, much like earlier campaigns against yellow fever and the subsequent one against smallpox.

In the 1960s, after AID was established, the agency focused on highly concessional loans to help finance and expand malaria eradication programs in Latin America. The use of DDT was the principal component of the program, primarily spraying it on the walls of houses and using spray teams to disseminate health information and monitor local health conditions. (Some of these health teams later became the backbone of child survival programs.) The DDT spraying was not intended to kill every mosquito, but to sufficiently interrupt malaria transmission so that existing parasites would die out.

Almost all Latin American countries mounted eradication campaigns, and all saw large declines in prevalence as a result. Cases in Colombia declined by approximately 80 percent, and while there was some resurgence from the peak of the program, malaria never returned to its remarkably deadly levels from before the application of DDT. By 1966, William Gaud, the head of AID, argued that more than 500 million people had been freed from the dangers of malaria as a result of AID's assistance.[53] More than 50 percent of the population of Latin America living in areas affected by malaria was free of the disease by 1964.[54] Large tropical areas around the globe, such as the Terai region of Nepal, became far more habitable and amenable for agriculture.

Yet malaria eradication efforts in the 1960s and 1970s were also subject to considerable criticism, both because malaria proved harder to eradicate than smallpox and because of the heavy use of DDT. With the publication of Rachael Carson's environmental treatise *Silent Spring* in 1962, opposition to the use of DDT surged, and it was ultimately banned in many countries, including the United States.

Consequently, malaria campaigns plateaued, and mosquitoes developed a degree of pesticide and drug resistance. Malaria cases, particularly in Africa, remained persistent, with children under five accounting for close to 90 percent of global deaths from the disease by the late 1980s. Many families were dedicating a substantial proportion of their meager incomes to pay for malaria treatments.

Thus, the renewed push under the Bush administration against malaria. The President's Malaria Initiative was very much a joint effort, and tremendous resources and energy were also brought to the table by the Global Fund, the World Health Organization, the World Bank, UNICEF, and other bilateral donors, including the United Kingdom.[55]

Malaria programs were seen as part and parcel of existing integrated maternal health and child survival programs. A large push was made to provide insecticide-treated bed nets, given their effectiveness in significantly reducing malaria. AID and its partners, including the Centers for Disease Control, also embraced a number of public–private partnerships—an increasingly important area of development cooperation—in the anti-malaria efforts. Putting over a billion dollars into the effort, the administration aimed to reduce mortality rates from malaria in fifteen African countries by 50 percent within five years.[56]

THE DOGS OF WAR

The United States invaded Iraq in March 2003, opening up a second front in what had been dubbed "the war on terror." However, the administration's dramatic case that the Iraq invasion was necessitated by the need to eliminate weapons of mass destruction in Iraq would ultimately prove flimsy.

The United States was now fighting hot wars in both Afghanistan and Iraq, and the administration presented no clear path toward a lasting peace in either country. Absent a viable diplomatic endgame, combat in both countries would last far longer than originally envisioned despite overwhelming US military superiority. The United States had simultaneously entered into two open-ended guerrilla conflicts.

AID, in ways that were highly reminiscent of Vietnam, was seen as a vital instrument in promoting stability in both countries as the fighting raged on. For AID staff the esprit de corps of the early days working out of the cobwebbed embassy in Kabul would give way to the grind of trying to promote development on a rapid timetable absent the security that is almost always a precursor to lasting progress.

The early years on the ground in Iraq and Afghanistan did not go well. AID was short-staffed in experienced managers after the merger battles of the 1990s, often slowed by its myriad bureaucratic restrictions, and not particularly well-equipped to make nimble, high-impact investments in war zones.

Program resources were not an issue after some initial delays in Afghanistan. In both Afghanistan and Iraq, AID eventually had more money than it knew how to get out the door. The agency was used to putting in place large grants and contracts that took years to plan and deploy. It struggled to implement small projects in real time that could demonstrate peace dividends. The Department of Defense, and to a lesser extent, the State Department and White House, expressed considerable frustration with AID's lack of speed, and had little patience with the agency's insistence that sound approaches to development took time and local buy-in.

Philip-Michael Gary recalls spending a lot of his time in Afghanistan with US military officers, trying to talk them out of giving away candy, cash, and trinkets to Afghans. "If not done in the proper manner, not only did it not ingratiate them, it made them hated."[57] The Pentagon pushed AID to build courthouses, which it did—despite the fact that the national police force was in shambles and there were virtually no lawyers.

Secretary of Defense Donald Rumsfeld was not a fan of AID, and AID's senior leadership was kept out of many of the early National Security Council coordination meetings regarding the situation in Iraq.[58]

Discussions about assistance to both countries came to be dominated to a remarkable degree by discussions of how quickly money could be spent rather than if assistance would be effective. Andrew Natsios spoke out repeatedly regarding his frustrations with the White House fixation on the "burn rate" in Afghanistan and Iraq.[59] The demand to spend quickly favored large contractors because they were the ones, as Natsios said, that "could spend the money faster than virtually any other international aid agency and certainly much faster than developing country governments."[60]

Department of Defense frustration with AID led it to create the Commanders' Emergency Response Program, which gave military officers pools of money that they could spend on priority local reconstruction needs. The US military was given extraordinarily broad discretion in how to spend this money, which would soon amount to billions of dollars in both conflicts. One civilian employee of the State Department lamented that the embassy's three key metrics for their success in Iraq were "[m]oney spent, number of projects reported, and size of our PowerPoint presentation claiming success."[61]

AID largely kept quiet as the Pentagon and Foggy Bottom spent towering sums of money on reconstruction programs that clearly would not work. Special inspector general reports for both Iraq and Afghanistan are full of examples of schools and hospitals built by the US military through Commanders' Emergency Response Programs that lay crumbling and unused just years after being constructed, all because the Defense Department did not stop and take the time to ask basic questions: Did the community need a school or hospital? Was there a school or hospital there before? Were doctors, nurses, or teachers available? Was there a maintenance budget to pay for the facility's upkeep? Would the community charge fees to use the facility? In the spirit of "can do," and driven by a naive belief that speed was always better, the Pentagon plunged ahead with all predictable results.

In Iraq and Afghanistan, the Department of Defense was eager to more directly manage AID's programs. AID's Office of Foreign Disaster Assistance had grown accustomed to having considerable autonomy on the ground in war zones and relief settings. Secretary of Defense Rumsfeld felt that AID's relief teams were excessively independent and wanted them to report directly to his field commanders. He wrote to Secretary of State Powell, making his case for them to do so. AID countered that most relief organizations would not want to work directly with the military. It took a meeting between Secretary of State Colin Powell, Secretary of Defense Donald Rumsfeld, Vice President Dick Cheney, and National Security Adviser Condoleezza Rice to defuse the situation.[62]

As in Vietnam, there was hope in Afghanistan and Iraq that combining expeditionary forces with AID officers in the field could win over the countryside. Provincial Reconstruction Teams of combined military and civilian units were created to conduct state building activities. The operations and structure of the Provincial Reconstruction Teams generated significant controversy, although their performance did seem to significantly improve over time.[63]

Here again we see echoes of earlier conflicts. The structure of these integrated civil-military teams was of far less importance than the key political and strategic decisions that shaped the landscapes upon which they worked.

"Donald Rumsfeld's view was that we should go in, take out Saddam, and leave, which was a terrible idea," argued Andrew Natsios."[64] The Iraqi military was rapidly demobilized with almost no planning put into finding onward employment or opportunity for the demobilized individuals—a routine step in almost any post-conflict setting. Making matters worse, as journalist Rajiv Chandrasekaran detailed, many of the key positions overseeing US reconstruction efforts in Iraq were handed out to political cronies of President George W. Bush, who knew almost nothing about development assistance or assisting a post-conflict country.[65] In Iraq, billions of dollars of cash were literally flown in on pallets, in what has been called "the largest airborne transfer of currency in the history of the world."[66]

As James Kunder of AID put it, "The hard lesson from both Afghanistan and Iraq was that development programs are not a good substitute for an effective diplomatic and military strategy."[67] This is all the more unfortunate, since earlier programs had managed a string of post-conflict reconstruction efforts—in Bosnia, Sierra Leone, Kosovo, and East Timor—that, while far from perfect, had brought a measure of stability on the ground.

This is not to say that AID didn't achieve some measure of real results in both Iraq and Afghanistan. Many AID programs in both countries were very well evaluated and managed successfully despite conditions on the ground. And while Andrew Natsios took deserved grief for his wildly off the mark assurance that US rebuilding costs in Iraq would not exceed $1.7 billion, he contends that some of the agency's best work was done in that country, and certainly the Bush administration would have been far better served if it had listened to its own reconstruction experts.[68]

AID was eager to highlight concrete examples of progress. In Iraq, the agency helped rehabilitate 2,800 Iraqi schools and trained close to 50,000 teachers and school administrators.[69] School supplies were distributed to 3 million children.

In Afghanistan, the most notable advances were in public health, with the agency arguing that improvements were nothing short of "miraculous."[70] Afghanistan's health started from a very low initial point after years of civil war and Taliban rule across much of the country. Infant and maternal mortality rates were some of the worst in the world. Working with the Ministry of Health, AID supported the government's efforts to deliver immunizations, restore the supply chain of essential drugs, deliver basic health services for mothers and newborns, combat communicable diseases, and rebuild health facilities. Much of the program was dependent on community health workers as frontline implementers. Within a decade, infant mortality had been cut by two-thirds and maternal mortality reduced by more than 75 percent (although some have challenged the credibility of these statistics).

These were historic and lifesaving advances, but they carry important caveats. The costs were enormous. Iraq and Afghanistan represented the largest aid program since the Marshall Plan, and the amount of assistance poured into both theaters was simply unsustainable.

Compared to the military costs of Iraq and Afghanistan, AID spending may have been an afterthought, but funding for programs administered by AID more than tripled in the decade after 9/11, going from around $6 billion a year at the turn of the century to around $22 billion by 2010—although it is important to remember that the increased level of global AIDS funding is also reflected in those figures.[71]

The high costs borne in the development efforts in Afghanistan and Iraq were not only financial; nearly 150 staff working with partner organizations funded by AID were killed during this period.[72]

Because such a large percentage of AID personnel ended up working in both Afghanistan and Iraq, an unusually large proportion of the agency's young staff cut their teeth working not in traditional development settings—poor, stable countries trying to generate economic growth, build competent institutions, and deliver basic social services—but in the dangerous hothouse transitions of war zones. The enduring lesson for these young professionals was one that had not changed much over the years: Foreign assistance was not very effective at advancing war aims.

During the Bush years, AID was also involved heavily in a very different conflict setting: Sudan. AID had long delivered large volumes of relief to the often-beleaguered population of Southern Sudan, and then became increasingly active with relief efforts in the Darfur region of Western Sudan as the crisis there intensified. Both Darfur and Southern Sudan were badly estranged from the ruling elite in Sudan's capital, Khartoum.

President Bush and Andrew Natsios were eager to achieve a durable peace in Sudan. Natsios has suggested that his familiarity with Sudan was one of the reasons why he was appointed by President Bush to lead AID in the first place. AID, under Natsios, was allowed the flexibility to become more involved in laying the groundwork for a peace process than normally would be the case given that such matters were usually the purview of the State Department. (Indeed, Natsios would become the president's special envoy for Sudan after he departed AID.)

And while the Bush administration's approach to the peace process, the situation in Darfur, and dealing with the Sudanese government were not without controversy, they were ultimately of significant import. In January 2005, the Sudanese government and the Sudan People's Liberation Movement signed an accord to end their long-running war—and set in motion the process that led to South Sudan becoming an independent country in 2011. Unfortunately, lasting stability in both Sudan and South Sudan remained elusive.

THE SQUEEZE

Shortly after Condi Rice was appointed secretary of state at the beginning of 2005, Andrew Natsios went to see her, eager to discuss several organizational issues.[73]

The year before, AID had issued a white paper, "US Foreign Aid: Meeting the Challenges of the Twenty-First Century," which made the case for "transformational development" where the agency would strengthen fragile states; deliver humanitarian assistance, deal with transnational concerns like HIV/AIDS; and advance US strategic interests in places like Pakistan, Afghanistan, and Iraq.

Natsios prepared a lengthy presentation to make his case for the importance of AID and foreign assistance in general. Secretary Rice stopped him almost immediately. She praised the agency's work in Eastern Europe, saying that she was impressed by its achievements. But she also argued that too many development programs lacked sufficient discipline.

A number of observers have suggested that Rice's view of AID was significantly shaped by an incident during her confirmation hearings when she was asked how much the US government was spending on democracy programs. Not having the answer in her briefing books or otherwise easily at hand, she promised to revert to the committee. Much to her frustration, no one seemed subsequently able to answer what seemed to be a straightforward question. She was told that many different parts of State and AID carried out programs with democracy elements; it would be almost impossible to get something that resembled an accurate answer. The idea of appointing someone with central authority over the budget of both AID and State assistance budgets began to have appeal.

"Condi, I've spent much of the last few years, since I became AID administrator," said Natsios, "fighting with the Defense Department, the National Security Council, Health and Human Services, the Labor Department, the State Department, the Agriculture Department—over our autonomy, our mission."

The two spent an hour discussing the situation. Natsios shared a short memo drafted by Steve Brent and Barbara Turner of the agency which called for the creation of a thirty-person office within State, headed by the AID administrator, who "would get control over all foreign aid federal spending on foreign assistance—not just in AID, at State, and in other federal agencies as well." The proposal was a more-sweeping version of the old concept by Hubert Humphrey in the 1970s to create a central authority over all assistance programs, this time putting the head of AID in such an oversight role. It was an unusually assertive effort by AID to grab back lost turf. Under the proposal, the AID administrator would be dual-hatted, running both the agency and the thirty-person office housed in the State Department, responsible for all federal foreign assistance funding.

Rice appeared receptive. She also made the case that the Foreign Service at both State and AID was still grossly understaffed, and that adding more bodies was essential "if you really want a highly effective agency." A follow-up discussion was scheduled with senior State Department executives. One of the additional attendees was Mike Gerson, the presidential speechwriter who had been so involved in both the creation of PEPFAR and the Millennium Challenge Corporation. According to Natsios, Gerson began drafting a presidential speech to announce the reforms. Natsios later recalled, "The president's concern was we were too much under the authority and control of the State Department, and its short-term diplomatic interests. That is the reason he wanted to announce statutory reforms for creating a more independent AID with an administrator with more stature and authority."

Then things started to go sideways.

The other federal agencies involved in foreign assistance programs were unwilling to give the AID administrator oversight of their respective budgets. Natsios learned from Gerson that the president didn't think a package of largely administrative reforms was worthy of a presidential address, and without a push from the White House there was no way such a proposal would make it through the bureaucracy.

Natsios decided that his time running the agency should come to an end. In 2005, he informed Condi Rice that he would be stepping down to teach at Georgetown University in mid-January 2006. As he departed, Natsios appeared exhausted with the long-running battles, saying that he'd left AID because he'd "done what he could do within the constraints of the position."[74]

A profile in the *New York Times* discussed his legacy: "Fans and detractors admire Mr. Natsios's straight talk, even if it is sometimes counterproductive. But such comments—combative, impolitic, impassioned—are characteristic of a man who took on unpopular battles, inside and outside the Bush administration, as he tried to restore the standing of the United States Agency for International Development, whose clout had declined steadily."[75]

Like Brian Atwood before him, Natsios was outspoken on his way out. He described the foreign assistance system as "constipated," choked by the snarl of congressional rules, regulations, and earmarks.[76] He also complained that domestic interest groups had assumed "intolerable" influence over the program.

Natsios's successor, Randall Tobias, was a rapidly rising star in the Bush administration. Tobias had earlier served as the CEO of pharmaceutical company Eli Lilly and had further cemented his position by serving as the first US global AIDS coordinator. While standing up the PEPFAR program had not been without its glitches, Tobias was widely regarded as an effective manager, and he had the personal clout to have his voice heard and respected by the president and the secretary of state. As Gerald Hyman noted of Tobias, "At PEPFAR, he required extraordinarily detailed plans and then commensurate quantitative measures for results. He brought that same accountancy mentality to his now-broadened role."[77]

Secretary Rice rolled out her plan for reforming foreign assistance shortly after Tobias's appointment. Calling foreign assistance "an essential component of our transformational diplomacy," Rice created the Office of the Director of Foreign Assistance, with Tobias as its head.[78] In the words of the administration, the new office would "[e]nsure the strategic and effective use of foreign assistance resources."[79] Rice's speech received major coverage, with the *New York Times* commenting, "AID has been an independent agency since it was founded in 1961, but Ms. Rice has made little secret of her frustration over what she has said is a lack of accountability."[80] On background, a senior State Department official assured the *Times*, "This is going to result in a more influential AID administrator."

It would have been easy to mistake the new plan for what had initially been proposed by Natsios. The language of "transformational diplomacy" echoed that of the white paper that Natsios had given Rice almost a year before. In terms of organization, the AID administrator was now dual-hatted, with the rank of a deputy secretary of state, controlling both the agency and the budget oversight office in the Department of State.

However, the differences from the original plan were substantial. The new office didn't have oversight of US foreign assistance budgets that the secretary of state didn't already effectively control. AID, rather than gaining greater control of assistance, effectively saw its own budgeting functions transferred out of the building. Worse still, AID's policy planning staff, the key hub within the agency for strategy and analysis, was moved over into what was dubbed the "F Bureau" at State. Instead of a staff of thirty, more than one hundred people were assigned to the office. Somewhat humiliatingly, the AID administrator was made to spend a significant amount of time sitting in a State Department office rather than in the administrator's office at AID.

The new office was created with very little advance congressional consultation, significantly angering members on both sides of the aisle who did not feel ownership of the new creation. Many questioned why the State Department was put in charge of long-term development budgets when it had no experience in this area.

"This has been a costly mistake for everyone in my view," reflected Peter McPherson, who had headed AID during the Reagan administration.[81] "The State Department bureaucracy has always wanted easier access to AID's money and more control over AID."

Almost every high-level effort to look at aid reform over the previous thirty years had agreed that the international affairs budget should be better coordinated, but to most in the development community the creation of the F Bureau felt more like an effort to marginalize AID, and for State to achieve by stealth what it had not been able to do with its plan to abolish AID a decade earlier.

Randall Tobias supported the plan, but his appointment was likely contingent on him doing so. Rice's plan to strip out budget and policy authorities from AID sent a discouraging signal to staff that Tobias was not going to protect them. Tobias, for his part, later argued that Rice's plan was "a very important effort to bring better strategic focus to the distribution and investment of our development dollars," but added that because the initiative came well into the president's second term, it could not get sufficient traction.[82]

Implementation of the new effort was bumpy and heightened tensions with field staff already fatigued by the bureaucratic burden generated by Washington. A 2007 Senate Foreign Relations report noted, "Field complaints about the 'F process' at State focus on the lack of transparency, the weeks of extra paperwork, the differing priorities between post and headquarters, as well as inconsistent demands, but the underlying, only sometimes unspoken, fight is about money."[83]

After Tobias had been on the job slightly more than a year, he became implicated in a high-profile prostitution scandal in April 2007. When call records from the notorious "DC Madam" were made public, the press reported that a number traced to Tobias's government-issued cell phone appeared on the list. Tobias's insistence that "no sex" was involved and that he only had the "gals come over to the condo to give me a massage" only added fuel to the uproar.[84] Tobias resigned the day after the allegations surfaced, but has consistently maintained since that time that the entire matter was a misunderstanding and that the press had taken his initial remarks out of context.[85]

Some in the development community could not help but observe that in his earlier role as the global AIDS coordinator, Tobias had supported measures to cut off funding from US NGOs trying to slow the spread of the pandemic by reaching out to sex workers. Tobias was the shortest-serving AID administrator.

Despite all the machinations around creating the F Bureau and moving greater budget control into the State Department, the office largely withered under the subsequent Obama administration, as President Obama simply left the director of foreign assistance position unfilled. However, the State Department, in a variety of forms, continued to exert significant influence over AID's budget.

TO THE FORE

It was not surprising that as part of the response to the Tobias scandal, the Bush administration turned to a woman—for the first time in the agency's history—to run AID. But AID's new chief, Henrietta Fore, was no token.

Fore was well served by her earlier stint as a political appointee at AID under the first President Bush, when she ran both the Asia and private sector bureaus. Taking leadership of AID, Fore's relatively brief tenure helped to markedly improve morale and recaptured, without ruffling feathers, some of the budget and policy turf that had been ceded to the State Department. This effort was considerably facilitated by the fact that Fore was coming out of the chief management job at the State Department, where she had helped to seize some of these very same authorities. Fore vigorously supported and nurtured numerous public–private partnerships at the agency, and partnerships between the business and development communities had become increasingly important since the launch of the Global Development Alliance in 2001.

Perhaps most importantly, following up on the commitment by Secretary Rice to restore Foreign Service personnel levels, Fore established the Development Leadership Initiative, with the goal of doubling AID's Foreign Service staff by 2012. The initiative was an essential palliative given that the agency's staff had shrunk to about half the size it had been twenty years earlier.

AID and the State Department had high-profile help in calling for reinforcements. Perhaps the most notable of the rhetorical endorsements came in a speech by Defense Secretary Robert Gates during his 2007 Landon Lecture at the University of Kansas, when he said: "What is clear to me is that there is a need for a dramatic increase in spending on the civilian instruments of national security—diplomacy, strategic communications, foreign assistance, civic action, and economic reconstruction and development."[86] Gates acknowledged that having a secretary of defense speaking in favor of spending for other agencies might strike some as a "man bites dog" story. Development advocates e-mailed his speech all over Washington.

While military support for aid programs always made it easier for Congress to support them, the growing securitization of America's approach to development was a discomfiting legacy of the post–September 11 period.

A COMPLICATED, SPRAWLING LEGACY

President George W. Bush had a profound impact on how US assistance was managed and directed. On balance, the Bush administration brought great sweeping, almost operatic, successes and failures along with a nearly unrivaled boom in resources.

Bush galvanized support for a colossal effort to confront the HIV and AIDS pandemic through the creation of the President's Emergency Plan for AIDS Relief and established the Millennium Challenge Corporation and its innovative, data-driven approach to development. Both of these efforts have stood the test of time, and both were notably established outside of AID.

Bush also dramatically increased the budget and set the wheels in motion to boost staffing levels. Bush pushed through more than twenty new foreign assistance initiatives, and US spending on official development assistance skyrocketed from $10 billion in 2000 to around $28 billion by the end of his second term.[87] The agency's direct-hire staff went from 2,007 in 2001 to 3,466 in 2012, an increase of more than 66 percent.[88] This also meant that AID grew radically younger. By 2012, two-thirds of AID's staff would have less than five years on the job, and the relative dearth of middle management forced the agency to rapidly promote junior staffers.

There were also steps forward in less high-profile areas. AID and other donors increasingly committed themselves to promoting aid effectiveness during this period. This resulted in what came to be known as the Paris Declaration, championing the principles of mutual accountability and country ownership of development programs, which was adopted in 2005 by more than one hundred developed and developing countries, as well as many international organizations and civil society groups at an OECD-sponsored conference.[89]

The other area of important reform by the Bush administration was in making the initial case for reforming US food aid programs—a system that still had more to do with placating large US agricultural and shipping concerns than it did promoting development. The Bush administration demonstrated political courage in taking on vested interests in the agricultural and shipping lobbies to promote long-called-for and common sense changes in the program. Unfortunately, AID was unable to hold together a sufficiently broad coalition in support of the changes, and consequently the push by the administration did not generate a great deal of traction. However, it did open the door for subsequent improvements to food aid.

The end of the administration brought another high-level review of the foreign assistance program, this time by the HELP Commission.[90] The commission decried the proliferation of assistance programs, the lack of effective coordination mechanisms, and the departure of technical expertise from the agency. AID's bureaucratic kudzu remained a growing burden.

The Bush administration shuddered to a close as a worldwide financial crisis shook the globe in September 2008 and amid the heat of the presidential race. The stock market plunged, and major US industries were in danger of disappearing overnight. And as history has often illuminated, when the globe's most advanced economies suffer, those of the developing world suffer more.

11

Ambition Constrained

Barack Obama was elected the forty-fourth President of the United States in 2008. With the global economy in tumult, his honeymoon was brief.

American job losses in 2008, the last year of the Bush presidency, had been the worst since World War II. The investment firm Lehman Brothers, an icon of Wall Street, dissolved into bankruptcy. The lenders Fannie Mae and Freddy Mac were taken over by the US Treasury. Another 800,000 Americans lost their jobs in Obama's first several months in the White House. Major American industries were in free fall. US carmakers teetered on the edge of collapse, eventually requiring a costly, but effective, government bailout.

In February 2009, President Obama's $787 billion economic stimulus package was approved by Congress—without a single vote from House Republicans (an initial indicator of the blanket opposition Obama was going to face from the GOP on a range of issues).

Further exacerbating the situation, the wars in Iraq and Afghanistan raged on, in what felt like deadly, painful distractions at a time when most Americans were preoccupied with a recession that was the worst since the Great Depression. In the face of the mounting costs and death toll overseas, there was little appetite for foreign adventurism.

As a candidate, Obama had pledged to double US foreign assistance by the end of his first term. Saying that he knew development assistance was "not the most popular" item on his agenda, Obama insisted that he would still make the case to the American people that it was the best investment in increasing the world's common security.[1] Obama also maintained that such a commitment reflected American values and would send a message abroad that said, "You matter to us. Your future is our future. And our moment is now." This was a rare pledge to support foreign aid by a politician before they had ascended to the White House, and it was particularly ambitious given the degree to which the assistance program had already expanded after September 11.

Secretary of Defense Robert Gates, who stayed on in his position despite the change in administrations, helped make the case. In March 2008, Gates said, "It has become clear that America's civilian institutions of diplomacy and development have been chronically undermanned and underfunded for far too long."[2] In July 2009 Gates called Senator Kent Conrad, the chairman of the Senate Budget Committee, to tell him: "It is in the Pentagon's interest to have a healthier foreign aid budget."[3]

Hopes were high in the development community that Obama would continue, and build upon, the momentum of the Bush years.

These hopes were buoyed by the appointment of Hillary Clinton as secretary of state. The appointment of Clinton was not only a fascinating move by Obama to heal the rift within the Democratic Party caused by his primary battle with Clinton, but it also put an ardent supporter of the aid program in command at Foggy Bottom. Many at AID remembered Clinton's pivotal support during the agency's battle with Senator Helms during the 1990s, and Clinton had seen scores of AID programs in person during her tenure as First Lady. It was no surprise to anyone that the Mexico City restrictions re-imposed on US family planning policies by the Bush administration were rescinded immediately after Obama came into office.

But the development community soon realized that the global economic crisis would limit the political space needed to make ramped-up assistance programs a reality. As early as March 2009, the *Christian Science Monitor* reported that administration officials were quietly acknowledging that "the economic downturn means the president is unlikely to reach his goal of doubling foreign aid."[4]

The developing world was hit hard by the financial crisis. The World Bank estimated that global GDP contracted by 1.7 percent in 2009, with South Asia and sub-Saharan Africa hit even harder.[5] In human terms, the Bank estimated that every 1 percent decline in developing country growth rates translated into 20 million more people falling into poverty.

There was also mounting angst that six months into the new administration the president had yet to nominate a new head of AID. On one level, it was predictable that a crushing global economic crisis and the conflicts in Iraq and Afghanistan had slowed movement on personnel. But some of the administration's initial delays on the development front were self-inflicted.

Appointees to AID had to be blessed by both the Obama White House and Secretary Hillary Clinton's team at the State Department—at a time when distrust between their respective staffs lingered despite the very public peacemaking between the president and secretary of state. Several potential AID appointees had fallen out of favor for being viewed as tilting too heavily toward the Obama or Clinton camps. The result was paralysis.

FEED THE FUTURE

While the economy dominated headlines in the United States and Europe, there was another global emergency unfolding with dire implications for the world's poorest—a global food crisis.

In the course of one year, from 2007 to 2008, commodity prices around the globe more than doubled.[6] The number of malnourished around the world spiked to over one billion people as a result, and food riots erupted in over thirty countries.

The situation further highlighted AID's previous shift away from agriculture. While still providing significant food aid around the globe, agriculture programs represented only around 5 percent of the agency's portfolio. While agriculture had been seen as the backbone of successful development in the 1960s and 1970s, and AID helped drive the Green Revolution, agriculture had become a backburner priority, not just for AID but for most donors, by the onset of the Obama administration. Health and humanitarian programs had grown by leaps and bounds as agricultural expertise had steadily been squeezed out.

The broad shift away from agriculture was counterintuitive because assistance programs in this area had always been well-regarded. Improving agricultural productivity helped to combat hunger, increased incomes in rural areas, and often had important spillover effects that allowed families to become healthier and better educated.

President Obama decided to launch his first major development initiative despite not having a new leader in place at AID. It was agreed that the food crisis should be a prominent topic on the agenda at the July 2009 G8 Summit being held in L'Aquila, Italy, where much of the focus remained on the global recession. Summit participants agreed that there had been long-standing underinvestment in agriculture and committed to pump $22 billion into agriculture over the following years, with President Obama pledging $3.5 billion—more than any other country.[7]

"The question is not whether we can end hunger, it's whether we will," said Secretary of State Hillary Clinton, while noting that undernutrition was costing developing countries up to 3 percent of their annual gross domestic product.[8] Stunting, which often accompanies chronic malnutrition, was pernicious, slowing cognitive and motor development, making individuals more susceptible to disease, and playing a role in up to 45 percent of all child deaths around the globe.[9]

The US government launched what came to be known as the Feed the Future initiative to meet its L'Aquila Summit commitment. Feed the Future promised to focus on improved agricultural productivity, expanded markets, resilience, and better nutritional outcomes. Like many of the Obama initiatives launched during an era of constrained resources, Feed the Future leaned heavily on public–private partnerships, in part because it was unrealistic to expect large pots of new money from Congress in the midst of a recession. Fortunately, because of the effort to begin rebuilding AID's staff launched by the Bush administration, more than one hundred new positions at the agency were set aside as agricultural officers.[10]

Feed the Future focused on small farmers, particularly women, in more than two dozen focus countries. In addition, the agency renewed its long-standing efforts to reform land tenure rights in the countries in which it worked, where laws and customs often prevented women from owning or inheriting land—a huge obstacle to progress.

AID teamed up with more than fifty American universities to create agricultural innovation labs designed to develop and scale new technologies to boost agricultural production.[11] These investments in research were supported by complementary efforts to address some of the other key obstacles to more-successful agriculture in these focus countries, including such things as improved transport from farm to market so that crops would not rot before they reached potential buyers.

The results from Feed the Future were positive. The L'Aquila Summit spending targets on agriculture were met. By the time of a 2015 progress report, Feed the Future claimed impressive gains, including doubling the rate of progress in reducing stunting in its focus countries.[12]

The Obama team would also make a later effort to reform the US food assistance program, building upon work begun in the Bush administration. Congress had long mandated that a significant percentage of all US international food aid be shipped aboard US-flagged vessels—i.e., ships registered in the United States. In 1985, Congress increased that percentage from 50 percent to 75. A study by researchers at Cornell University concluded that this subsidy of US shipping companies cost American taxpayers $140 million in unnecessary transportation costs during 2006 alone.[13] The Government Accountability Office noted that between 2006 and 2008, US food aid funding increased by nearly 53 percent, but the amount of food delivered decreased by 5 percent. Why? Because US food aid policies were heavily swayed by the agribusiness and maritime industries that stressed buying American, rather than securing both food and transport at the best prices in locations closest to where the food was needed. One estimate from this period observed that only 41 percent of the cost of food shipped from the United States was food itself; the rest went for shipping and handling.[14]

As Barry Riley noted in his history of the US food aid program:

> Over the past two centuries American food aid has been used as a tool of foreign policy and as a response to famine; as a political device to win the votes of American farmers in congressional and presidential elections; and as a useful chip in Cold War poker games. It has been a means of bolstering the US maritime industry and American agribusinesses and a balancing item in Arab–Israeli peace negotiations. It was a weapon used to blunt the advances of bolshevism in post–World War I Europe and communism after World War II. It has created antagonisms with other food-exporting countries who believe it to be nothing more than ill-disguised export promotion, harmful to their own food exports, while at the same time it has been received with overwhelming gratitude by millions of under-nourished households in some of the poorer corners of the world.[15]

President Obama, with the help of an increasingly vocal humanitarian community, was able to make modest progress in instituting food aid reforms given the increasing outcry over the obvious inefficiencies imposed by Congress and the shipping and agriculture industries.

DUELING REVIEWS

While AID still awaited announcement of its new head, the Obama administration—in what veers on parody by this point in the agency's history—launched simultaneous competing reviews of the assistance program. At the same time, Democratic congressman Howard Berman of California led an effort to pass major foreign aid reform legislation, but the Obama administration was cool to any congressional plan moving forward before it completed its internal assessments.

In July of 2009, Secretary of State Clinton announced the launch of the Quadrennial Diplomacy and Development Review, or QDDR, modeled on a strategic planning exercise at the Department of Defense. It was intended to help both State and AID strengthen their capacity "to meet 21st Century demands" on diplomacy and development.[16]

The next month, President Obama approved a Presidential Study Directive of US global development policy. The QDDR, while a joint State–AID undertaking, was initiated and led by the State Department, while the Presidential Study Directive was run out of the National Security Council with broad participation by federal agencies interested in development policy. AID, lacking political appointees in its senior-most positions, was at a distinct disadvantage in its ability to influence either.

Secretary Clinton had strong opinions about the assistance program and how it should best be used. "I've always thought the debate between 'aid for aid's sake' and 'aid for strategic ends' was somewhat beside the point. We need to do both," said Clinton.[17] "I argued that we needed to draw a clear link between our aid work and US national security," she added. "There were some development professionals who disagreed with that view, but the president eventually accepted the premise that natural disasters, poverty, and disease in other countries were also threats to US strategic interests."

A central strand within both the Presidential Study Directive and the QDDR was to recognize the significantly evolving landscape for US assistance. Total donor assistance, which had been in decline through the post–Cold War 1990s, had spiked after September 11, 2001, roughly doubling from 1999 to 2009, and America regained its position as the largest single foreign assistance donor in the world, but the United States only represented about 22 percent of total official development assistance.[18] About half of the US non-military aid budget was dedicated to health programs and humanitarian relief.[19]

Large private entities, like the Bill & Melinda Gates Foundation, were now also donating billions of dollars to development. And unlike AID, such foundations were not ensnarled in endless layers of earmarks and red tape, making it easier for them to take risks and invest in innovative and over-the-horizon technologies. US private capital flows to the developing world now surpassed the foreign aid program by a factor of ten, and remittances alone also surpassed the size of AID's entire budget.

There were mounting concerns as both the QDDR and the Presidential Study Directive unfolded. The QDDR sprawled into a seemingly never-ending series of working groups exploring virtually every aspect of the operations at State and AID.

As deadline after deadline shifted, the wait for the QDDR became something of a running joke among think tanks and nongovernmental organizations in Washington. As Nancy Birdsall, the president of the Center for Global Development, commented, "The feeling then was: 'What is going on? Is it all about process?'"

There was also alarm about the lack of leadership at the agency. After nine months with no nominee to head AID, Republican senator Richard Lugar and Democratic senator John Kerry pleaded with the administration in a joint letter: "We believe that time is of the essence, and that the longer we wait for a new leader for the agency, the more serious the problems become."[20]

The physician Paul Farmer briefly emerged as a leading candidate to run AID before pulling his name from consideration. Alonzo Fulgham, a career officer at the agency who served as the acting AID administrator for most of 2009, deserves credit for running AID without the full political backing of Senate approval as the increasingly impatient aid community waited for word of a nominee.

Eventually the various logjams broke. Rajiv Shah was confirmed as administrator of AID the day before Christmas of 2009, and sworn into his post in early January 2010. President Obama had left the post vacant for 25 percent of his first term.

A physician by training, Shah briefly served as an under secretary and the chief scientist at the Department of Agriculture. His selection seems to have been considerably facilitated by the fact he had been confirmed for his position at the Department of Agriculture not long before. Shah had also served a seven-year stint at the Bill & Melinda Gates Foundation, where he had been director of agricultural development.

Shah's early comments made clear that he would bring a technocratic bent to the position. "I expect us to succeed in some of our efforts, and to fall short in others. I expect a strong evaluation function and feedback loop that enables us to be accountable in both cases, and to learn from each."[21]

While Obama and Shah were eager to put their stamp on the development program, there was also a clear realization that they were at a severe disadvantage vis-à-vis the Bush administration in their prospects for creating such a legacy. The Bush team had created the Millennium Challenge Corporation and PEPFAR, massive new commitments on top of already-inflated wartime investments in reconstruction in Afghanistan and Iraq. With the economic crisis and Republicans in Congress increasingly reflexive in their opposition to anything proposed by President Obama, the days of new money and new authorities were largely over. Consequently, the Obama administration's vision for development had to be harnessed around making existing programs work better and bringing the resources of new partners to the table.

A BATTERED HAITI

On January 12, 2010, just six days after Shah had been sworn in, Haiti was hit by 7.0-magnitude quake, with its epicenter a mere sixteen miles away from its capital, Port-au-Prince. The result was stunning devastation.

Haiti was already the poorest country in the western hemisphere, its development long stunted by a complex history of foreign exploitation, internal political turmoil, and violence. The country's building codes were lax to nonexistent, as was earthquake preparedness, and the country still had not fully recovered from a pair of major hurricanes in 2008.

Buildings across the country crumbled like poorly built towers of toy blocks. The three major hospitals suffered major damage. The National Palace, the National Assembly, Port-au-Prince cathedral, UN headquarters, and countless other buildings collapsed. The ports and airport in the capital were impassable. Hundreds of thousands of private homes, particularly those of the poorest, effectively disintegrated.

Haiti's infrastructure was already so limited, and the devastation so widespread, that the death toll from the quake remains a terrible unknown to this day, with estimates ranging from 80,000 to 300,000 fatalities. More than a million and a half people were left homeless. According to a study released at the time by the Inter-American Development Bank, which compared the earthquake to more than 1,700 other global disasters in the preceding decades, the Haiti earthquake was found to be one of the world's most devastating natural disasters since World War I when accounting for Haiti's size and economy.[22]

Footage of the wreckage helped trigger an enormous outpouring of donations and support from all over the world. International resources were mobilized to a remarkable degree. Within hours, AID had dispatched urban search-and-rescue teams from Florida and Virginia to help pull survivors from the rubble. In tense scenes, the teams from the United States and elsewhere, aided by specially trained dogs, pulled almost 150 people from collapsed structures.[23] AID would establish the largest Disaster Assistance Response Team it had ever mobilized for a natural disaster.

With the hospitals inoperable, the United States and the United Kingdom airlifted wounded earthquake victims to hospital ships positioned off the coast, but this would only provide for a fraction of those in need.

Efforts to deliver the enormous amounts of humanitarian assistance required were hindered by the collapse of the electric and telecommunications grids (which had been in poor shape even before the quake), blocked roads, and struggles to get the ports functioning. The search for survivors shifted to efforts to recover remains. Seven days after the quake, there were few signs that relief was reaching those outside the capital.

With more than a million people living without shelter, it was a race against time. AID and a range of partners made access to safe drinking water in the capital a priority, and it was an early, important success story in saving lives. Roughly three weeks after the quake, the municipal water authority in Port-au-Prince was producing a greater volume of clean water than it had before the earthquake.[24] More than a million people were receiving properly treated water by the end of April.

Back in Washington, AID was buffeted by political pressures and suffering to an extent from the slow pace of White House appointments. Not only had Rajiv Shah been on the job less than a week, all of the agency's senior positions, including the heads of the disaster office and the agency's overall humanitarian bureau, were filled by career officials in an "acting" capacity.

However, press coverage of Shah's response to the crisis at the time was glowing, with the *Washington Post* reporting that Shah "wowed the White House and State Department, with top officials in both places praising his steady leadership and command of the evolving operations in Port-au-Prince."[25] Shah's critical role in the Haiti response significantly raised his profile within the administration and with the president himself. As David Beckmann, the president of Bread for the World, put it, "The only good thing that came out of the Haiti earthquake is that it raised Raj Shah to be a partner of the president."[26]

The interest in the White House and the State Department in the Haiti situation was intense. Secretary Clinton had commissioned her chief of staff, Cheryl Mills, to prepare a series of recommendations on Haitian development even before the quake. This effort was near completion when the quake struck, and ultimately guided many of the efforts that followed.[27]

Former president Bill Clinton was named as a UN special envoy to Haiti to coordinate a remarkably disparate set of relief activities from organizations and charities large and small. There were signs of frustration all around. Haitian prime minister Jean-Max Bellerive complained that the patchwork of NGOs operating on the ground weren't keeping the government informed, making it impossible for the government to determine how it should deploy its own resources. NGOs countered that the government of Haiti was even more of a mess than usual, and that waiting for government approval or coordination would mean more lives lost.

An after-action report on AID's involvement in Haiti noted that many of the relief professionals at the agency did not fully appreciate the political sensitivities around the situation in Haiti.[28] President Obama's team, having seen how President Bush had been lambasted for the poor domestic response to Hurricane Katrina, wanted relief delivered with urgency. The White House also worried that a stalled relief effort could trigger a flood of refugees headed for Florida. Secretary Clinton—with her staff having been involved in Haiti planning before the quake, and her husband appointed the UN secretary general's special envoy—saw her office as a wellspring for reconstruction plans.

These dynamics combined to create a situation where AID was violating one of its core tenets of relief work: Plans and supplies were being "pushed" out of Washington rather than being "pulled" down by teams on the ground as they identified their needs and priorities.

Resources were not the problem. The US government allocated more than a billion dollars for Haiti in the years following the quake. Instead, the greatest problems stemmed from efforts to move from immediate lifesaving assistance to longer-term reconstruction that would rebuild housing and revitalize a dysfunctional economy.

Six months after the quake, hundreds of thousands of people were still living in tents. Significant numbers of Haitians fled to the countryside rather than remain squatting in precarious situations in the capital. Adding to the already precarious situation, in October 2010, a cholera outbreak erupted, tragically caused by a Nepalese contingent of UN peacekeepers. Close to ten thousand people were killed in the outbreak, with hundreds of thousands more sickened by the illness.

AID subsequently came under considerable criticism for both the tempo and quality of its reconstruction work. A June 2013 Government Accounting Office report found that AID, which was responsible for spending more than half of the total funds dedicated to Haiti, had only disbursed about one-third of the money available.[29] Attempts to rebuild a large port that serviced the Caracol Industrial Park ran two years behind schedule, and the agency's estimate of the number of houses it could rebuild was reduced by some 80 percent as a result of escalating costs.

BATTLING THE BELTWAY

In September 2010, Obama finally rolled out the Presidential Policy Directive defining a US global development policy, and in December of that same year, Clinton released the QDDR.

In a speech presenting the new development policy at the United Nations, President Obama argued that the review had made clear that progress depended on the choices of political leaders and the quality of institutions. He also indicated that the United States needed to make hard choices: "We must be more selective and focus our efforts where we have the best partners and where we can have the greatest impact."[30]

The strategic vision was straightforward. Once America selected a country to focus on as a good development partner, its revamped aid system would focus on sustained economic growth, innovation, and country "ownership"—that is, getting local input to determine priorities and tailor aid to meet those needs. In many ways, this expanded the core tenets of the Millennium Challenge Corporation and applied them more broadly.

But the hurdles to AID being more selective remained considerable, and the discipline which President Obama advocated was not always realized.

The Obama team approached the legacy of the Bush administration with considerable care. The Obama administration preserved the Millennium Challenge Corporation and maintained the overarching commitment to combat HIV/AIDS through PEPFAR.

In a move lauded by health experts, Obama also incrementally, but decidedly, shifted AIDS programming to focus more heavily on building up the health systems in developing countries rather than working around them to deliver emergency assistance. The United States would remain the global leader in combating HIV and AIDS, but developing countries would have to share a portion of that burden and better manage their own approach to health.

By 2012 the Obama administration targeted a once unthinkable goal: creating an AIDS-free generation, a remarkable shift from the despair of the early 2000s.[31] The core of the strategy was to further scale up prevention efforts, reduce the many gender barriers women and girls faced in accessing HIV-related services, and end discrimination against people living with HIV and AIDS. While the world is still far from achieving its goal of an AIDS-free generation, progress in stemming its tide still stands as a major accomplishment.

The Obama administration continued to make often unheralded progress against malaria. The World Health Organization estimated that more than six million deaths were averted between 2000 and 2015 as a result of global malaria control.[32] Most lives saved were those from a particularly vulnerable group: children under the age of five living in sub-Saharan Africa. Distributing millions of treated bed nets to keep mosquitoes away from people while they were sleeping was obviously an important part of the equation, but equally important to success was the increased use of data to inform how the program was managed, and increased reliance on household surveys to gain a more-accurate picture of how families were confronting malaria.

Obama also reversed a number of Bush-era approaches that he didn't think made sense. The Obama administration reestablished a policy office at AID and slowly gave AID back some, but not all, of the authority over its budget. And while this may sound like mere bureaucratic box shuffling, a federal agency without control of its budget or the ability to formulate policy is effectively neutered. As Nora O'Connell of Save the Children observed, reestablishing the policy shop at AID was "one of the biggest successes" of the early strategy reviews, and it helped reestablish AID as a thought leader on development and give it a seat at the table in broader discussions with the State Department and the White House.[33]

The Quadrennial Diplomacy and Development Review, when it was finally released, received more mixed reviews than the Presidential Policy Directive on development. Weighing in at 210 pages, the QDDR was a far longer document than the concise presidential directive and it reflected the long-running internal turf battles that had been fought beneath its surface.

Secretary Clinton, like Secretary Rice before her, wanted a stronger, better-funded AID. And, like Rice, she also wanted AID more closely under her control. The report included a call to add 5,500 new Foreign Service and civil service personnel. There was also considerable emphasis on the importance of "smart power" that projected America's influence through means other than raw military force.

Through the QDDR, the State Department assigned itself as the lead in all complex crises, eroding what had been AID's traditional lead role in dealing with man-made humanitarian emergencies through its Office of Foreign Disaster Assistance. Most such crises can only be effectively resolved by adroit diplomacy, but it was not obvious why the State Department saw the need to put itself in charge of operational aspects of response, such as the delivery of humanitarian assistance where it had little expertise.

Gerald Hyman expressed frustration that AID had gone from being an independent development agency to being steadily integrated into the State Department, and that this steady erosion had "discernable, negative effects on the quality of analysis, internal discourse, and decision-making."[34]

The QDDR and the Presidential Policy Directive presented almost competing visions for development, and AID's contribution to both had been hampered at the outset by its lack of senior political appointees in position as the strategies were crafted.

Regrettably, by the time the QDDR was released in 2010, the window for a collaborative approach to reform legislation had closed because Democrats had lost control of the House. Republicans gained a large majority in the House and narrowed Democratic Senate control to a razor-thin majority. On a whole range of issues, Obama would soon face unprecedented obstructionism from Congress, although—curiously—foreign assistance usually was not one of those issues.

For Raj Shah, there was little to be gained, and much to be lost, in giving priority to the messy churn of organizational debates that were swirling at the time he was appointed. But Shah did use these broader reviews as a chapeau under which he bundled a number of his key reforms and initiatives, branded somewhat amorphously as "USAID Forward."

He led the agency to release a series of formal policy papers on thematic issues on everything from global health to countering violent extremism. Not surprisingly, given his background, Shah supported the push already under way to restore the agency as a key player in agricultural development.

Shah placed considerable emphasis on AID embracing technology and innovation, which had been a hallmark of its approach in earlier decades, at a time when technology was unleashing new dynamism in developing countries. M-Pesa—a money-transfer system which British aid agency funding had helped to pioneer in Kenya—worked via mobile phone and was suddenly allowing millions of people access to banking services for the first time. AID pushed to expand these systems in multiple countries. One study found that mobile phone coverage in South Africa was associated with an increase of employment by 15 percent.[35]

Under his leadership, and generally in line with global trends, Shah made AID's program and budget data more transparent. The agency developed a new evaluation policy which it published in January 2011, and it made publicly available a wide range of its own evaluation reports from across the globe. Such monitoring and evaluation efforts were routine at the agency for much of its existence, yet were virtually eliminated after steep operating expense budget cuts in the late 1990s. Building on the earlier work of Andrew Natsios and Henrietta Fore, Shah placed considerable emphasis on the potential of public–private partnerships.

In January 2011 Shah unveiled his first major reform that he seemed to own from conception to implementation, although it had been shaped heavily by input from his mission directors. Driven by the agency's operations in Iraq and Afghanistan, AID had found that it was much harder to work with ministries and local officials in both countries through the filter of contractors. If AID was going to be held to account for results, it wanted the ability to engage much more directly in dialogue with the institutions that would be the real agents of change.

In blazing remarks, Shah drew parallels between the agency's reliance on for-profit firms and President Eisenhower's warnings about the emergence of powerful defense contractors. Shah complained that the "aid-industrial complex" of large contractors and grantees that worked with the agency had become an obstacle to effective development.

"Our industry is full of incentives designed to prolong our efforts rather than reduce them or enable transitions," said Shah. "As a result, handoffs rarely happen. Projects are extended in perpetuity while goals remain just out of reach. There's always another high-priced consultant that must take another flight to another conference or lead another training."[36] Shah pointed out that more than 90 percent of AID's grants and contracts went to US NGOs and for-profit firms, and insisted that AID would no longer be "writing big checks to big contractors and calling it development."

The data backed Shah up. At that point, AID's contractors received more than $3.19 billion a year, and more than 27 percent of the agency's overall funding was directed to American for-profit firms. To put this in perspective, if the for-profit contractor Chemonics were a country, it would have been the third-largest recipient of AID funding in the world in 2011, behind only Afghanistan and Haiti.

Shah's solution: to have 30 percent of the budget for implementing field missions' programs go to institutions and organizations in the developing world rather than to US NGOs and for-profit firms. Shah had considerable merit when arguing that building the capacity of local partners should be a high priority and that the agency had become far too reliant on American firms and nonprofits to carry out its work.

But the rollout of this new plan underscored how green Shah was in the ways of Washington.

Shah's rhetoric was ham-handed, and he had done little work in advance to build support for his plan on the Hill or in the development community more broadly. Shah unconstructively lumped together both for-profit contractors and nonprofit charities in his broadside. For-profit contractors quickly mobilized against the agenda with adroit and expensive lobbying on the Hill that claimed giving more money directly to developing countries would mean waste, fraud, and abuse. AID was forced to engage in extensive damage control.

Eventually, the administration came to realize more fully the difficulties of building capacity on the ground. It was labor-intensive and required considerable time and patience. NGOs warmed to the idea that more needed to be invested in local partners and capacities. While for-profit contractors were still not enamored of the idea, they achieved a détente with the administration after Shah and others walked back their commitment to hit a hard 30 percent target, calling this an "aspirational" goal.[37]

AID estimated that it more than doubled the aid dollars flowing to local partners, and a 2013 study by Oxfam America found that local development leaders gave AID positive marks for the efforts.

An interesting example of AID's increased reliance on local partners was AID's work with the Afghan Health Ministry, which helped foster a twenty-year jump in life expectancy in little more than a decade. An analysis by the Center for Global Development cited several important elements for this progress beyond the enormous level of resources which the United States funneled into Afghanistan.[38] The program was directed through the Ministry of Health rather than through outside contractors. The United States pooled funding with other donors, something it is usually reluctant to do. And most importantly, Johns Hopkins School of Public Health was contracted to evaluate whether the system was working and to provide continuous feedback.

Working with such local partners is obviously most effective in countries that have strong institutional capacity, but the lessons from AID's work with the Afghan Health Ministry suggest that it also has some applications in transition settings. Investing in local capabilities is ultimately the best way to achieve development that stands the test of time, yet it remained controversial more than fifty years into AID's existence.

A NEW TAKE

Expectations for President Obama from Africa were high, and highly unrealistic, from the start of his administration. Many assumed that since the president was African American, he would naturally devote disproportionate time and attention to the continent. Kenya declared a national holiday upon his election, and one Kenyan proclaimed to National Public Radio, "This is just a blessing from god."[39]

The fact that the administration knew it would not be in a position to deliver traditional big-ticket deliverables to Africa helped push the administration toward a more mature approach. Most African states also increasingly recognized that foreign aid alone would not drive lasting economic growth and prosperity. Perhaps the best single embodiment of this new attitude was the establishment of a common African position on key development priorities endorsed by African Union members in 2014.

President Obama also hosted the first-ever US–Africa leaders' summit which brought the leaders of fifty of the fifty-four African countries to Washington. One of the key concerns repeatedly expressed by the African leaders: expanding access to electricity. Energy poverty remained an enormous issue on the continent. To put it in perspective, the average American's refrigerator alone consumed about three times as much energy annually as did all the energy uses by the average Kenyan.[40] Some 90 percent of children in sub-Saharan Africa went to primary schools that did not have electricity.[41] That lack of power reduced productivity and limited educational opportunities.

President Obama launched the Power Africa initiative, with the goal of doubling access to electricity across sub-Saharan Africa. Power Africa used relatively modest amounts of US assistance to catalyze private-sector investment to improve Africa's electrification. The administration claimed that the program leveraged more than $20 billion of funding within two years.[42] While it is in many ways still early to judge how effective Power Africa is as a program, because electrification is by its nature a long-term endeavor, it was far more attuned to what African leaders cited as their key priorities than many traditional aid programs. It also seemed to symbolize a willingness to have AID operate differently than it had traditionally. Power Africa took on a set of issues where there wasn't already a strong programmatic focus at AID and underscored that if the agency was going to stay relevant, it would need at times to move out of its comfort zone of dealing predominantly with health and humanitarian assistance.

Power Africa was warmly received by congressional Republicans and Democrats. A Democratic administration got positive reviews for tackling an issue where private-sector leadership was essential. And in many ways, Power Africa may have been the administration's most sophisticated development package in that it was built around public–private partnerships, used limited US assistance dollars to mobilize funding from other sources, focused on practical policy reforms, and met an area of genuine need. This also spoke to Raj Shah's increasingly attuned political ear, and the considerable hard work he had invested in building up relationships on the Hill and across the development community.

There was growing recognition that Africa remained the next great developing market with both opportunities and challenges presenting themselves on an enormous scale. As a result of shifting attitudes and a less-paternalistic approach, assistance was being offered more in the spirit of partnership than it previously had been. In a welcome throwback to AID's early days, President Obama also established the Young African Leadership Initiative to train and invest in building the skills of emerging young civic leaders and entrepreneurs. The model was soon expanded to both Southeast Asia and the Americas.

Shah, to his credit, was eager to return the agency to the days when it had been known as a global innovator of new technologies and approaches to development. In the spring of 2014, AID launched its Global Development Laboratory, a cornerstone effort into which Shah invested years of work to ramp up research and attempt to bring new technologies to scale. Linked to this, AID also launched a Global Innovation Fund to pilot new social innovations in development. Although the culture at AID still remained significantly risk-averse, Shah thought the agency could afford to take more risks if it partnered smartly with universities and the private sector.

The emphasis on innovation carried through to AID's response to the Ebola epidemic that swept through West Africa in 2014. Shah announced an Ebola Grand Challenge to help design better gear for frontline medical responders. The winning team from Johns Hopkins University included Jill Andrews, a wedding dress designer from Baltimore. The team developed a protective medical suit that was far easier to use than the gear that was being used at the time—requiring eight, rather than twenty, steps to put on and take off, making it far less likely that first responders would be exposed to the deadly disease.

Shah's penchant for technology served the agency less well at other times, particularly when it came to light that AID had been operating Twitter accounts clandestinely in an effort to get young Cubans to revolt against the government. Senator Patrick Leahy of Vermont called the plan, "dumb, dumb, dumb" after it was revealed.[43] At the time the effort came to light, Leahy had been involved in efforts to release an AID contractor, Alan Gross, who had been arrested in Cuba in 2010, and the senator was concerned that the revelations would imperil efforts to release Gross.[44]

In 2015, Shah departed the administration after about five years on the job. (Interestingly, on the day he announced his departure, Cuba officially agreed to release Gross.[45]) "He was the rare administration official who drew support from Democrats and Republicans on Capitol Hill," reflected a *New York Times* profile. "As administrator, Mr. Shah sought to change the way America provided foreign aid. Rather than pouring billions of public dollars into programs to fight poverty, the agency used loan guarantees to get local banks and businesses to finance big projects, gave money directly to foreign development groups instead of to American contractors, and helped push for changes in the way the United States ran its program for international food aid."[46] Republican senator Lindsey Graham of South Carolina praised Shah as "a smart coalition builder who has brought a long overdue, transparent and businesslike approach" to running the agency.

Shah's relationship with Secretary of State Hillary Clinton was sufficiently strong that he was able to restore many of the policy and budget functions that had been stripped away during the Bush administration, but not so strong that he was able to entirely wrest budget control away from the State Department. And if there was a major complaint about Shah's tenure, it was that he pushed ideas forward faster than his own bureaucracy could digest them.

After some considerable delays in the confirmation process, Shah was succeeded by Gayle Smith in December 2015, the second woman to run the agency. Although Smith's time running the agency was fairly brief, she brought a wealth of experience to the post. Indeed, in many ways her appointment was recognition for a long career of service in Africa and international development.

Smith had spent two decades as a freelance reporter working across Africa and had served at the National Security Council, working on Africa and international development issues under both President Clinton and President Obama. She had helped lead Obama's Presidential Study Directive on global development. Although some human rights activists grumbled that Smith was too supportive of a number of African strongmen during her stints in government, her appointment was warmly received. Rock musician and Africa advocate Bono proclaimed, "Gayle's quick mind and wit are matched only by her huge heart and her tenacious, get-shit-done spirit."[47]

A BURST OF AGREEMENT

The Obama administration is in many ways remembered for its growing polarization, with many Republicans eager to delegitimize his presidency, questioning his citizenship, religion, and values. On most fronts, the Republican majorities in the House and Senate simply refused to consider legislation supported by the president.

There was one significant, and decidedly odd, exception: foreign aid. The tail end of the Obama administration saw a burst of action on a range of bipartisan legislation to improve the effectiveness of the foreign aid program, starting with the Water for the World Act in 2014, which emphasized the importance of clean drinking water in developing countries.

In February 2016, President Obama signed the Electrify Africa Act, which essentially codified Power Africa with bipartisan sponsors in both the House and the Senate. In July 2016, Obama signed into law the Global Food Security Act, cementing many elements of the administration's Feed the Future Initiative into law, again with bipartisan backing. Also in July 2016, Obama signed into law the Foreign Aid Transparency and Accountability Act, which required better monitoring and evaluation of US foreign assistance programs and made such evaluations more easily accessible to the public.

The burst of constructive, bipartisan congressional engagement around foreign assistance was in many ways a testament to the long hours Raj Shah and Gayle Smith had both put into cultivating personal relationships with members of Congress.

This period also saw a number of important global agreements on development. In 2011, former AID head Brian Atwood, then chair of the OECD Development Assistance Committee, helped major donors reach agreement on principles for effective development cooperation at a conference in Busan, South Korea.

And while the Bush administration had been initially cool to the Millennium Development Goals—a set of fifteen-year development targets set in 2000—the Obama administration was heavily involved in negotiating and championing the successor Sustainable Development Goals affirmed by the United Nations in 2015. Global interest in these goals was intense, and the process of formulating them took two years, including more than eight months of arduous negotiations among UN member states in New York.

Former White House chief of staff John Podesta, an ardent supporter of international development, was part of the United Nations panel that helped forge what was essentially the first draft of the Sustainable Development Goals, and he exerted considerable influence behind the scenes in getting agencies, including AID, to embrace some of the stretch positions within the goals.

Perhaps most notably, it was Podesta who helped convince President Obama to accept what became the tent pole within the Sustainable Development Goals: the commitment to end extreme poverty by 2030. In his 2013 State of the Union speech, Obama declared, "In many places, people live on little more than a dollar a day. So the United States will join our allies to eradicate such extreme poverty in the next two decades."[48]

This was a historic commitment, and it helped lend considerable impetus to the negotiations. In a significant change from the Millennium Development Goals, the Sustainable Development Goals also included a sweeping declaration to "leave no one behind" and ensure explicitly that groups that had traditionally been excluded in their own societies because of their gender, ethnicity, or caste would be included.

Lastly, and while obviously a larger issue than AID, the Obama administration helped lead the way in securing the Paris Agreement on climate change. While there are climate skeptics, they were relatively rare in the development community because most recognized that the impact of climate change is being felt disproportionately by the developing world—a cruel irony, given how little these countries had to do with driving climate change in the first place. And there is broad understanding in the development community that without far more rapid progress in addressing climate change, the development gains of the last several decades are acutely vulnerable.

Obama deserves credit for being the first US president to try to seriously come to grips with climate change and its implications for the global community.

The flurry of agreements at the end of the Obama administration struck hopeful notes for the development community. These agreements very much reflected Obama's approach: collaborative, multilateral, and evolutionary rather than revolutionary. Despite the worst global recession since the Great Depression and ongoing wars in Afghanistan and Iraq, Obama successfully maintained the increase of US assistance levels made during the Bush administration, a rather remarkable feat.

But there were lingering concerns that the reforms of the Obama years lacked deep roots. It was a proposition that would soon be tested.

12

Do as We Say, Not as We Do

On November 8, 2016, Donald Trump won the US presidential election in a result that stunned everyone involved, including Trump. Republicans also retained control of both the House and Senate.

For AID and the broader development community, the shock was difficult to describe. Development experts, including Republicans, had been unusually vocal in their opposition to Trump. More than 120 senior development and foreign policy leaders who had served in previous Republican administrations signed a letter during the election calling Trump unfit for office because of what they called his dishonesty, hateful anti-Muslim rhetoric, and admiration of foreign dictators.[1] With the distance of history, the charges may sound intemperate, but they were not unfounded.

Trump had made raw nativist appeals a central part of his platform and his identity. It was unsurprising then that he regularly bashed international assistance, saying "we should stop sending foreign aid to countries that hate us."[2]

President Trump also had a long and troubling record of embracing disinformation on important global health issues. In the early 1990s, he claimed that AIDS patients were intentionally spreading the disease.[3] In 2009, during an outbreak of swine flu, he argued that Americans should avoid flu vaccines.

Many at AID and elsewhere recalled Trump's extended Twitter commentary during the 2014 Ebola crisis in West Africa when he had called for US borders to be closed. A characteristic tweet declared, "People that go to faraway places to help out are great—but must suffer the consequences!"[4] As Gabriel Schoenfeld, an adviser to Mitt Romney, was left to lament, "The heartless panic-monger who launched this fusillade of tweets was a private citizen. Today, he is the president of the United States with responsibility for managing a public health crisis that could arrive on our shores."[5]

Career staffers at AID, as they do with every presidential transition, prepared lengthy briefing books for the incoming Trump team to help new political appointees get up to speed on key policy and managerial issues. Most at AID had assumed they would be handing those briefing books to Hillary Clinton staffers the day after the election. But with Clinton's loss, AID staff awaited the appearance of the Trump transition officials. Weeks and weeks passed, and no officials from the Trump team appeared. Managing AID did not appear to be a priority for Team Trump.

Many in the development community and at AID tried to put on a brave face as they waited with mounting anxiety for the administration to signal its intentions on development. Some felt that Trump would warm to the importance of foreign assistance as had earlier Republican presidents, such as Ronald Reagan.

Others argued that to fulfill Trump's campaign slogan to "Make America Great Again" would require renewed investments in development to nurture future markets. In the *New York Times*, former Republican senator Bill Frist of Tennessee pushed to maintain support for the President's Emergency Plan for AIDS Relief, insisting that combating AIDS was "a key element of America's national security strategy."

Like many presidents, Trump's first appointment on the international front was the secretary of state, with former oil company executive Rex Tillerson confirmed for the position. A series of questions from the Trump transition team were directed to career staffers at the State Department. Among the queries: "With so much corruption in Africa, how much of our funding is stolen?"[6] "Why should we spend these funds on Africa when we are suffering here in the U.S.?" "Are we losing out to the Chinese?"

Trump signed an executive order, which was subsequently legally contested at length, imposing a temporary ban on the United States accepting even a small, heavily vetted number of refugees from around the globe who had been displaced by war, conflict, and repression.

Another executive order, urged on the president by Vice President Mike Pence, expanded the Mexico City policy on international family planning programs far beyond the actions of any other Republican president, applying it not only to limit grants to family planning programs but to constrain all global health programs.

But research in the medical Journal *The Lancet* found that the Mexico City policy tended to increase abortions in the countries it examined by about 40 percent because it also usually came along with significantly reduced access to contraception.[7] "Regardless of what people personally believe about abortion," said Grant Miller, one of the co-authors of the study, "our evidence is consistent with what aid organizations have been saying, which is that this leads to a pretty big increase in abortions."[8]

Trump complained of foreign aid, "We give money to countries, but we don't give money to our own country," and claimed that Democrats didn't "even know the name" of the nations to which they directed foreign aid.[9] He also denounced developing countries for not being more grateful, adding, "They do nothing for us."

The US commitment to international development appeared to be facing a potential extinction-level event.

AN UNUSUAL RESISTANCE

Foreign assistance programs were targeted for substantial budget cuts. In keeping with Trump's intent to increase defense spending by $54 billion and pursue large tax cuts, White House officials announced that it would seek deep reductions of more than 30 percent to the aid program.[10] An indefinite hiring freeze was instituted at AID.

The proposed cuts to AID's budget included high-impact, low-cost efforts like the Famine Early Warning System, which was slated for elimination, as were a range of programs dealing with climate and gender. When the director of the Office of Management and Budget, Mick Mulvaney, unveiled the administration's budget blueprint in March 2017, he stated, "It is not a soft-power budget. This is a hard-power budget."[11]

Congress, including many Republicans, reacted with anger to President Trump's plans to sharply curtail the foreign aid program—a program that every Republican and Democratic president since World War II had supported.

Republican senator Lindsey Graham, often one of Trump's most unquestioning supporters, declared that Trump's cuts would be "dead on arrival."[12] Republican senator Marco Rubio of Florida said on Twitter that "foreign aid is not charity," and pointed out that it constituted less than 1 percent of the budget. Even Senate Majority Leader Mitch McConnell argued, "The diplomatic portion of the federal budget is very important, and you get results a lot cheaper frequently than you do on the defense side."

More than 120 retired generals and admirals signed a joint letter in response to the proposed foreign assistance cuts:

> We know from our service in uniform that many of the crises our nation faces do not have military solutions alone—from confronting violent extremist groups like ISIS in the Middle East and North Africa to preventing pandemics like Ebola and stabilizing weak and fragile states that can lead to greater instability. There are 65 million displaced people today, the most since World War II, with consequences including refugee flows that are threatening America's strategic allies in Israel, Jordan, Turkey, and Europe.[13]

Further adding to the anxiety over AID's fate, the White House issued an executive order calling for major reorganization plans for the executive branch. The old effort by Senator Helms to fold AID into the State Department appeared to be under renewed consideration. Secretary Tillerson's views toward foreign assistance remained largely opaque, although he seemed convinced that both State and AID could achieve the same results with significantly fewer staff. Tillerson had led ExxonMobil through a major reduction in its personnel, and he brought that same guiding philosophy with him to his new post.

Tillerson spent more than $10 million on outside consulting fees exploring how to reorganize both State and AID, and he warmed to the idea of cutting more than 2,300 posts at the two agencies.[14] AID, with no senior political leadership in place, was poorly positioned to advocate for its staff or its budget.

GOING GREEN

In May 2017, President Trump announced his nomination of Mark Green to head AID. The decision was striking in its normality. While many had feared the appointment of an ideologue fundamentally opposed to foreign aid in both concept and practice to pave the way for AID's elimination, Green would have been an unsurprising choice in almost any administration.

Green had been a four-term Republican congressman from Wisconsin and had served as the US ambassador to Tanzania under the second President Bush. His development credentials were solid: He had served as president of the International Republican Institute, which promotes democracy abroad, and he had served on the board of the Millennium Challenge Corporation and the nonprofit Malaria No More. He and his wife had taught English in Kenya as volunteers after graduating from college.[15]

In choosing leadership for the foreign aid program, Trump selected an individual who embraced the idea that foreign assistance both reflected American values and advanced core national interests, and who enjoyed considerable credibility with both Congress and the development community.

The appointment was in some ways an accident of geography: Green's nomination had been championed by White House Chief of Staff Reince Priebus and Speaker of the House Paul Ryan, who both hailed from Green's home state of Wisconsin. Neither Ryan nor Priebus would stay in Trump's good graces for long, and it is unlikely that Green would have gotten the nod at any different juncture during the Trump presidency.

Green's appointment evinced a sigh of relief among AID staff, development professionals, and allies. "Green's confirmation is a sign of hope," said Scott Morris of the Center for Global Development. "We will at least have a responsible actor overseeing this difficult and fraught process."[16] Few could imagine that Green would have accepted the job if his sole mission was to dismantle the agency or completely hobble its programs. The fact that Green had also served in Congress also sent a reassuring message that he would maintain good, if quiet, ties to the bipartisan group of senators and congressmen that supported the aid program.

During his confirmation hearings, Green struck a nonideological tone, saying, "[International development is one of those quiet places where Republicans and Democrats have long come together on a bipartisan basis. It was, after all, President

Bush who created MCC and PEPFAR, and then President Obama who launched Power Africa and Feed the Future."[17] Not surprisingly, Green also leaned heavily into the importance of public–private partnerships, maintaining, "There are literally trillions of dollars that could be mobilized for development."

Green's confirmation hearings were without controversy, and his nomination was easily approved. In many ways, Green became one of the least-criticized heads of AID in its history—primarily because those who cared about development felt that any replacement would likely be far worse. As Sarah Rose and Erin Collinson of the Center for Global Development said of Green, "He managed to walk a fine line to avoid appearing at odds with the administration, while simultaneously avoiding provoking lawmakers with a full-throated embrace of deep budget cuts."[18]

Thanks to strong bipartisan support on the Hill, funding for aid programs remained relatively flat. The Trump administration periodically requested large cuts in foreign assistance, but those efforts felt increasingly halfhearted, sometimes not even including details on which countries or programs the administration wanted to reduce. These efforts were consistently rejected by Congress.

COGNITIVE DISSONANCE

In January 2018, President Trump made headlines when his comments from a closed-door meeting at the White House with lawmakers from both parties were leaked to the press.[19] When a discussion about immigration turned to Africa, Trump interjected that America did not want immigrants from "all these shithole countries," saying he preferred immigrants from places "like Norway." In reference to Haitians the president asked, "Why do we need more?," adding, "Take them out."

The *New York Times* had reported a month earlier that Trump had complained in an immigration meeting that Haitian immigrants "all have AIDS," and that if Nigerian immigrants were allowed to enter the United States, they would never "go back to their huts."[20]

The United Nations Human Rights Office denounced Trump's comments as shameful and racist. Across Africa, US ambassadors were called in to foreign ministries and asked whether the president viewed their countries so poorly. The African Union expressed alarm with the president's remarks.

It felt like a candid moment for President Trump. He appeared to view the developing world as largely a place of pestilence and deprivation. He almost never articulated a reason why the United States would want to engage with such countries other than securing the rights to their oil and minerals. There was no recognition that the United States had enormously benefited over decades by engaging the developing world in commerce, the arts, science, and culture.

Trump and some of his key advisers, such as Steve Bannon, advocated spending as much on the military—and as little on diplomacy and development—as possible. Yet most generals recognized there were limits to the use of force. Just as diplomats could help prevent wars, international development saved countless lives through immunization programs and combating highly infectious diseases while shoring up critical institutions.

Trump consistently framed foreign aid as a transaction. Trump and other senior administration officials, such as Ambassador to the United Nations Nikki Haley, spoke about the importance of foreign aid for winning votes at the United Nations.[21] Using foreign aid to buy votes at the UN had proven neither smart nor effective over the years, and diplomats that needed aid dollars to swing ballots in New York tended not to be very good diplomats.

Trump and his team launched a Presidential Study Directive around the notion that foreign aid should first and foremost be about influence. "Moving forward, we are only going to give foreign aid to those who respect us and, frankly, are our friends," Trump told the United Nations.[22] An early draft of the directive argued that the United States should "reduce or eliminate foreign assistance to countries and international organizations that are working against or do not support United States interests." Nikki Haley accused developing countries of biting the hand that fed them, and it was clear that the administration deeply distrusted multilateral institutions, even though the United States had an outsized voice in shaping and directing them.

At AID, Mark Green steered clear of such inflammatory language. Although AID was experiencing growing tensions with Secretary Tillerson and his staff over potential reorganization proposals, Tillerson had fallen out of favor with the White House. (Among other transgressions, Tillerson was reported to have called Trump a "moron" in a meeting with Pentagon and National Security Council staffers. He also objected to the frequently problematic freelance diplomacy by Trump's son-in-law Jared Kushner across the Middle East.)

During a March 2018 tour of Africa launched in part to help contain the damage of President Trump's "shithole" remarks, Secretary Tillerson was fired over the phone by White House Chief of Staff Reince Priebus.

In April 2018, Mark Green unveiled a series of proposed reforms for AID. Tillerson's reorganization plans had effectively disappeared with his dismissal, and Green shrewdly used the window between Tillerson's departure and the confirmation of Mike Pompeo as the next secretary of state to make his case. Unlike Tillerson, Green's plans had been developed largely by his own career staff rather than consultants.

Green quietly worked behind the scenes and rolled out a reorganization effort that did its best to bridge the considerable gulf between the president's dismissive rhetoric about foreign aid and responsible development.

Green's signature approach to development was built around what he called the "journey to self-reliance." He argued that one of the guiding principles of the aid program should be charting a collaborative course with recipients to move them as quickly away from the need for assistance as possible. Green wanted to use extensive metrics and data to measure progress toward the goal of self-reliance and weave those advanced measurements into budget and program decisions. Toward that end, he developed a system of "roadmaps" as a tool to chart each aid recipient country's capacity and commitment as measured by objective criteria.[23]

The language bore striking resemblance to that used by presidents Kennedy and Johnson almost sixty years before. Green, unlike most of his predecessors in the modern era, did not stress initiatives built around specific sectors, but rather an approach to development in a country as a whole. And while this renewed country focus and emphasis on cross-cutting capacity building and commitment was welcome, congressional distrust of the administration's approach to development spurred a rash of new spending directives from Capitol Hill aimed at narrowing AID's flexibility.

Green also wanted to better organize the agency's humanitarian and conflict work, in part by merging offices that dealt with humanitarian relief and food aid. Green argued that his preferences were not driven by the draconian budget cuts that his own president repeatedly floated. "Our redesign has never been about the budget or a response to a budget. It's never been about staff size," Green told his staff. "It's been about pulling together the best ideas that we can find, some of them new, some of them not so new."[24] AID also showed a new willingness to measure the effectiveness of its programs against simply giving poor households cash.

As President Trump repeatedly sang the praises of authoritarian strongmen, Green argued in December 2018, "We don't just hand out money, and we won't just prop up the powerful. We insist upon the rule of law."[25]

AID also increasingly tried to position itself as an important counterbalance to Chinese influence in the developing world, an argument that resonated with the China hawks in important senior positions in the US government. Green argued that Chinese aid was really "predatory lending dressed up as assistance. It lures borrowers with promises of easy money but then straddles them with unsustainable levels of debt." He added, "Our approach—the American approach, on the other hand—moves countries from being recipients, to partners, to fellow donors. It's based upon the notion of a hand up, not a handout." The language here too harkened back to the Cold War, but as noted, few development practitioners were going to give Green a hard time given the political climate in which he was operating.

By mid-2019, Green had received congressional approval for the bulk of proposed organizational changes, a victory for Green's steady, low-key approach.[26] Where Secretary Tillerson had given serious consideration to dissolving AID, Secretary Pompeo seemed largely content to let Green manage the agency as he saw fit.

THE COST

In December 2019, China identified a growing cluster of pneumonia cases in the city of Wuhan, initially traced back to a seafood and poultry market. The virus was soon identified as COVID-19. Deaths quickly spiraled in Wuhan, and the city of more than ten million people was blocked off by Chinese authorities, with strict restrictions placed on movement and gatherings. By the end of January, the World Health Organization declared COVID-19 to be a global health emergency.

By February, deaths outside China began popping up, accelerated by the pace of international travel in a highly globalized age, with cruise ships particularly hard hit. Iran and Italy soon emerged as COVID-19 hot spots.

As the first case was identified in the United States in late January 2020, President Trump declared of COVID-19, "We have it totally under control."[27] A month later, as the number of cases continued to accelerate, Trump claimed that the number of cases in the United States would "be down close to zero" within days.[28]

Trump's proclivity to dismiss science and evidence in global public health would have devastating results as the United States faced the brunt of a global pandemic. The Trump administration had dismantled a pandemic task force led out of the National Security Council and sharply cut back the Centers for Disease Control staff in China.[29] Public health officials in the administration were dismissed from their posts for warning about the significant likely impact of COVID-19. The United States stumbled through early efforts to test and track COVID-19, and the president was often publicly skeptical of the measures recommended by his own epidemiological experts, such as social distancing and wearing a face mask, to slow COVID-19's spread.

It did not seem coincidental that three of those countries hardest hit—the United States, the United Kingdom, and Brazil—were all led by populist leaders who initially downplayed the severity of the pandemic and the need to prepare for it.

Not only did the United States suffer more than 400,000 dead as a result of the Trump administration's inept response to COVID-19, far more than any other country, it also marked the first time since the end of World War II that US leadership in response to a major global crisis was almost invisible. As the *Financial Times* observed, "American leadership in any disaster, whether a tsunami or an Ebola outbreak, has been a truism for decades," and yet in the face of a global pandemic, "History will mark COVID-19 as the first time that ceased to be true."[30] Rather remarkably, President Trump decided to freeze funding to the World Health Organization during the peak of the crisis, blaming the organization for not being more aggressive in its reporting about COVID-19 in China during the early stages of the pandemic. The move was roundly condemned.[31] Trump then gave notice that the United States intended to withdraw from the World Health Organization.

"Trump's handling of the pandemic at home and abroad has exposed more painfully than anything since he took office the meaning of America First," said William Burns, who had been the senior-most career US diplomat at the State Department before he left to head the Carnegie Endowment.[32] "America is first in the world in deaths, first in the world in infections, and we stand out as an emblem of global incompetence. The damage to America's influence and reputation will be very hard to undo."

AID was effective where it could be. It established a working group on COVID by January 2020 and activated an internal task force led by Dr. Ken Staley (who had earlier led US anti-malaria efforts) by March. Congress granted AID some additional funding and hiring flexibility in order to deal with the crisis. But as the United States moved into virtual lockdown and its economy reeled as more than twenty million people became unemployed in April 2020 alone, it was also clear that America had entered a period when it was going to be more focused on problems at home rather than abroad.[33]

The impact of COVID was felt throughout the developing world, even in locations where the number of infections was relatively low. The sharp decline of global economic growth and restrictions on travel and trade, as always, were felt most acutely by those living on the margins. The World Bank estimated that between forty to sixty million people would slip back into extreme poverty as a result of the pandemic.[34]

Amid this tumult, Mark Green announced that he was stepping down as head of AID in April 2020. The move had long been rumored, but it left the agency adrift at a crucial time. Green, as he did throughout his tenure, offered comments in defense of foreign assistance without directly criticizing his own administration's approach. "I think the crisis that we're all facing right now should serve as a reminder that these kinds of investments are important," said Green, "not just for our partners, they're important for us."[35]

Green deserves credit for guiding the agency through a tumultuous, exhausting period, and his departure brought kind words from a wide variety of quarters about his performance. Members of Congress, from both parties, also deserve considerable praise for acting in a bipartisan fashion to repeatedly turn back the deep and ill-advised budget cuts proposed by the White House. There has probably never been a broader, more-effective bipartisan coalition on Capitol Hill around foreign assistance than during the Trump era. The damage to the cause of development clearly could have been far worse.

That said, it is difficult to consider the record of the Trump years as anything other than wanton, careless destruction. Trump needlessly frayed the transatlantic alliance that has been the backbone of so much global progress to near a breaking point. He largely closed American shores to refugees. He sought to undermine many of the international institutions which the United States helped create to advance core goals in global health, trade, and peace. He essentially denied that climate change, perhaps the most serious issue facing the developing and developed worlds alike in coming years, existed. He slashed aid to Central America because of his anger with both legal and illegal immigration from these countries, making it harder, not easier, to address the underlying conditions which drove immigration in the first place.

Without Mark Green at the helm, AID increasingly became a dumping ground for Trump political appointees with more-extremist views. The White House appointed a religious freedom adviser at AID with a long history of anti-Muslim views who had earlier cheered mass incarceration of those practicing Islam.[36] The deputy White House liaison had a record of denouncing liberal democracy and feminism. The deputy chief of staff was an anti-transgender activist. In the waning months of the Trump administration the deputy administrator of AID, a Trump political appointee, was summarily dismissed via e-mail to allow the acting administrator to serve longer without being in violation of the law.

This period also underscores the fact that the overall effectiveness of US foreign assistance programs is deeply tied to the broader vision supporting them. Offering other nations assistance is not a dry, technical exercise. Foreign aid has always been most effective when coupled with a view of shared prosperity, values, and partnership. So, while AID continued to carry out democracy and governance programs during the Trump years, the impact of those programs was continually diminished by having a US president scoff at the notion that human rights and the rule of law were fundamental values. Trump's bitter fight to contest the presidential race he had so self-evidently lost in 2020 further corroded the long-cherished ideal that democracy in the United States was built around the stable and orderly transfer of power in free elections.

There was never a US president less committed to the intrinsic value of helping the poor and underprivileged of the developing world than Trump. Never was there a US president in the modern era who appeared to have such callous disregard of the basic human condition of those suffering from discrimination and a lack of opportunity. The fact that Trump himself was hospitalized with COVID-19 in October 2020 as he fought a losing re-election campaign against Joe Biden seemed an all-too-predictable coda to his presidency.

Trump's worldview, most often packaged under the "America First" banner, was that all international interactions were zero-sum in nature. Every deal, every agreement, and every exchange must have a winner and a loser. In sharp contrast, international development as an endeavor has always been built around an understanding that cooperation to support human development is a win-win. The People of Ghana, Zimbabwe, Laos, and Nepal can become healthier, better educated, and more prosperous with the people of the United States benefiting as well. The last smallpox case was eradicated in Somalia, thousands of miles from the shores of the United States, but the United States benefited enormously from that moment and many more like it. In many ways it seemed only fitting that the day after the US presidential election in 2020, Trump's withdrawal from the Paris Agreement on climate change became formal.

13

Conclusion

The United States Agency for International Development has been in existence for sixty years, and foreign assistance has been established as an important part of the American ethos.

If there is a single lesson about foreign assistance, it is that the people of the developing world are by far the greatest determinant of its success or failure. Foreign aid can provide resources, build the capacity of both individuals and institutions, and transfer vital knowledge about shared problems. Aid can provide incentives for reform and encouragement and support to local reformers. But it cannot, by itself, overcome entrenched resistance by those who benefit from bad policies or corrupt politics. Lasting development requires vision, resources, and commitment.

It is courageous local leaders, activists, entrepreneurs, academics, scientists, and advocates that ultimately bend a country's arc toward greater freedoms, better human conditions, and lasting prosperity. Those people are the ultimate heroes of this story.

Given the contentious history of foreign assistance, it is no surprise that debates about it have often been reduced to a single common denominator: *Does it work?* Over the years, the scholarly literature has, for the most part, answered with a qualified "Yes, some of the time; but it depends on the circumstances."[1]

There has certainly been a cottage industry highly critical of foreign aid. Books with titles like *The Road to Hell* and *Dead Aid* leave little suspense as to their view of assistance, painting these efforts as everything from incompetent to evil. Foreign aid has been criticized for interfering with the proper functions of free markets, propping up dictatorial strongmen, and lining the pockets of corrupt bureaucrats—all of which it has done at different times. On a more philosophical level, conservative political scientist Edward Banfield argued that "government may take from citizens and give to foreigners," but not if "all advantage will accrue to foreigners and none to citizens."[2]

Economists, by and large, have struggled to separate the impact of aid from the multitude of other forces influencing economic growth, accountable governance, education, and human health. Assistance has been offered across remarkably diverse geographies, political settings, and local conditions even before AID's creation. Trying to precisely attribute its impact rarely delivers tidy, linear judgments. The dynamics driving any country forward or back are extremely complex and driven by a host of interlocking historical, political, cultural, economic, and environmental factors, of which foreign assistance is only one.

Nobel Prize–winning economist Angus Deaton once huffed, "When the conditions for development are present, aid is not required. When local conditions are hostile to development, aid is not useful; and it will do harm if it perpetuates those conditions."[3]

One should look at the distress of economists such as Deaton with a degree of sympathy. How do you fairly evaluate US foreign assistance overall when, on the one hand, it helped make South Korea and Taiwan economic powerhouses but, on the other hand, squandered billions in Iraq, Afghanistan, and Vietnam? How do you properly value the worth of the foreign assistance that directed tens of millions of dollars to Mobutu Sese Seko in Zaire and which introduced simple, lifesaving health interventions that have saved the lives of millions of children around the globe? What is the value of a life saved? What is the cost of a strategic blunder?

The relative merits of aid become clearer when we step back and look at the world when AID was created compared to conditions today. In 1960, women in low- and middle-income countries had an average of more than five children. As of 2017, that number was more than halved.[4]

In 1960, life expectancy at birth in low- and middle-income countries was forty-seven years; by 2017, this number had risen to seventy-one.[5] Think of this figure not as a dry statistic but as a practical reality: The average person in the developing world was enjoying twenty-four more years of life in 2017 than in 1960. That is a remarkable advancement of the human condition within a breathtakingly short period of time.

In 1960, global GDP per capita in current US dollars was $452; by 2015 that number, adjusted for inflation, had leapt to more than $10,000.[6] Even for the countries categorized as least developed by the UN, GDP per capita rose from about $300 in 1980 to over $1,000 in 2015.[7]

While global data sources dating back to the 1960s are scarce in many important areas, between 1990 and 2018—again, a very narrow slice of time—the total number of deaths under the age of five dropped almost 58 percent—from 12.5 million to 5.3 million a year in the developing world.[8] In 1990, roughly a billion people were undernourished, a figure that was cut by almost 20 percent by 2018.[9]

The percentage of people living in extreme poverty—defined as living on less than $1.90 a day—fell from roughly 36 percent in 1990 to 10 percent in 2015.[10]

In 1976, the global adult literacy rate was 65 percent, with female adult literacy at only 56 percent.[11] By 2018, the global adult literacy rate stood at 86 percent,[12] with female adult literacy rates having climbed to roughly 83 percent.[13] And again, these are not just numbers. Access to education for girls means they live longer, achieve higher earnings, and have significantly healthier families.

Of course, the degree of credit foreign assistance deserves in this wave of progress is a complicated question. But when we take a step back, the debate over the efficacy of foreign aid is almost laughable. As this history has described, the United States and other donors have delivered lifesaving humanitarian assistance to millions upon millions of people since 1960; without that assistance the death toll from wars and famines during this period would have been far, far higher. There have been major, long-running campaigns against cholera, smallpox, malaria, and polio—with polio pushed to the brink of eradication and smallpox eliminated. Child survival programs, driven by oral rehydration therapy and immunizations, have been the driving force in the sharp reduction in infant mortality.

The push from donors helped millions of girls receive a basic education for the first time, and international family planning programs have been absolutely essential in allowing women to have smaller, better-cared-for families where they are not forced to constantly have more babies simply to stay one step ahead of grim actuarial odds. Advances in agricultural technology—most importantly, the Green Revolution—were often funded by foreign aid when there was not a clear market incentive to assist poor, smallholder farmers, and they have led to significant jumps in production and incomes. Market reforms have fueled major gains in growth across the developing world.

US leadership helped to put democracy promotion on the international development agenda, and while uneven, has had a positive impact on the growth of free governments over the years.[14]

In reality, any single one of these accomplishments would more than justify the rather paltry 1 percent of the federal budget that the United States expends on foreign assistance. How could an effort that saved millions of lives not be worth it? How could an endeavor, even though flawed, that contributed to the most rapid gains in human health and well-being in history, not be money well spent?

As William Gaud, one of AID's early leaders, argued, there are two basic reasons to provide foreign assistance: It is in our self-interest, and it is the right thing to do.[15] Foreign assistance has often been the embodiment of an effective "soft power" approach to the world for the United States, i.e., the ability to attract allies and partners rather than coerce them.

But of course, we can and should learn from what at times have been serious missteps.

First and foremost, we should recognize that AID's most prominent failures have come in instances where the United States tried to use foreign assistance as a blunt strategic instrument. Instrumentalizing foreign aid to help achieve short-term military or diplomatic aims has never worked well, and there is no indication it will do so in the future. This has often meant that bigger has not been better for the agency. Locations where AID has had its largest field presence have often delivered the most disappointing results: Vietnam in the 1960s and 1970s; Egypt in the 1980s and 1990s; and Afghanistan and Iraq in the wake of September 11.

Each of these settings involved high-profile national security priorities where resources and manpower were almost unlimited, but there was very little willingness to question how, or even if, development could work under such conditions.

As the persistent debate about merging AID into the State Department has highlighted, there have always been divergent strategic views of aid. Indeed, this debate represents a continuation of an argument that dates back to the origins of the Marshall Plan. When he formed AID, President Kennedy saw its central strategic goal as expanding the number of free-market democracies over the long run, which he in turn believed would make the United States more secure and more prosperous. Development was, in and of itself, achieving an important strategic aim fundamentally in line with our national character. The alternative view has been to use aid to gain short-term leverage and influence in countries willing to oppose communism or terrorism regardless of their actual commitments to democracy and free markets.

The tension between these two approaches has never been reconciled, and it is the reason that some of the secretaries of state most renowned for their diplomatic prowess seemed to value development the least. James Baker, under the first President Bush, helped appoint Ron Roskens to run the agency only to have him subsequently almost drive the agency off a cliff. Henry Kissinger wanted to dismantle the entire bilateral assistance program and place its functions in the World Bank. Kissinger and Nixon's systematic efforts to deny lifesaving humanitarian assistance to those reeling from the violence in East Pakistan in 1970 and 1971 as that country split apart from West Pakistan is a particularly shameful example of essentially weaponizing the assistance program.

Foreign aid should reflect the Kennedy strategic vision of democratic societies— free markets and free people; it should not be about getting countries to like the United States or to vote with it at the United Nations. The United States wants stable and prosperous democratic partners that are reliable allies in the long run. Sensible assistance programs can help build these relationships, even when the countries receiving assistance disagree with Washington on specific policy issues. For example, the Reagan administration did not approve when Costa Rica tried to broker peace in the conflicts raging in Central America during the 1980s. But it provided much-needed assistance that helped Costa Rica restore its battered economy and preserve that nation's leading role as a champion of democracy, human rights, and free trade in the region. Similarly, the United States and India were badly estranged at different points during the Cold War, but India remains the world's largest democracy and has emerged as one of America's most important allies in Asia—a good return on US assistance.

In short, when people talk about aid as merely a tool of diplomacy, they have it exactly backwards. Instead we should be talking about how diplomacy, like aid, is a critical tool to help achieve development. US ambassadors who encourage market reforms and investments in health and education by the countries where they are posted, rather than looking at the AID mission to help launch projects to curry favor with the government, are better serving US interests.

This is also why the aid program has often been its most effective when there has been strong presidential support for achieving key development goals, whether it was the Green Revolution or PEPFAR. What was often most striking in looking at AID's early historical records was the degree to which the White House directly involved itself in development planning and the willingness of presidents and their key advisers to directly push developing countries to embrace reform. When the White House makes development an important US foreign policy objective, it has enormous influence on the attitudes of the leaders of developing countries, the Departments of State, Treasury, and Defense, Congress, and public opinion.

Direct presidential involvement in the development program has waned over the years and speaks to a certain diminishment of AID as an agency. In AID's early years, the United States maintained outsized influence around the world and across much of the developing world, particularly Latin America. Other donors, and other sources of finance—either public or private—were just beginning to provide substantial flows to the developing world. This meant that AID as a donor, and as a vehicle for development policy, dominated the landscape as developing countries faced a stark choice between embracing Washington or aligning with global communism.

Today, there are dozens of donors around the globe. Almost all of them at one time or another have benefited from receiving US assistance, from the Marshall Plan onward. This is a notable achievement. Growing the community of donors was one of AID's foundational goals. By that measure, US leadership has been an unmitigated success, helping to mobilize enormous additional resources for development. In addition, as developing economies have grown, they have become increasingly attractive destinations for private capital and long-term investment, which was always the intended goal.

To take another example, growth and globalization have taken place so rapidly since AID's inception that remittances—the money sent back to the developing world from people now working outside of it—now dwarf the total sum of assistance provided by all donors combined. Overall, as more countries have grown out of poverty, their domestic resources and commercial and private transfers have become far more important than aid as sources of financing for their own development. So, in this sense, it becomes entirely understandable how AID, and US development policy in general, is far less influential than it was during the 1960s and 1970s. AID is but one voice of many, and that is not a bad thing.

But AID has also become less influential over the years for more troubling reasons. There is probably not a single member of the development community who feels that AID has not become excessively bogged down in rules, regulations, reporting, and earmarks imposed by Congress and its own bureaucracy. Requirement after requirement has been layered onto AID over the years as process has often crowded out substance. (This also explains why initiatives like PEPFAR and the Millennium Challenge Corporation were placed outside AID in recent years.)

Other than humanitarian assistance, it has become almost impossible for the agency to spend small amounts of money nimbly. AID today most likely could not do the innovative work it did in South Africa in the late 1980s in supporting anti-apartheid activists. Many projects now take years to get from design through approval to the point of being implemented. As *The Economist* argued, AID's "outdated and increasingly baroque legal and regulatory framework" continues to serve as a major drag upon its impetus.

Large, for-profit (and some nonprofit) development contractors have come to consume an outsized proportion of AID's budget—in part because they have program and management skills that are now in short supply at AID, as staff has been reduced, and in part because they are well-equipped to comply with all the rules and regulations required to compete for AID contracts and wait, usually for many months, until they are awarded.

AID's emphasis on compliance and perpetual concerns about being hectored by Congress has resulted in an excessive emphasis on investments that are easy to measure. While the emphasis on data and results are welcome, some of the most important parts of development are more challenging to measure and take a long time to produce quantifiable results. The agency, then, feels pressured to do two very different things: design and implement projects that achieve measurable improvement in key project indicators in the short term, while simultaneously fostering complex behavioral change and structural transformations over the long term.

Building up people and the institutions in which they serve is in many ways the heart of development. AID veterans broadly hail participant training programs, often involving American universities, as being central to some of the agency's most important successes. Large numbers of those trained by US assistance became highly influential in their own societies. Yet, long-term training of people, often with a generalist bent, is a classic example of an approach that has been abandoned over the years—not because it isn't effective, but simply because it was a hard-to-measure effort that fell out of favor.

Consider also the case of Peruvian economist Hernando de Soto, whose research AID largely underwrote for more than two decades. His groundbreaking findings on property rights helped illuminate the fact that millions of poor held property but lacked a legal title to such land, meaning that such informal holdings couldn't be used as collateral for lending.[16] De Soto changed how economists and development experts think about poverty and the informal economy, yet a strict evaluation of his work in its first several years would not have produced the kind of short-term hard results that Congress and others frequently expect out of AID.

Institution building is, by its nature, a long-term endeavor where immediate results are muddy. This history has noted many examples—the Korean Institute of Technology, Indian agricultural universities, and many more—which have had a tremendous payoff. Even so, Congress and many administrations have preferred more-instant gratification.

AID has taken on an increasingly disaggregated approach to development since the passage of New Directions legislation in the early 1970s. By focusing more heavily on specific sectors such as health and humanitarian assistance, the agency has maintained a reasonably effective constituency for its work. Unfortunately, at times it has also lost sight of the forest for the trees. The focus should remain on truly transformative change of economies, institutions, and societies as a whole, and AID has too often drifted away from that approach.

So, is there still a role for AID and US foreign assistance going forward? As the impact of COVID-19, its profound economic impact, and the slide backward toward poverty for tens of millions has made clear, there is still enormous work to be done in international development. Decades' worth of development progress is suddenly at risk. There remain millions of deaths that are easily preventable every year, and far too many people who remain trapped in despair simply by the accident of the conditions into which they were born. New technologies are opening up possibilities for transformation never seen before, and the decades of development experience have resulted in invaluable lessons of what works and what does not.

But it is also clear that AID itself is in need of more-radical transformation if it is going to address a new generation of challenges, such as climate change, helping countries fully take advantage of digital technologies, and better investing in fostering local capacity and commitment. Entropy and bureaucracy have steadily corroded America's ability to lead in development. Rather than yet another reorganization effort, the US government needs a far more drastic rethink about how it engages with the world.

Lastly, if the United States wants its commitment to development to be most effective, it must also examine itself with a more-critical eye. If the United States wishes to promote individual liberty in Africa, South Asia, and beyond, it must demonstrate respect for the rule of law at home. If Washington wants developing countries to embrace free markets, it should dismantle its own wasteful subsidies. If America wants developing countries to redress the conditions that leave too many of their citizens marginalized, it will need to be more forthright in addressing its own deep-seated patterns of discrimination. Foreign assistance remains a window to the world and a lasting reflection of ourselves—as powerful as it has been imperfect.

Acknowledgments

First, I want to acknowledge the innumerable contributions made by all the people at AID, past and present, who go about their jobs often under the most demanding conditions, and usually with little fanfare. Their talent and dedication have made the world a better place.

I owe thanks to many for their help and insight along the journey that was writing this book.

My family has been incredibly supportive of my work, even through the seemingly endless travails of 2020. Brenda, my wife, remains my best and truest muse and guide.

Carolyn Kenney was a fantastic research assistant and thought partner throughout and marched with good spirits through an incredible volume of material, covering more than six decades.

I also want to thank the many people who reviewed the text, including a handful of former AID administrators, who saved me from any number of self-inflicted blunders. Thanks also to Charles Kenny, a good friend and a fine author, who helped bring better focus to these pages, as did Curt Tarnoff and Larry Nowels, both formerly of the Congressional Research Service.

I want to express particular gratitude to the USAID Alumni Association for their support. Alexander Shakow, Carol Peasley, James Michel, Dan Runde, and the late John Sanbrailo all provided incredibly useful feedback, and they could not have been more gracious along the way. In addition, the alumni association helped underwrite my research efforts—although the words and opinions expressed here are solely my own.

I also appreciate the help and support from my terrific agent, Gail Ross, and the whole team at Rowman, particularly Jon Sisk, who first reviewed my manuscript. And lastly, I would like to thank you, the reader. I always welcome your feedback, criticism, and inquiries.

Endnotes

CHAPTER 1

1. US Department of State, *Highlights of President Kennedy's New Act for International Development* (Washington, DC: US Government Printing Office, 1961), 4–8.

2. Fritz Ermarth, *The Soviet Union in the Third World: Purpose in Search of Power* (Santa Monica, CA: Rand Corp, 1969), 1.

3. Jacob A. Rubin, *Your Hundred Billion Dollars: The Complete Story of American Foreign Aid* (Philadelphia: Chilton Company, 1964), 117.

4. James M. Hagen and Vernon W. Ruttan, *Development Policy Under Eisenhower and Kennedy* (Minneapolis: University of Minnesota, Economic Development Center, 1987), 8.

5. John A. Farrell, *Richard Nixon: The Life* (New York: Random House LLC, 2017), 264–66.

6. Thomas Oliphant and Curtis Wilkie, *The Road to Camelot: Inside JFK's Five-Year Campaign* (New York: Simon & Schuster, 2017), 90.

7. Dr. Michael Pillsbury, *Secret Successes of AID: With Declassified Documents on Economic Policy Reforms in Asia* (Washington, DC: National Defense University Press, 1999), 38.

8. Arthur M. Schlesinger Jr., *A Thousand Days: John F. Kennedy in the White House* (Boston: Mariner Books, 1965, 2002), 554.

9. Oliphant and Wilkie, *The Road to Camelot*, 91–92.

10. John Sanbrailo, "Extending the American Revolution Overseas: Foreign Aid, 1789–1850," *Foreign Service Journal* (March 2016), http://www.afsa.org/extending-american-revolution-overseas-foreign-aid-1789-1850; and David Cushman Coyle, "A Brief Survey of United States Foreign Economic Cooperation since 1945" (New York: The Church Peace Union, 1957), 1.

11. Foreign Policy Association, "Seminar Number One: The United States and the Developing Nations," American Leadership Seminars, Background Folio III, 1.

12. Robert C. Kennedy, "The First Mountain to Be Removed," *New York Times*, July 22, 1905, https://archive.nytimes.com/www.nytimes.com/learning/general/onthisday/harp/0722.html.

13. William E. Leuchtenburg, *Herbert Hoover: The American Presidents Series: The 31st President, 1929–1933* (New York: Henry Holt and Company, 2009), 161.

14. Jimmy Goodman, "Happy Birthday, Herbert Hoover: The Lost Legacy of a Hated President," *The Atlantic*, August 10, 2011, https://www.theatlantic.com/politics/archive/2011/08/happy-birthday-herbert-hoover-the-lost-legacy-of-a-hated-president/243406/.

15. US National Park Service, "The Emergence of the Great Humanitarian," Herbert Hoover National Historic Site, last updated October 25, 2018, https://www.nps.gov/articles/emergence-of-the-great-humanitarian.htm.

16. Franklin D. Roosevelt Presidential Library and Museum, "Our Documents: Lend Lease," http://docs.fdrlibrary.marist.edu/odlendls.html.

17. G. Edward Schuh, et al., "International Cooperation for Sustainable Economic Growth: The US Interest and Proposals for Revitalization," Report of a Task Force on Development Assistance and Economic Growth (1992), 11–12.

18. Congressional Budget Office, "The Role of Foreign Aid in Development" (May 1997), 16.

19. Schuh, et al., "International Cooperation for Sustainable Economic Growth," 21.

20. The Executive Secretariat of the International Cooperation Administration, "Economic Strength for the Free World, May 1953," in "Certain Reports and Proposals on Foreign Aid," (1956), 23.

21. Robert J. Donovan, *The Second Victory: The Marshall Plan and the Postwar Revival of Europe* (Lanham, MD: Madison Books, 1987), 28.

22. Ibid.

23. R. R. Palmer and Joel Colton, *A History of the Modern World* (New York: McGraw-Hill Publishing Company, 1984), 850.

24. US Department of Agriculture Famine Emergency Committee press release, April 5, 1946.

25. Donovan, *The Second Victory*, 31.

26. Ibid., 47.

27. John Norris, "Special Feature: A History of American Public Opinion on Foreign Aid," *Devex*, August 15, 2017, https://www.devex.com/news/special-feature-a-history-of-american-public-opinion-on-foreign-aid-90732.

28. Ibid.

29. Donovan, *The Second Victory*, 60.

30. Greg Behrman, *The Most Noble Adventure: The Marshall Plan and the Time When America Helped Save Europe* (New York: Simon & Schuster, 2007), 5.

31. Paul Fisher, *A Short History of the US Aid Program: The Development of Key Aid Concepts* (Washington, DC: US Agency for International Development, 1963), 25.

32. The Avalon Project, "Inaugural Address of Harry S. Truman," Yale Law School, https://avalon.law.yale.edu/20th_century/truman.asp.

33. US Library of Congress, Congressional Research Service, *Development Assistance Policy: A Historical Overview*, by Theodor W. Galdi (April 6, 1988), 4–5.

34. Samuel Hale Butterfield, *US Development Aid—An Historic First: Achievements and Failures in the Twentieth Century* (Westport, CT: Praeger, 2004), 3.

35. Harry S. Truman, *Memoirs by Harry S. Truman, Volume Two: Years of Trial and Hope* (Garden City, NY: Doubleday and Co., 1956), 232.

36. Butterfield, *US Development Aid*, 18–19; and Norris, "Special Feature: A History of American Public Opinion on Foreign Aid."

37. US Congressional Budget Office, "Enhancing US Security through Foreign Aid" (1994): 79, https://www.cbo.gov/sites/default/files/103rd-congress-1993-1994/reports/doc21.pdf.

38. Dawn M. Liberi, *No Longer on the Front Lines: US Bi-Lateral Assistance and the Role of the Agency for International Development* (Washington, DC: National Defense University, 1992), 4.

39. Commission on Foreign Economic Policy, *Report to the President and the Congress* (Washington, DC, 1954), 9.

40. Michael Meyer, "Still 'Ugly' After All These Years," *New York Times*, July 10, 2009, http://www.nytimes.com/2009/07/12/books/review/Meyer-t.html.

41. William J. Lederer and Eugene Burdick, *The Ugly American* (Greenwich, CT: Crest Giant, 1960).

42. US International Cooperation Administration, *Reply to Criticism in* The Ugly American (Washington, DC: The Administration, 1959), https://babel.hathitrust.org/cgi/pt?id=uc1.a0012146023;view=1up;seq=1#main.

43. Allen McDuffee, "'The Ugly American' Was a Scathing Critique of Our Bad Behavior Abroad—and It Became a Best Seller," *Timeline*, May 6, 2017, https://timeline.com/ugly-american-burdick-lederer-511f37a41590.

44. James M. Hagen and Vernon W. Ruttan, *Development Policy Under Eisenhower and Kennedy* (Minneapolis: University of Minnesota, Economic Development Center, 1987), 11.

45. US Congress, Senate Committee on Foreign Relations, *Technical Assistance in the Far East, South Asia, and Middle East*, Report of Senator Theodore Francis Green on a Study Mission (1956), 49–50.

46. Michael P. Todaro and Stephen C. Smith, *Economic Development*, 8th ed. (Boston: Addison Wesley, 2003), 112.

47. Hagen and Ruttan, *Development Policy Under Eisenhower and Kennedy*, 32–33.

48. The existing foreign assistance programs at that point included the International Cooperation Administration, the Development Loan Fund, the Agricultural Surplus programs (PL 480) run out of the Department of Agriculture, and the "soft loans" administered through the EXIM Bank. See Sean P. Duffy, *The Origins of the Agency for International Development: Foreign Assistance Reorganization in 1961* (Washington, DC: Agency for International Development, 1991), 1.

49. The Executive Secretariat of the International Cooperation Administration, "Certain Reports and Proposals on Foreign Aid," 73–74.

50. Rubin, *Your Hundred Billion Dollars*, 111.

51. The White House, "The Reorganization of Foreign Aid of 1961, Part I: The Foreign Aid Message of March 22, Prelude to Reorganization," Rough First Draft, Not for Distribution or Quotation, 20.

52. Oliphant and Wilkie, *The Road to Camelot*, 94.

53. Maurice Williams, interview by W. Haven North, May 15, 1966, ADST Oral History, 46, https://adst.org/wp-content/uploads/2013/12/Williams-Maurice.pdf.

54. Pillsbury, *Secret Successes of AID*.

55. Maurice Williams, "Foreword," in *US Development Aid: An Historic First* by Samuel Hale Butterfield (Westport, CT: Praeger, 2004), x.

56. Max F. Millikan and W. W. Rostow, "A New Foreign Economic Policy for the United States," *Christian Science Monitor*, May 31, 1956.

57. Ibid.

58. Pillsbury, *Secret Successes of AID*, 36, 54.

59. Ibid., 273.

60. Millikan and Rostow, "A New Foreign Economic Policy for the United States."

61. J. Galbraith, "A Positive Approach to Economic Aid," *Foreign Affairs*, 39 (1961): 444–57.

62. Pillsbury, *Secret Successes of AID*, 55–56.

63. Walt W. Rostow, "Walt W. Rostow Oral History Interview—JFK #1, 4/11/1964," interview by Richard Neustadt, John F. Kennedy Presidential Library and Museum (April 11, 1964), https://www.jfklibrary.org/sites/default/files/archives/JFKOH/Rostow%2C%20 Walt%20W/JFKOH-WWR-01/JFKOH-WWR-01-TR.pdf.

64. Oliphant and Wilkie, *The Road to Camelot*, 100–2.

65. The White House, "The Reorganization of Foreign Aid of 1961, Part I," 18.

66. Ibid.

67. Extract from "Report to the Honorable John F. Kennedy: Summary of Recommendations from the Task Forces," December 31, 1960, unpublished but available at the OMB Library, Washington, DC.

68. The White House, "The Reorganization of Foreign Aid of 1961, Part I," 31.

69. National Academy of Public Administration, "Making Organizational Change Effective: Case Analyses of Attempted Reforms in Foreign Affairs," A Report to the Commission on the Organization of the Government for the Conduct of Foreign Policy (1974), 7.

70. The White House, "The Reorganization of Foreign Aid of 1961, Part I," 25–26.

71. John F. Kennedy, "Inaugural Address," January 20, 1961, John F. Kennedy Presidential Library and Museum, https://www.jfklibrary.org/archives/other-resources/ john-f-kennedy-speeches/inaugural-address-19610120.

72. The White House, "The Reorganization of Foreign Aid of 1961, Part I," 50.

73. Schlesinger Jr., *A Thousand Days*, 591.

74. Duffy, *The Origins of the Agency for International Development*, 4–5.

75. Ibid., 4.

76. David E. Bell, "David E. Bell Oral History Interview—JFK #2, 1/2/1965," interview by William T. Dentzer Jr., John F. Kennedy Presidential Library and Museum (January 2, 1965), https://archive2.jfklibrary.org/JFKOH/Bell,%20David%20E/JFKOH-DEB-02/ JFKOH-DEB-02-TR.pdf.

77. Duffy, *The Origins of the Agency for International Development*, 4–5.

78. Schlesinger Jr., *A Thousand Days*, 590.

79. National Academy of Public Administration, "Making Organizational Change Effective," 12.

80. Hagen and Ruttan, *Development Policy Under Eisenhower and Kennedy*, 22.

81. Barry Riley, *The Political History of American Food Aid: An Uneasy Benevolence* (New York: Oxford University Press, 2017), 215.

82. Hagen and Ruttan, *Development Policy Under Eisenhower and Kennedy*, 25.

83. Bell, "David E. Bell Oral History Interview—JFK #2, 1/2/1965."

84. The White House, "The Reorganization of Foreign Aid of 1961, Part I," 86–87.

85. Bell, "David E. Bell Oral History Interview—JFK #2, 1/2/1965."

86. Jerome Levinson and Juan de Onis, *The Alliance That Lost Its Way* (Chicago: Quadrangle Books, 1970), 34.

87. John F. Kennedy, "Address at a White House Reception for Members of Congress and for the Diplomatic Corps of the Latin American Republics, March 13, 1961," John F. Kennedy Presidential Library and Museum, https://www.jfklibrary.org/archives/other-resources/john-f-kennedy-speeches/latin-american-diplomats-washington-dc-19610313.

88. Schlesinger Jr., *A Thousand Days*, 205.

89. *New York Times*, "A New 'Alliance for Progress,'" December 10, 1961, 8.

90. Tad Szulc, "'Allianza' Pleases Latins: Kennedy's Program to Provide for Development Wins Warm Response from Most Quarters," *New York Times*, March 18, 1961.

91. John F. Kennedy, "Special Message to the Congress on Foreign Aid," March 22, 1961, The American Presidency Project, https://www.presidency.ucsb.edu/documents/special-message-the-congress-foreign-aid-1.

92. Ibid.

93. This became the Development Assistance Committee of the OECD. See Helmut Fuhrer, *The Story of Official Development Assistance: A History of the Development Assistance Committee and the Development Co-Operation Directorate in Dates, Names and Figures* (Paris: Organisation for Economic Co-Operation and Development, 1996), 8–13, http://www.oecd.org/dac/1896816.pdf.

94. Joseph R. L. Sterne, "Kennedy Asks Long-Term Foreign Loans," *Baltimore Sun*, March 23, 1961.

95. Ibid.

96. Hagen and Ruttan, *Development Policy Under Eisenhower and Kennedy*, 17.

97. Butterfield, *US Development Aid*, 64.

98. Duffy, *The Origins of the Agency for International Development*, 4.

99. The White House, "The Reorganization of Foreign Aid of 1961, Part II: The Preparation of the President's Legislative Recommendations of May 26," Rough First Draft, 211–12.

100. Ibid., 50.

101. William S. Gaud, "William S. Gaud Oral History Interview—JFK #1, 2/16/1966," interview by Joseph E. O'Connor, John F. Kennedy Presidential Library and Museum (February 16, 1966), https://archive2.jfklibrary.org/JFKOH/Gaud,%20William%20S/JFKOH-WSG-01/JFKOH-WSG-01-TR.pdf.

102. Rubin, *Your Hundred Billion Dollars*, 113.

103. "Congressional Presentation: Hearings Begin on the Act for International Development," *ICA Digest*, June 9, 1961, 1–3, as cited in Duffy, *The Origins of the Agency for International Development*.

104. Ibid. As previously noted, George Ball had obtained international agreement to establish the Development Assistance Committee as a formal part of the new Organization for Economic Cooperation and Development. (See text accompanying note 128.)

105. "A Decade of Development," A Report on the Eighth National Conference on International and Social Development (Washington, DC, 1961), as cited in Duffy, *The Origins of the Agency for International Development*.

106. "Congressional Presentation: Hearings Begin on the Act for International Development," *ICA Digest* (1961): 1–3, as cited in Duffy, *The Origins of the Agency for International Development*.

107. Hagen and Ruttan, *Development Policy Under Eisenhower and Kennedy*, 19–20.

108. Ibid.

109. "Friends, Foes of Foreign Aid Join Issue: Clash on Capitol Hill," *ICA Digest* (1961): 1–4, as cited in Duffy, *The Origins of the Agency for International Development.*

110. William Gaud, "William Gaud Oral History Interview I," interview by Paige E. Mulhollan, November 28, 1968, LBJ Presidential Library, 3–4.

111. Bell, "David E. Bell Oral History Interview—JFK #2, 1/2/1965."

112. Levinson and de Onis, *The Alliance That Lost Its Way*, 64.

113. Ibid., 62.

114. Ibid., 65.

115. Ibid., 33.

116. Elliott R. Morss and Victoria A. Morss, *US Foreign Aid: An Assessment of New and Traditional Development Strategies* (Boulder, CO: Westview Press, 1982), 24.

117. *Reunion extraordinaria del Consejo Interamerican Economico y Social al nivel ministerial* (Washington, DC: Pan American Union, 1961), as cited in Levinson and de Onis, *The Alliance That Lost Its Way.*

118. Levinson and de Onis, *The Alliance That Lost Its Way*, 66–67.

119. L. Ronald Scheman, "The Alliance for Progress: Concept and Creativity," in *The Alliance for Progress: A Retrospective*, ed. Ronald L. Scheman (New York: Praeger, 1988), 12–13.

120. Duffy, *The Origins of the Agency for International Development*, 4.

121. The US Agency for International Development's name has been abbreviated in a wide and often confusing variety of ways since its creation, including, but not limited to: Aid, A.I.D., AID, US AID; USA.I.D., and AID. For purposes of clarity, the acronym used throughout the text here is simply "AID," even in cases where it was presented in one of its alternative forms in original text.

122. Hagen and Ruttan, "Development Policy Under Eisenhower and Kennedy."

123. Rubin, *Your Hundred Billion Dollars*, 100–1.

124. Fowler Hamilton, "Fowler Hamilton Oral History Interview—JFK, 8/18/1964," interview by Edwin R. Bayley, August 18, 1964, John F. Kennedy Presidential Library and Museum, https://archive2.jfklibrary.org/JFKOH/Hamilton,%20M.%20Fowler/JFKOH-MFH-01/JFKOH-MFH-01-TR.pdf.

125. César J. Ayala and Rafael Bernabe, Puerto Rico in the American Century: A History Since 1898 (Chapel Hill: University of North Carolina Press, 2007), 315.

126. Bell, "David E. Bell Oral History Interview—JFK #2, 1/2/1965."

127. *Washington Post*, "Injection of Vigor," November 8, 1961, https://search-proquest-com.dclibrary.idm.oclc.org/docview/141319319/A3B8110DFC27496BPQ/2?accountid=46320.

128. Robert H. Nooter, interview by W. Haven North, January 6, 1996, ADST Oral History, 6, 9–11, http://adst.org/wp-content/uploads/2013/12/Nooter-Robert-H.pdf.

129. By Executive Order 10973 of November 3, 1961, President Kennedy delegated to the secretary of state the bulk of his functions under the Foreign Assistance Act of 1961. (Some functions went to Treasury, Defense, and others.) The Executive Order directed the secretary of state to "establish an agency in the Department of State to be known as the Agency for International Development" to be "headed by an Administrator who shall be the officer provided for in section 624(a) (1) of the Act." (That means the officer "primarily responsible for carrying out Part I of the Act." The secretary of state, in turn, delegated many of those functions to the administrator, initially by letter and then by Delegation of Authority 104. So, technically, the Agency was formally established through a two-step process involving action, first, by the president, and then, second, by the secretary of state. The Executive Order and the

initial delegation to Administrator Fowler from Acting Secretary Chester Bowles were both published at https://www.govinfo.gov/content/pkg/FR-1961-11-07/pdf/FR-1961-11-07.pdf. Both documents have now been superseded.

130. David Martin, "JFK's Personal Connection to Army's Green Berets," *CBS News*, November 25, 2013, https://www.cbsnews.com/news/jfks-personal-connection-to-armys -green-berets/.

131. W. W. Rostow, *Eisenhower, Kennedy and Foreign Aid* (Austin: University of Texas Press, 1985).

CHAPTER 2

1. US Department of State, *Highlights of President Kennedy's New Act for International Development* (Washington, DC, 1961), 20.

2. Ibid.

3. UNICEF, "Progress in Reducing Child Deaths in Latin America and the Caribbean Has Been Substantial in the Past 40 Years," November 4, 2004, https://www.unicef.org/ progressforchildren/2004v1/latinCaribbean.php.

4. Richard Podol, interview by W. Haven North, September 12, 1996, ADST Oral History, 11, http://adst.org/wp-content/uploads/2013/12/Podol-Richard.pdf.

5. Charles Kenny and John Norris, "The River that Swallows All Dams," *Foreign Policy*, May 8, 2015, https://foreignpolicy.com/2015/05/08/the-river-that-swallows-all-dams-congo -river-inga-dam/.

6. Vincent W. Brown, interview by W. Haven North, May 1997, ADST Oral History, 19, 21, https://adst.org/wp-content/uploads/2013/12/Brown-Vincent-W.pdf.

7. Harvey E. Gutman, interview by Stuart Van Dyke, August 26, 1997, ADST Oral History, 6, 8, 11, http://adst.org/wp-content/uploads/2013/12/Gutman-Harvey-E.pdf.

8. Fowler Hamilton, "Fowler Hamilton Oral History Interview—JFK, 8/18/1964." AID is staffed by a complex mix of Foreign Service and civil service employees, Foreign Service nationals from the countries in which it works, a variety of contractors, and personnel detailed to AID from other US government agencies.

9. Ibid.

10. Schlesinger Jr., *A Thousand Days*, 594.

11. William S. Gaud, "William S. Gaud Oral History Interview—JFK #1, 2/16/1966."

12. Archibald Gordon MacArthur, interview by W. Haven North, February 12, 1999, ADST Oral History, 7, https://adst.org/wp-content/uploads/2013/12/MacArthur-Archibald -Gordon.pdf.

13. Foreign Policy Association, "Seminar Number One: The United States and the Developing Nations," American Leadership Seminars, Background Folio III, 17–18, date unknown.

14. Ibid.

15. Samuel H. Butterfield, interview by Harry Missildine, May 10, 1996, ADST Oral History, 13, https://adst.org/wp-content/uploads/2013/12/Butterfield-Samuel-H.pdf.

16. Melbourne L. Spector, interview by W. Haven North, September 12, 1996, ADST Oral History, 57, http://adst.org/wp-content/uploads/2013/12/Spector-Melbourne-L.-1996 .pdf.

17. Schlesinger Jr., *A Thousand Days*, 594.

18. Butterfield, *US Development Aid*, 61–62.

19. Spector, interview by W. Haven North.

20. John B. Rehm and Theodore Tannenwald Jr., interview by Melbourne Spector, January 21, 1997, ADST Oral History, 14, https://adst.org/wp-content/uploads/2013/12/Rehm-John-B.-and-Tannenwald-Theodore-Jr.pdf.

21. Rubin, *Your Hundred Billion Dollars*, 100–1.

22. Schlesinger Jr., *A Thousand Days*, 596.

23. Joseph Toner, interview by Melbourne Spector, October 31, 1989, ADST Oral History, 12, https://www.adst.org/OH%20TOCs/Toner,%20Joseph.toc.pdf.

24. Peter Askin, "The Great Turnaround in Latin America," in *Fifty Years in AID: Stories from the Front Lines*, eds. Janet C. Ballantyne and Maureen Dugan (Arlington, VA: Arlington Hall Press, 2012).

25. US Library of Congress, Congressional Research Service, *US Agency for International Development (AID): Background, Operations, and Issues* by Curt Tarnoff (2015), 5, https://fas.org/sgp/crs/row/R44117.pdf.

26. Walt Rostow, "Walt W. Rostow Oral History Interview—JFK#1, 4/11/1964," interview by Richard Neustadt, John F. Kennedy Presidential Library and Museum (April 11, 1964), 14, https://archive1.jfklibrary.org/JFKOH/Rostow,%20Walt%20W/JFKOH-WWR-01/JFKOH-WWR-01-TR.pdf.

27. Levinson and de Onis, *The Alliance That Lost Its Way*, 77. Quadros was succeeded by Vice President João Goulart, who was overthrown by a military coup in 1964.

28. Lawrence E. Harrison, interview by W. Haven North, December 12, 1996, ADST Oral History, 6–7, http://adst.org/wp-content/uploads/2013/12/Harrison-Lawrence-E.pdf.

29. Bernard Diederich, Somoza and the Legacy of US Involvement in Central America (New York: Dutton, 1981), 21.

30. David Jickling, interview by W. Haven North, September 14, 1998, ADST Oral History, 10–11, 13–14, http://adst.org/wp-content/uploads/2013/12/Jickling-David.pdf.

31. Rubin, *Your Hundred Billion Dollars*, 178.

32. Robert D. Schulzinger, *US Diplomacy Since 1900* (New York: Oxford University Press, 1998), 262.

33. Jickling, interview by W. Haven North, 23.

34. Carlos Osorio and Marianna Enamoneta, "To Save Dan Mitrione Nixon Administration Urged Death Threats for Uruguayan Prisoners," *National Security Archive Electronic Briefing Book* 324 (2010), https://nsarchive2.gwu.Juneedu/NSAEBB/NSAEBB324/index.htm.

35. Richard R. Fagen, "Death in Uruguay," *New York Times*, June 25, 1968, https://www.nytimes.com/1978/06/25/archives/death-in-uruguay-uruguay.html.

36. Such assistance was banned in 1974, and only later incrementally reauthorized in the 1980s and 1990s within the broader context of support for democratic governance, combating narcotics traffic, and counterterrorism.

37. Bell, "David E. Bell Oral History Interview—JFK #2, 1/2/1965."

38. Schlesinger Jr., *A Thousand Days*, 595.

39. Jickling, interview by W. Haven North, 10–11, 13–14.

40. Donor M. Lion, Letter to David E. Bell, August 11, 1966.

41. Judy C. Bryson, interview by W. Haven North, March 13, 1998, ADST Oral History, 14, https://adst.org/wp-content/uploads/2013/12/Bryson-Judy.oh1_.pdf.

42. Schlesinger Jr., *A Thousand Days*, 551.

43. Ibid.

44. Madeleine G. Kalb, "The C.I.A. and Lumumba," *New York Times*, August 2, 1981, https://www.nytimes.com/1981/08/02/magazine/the-cia-and-lumumba.html.

45. Williams, interview by W. Haven North.

46. Harvey E. Gutman, interview by Stuart Van Dyke, August 26, 1997, ADST Oral History, http://adst.org/wp-content/uploads/2013/12/Gutman-Harvey-E.pdf.

47. W. Haven North and Jeanne Foote North, "Transformation Trends in Government and Democracy—US Bilateral Foreign Economic Assistance (USFEA): Perpetual Transformations," June 20, 2006, draft.

48. Schlesinger Jr., *A Thousand Days*, 555.

49. Ibid., 558.

50. Bell, "David E. Bell Oral History Interview—JFK #2, 1/2/1965."

51. Schlesinger Jr., *A Thousand Days*, 558.

52. Anthony Miles Schwarzwalder, interview by W. Haven North, ADST Oral History (December 27, 1997), 4–6, https://adst.org/wp-content/uploads/2013/12/Schwarzwalder Anthony-M-1.pdf.

53. Ibid.

54. Anne O. Krueger and Vernon W. Ruttan, "The Development Impact of Economic Assistance to LDCs, Volume 1," Prepared for the Agency for International Development and the Department of State (1983), 15–1.

55. Daniel Yergin and Joseph Stanislaw, *The Commanding Heights: The Battle Between Government and the Marketplace that Is Remaking the Modern World* (New York: Simon & Schuster, 1998), 83–88.

56. Thomas G. Patterson, ed., *Kennedy's Quest for Victory: American Foreign Policy, 1961–1963* (New York: Oxford University Press, 1992), 280.

57. Schlesinger Jr., *A Thousand Days*, 573.

58. *Washington Post*, "How the Aluminum Deal Foiled Ghana," December 14, 1980, https://www.washingtonpost.com/archive/opinions/1980/12/14/how-the-aluminum-deal-foiled-ghana/f8bc342e-8ecc-48bf-b5e1-456d2e92c8df/.

59. Yergin and Stanislaw, *The Commanding Heights*, 83–88.

60. *Washington Post*, "How the Aluminum Deal Foiled Ghana."

61. J. N. Fobil, Remediation of the Environmental Impacts of the Akosombo and Kpong Dams in Ghana (Horizon Solutions, 2008), https://www.solutions-site.org/node/76.

62. *Washington Post*, "How the Aluminum Deal Foiled Ghana."

63. Hariadene Johnson, interview by W. Haven North, September 8, 1998, ADST Oral History, 19, http://adst.org/wp-content/uploads/2013/12/Johnson-Hariadene.pdf.

64. Barbara Ward, "Personal and Confidential Memo to David Bell—Assistance to India and Pakistan," June 14, 1965.

65. Butterfield, *US Development Aid*, 73–75; and John P. Lewis, "Reviving American Aid to India: Motivation, Scale, Uses, Constraints," in *India: A Rising Middle Power*, ed. John W. Mellor (Boulder, CO: Westview Press, 1979), 321.

66. Ibid.

67. Foreign Policy Association, "Seminar Number One—The United States and the Developing Nations," American Leadership Seminars, Background Folio III, 29–30, no date.

68. Ward, "Personal and Confidential Memo to David Bell."

69. US Agency for International Development, "Principles from East Asia: The Case of Taiwan" (Washington, DC: USAID Development Information Services, 2003), 2–5.

70. Pillsbury, *Secret Successes of AID*, 88, 94, 98.

71. US Library of Congress, Congressional Research Service, *US Agency for International Development (AID): Background, Operations, and Issues*, by Curt Tarnoff (2015), 5, https://fas.org/sgp/crs/row/R44117.pdf.

72. US Agency for International Development, "Principles from East Asia," 2–5.

73. Butterfield, *US Development Aid*, 205.

74. US Agency for International Development, "Principles from East Asia," 2–5.

75. Butterfield, *US Development Aid*, 204–5.

76. US Agency for International Development, "Principles from East Asia," 2–5.

77. Pillsbury, *Secret Successes of AID*, 88, 94, 98.

78. Ibid.

79. David E. Bell, Handwritten Notes, "Beyer—Hong Kong—2 Jan 63," January 2, 1963.

80. US Agency for International Development, "Principles from East Asia," 2–5.

81. Bell, "David E. Bell Oral History Interview—JFK #2, 1/2/1965."

82. Ibid.

83. Rufus Phillips, *Why Vietnam Matters: An Eyewitness Account of Lessons Not Learned* (Annapolis, MD: Naval Institute Press, 2008), 76–77.

84. Rufus Phillips, "Counterinsurgency in Vietnam: Lessons for Today," *Foreign Service Journal* (2015), http://www.afsa.org/counterinsurgency-vietnam-lessons-today.

85. Butterfield, *US Development Aid*, 91–92.

86. Ibid., 90–93.

87. William S. Gaud, "The Role of Foreign Aid in US Foreign Policy," Presentation to the Cabinet, August 25, 1966, LBJ Presidential Library.

88. Harvey E. Gutman, interview by Stuart Van Dyke, August 26, 1997, ADST Oral History, 17, http://adst.org/wp-content/uploads/2013/12/Gutman-Harvey-E.pdf.

89. US Department of State Office of the Historian, "Memorandum from Robert H. Johnson of the Policy Planning Council to the Director of the Council (Rostow)," by Robert H. Johnson (February 15, 1962), https://history.state.gov/historicaldocuments/frus1961-63v02/d63.

90. Phillips, *Why Vietnam Matters*, 103.

91. Ibid., xiv.

92. Ambassador Princeton Lyman, interview by Charles Stuart Kennedy, May 12, 1999, ADST Oral History, 16–17, http://www.adst.org/OH%20TOCs/Lyman,%20Princeton.toc.pdf.

93. Seth Jacobs, *Cold War Mandarin: Ngo Dinh Diem and the Origins of America's War in Vietnam, 1950–1963* (Lanham, MD: Rowman & Littlefield, 2006), 123–25.

94. Phillips, *Why Vietnam Matters*, 183–86.

95. David E. Bell, "Notes Made During a Visit to Special Forces HR, Ft. Bragg, NC, 1964," November 25, 1964.

96. Thomas Lueck, "Otto Passman, 88, Louisiana Congressman Who Fought Spending," *New York Times*, August 14, 1988.

97. Rubin, *Your Hundred Billion Dollars*, 104–5.

98. William S. Gaud, "William S. Gaud Oral History Interview—JFK #1, 2/16/1966."

99. Foreign Policy Association, "Seminar Number One—The United States and the Developing Nations," 17–18.

100. Lueck, "Otto Passman, 88, Louisiana Congressman Who Fought Spending."

101. Gaud, "William Gaud Oral History Interview I," 13.

102. David E. Bell, "Remarks of David E. Bell, Administrator, Agency for International Development at the Arkansas Economic Education Workshop," July 11, 1963, Little Rock, Arkansas.

103. Fisher, *A Short History of the US Aid Program: The Development of Key Aid Concept*, 20.

104. Rubin, *Your Hundred Billion Dollars*, 111.

105. Ibid., 110.

106. Foreign Policy Association, "Seminar Number One—The United States and the Developing Nations," 27–28.

107. William S. Gaud, "William S. Gaud Oral History Interview—JFK #2, 2/21/1966," interview by Joseph E. O'Connor, February 21, 1966, John F. Kennedy Presidential Library and Museum, https://archive2.jfklibrary.org/JFKOH/Gaud,%20William%20S/JFKOH -WSG-02/JFKOH-WSG-02-TR.pdf.

108. Edwin R. Bayley, "Edwin R. Bayley Oral History Interview—JFK #2, 12/19/1968," interview by Larry J. Hackman, December 19, 1968, John F. Kennedy Presidential Library and Museum, http://archive1.jfklibrary.org/JFKOH/Bayley,%20Edwin%20R/JFKOH-ERB-02/JFKOH-ERB-02-TR.pdf.

109. Bell, "David E. Bell Oral History Interview—JFK #2, 1/2/1965."

110. David E. Bell, "David E. Bell Oral History Interview—JFK #1, 7/11/1964," interview by Robert C. Turner, Transcript, July 11, 1964, John F. Kennedy Presidential Library and Museum, https://archive1.jfklibrary.org/JFKOH/Bell,%20David%20E/JFKOH-DEB-01/JFKOH-DEB-01-TR.pdf.

111. Rubin, *Your Hundred Billion Dollars*, 53.

112. David E. Bell, "David E. Bell Oral History Interview—JFK #1, 7/11/1964."

113. Schlesinger Jr., *A Thousand Days*, 597.

114. David Bell, "David Bell Oral History Interview I," interview by Paige E. Mulhollan, December 27, 1968, LBJ Presidential Library, 16–18, 20.

115. Bell's credentials going into the job were solid. He had served as an administrative executive to President Truman and Kennedy's budget director. Equally important, he had served as an economic adviser in Pakistan during the Eisenhower administration.

116. Butterfield, *US Development Aid*, 60–61.

117. Ambassador Princeton Lyman, interview by Charles Stuart Kennedy, 18.

118. Vernon W. Ruttan, *United States Development Assistance Policy: The Domestic Politics of Foreign Economic Aid* (Baltimore, MD: Johns Hopkins University Press, 1996), 209.

119. Schlesinger Jr., *A Thousand Days*, 597.

120. David E. Bell, Handwritten Notes, "Presidential Call in High Dudgeon," June 14, 1981.

121. Ibid.

122. General Lucius D. Clay, "Press Briefing to the Committee to Strengthen the Security of the World," March 22, 1963.

123. Ibid.

124. L. D. Clay, *The Scope and Distribution of US Military and Economic Assistance Programs* (Washington, DC: US Department of State, 1963).

125. Schlesinger Jr., *A Thousand Days*, 598.

126. David E. Bell, Handwritten Notes, "Presidential Call in High Dudgeon."

127. Bell, "David E. Bell Oral History Interview—JFK #2, 1/2/1965."

128. *Business Week*, "Foreign Aid Cuts Jolt White House," August 31, 1963.

129. Ibid.

130. Rubin, *Your Hundred Billion Dollars*, 114.

131. Senator Gale W. McGee, *Personnel Administration and Operations of Agency for International Development—Report of Senator Gale W. McGee to the Committee on Appropriations* (Washington, DC: US Government Printing Office, 1963), 24.

132. Rubin, *Your Hundred Billion Dollars*, 55.

133. W. W. Rostow, Memo to AID—David Bell, "Future of Foreign Aid," November 13, 1963.

134. At that time, membership of the US-led OECD Development Assistance Committee had expanded to include Belgium, Canada, Denmark, France, Germany, Italy, Japan, Netherlands, Portugal, United Kingdom, United States, and the Commission of the EEC.

135. Ruttan, *United States Development Assistance Policy*, 266.

136. Robert Dallek, *An Unfinished Life: John F. Kennedy, 1917–1963* (New York: Back Bay Books, 2003).

137. *WBUR*, "Kennedy Records Private Thoughts on Vietnam," November 21, 2013, http://www.wbur.org/news/2013/11/21/kennedy-records-private-vietnam.

138. Spector, interview by W. Haven North, September 12, 1996, 62.

139. Bell, "David E. Bell Oral History Interview—JFK #2, 1/2/1965."

140. Ibid.

141. Schlesinger Jr., *A Thousand Days*, 1029.

142. Gordon W. Evans, interview by Barbara S. Evans, December 9, 1988, ADST Oral History, 32, http://adst.org/wp-content/uploads/2013/12/Evans-Gordon-W.pdf.

143. Robert H. Nooter, interview by W. Haven North, January 6, 1996, ADST Oral History, 6, 9–11, http://adst.org/wp-content/uploads/2013/12/Nooter-Robert-H.pdf.

CHAPTER 3

1. Adam Wernick, "LBJ Knew the Vietnam War Was a Disaster in the Making. Here's Why He Couldn't Walk Away," *The World*, September 8, 2017, https://www.pri.org/stories/2017-09-08/lbj-knew-vietnam-war-was-disaster-making-heres-why-he-couldnt-walk-away.

2. Executive Office Building, "Memorandum for the Record of a Meeting," FRUS 1961–1963, vol. 4 (Washington, DC, November 24, 1963), Vietnam, 635–37, as cited in Phillips, *Why Vietnam Matters*.

3. Phillips, *Why Vietnam Matters*, 217.

4. William Walker, "Mixing the Sweet with the Sour," in *The Diplomacy of the Crucial Decade: American Foreign Relations During the 1960s*, ed. Diane B. Kunz (New York: Columbia University Press, 1994), 89–92.

5. Stephen G. Rabe, *The Most Dangerous Area in the World: John F. Kennedy Confronts Communist Revolution in Latin America* (Chapel Hill: University of North Carolina Press, 1999), 173.

6. *New York Times*, "US May Abandon Effort to Deter Latin Dictators," March 19, 1964, https://www.nytimes.com/1964/03/19/archives/us-may-abandon-effort-to-deter-latin-dictators-mann-is-said-to-be.html.

7. US Department of State, Office of the Historian, "Foreign Relations of the United States, 1964–1968, Volume XXXI, South and Central America; Mexico," https://history.state.gov/historicaldocuments/frus1964-68v31/d10.

8. Max Holland, ed., "Lyndon Johnson, John McCormack, and Otto Passman on 29 November 1963," Tape K6311.05, PNO 12, Presidential Recordings Digital Edition—The Kennedy Assassination and the Transfer of Power, vol. 1 (Charlottesville: University of Virginia Press, 2014), http://prde.upress.virginia.edu/conversations/9010163.

9. Robert David Johnson and David Shreve, eds., "Lyndon Johnson and Larry O'Brien on 12 December 1963," Tape K6312.08, PNO 4, Presidential Recordings Digital Edition—The Kennedy Assassination and the Transfer of Power, vol. 2 (Charlottesville: University of Virginia Press, 2014), http://prde.upress.virginia.edu/conversations/9020167.

10. Felix Belair Jr., "House Panel Cuts Aid $800 Million; Defies President," *New York Times*, December 14, 1963.

11. Lyndon B Johnson, "Notes from George Ball Telcon," May 13, 1964, LBJ Presidential Library.

12. George Ball and David Bell, "George Ball–David Bell Telephone Transcript, 12:45 p.m., 14 December 1963," Box 2, George Ball Papers, LBJ Presidential Library.

13. Robert Komer and George Ball, "Telephone Conversation, 6:55 p.m., 13 December 1963," Box 2, George Ball Papers, LBJ Presidential Library.

14. Office of the White House Press Secretary, Press Release, December 14, 1963.

15. Robert David Johnson and David Shreve, eds., "Lyndon Johnson, John McCormack, and Carl Albert on 20 December 1963," Tape K6312.12, PNOs 3 and 4, Presidential Recordings Digital Edition—The Kennedy Assassination and the Transfer of Power, vol. 2 (Charlottesville: University of Virginia Press, 2014), http://prde.upress.virginia.edu/conversations/9020265; and Robert David Johnson and David Shreve, eds., "Lyndon Johnson and Albert Thomas on 20 December 1963," Tape K6312.12, PNO 1, Presidential Recordings Digital Edition—The Kennedy Assassination and the Transfer of Power, vol. 2 (Charlottesville: University of Virginia Press, 2014), http://prde.upress.virginia.edu/conversations/9020263.

16. Lyndon Johnson and Jack Brooks, "LBJ on the Foreign Aid Budget," December 20, 1963, Conversation No. K6312-13-05, Miller Center, https://millercenter.org/the-presidency/educational-resources/lbj-on-the-foreign-aid-budget.

17. Max Frankel, "Funds for Foreign Aid," New York Times, December 22, 1963, 4.

18. US House of Representatives, "A Rare Christmas Eve Session," December 24, 1963, https://history.house.gov/HistoricalHighlight/Detail/35448?ret=True.

19. R. Dungan, "Notes on George Ball Telcon, December 16, 1963," LBJ Presidential Library.

20. Rowland Evans and Robert Novak, *Lyndon B. Johnson: The Exercise of Power: A Political Biography* (New York: New American Library, 1966), 354–55.

21. Edwin R. Bayley, "Edwin R. Bayley Oral History Interview—JFK #2, 12/19/1968," interview by Larry J. Hackman, December 19, 1968, John F. Kennedy Presidential Library and Museum, http://archive1.jfklibrary.org/JFKOH/Bayley,%20Edwin%20R/JFKOH-ERB-02/JFKOH-ERB-02-TR.pdf.

22. Robert David Johnson and David Shreve, eds., "Lyndon Johnson and Ralph Dungan on 17 December 1963," Tape K6312.09, PNO 10, Presidential Recordings Digital Edition—The Kennedy Assassination and the Transfer of Power, vol. 2 (Charlottesville: University of Virginia Press, 2014), http://prde.upress.virginia.edu/conversations/9020205.

23. Robert David Johnson and David Shreve, eds., "Lyndon Johnson and Wayne Morse on 23 December 1963," Tape K6312.16, PNOs 9 and 10, Presidential Recordings Digital Edition—The Kennedy Assassination and the Transfer of Power, vol. 2 (Charlottesville: University of Virginia Press, 2014), http://prde.upress.virginia.edu/conversations/9020331.

24. Associated Press, "AID Panel: Split-Up Studied," *New York Herald Tribune*, December 28, 1963.

25. Tad Szulc, "Drastic Change Sought in Goals for Foreign Aid," New York Times, January 4, 1964.

26. Ibid.

27. Senate Foreign Relations Committee Report No. 588 of October 22, 1963, as cited in the President's Committee to Examine the Foreign Assistance Program, "Hall Working Group Outline," December 26, 1963.

28. David Bell, "David Bell Oral History Interview I."

29. Guian A. McKee, ed., "Lyndon Johnson and Ralph Dungan on 28 April 1964," Tape WH6404.14, Citation #3161, Presidential Recordings Digital Edition—Toward the Great Society, vol. 6 (Charlottesville: University of Virginia Press, 2014), http://prde.upress.virginia.edu/conversations/9060098.

30. Orville Freeman, "Orville Freeman Oral History Interview III," interview by T. H. Baker, July 21, 1969, LBJ Presidential Library, 2–4, 6, http://www.lbjlibrary.net/assets/documents/archives/oral_histories/freeman/freeman%20web%203.pdf.

31. Riley, *The Political History of American Food Aid*, 288.

32. Ibid., 233.

33. "Notes from AID/Gaud—George Ball Telcon," October 7, 1965, LBJ Presidential Library.

34. David Bell, "David Bell Oral History Interview I," 42.

35. John Deaver, note to McGeorge Bundy containing "a draft of a memorandum on Mr. Clifford's Non-Committee," December 3, 1965, LBJ Presidential Library.

36. Gordon Chase, "The Foreign Assistance Program—A Survey of the Record," Remarks made February 20, 1967, St. Joseph, Michigan, 8–9.

37. Donald S. Brown, interview by W. Haven North, December 4, 1996, ADST Oral History, 16, https://adst.org/wp-content/uploads/2013/12/Brown-Donald-S.pdf.

38. Rowland Evans and Robert Novak, "Inside Report . . . Black Days for Otto," Washington Post, May 22, 1964.

39. "The World Food Problem," Discussion Paper for NSC Meeting on July 19, 1966, LBJ Presidential Library.

40. Alan Berg, "AID's Nutrition History (The Early Years)," 2–3. Unpublished paper written to contribute to "Nourishing Lives and Building the Future: The History of Nutrition at USAID," June 25, 2019.

41. "The World Food Problem," Discussion Paper for NSC Meeting on July 19, 1966.

42. Butterfield, *US Development Aid*, 86.

43. Riley, *The Political History of American Food Aid*, 237.

44. Berg, "AID's Nutrition History," 2–3.

45. Krueger and Ruttan, "The Development Impact of Economic Assistance to LDCs," 8-1 to 8-2, 8-7 to 8-8, 8-21 to 8-22.

46. Ibid.

47. The President's Committee to Study the United States Military Assistance Program, "Volume 1: Composite Report of the President's Committee to Study the United States Military Assistance Program," (Washington, DC, 1959), 94–97, http://edocs.nps.edu/2012/December/pcaaa444.pdf.

48. Phyllis Tilson Piotrow, *World Population Crisis: The United States Response* (Westport, CT: Praeger, 1973), 45.

49. Schlesinger Jr., *A Thousand Days*, 600.

50. John Norris, "Kennedy, Johnson and the Early Years," *Devex*, July 23, 2014, https://www.devex.com/news/kennedy-johnson-and-the-early-years-83339.

51. W. Haven North and Jeanne Foote North, "Transformations in US Foreign Economic Assistance," in *Foreign Aid and Foreign Policy—Lessons for the Next Half-Century*, eds. Louis A. Picard, Robert Groelsema, and Terry F. Buss (New York: M. E. Sharpe, 2008), 272.

52. Robert W. Barnett, "Population: Policy and Program," March 25, 1966, College of Physicians and Surgeons at Columbia University, LBJ Presidential Library.

53. Schlesinger Jr., *A Thousand Days*, 601.

54. Barnett, "Population: Policy and Program."

55. Butterfield, *US Development Aid*, 86.

56. Barnett, "Population: Policy and Program."

57. James Howe, interview by Samuel Butterfield, April 24, 1997, ADST Oral History, 12, http://adst.org/wp-content/uploads/2013/12/Howe-James.pdf.

58. Herman Kleine, interview by W. Haven North, February 14, 1996, ADST Oral History, 54–55, http://adst.org/wp-content/uploads/2013/12/Kleine-Herman.pdf.

59. Marshall D. Brown, interview by W. Haven North, December 4, 1996, ADST Oral History, 23, https://adst.org/wp-content/uploads/2013/12/Brown-Marshall-D.pdf.

60. Stuart Van Dyke, interview by Scott Behoteguy, September 18, 1997, ADST Oral History, 10–12, http://adst.org/wp-content/uploads/2013/12/Van-Dyke-Stuart.pdf.

61. Lawrence E. Harrison, interview by W. Haven North, December 12, 1996, ADST Oral History, 11–15, http://adst.org/wp-content/uploads/2013/12/Harrison-Lawrence-E.pdf.

62. Jack Heller and Charles Montrie, "Mid-Decade Evaluation—Alliance for Progress," August 9, 1965, memo to James Howe.

63. US Congress, Senate, Committee on Foreign Relations, *Some Important Issues in Foreign Aid*, report prepared by the Legislative Reference Service of the Library of Congress at the request of Senator Bourke B. Hickenlooper (Washington, DC: US Government Printing Office, August 4, 1966), 21–22.

64. Joseph Kraft, "Food for Aid," *New York Times*, November 24, 1965, 12.

65. W. W. Rostow, "Program for the OAS Summit," January 27, 1967, Memorandum for the President, LBJ Presidential Library.

66. See troop levels reported at https://www.americanwarlibrary.com/vietnam/vwatl.htm.

67. Butterfield, *US Development Aid*, 93–94; and Fraleigh, quoted from Harvey C. Neese and John O'Donnell, eds., *Prelude to Tragedy: Vietnam, 1960–1965* (Annapolis, MD: Naval Institute Press, 2001), 116.

68. Neese and O'Donnell, *Prelude to Tragedy*, 231–32.

69. Ruttan, *United States Development Assistance Policy*, 276–77.

70. McGeorge Bundy, "The Situation in Vietnam," February 7, 1965, Memorandum for the President, LBJ Presidential Library.

71. Notes from the 547th NSC Meeting, "Subject: David Bell's Return," February 8, 1965, LBJ Presidential Library.

72. R. W. Komer, Memorandum for Secretary McNamara, March 29, 1967, LBJ Presidential Library.

73. North and North, "Transformations in US Foreign Economic Assistance," 274.

74. Bradshaw Langmaid, interview by W. Haven North, July 14, 1998, ADST Oral History, 8, http://adst.org/wp-content/uploads/2013/12/Langmaid-Bradshaw.pdf.

75. NSC Papers, "Cabinet AID Review: Summary (Draft)," November 3, 1965, LBJ Presidential Library.

76. Krueger and Ruttan, "The Development Impact of Economic Assistance to LDCs," 13-25.

77. Princeton Lyman, "Building a Political-Economic Approach to Development," The American Political Science Association (1970), 16.

78. Vernon W. Ruttan, *The Future of US Foreign Economic Assistance* (Minneapolis: University of Minnesota, Department of Agriculture and Applied Economics, 1991), 6.

79. Pillsbury, *Secret Successes of AID*, 101.

80. Nooter, interview by W. Haven North, 37–39.

81. Pillsbury, *Secret Successes of AID*, 105.

82. Ambassador Princeton Lyman, interview by Charles Stuart Kennedy, 19–20.

83. Eric Chetwynd, interview by W. Haven North, May 17, 1999, ADST Oral History, 22, 26, https://adst.org/wp-content/uploads/2013/12/Chetwynd-Eric-Jr.pdf.

84. Krueger and Ruttan, "The Development Impact of Economic Assistance to LDCs," 13-7.

85. Butterfield, *US Development Aid*, 206–7.

86. Roger Ernst, interview by Arthur Lowrie, March 3, 1997, ADST Oral History, 37–38, available at http://adst.org/wp-content/uploads/2013/12/Ernst-Roger.pdf.

87. Vincent W. Brown, interview by W. Haven North, May 1997, ADST Oral History, 24–27, available at https://adst.org/wp-content/uploads/2013/12/Brown-Vincent-W.pdf.

88. Ibid.

89. Krueger and Ruttan, "The Development Impact of Economic Assistance to LDCs," 13-43 to 13-44.

90. Butterfield, *US Development Aid*, 206–7.

91. Lane Holdcroft, interview by Charles Christian, September 18, 1995, ADST Oral History, 7–8, http://adst.org/wp-content/uploads/2013/12/Holdcroft-Lane.pdf.

92. Ambassador Princeton Lyman, interview by Charles Stuart Kennedy, 25.

93. Krueger and Ruttan, "The Development Impact of Economic Assistance to LDCs," 13-47 to 13-49.

94. Leonard Rogers, interview by Mark Tauber, April 18, 2017, ADST Oral History, 19, https://adst.org/wp-content/uploads/2013/12/Rogers-Leonard-1.pdf.

95. David C. Cole, *Lucky Me: Engaging a World of Opportunities and Challenges* (CreateSpace, 2014), 150.

96. US Congress, Senate, Committee on Appropriations, *Personnel Administration and Operations of Agency for International Development*, report of Senator Gale W. McGee to the Committee on Appropriations (Washington, DC: US Government Printing Office, November 29, 1963), 1–18.

97. Lyman, interview by Charles Stuart Kennedy, 28.

98. Vincent W. Brown, interview by W. Haven North, 24–27.

99. "Note on Korea Aid Prepared for the 1965 Cabinet Review of Foreign Aid," December 25, 1965, LBJ Presidential Library.

100. Annex Paper on "Self-Help and Foreign Aid," to a Memorandum on "A New Self-Help Provision in the Foreign Assistance Legislation," December 9, 1966, LBJ Presidential Library.

101. Pillsbury, *Secret Successes of AID*, 105.

102. James Fox, *Applying the Comprehensive Development Framework to AID Experiences* (The World Bank, 2000), 3–6.

103. North and North, "Transformations in US Foreign Economic Assistance," 274.

104. David Reynolds, *One World Divisible: A Global History Since 1945* (New York: W. W. Norton, 2000).

105. North and North, "Transformations in US Foreign Economic Assistance," 274.

106. Fox, *Applying the Comprehensive Development Framework to AID Experiences*, 3–6.

107. Reynolds, *One World Divisible*.

108. Vincent W. Brown, interview by W. Haven North, 24–27.

109. Madison Broadnax, interview by W. Haven North, September 18, 1998, ADST Oral History, 23, http://adst.org/wp-content/uploads/2013/12/Broadnax-Madison.pdf.

CHAPTER 4

1. Krueger and Ruttan, "The Development Impact of Economic Assistance to LDCs," 12-7 to 12-8, 12-12 to 12-17.

2. R. W. Komer, Memorandum for the President, August 31, 1965, LBJ Presidential Library.

3. David Reiff, "Where Hunger Goes: On the Green Revolution," *The Nation*, February 17, 2011, https://www.thenation.com/article/archive/where-hunger-goes-green-revolution/.

4. Riley, *The Political History of American Food Aid*, 256–58.

5. Ibid., 264–65.

6. US Congress, Senate, Committee on Foreign Relations, *Some Important Issues in Foreign Aid*, 36, 49.

7. John P. Lewis, "Policy Based Assistance: An Historical Perspective on A.I.D.'s Experience and Operations in India/Asia in a Bilateral and Multilateral Context," July 1989, as cited in Pillsbury, *Secret Successes of AID*.

8. Freeman, "Orville Freeman Oral History Interview III," interview by T. H. Baker, 2–4, 6.

9. John Lewis, *India's Political Economy* (Delhi: Oxford University Press, 1997), 126.

10. Rob W. Komer, "RWK Memos to the President and Mr. Bundy on Expiration of PL 480 Agreement W/ India (April 30–June 17, 1965)," John F. Kennedy Presidential Library and Museum.

11. Rob W. Komer, Letter to McGeorge Bundy, June 18, 1965, LBJ Presidential Library.

12. Ibid.

13. US Agency for International Development, *AID's Legacy in Agriculture Development: 50 Years of Progress* (Washington, DC: USAID, November 2013), 29, https://www.AID.gov/sites/default/files/documents/1867/AID-Legacy-in-Agricultural-Development.PDF.

14. John P. Lewis, "Policy Based Assistance."

15. Ibid.

16. McGeorge Bundy and R. W. Komer, "India and Pakistan," October 5, 1965, Memorandum for the President, LBJ Presidential Library.

17. NSC Papers, "Cabinet AID Review: Summary (Draft)," November 3, 1965, LBJ Presidential Library.

18. David E. Bell, Memorandum for the Secretary, December 29, 1965, LBJ Presidential Library.

19. Riley, *The Political History of American Food Aid*, 245.

20. Lewis, *India's Political Economy*, 130.

21. R. W. Komer, "President's Meeting with Indian Ambassador Nehru," February 3, 1966, Memorandum for the record, LBJ Presidential Library.

22. John P. Lewis, "Indian Economic Prospects on the Eve of the Prime Minister's Visit to the President," March 21, 1966, letter to Robert W. Komer, LBJ Presidential Library.

23. Lewis, *India's Political Economy*, 130.

24. Freeman, "Orville Freeman Oral History Interview III," interview by T. H. Baker 9–11.

25. Riley, *The Political History of American Food Aid*, 293.

26. Ibid., 288.

27. David Bell, "David Bell Oral History Interview I," 35–41.

28. Williams, interview by W. Haven North, 49–51.

29. Ibid., 49–51.

30. David Bell, "David Bell Oral History Interview I," 35–41.

31. Riley, *The Political History of American Food Aid*, 299.

32. Ibid., 303.

33. *Time* magazine, "The Administration: Bell's Toll," July 8, 1966.

34. Guian A. McKee, ed., "Lyndon Johnson and Richard Russell on 11 June 1964," Tape WH6406.05, Citations #3680 and #3681, Presidential Recordings Digital Edition—Mississippi Burning and the Passage of the Civil Rights Act, vol. 7 (Charlottesville: University of Virginia Press, 2014), http://prde.upress.virginia.edu/conversations/9070062.

35. Felix Belair Jr., "Bell Quits Post as AID Director," *New York Times*, June 28, 1966.

36. Donald S. Brown, interview by W. Haven North, 16.

37. *Evening Star*, "Gaud, AID Nominee, Known as Workhorse," June 29, 1966.

38. *Washington Post*, "Promotion at A.I.D.," July 16, 1965.

39. Office of the White House Press Secretary, "Remarks of the President at the Swearing-In Ceremony for William Gaud as Administrator of the Agency for International Development," August 3, 1966.

40. Krueger and Ruttan, "The Development Impact of Economic Assistance to LDCs," 12-38 to 12-39.

41. US Department of State, "India-Pakistan Problems," August 17, 1966, Memorandum of conversation, LBJ Presidential Library.

42. Lyndon B. Johnson, notes on a memo from Bromley Smith, August 24, 1966, LBJ Presidential Library.

43. Harold Saunders and W. Howard Wriggins, "Indian Food: Odds and Ends," December 2, 1966, Memorandum for WWR, LBJ Presidential Library.

44. William S. Gaud, "Task Force on Foreign Aid," Memorandum for The Honorable Joseph A. Califano Jr., Special Assistant to the President, November 23, 1966, LBJ Presidential Library.

45. Summary paper on "India's Food Crisis, 1965–67," no author, no date, LBJ Presidential Library.

46. Nicholas deb. Katzenbach and William S. Gaud, "India Food," August 9, 1967, Memorandum for the President, LBJ Presidential Library.

47. Eugene V. Rostow, "India Food: Conditions for Food Matching Our Commitment," August 19, 1967, Memorandum for the Secretary, LBJ Presidential Library.

48. J. Anthony Lukas, "US Delay on Food Is Assailed in India," *New York Times*, November 29, 1966, https://search-proquest-com.dclibrary.idm.oclc.org/docview/117635934/AC2E 6DD33A8247E0PQ/1?accountid=46320.

49. Robert Komer, "Robert Komer Oral History Interview I," interview by Joe B. Frantz, January 30, 1970, LBJ Presidential Library, 29–31, 34.

50. Ibid.

51. Charles C. Mann, *The Wizard and the Prophet: Two Remarkable Scientists and Their Dueling Visions to Shape Tomorrow's World* (New York: Alfred A. Knopf, 2018), 95 and 153.

52. Ibid., 130.

53. US Agency for International Development, *AID's Legacy in Agriculture Development*, 29.

54. John Norris, "Kennedy, Johnson and the Early Years," *Devex*, July 23, 2014, https://www.devex.com/news/kennedy-johnson-and-the-early-years-83339.

55. US Library of Congress, Congressional Research Service, *US Agency for International Development (AID): Background, Operations, and Issues*, by Curt Tarnoff, 7–8.

56. Gordon Conway, *One Billion Hungry: Can We Feed the World?* (Ithaca: Cornell University Press, 2012), 50–51.

57. US Agency for International Development, *AID's Legacy in Agriculture Development*, 39; and Lawrence Busch, *Universities for Development: Report of the Joint Indo-US Impact Evaluation of the Indian Agricultural Universities* (Washington, DC: US Agency for International Development, 1988).

58. Ibid., 50.

59. Ibid., 39.

60. Ibid., 50.

61. Mann, *The Wizard and the Prophet*, 431.

62. Norris, "Kennedy, Johnson and the Early Years."

63. US Agency for International Development, *AID's Legacy in Agriculture Development*, 29; and Fox, *Applying the Comprehensive Development Framework to AID Experiences*, 18.

64. US Agency for International Development, *AID's Legacy in Agriculture Development*, xiii–xiv, 36.

65. Allison Butler Herrick, interview by W. Haven North, April 1, 1996, ADST Oral History, 46, http://adst.org/wp-content/uploads/2013/12/Herrick-Allison-Butler.pdf.

66. Peter Hazell, "Think Again: The Green Revolution," *Foreign Policy*, September 22, 2009, https://foreignpolicy.com/2009/09/22/think-again-the-green-revolution/.

67. Steven Ross Pomeroy, "Green vs. the Green Revolution," *Forbes*, March 10, 2014, https://www.forbes.com/sites/rosspomeroy/2014/03/10/greens-vs-the-green-revolution/#59d06d0f5aa3.

68. Norman Borlaug, "The Green Revolution, Peace, and Humanity," December 11, 1970, Nobel Lecture, https://www.nobelprize.org/prizes/peace/1970/borlaug/lecture/.

69. US Agency for International Development, *Making a World of Difference: Celebrating 30 Years of Development Progress* (Washington, DC, 1998), 3.

70. Lyndon Baines Johnson, *The Vantage Point: Perspectives of the Presidency, 1963–1969* (New York: Holt, Rinehart and Winston, 1971).

71. Harold H. Saunders, NSC Paper, January 1, 1969, LBJ Presidential Library.

72. Pillsbury, *Secret Successes of AID*, 119–34.

73. Lewis, *India's Political Economy*, 131.

74. Owen Cylke, interview by W. Haven North, November 6, 1996, ADST Oral History, 55–57, https://adst.org/wp-content/uploads/2013/12/Cylke-Owen.pdf.

75. US Congress, Senate, Committee on Foreign Relations, *Some Important Issues in Foreign Aid*, 53–54.

76. Reimert Thorolf Ravenholt, interview by Rebecca Sharpless, July 18–20, 2002, Population and Reproductive Health Oral History Project, Sophia Smith Collection, 85–86, https://www.smith.edu/libraries/libs/ssc/prh/transcripts/ravenholt-trans.pdf.

77. Ibid.

78. Butterfield, *US Development Aid*, 9101–102.

79. Stephen Engelberg, "Conservatives Hope to Link Abortion with Overseas Aid," *New York Times*, June 24, 1984.

80. Norris, "Kennedy, Johnson and the Early Years."

81. Phyllis Tilson Piotrow, *World Population Crisis: The United States Response* (Westport, CT: Praeger, 1973), 4106.

82. Ravenholt, interview by Rebecca Sharpless, 90–91.

83. Steve Sinding, "Population Programs and Problems," in *Fifty Years in AID: Stories from the Front Lines*, eds. Janet C. Ballantyne and Maureen Dugan (Arlington, VA: Arlington Hall Press, September 2012).

84. Piotrow, *World Population Crisis*, 104.

85. Judy C. Bryson, interview by W. Haven North, March 13, 1998, ADST Oral History, 18–19, https://adst.org/wp-content/uploads/2013/12/Bryson-Judy.oh1_.pdf.

86. Andrea Strano, "Foreign Service Women Today: The Palmer Case and Beyond," *Foreign Service Journal* (March 2016): 24–25, https://www.afsa.org/sites/default/files/march2016fsj.pdf.

87. Barbara Turner, interview by Ann Van Dusen, September 26, 2017, ADST Oral History, 7–9, http://adst.org/wp-content/uploads/2018/01/Turner-Barbara.pdf.

88. Tanya Himelfarb, *50 Years of Global Health: Saving Lives and Building Futures* (Washington, DC: US Agency for International Development, June 2014), 26, https://www.usaid.gov/sites/default/files/documents/1864/USAID_50-Years-of-Global-Health.pdf.

89. John R. Schott, *Title IX: A New Dimension in US Foreign Aid?* prepared for delivery at the Annual Meeting of the International Studies Association (San Francisco, 1969), 8.

90. Ibid., 2–4.

91. Ibid.

92. Thomas Carothers and Diane De Gramont, *Development Aid Confronts Politics: The Almost Revolution* (Washington, DC: Carnegie Endowment for International Peace, 2013), 31.

93. US Congress, Congressional Budget Office, *Bilateral Development Assistance Background and Options* (February 1977), 7.

94. Walt Rostow, "The Korry Report on Development Policies and Programs in Africa," August 9, 1966, Memorandum for the President, LBJ Presidential Library.

95. David Shear, interview by W. Haven North, January 13, 1998, ADST Oral History, 32, https://adst.org/wp-content/uploads/2013/12/Shear-David.pdf.

96. US Congress, Congressional Research Service, *A Concise Survey of US Foreign Aid*, by Allan S. Nanes (February 26, 1975), 6.

97. Roger Morris, "Chronology of Presidential Involvement in President Johnson's OAU Speech, May 26, 1966," LBJ Presidential Library.

98. Roger Morris, "Papers on Presidential Decisions in Foreign Policy—President Johnson's Speech of May 26, 1966 on African Policy," LBJ Presidential Library.

99. "Why Are We Aiding So Many African Countries?" November 20, 1965, Africa Bureau to Bundy, LBJ Presidential Library.

100. Stephen Hicks, "Smallpox: Jenner's Ending the Scourge," January 29, 2016, https://www.stephenhicks.org/2016/01/29/smallpox-jenners-ending-the-scourge/.

101. Fox, *Applying the Comprehensive Development Framework to AID Experiences*, 7–11.

102. Jane Seymor, "Case 1: Eradicating Smallpox," *Center for Global Development*, https://www.cgdev.org/page/case-1-eradicating-smallpox.

103. D. A. Henderson and Petra Klepac, "Lessons from the Eradication of Smallpox: An Interview with D. A. Henderson," *Philosophical Transactions of the Royal Society B: Biological Sciences* (2013), doi: 10.1098/rstb.2013.0113.

104. Jonathan B. Tucker, "A Pox on Smallpox," *Issues in Science and Technology* XXVI.1 (2009), https://issues.org/br_tucker-5/.

105. Henderson and Klepac, "Lessons from the Eradication of Smallpox."

106. Himelfarb, *50 Years of Global Health*, 21–23.

107. Henderson and Klepac, "Lessons from the Eradication of Smallpox."

108. Fox, *Applying the Comprehensive Development Framework to AID Experiences*, 7–11. Anecdote drawn from (Ogden, 1987, 35).

109. Donald Henderson, "Acceptance Remarks," 1976 Lasker Awards Ceremony, http://www.laskerfoundation.org/awards/show/smallpox-eradication/.

110. Fox, *Applying the Comprehensive Development Framework to AID Experiences*, 7–11.

111. Seymor, "Case 1: Eradicating Smallpox."

112. Nicholas deB. Katzenbach, "Viet-Nam," November 16, 1967, Memorandum for the President, LBJ Presidential Library.

113. Liberi, *No Longer on the Front Lines*, 12.

114. US Congress, Congressional Research Service, *Development Assistance Policy: A Historical Overview*, by Theodor W. Galdi, 24.

115. Ibid., 24.

116. Nooter, interview by W. Haven North, 86.

117. Gaud, "William Gaud Oral History Interview I," 29–30.

118. L. Wade Lathram, interview by William E. Knight, June 2, 1993, ADST Oral History, 10–11, http://www.adst.org/OH%20TOCs/Lathram,%20Wade.toc.pdf.

119. US Congress, Senate, Committee on Foreign Relations, *Some Important Issues in Foreign Aid*, 24–25.

120. Ibid.

121. L. Wade Lathram, interview by William E. Knight, 12–13.

122. Phillips, "Counterinsurgency in Vietnam: Lessons for Today."

123. Ambassador Clayton E. McManaway Jr., interview by Charles Stuart Kennedy, June 29, 1993, ADST Oral History, 10, 13–20, https://www.adst.org/OH%20TOCs/McManaway,%20Clayton%20E.%20Jr.toc.pdf.

124. Norris, "Kennedy, Johnson and the Early Years."

125. Julius E. Coles, interview by Stuart Kennedy, August 22. 2008, ADST Oral History, 43–48, https://adst.org/wp-content/uploads/2013/12/Coles-Julius-1.pdf.

126. Robert Komer, "Robert Komer Oral History Interview II," interview by Joe B. Frantz, August 18, 1970, LBJ Presidential Library, 25–48.

127. William P. Schoux, *The Vietnam Cords Experience: A Model of Successful Civil-Military Partnership?* (Washington, DC: US Agency for International Development, 2006), 16–17.

128. Julius E. Coles, "Trying to Win the Hearts and Minds of the People of Vietnam," in *Fifty Years in AID: Stories from the Front Lines*, eds. Janet C. Ballantyne and Maureen Dugan (Arlington, VA: Arlington Hall Press, September 2012).

129. Norma Parker, *Lessons Learned: AID Perspectives on the Experience with Provincial Reconstruction Teams (PRTs) in Afghanistan* (June 2013), 5–6.

130. John Norris, "How to Balance Safety and Openness for America's Diplomats," *The Atlantic*, November 4, 2013, https://www.theatlantic.com/international/archive/2013/11/how-to-balance-safety-and-openness-for-america-s-diplomats/281123/.

131. Phillips, *Why Vietnam Matters*, 283–84.

132. L. Wade Lathram, interview by William E. Knight, 10–11.

133. Ibid., 17–18.

134. John Hummon, interview by W. Haven North, May 11, 1999, ADST Oral History, 17, http://adst.org/wp-content/uploads/2013/12/Hummon-John.pdf.

135. Williams, interview by W. Haven North, 49–51.

CHAPTER 5

1. John Norris, "The Cold War and Its Aftermath," *Devex*, July 23, 2014, https://www.devex.com/news/the-cold-war-and-its-aftermath-83340.

2. Stephen E. Ambrose, *Nixon, Volume Two: The Triumph of a Politician, 1962–1972* (New York: Simon & Schuster, 1989), 111–12.

3. Ibid., 112.

4. Williams, interview by W. Haven North, 56–59.

5. US Congress, House of Representatives, Committee on International Relations, Subcommittee on International Development, *Hearing on Rethinking United States Foreign Policy toward the Developing World: A Critical Review of AID*, August 4, 1977.

6. Norris, "The Cold War and Its Aftermath."

7. Hummon, interview by W. Haven North, 20–21.

8. US Congress, Congressional Research Service, *Foreign Aid Reform: Studies and Recommendations*, by Susan B. Epstein and Matthew C. Weed (December 17, 2008), 4.

9. "A New Look at Foreign Aid Organization," Richard M. Nixon Presidential Library and Museum Documents.

10. Henry A. Kissinger, "National Security Council Meeting of March 26 on Foreign Aid," March 25, 1969, Memorandum for the President, Richard M. Nixon Presidential Library and Museum Documents.

11. Henry A. Kissinger, "Talking Points: National Security Council—AID," April 15, 1970, Richard M. Nixon Presidential Library and Museum Documents.

12. Richard Nixon, "Report by President Nixon to the Congress," February 18, 1970, US Department of State Office of the Historian, https://history.state.gov/historicaldocuments/frus1969-76v01/d60.

13. Kissinger, "Talking Points: National Security Council—AID," April 15, 1970.

14. Henry A. Kissinger, "Issues for Decision," July 14, 1970, Memorandum for the President, Richard M. Nixon Presidential Library and Museum Documents.

15. Task Force on International Development, *US Foreign Assistance in the 1970s: A New Approach—Report to the President* (Washington, DC: Government Printing Office, 1970).

16. Henry A. Kissinger, "Your Meeting with Rudolph Peterson on March 2 at 11 a.m." March 1, 1971, Memorandum for the President, Richard M. Nixon Presidential Library and Museum Documents.

17. Richard Nixon, "Special Message to the Congress on Foreign Aid," May 28, 1969, *The American Presidency Project*, http://www.presidency.ucsb.edu/ws/?pid=2073.

18. Williams, interview by W. Haven North, 56–59.

19. Butterfield, *US Development Aid*, 79, 179.

20. John H. (Jack) Sullivan, interview by W. Haven North, October 29, 1996, ADST Oral History, 12, http://adst.org/wp-content/uploads/2013/12/Sullivan-John-H.-Jack.pdf.

21. Gary J. Bass, *The Blood Telegram: Nixon, Kissinger, and a Forgotten Genocide* (New York: Alfred Knopf, 2013), 56.

22. Ambrose, *Nixon, Volume Two*, 253–54.

23. Henry A. Kissinger, "Your Meeting on Biafra," January 10, 1969, Memorandum for Mrs. Nixon, Richard M. Nixon Presidential Library and Museum Documents.

24. Roger Morris, "The Biafran Relief Decision," February 12, 1969, Memorandum for Henry Kissinger, Richard M. Nixon Presidential Library and Museum Documents.

25. Roger Morris, "Action Items on Nigeria," January 15, 1970, Memorandum for Henry Kissinger, Richard M. Nixon Presidential Library and Museum Documents.

26. Henry A. Kissinger, "Nigerian Relief Status Report," January 19, 1970, Memorandum for the President, Richard M. Nixon Presidential Library and Museum Documents.

27. Richard Nixon, handwritten notes on Henry A. Kissinger's Memorandum for the President on "Status Report on the Nigerian Civil War," April 8, 1969, Richard M. Nixon Presidential Library and Museum Documents.

28. Roger Morris, "Next Steps in Nigeria," July 3, 1969, Memorandum for Henry Kissinger, Richard M. Nixon Presidential Library and Museum Documents.

29. Alexander P. Butterfield, Memorandum for Henry Kissinger, July 14, 1969, Richard M. Nixon Presidential Library and Museum Documents.

30. W. Haven North, "The Nigerian Civil War and Relief Operations," in *Fifty Years in AID: Stories from the Front Lines*, eds. Janet C. Ballantyne and Maureen Dugan (Arlington, VA: Arlington Hall Press, September 2012).

31. Frederick E. Gilbert, interview by W. Haven North, September 4, 1997, ADST Oral History, 51–54, http://adst.org/wp-content/uploads/2013/12/Gilbert-Frederick-E.pdf.

32. Hariadene Johnson, interview by W. Haven North, September 8, 1998, ADST Oral History, 26, http://adst.org/wp-content/uploads/2013/12/Johnson-Hariadene.pdf.

33. Ibid.

34. David Shear and Roy A. Stacy, "Reclaiming the African Sahel," in *Fifty Years in AID: Stories from the Front Lines*, eds. Janet C. Ballantyne and Maureen Dugan (Arlington, VA: Arlington Hall Press, September 2012).

35. John D. Pielemeier, interview by W. Haven North, September 24, 1997, ADST Oral History, 43, http://adst.org/wp-content/uploads/2013/12/Pielemeier-John-D.pdf.

36. Alan Berg, "AID's Nutrition History (The Early Years)," 5.

37. Bass, *The Blood Telegram*.

38. Ibid., 30.

39. Desaix "Terry" Myers, interview by Alexander Shakow, January 17, 2017, ADST Oral History, 24–27, http://adst.org/wp-content/uploads/2017/12/Myers-Desaix-Terry.pdf.

40. Williams, interview by W. Haven North, 65–67.

41. Bass, *The Blood Telegram*, 88.

42. Desaix "Terry" Myers, interview by Alexander Shakow, 24–27.

43. Bass, *The Blood Telegram*, 77.

44. Riley, *The Political History of American Food Aid*, 321.

45. Ambrose, *Nixon, Volume Two*, 450, 482.

46. Riley, *The Political History of American Food Aid*, 323; and Bass, *The Blood Telegram*, 144.

47. Ibid., 330.

48. Ambrose, *Nixon, Volume Two*, 483.

49. Riley, *The Political History of American Food Aid*, 329.

50. Gordon W. Evans, interview by Barbara S. Evans, December 9, 1998, ADST Oral History, 23–24, http://adst.org/wp-content/uploads/2013/12/Evans-Gordon-W.pdf.

51. Nooter, interview by W. Haven North, 53.

52. Norris, "How to Balance Safety and Openness for America's Diplomats."

53. John R. Brown III, Memorandum for Dr. Kissinger, December 16, 1969, Richard M. Nixon Presidential Library and Museum Documents.

54. Tim Weiner, "Robert Komer, 78, Figure in Vietnam, Dies," *New York Times*, April 12, 2000, http://www.nytimes.com/2000/04/12/world/robert-komer-78-figure-in-vietnam-dies.html.

55. Robert Lester, interview by Ann Van Dusen, November 15, 2016, ADST Oral History, 16–18, 20, http://adst.org/wp-content/uploads/2013/12/Lester-Robert.pdf.

56. Miles Wedeman, interview by John Kean, September 12, 1995, ADST Oral History, 39–40, https://adst.org/wp-content/uploads/2013/12/Wedeman-Miles.pdf.

57. Williams, interview by W. Haven North, 89.

58. Tim Weiner, "Robert Komer, 78, Figure in Vietnam, Dies."

59. John Norris, "Special Feature: A History of American Public Opinion on Foreign Aid," *Devex*, August 15, 2017, https://www.devex.com/news/special-feature-a-history-of-american-public-opinion-on-foreign-aid-90732.

60. Daniel P. Moynihan, Memorandum for Honorable William P. Rogers, Secretary of State, July 15, 1969, Richard M. Nixon Presidential Library and Museum Documents.

61. Daniel P. Moynihan and Henry A. Kissinger, "Reports on International Population Problems," February 25, 1970, Memorandum for the President, Richard M. Nixon Presidential Library and Museum Documents.

62. John A. Hannah, "Memorandum for A.I.D. Employees," Office of the Administrator, January 24, 1972.

63. Steven W. Sinding, interview by W. Haven North, February 27, 2001, ADST Oral History, 9–16, http://adst.org/wp-content/uploads/2013/12/Sinding-Steven-W.pdf.

64. Himelfarb, *50 Years of Global Health*, 30.

65. Ibid., 45.

66. Ibid., 36.

67. Joseph C. Wheeler, interview by W. Haven North, June 17, 1998, ADST Oral History, 40–41, https://adst.org/wp-Acontent/uploads/2013/12/Wheeler-Joseph-C.pdf.

68. Sinding, "Population Programs and Problems."

69. Butterfield, *US Development Aid*, 104.

70. Richard Elliott Benedick, interview by Raymond Ewing, August 31, 1999, ADST Oral History, 41, https://adst.org/wp-content/uploads/2013/12/Benedick-Richard-Elliott-1.pdf.

71. Sinding, interview by W. Haven North.

72. Edgar Owens and Robert Shaw, *Development Reconsidered: Bridging the Gap Between Government and the People* (Lexington, MA: DCHeath and Co., 1974,1972), xv.

73. Lawrence E. Harrison, interview by W. Haven North, December 12, 1996, ADST Oral History, 6–7, http://adst.org/wp-content/uploads/2013/12/Harrison-Lawrence-E.pdf.

74. US Agency for International Development, *A Review of Alliance for Progress Goals*, a report by the Bureau for Latin America (March 1969), 1.

75. Ibid., 1.

76. Ibid., 34.

77. David Lazar, interview by W. Haven North, March 20, 1997, ADST Oral History, 63, https://adst.org/wp-content/uploads/2013/12/Lazar-David.pdf.

78. Donor M. Lion, interview by W. Haven North, June 25, 1997, ADST Oral History, 27, http://adst.org/wp-content/uploads/2013/12/Lion-Donor-M.pdf.

79. US Agency for International Development, *AID's Legacy in Agriculture Development*, 52.

80. Stuart Van Dyke, interview by Scott Behoteguy, September 18, 1997, ADST Oral History, 16–17, http://adst.org/wp-content/uploads/2013/12/Van-Dyke-Stuart.pdf.

81. Williams, interview by W. Haven North, 104.

82. Richard M. Nixon, handwritten notes on John A. Hannah's Resignation Letter, September 4, 1973, Richard M. Nixon Presidential Library and Museum Documents.

83. Leonard Sloane, "Nominee to Direct Foreign Aid Daniel Safford Parker," *New York Times*, September 8, 1973, https://www.nytimes.com/1973/09/08/archives/nominee-to-direct-foreign-aid-daniel-safford-parker-aid-to-campaign.html.

84. Lloyd Jonnes, interview by W. Haven North, August 19, 1996, ADST Oral History, 52–53, http://adst.org/wp-content/uploads/2013/12/Jonnes-Lloyd.pdf.

85. Ibid.

86. Hannah, "Memorandum for A.I.D. Employees."

87. Ken Hughes, ed., "Richard Nixon and Henry A. Kissinger on 29 October 1971," Conversation 013-043, Presidential Recordings Digital Edition—Nixon Telephone Tapes 1971 (Charlottesville: University of Virginia Press, 2014), http://prde.upress.virginia.edu/conversations/4006648.

88. US Congress, Congressional Research Service, *Development Assistance Policy: A Historical Overview*, by Theodor W. Galdi, 24.

89. Sullivan, interview by W. Haven North, 9, 11.

90. John A. Hannah, "A.I.D. General Notice: Designation of A.I.D. Coordinator for Supporting Assistance," Office of the Administrator, July 1, 1971; and Hannah, "Memorandum for A.I.D. Employees."

91. John Norris, "Special Feature: Ghana, Grandma and the Factors Affecting American Public Opinion on Foreign Aid," *Devex*, August 22, 2017, https://www.devex.com/news/special-feature-ghana-grandma-and-the-factors-affecting-american-public-opinion-on-foreign-aid-90733.

92. US Congress, Congressional Research Service, *Foreign Aid Reform: Studies and Recommendations*, by Susan B. Epstein and Matthew C. Weed (December 17, 2008), 4.

93. Sullivan, interview by W. Haven North, 9, 11.

94. North and North, "Transformations in US Foreign Economic Assistance," 276–78.

95. H. W. Arndt, *Economic Development, the History of an Idea* (Chicago: University of Chicago Press, 1987), 110.

96. Himelfarb, *50 Years of Global Health*, 40.

97. US Library of Congress, Congressional Research Service, *US Agency for International Development (AID): Background, Operations, and Issues*, by Curt Tarnoff, 6–7.

98. US Agency for International Development, *AID's Legacy in Agriculture Development*, 6–7.

99. Frederick E. Gilbert, interview by W. Haven North, September 4, 1997, ADST Oral History, 179–80, http://adst.org/wp-content/uploads/2013/12/Gilbert-Frederick-E.pdf.

100. US Congress, Congressional Budget Office, *Bilateral Development Assistance Background and Options* (February 1977), viii.

101. North and North, "Transformations in US Foreign Economic Assistance," 286.

102. Alexander Ray Love, interview by W. Haven North, February 10, 1998, ADST Oral History, 49, http://adst.org/wp-content/uploads/2013/12/Love-Alexander-Ray.pdf.

103. Fox, *Applying the Comprehensive Development Framework to AID Experiences*, 21–22.

104. Butterfield, *US Development Aid*, 181.

105. Lion, interview by W. Haven North, 77.

106. William White, interview by W. Haven North, May 23, 1996, ADST Oral History, https://adst.org/wp-content/uploads/2013/12/White-William.pdf.

107. Dr. John R. Eriksson, interview by W. Haven North, April 17, 1995, ADST Oral History, 12, http://adst.org/wp-content/uploads/2013/12/Eriksson-John-R.pdf.

108. Dan Carter, *The Agency for International Development: An Assessment of the Agency Operations as a Result of Changes in the Foreign Assistance Act of 1973* (September 29, 1977), 29.

109. Sullivan, interview by W. Haven North, 17–18.

110. Frederick E. Gilbert, interview by W. Haven North, September 4, 1997, ADST Oral History, 178, http://adst.org/wp-content/uploads/2013/12/Gilbert-Frederick-E.pdf.

111. Norris, "Special Feature: Ghana, Grandma and the Factors Affecting American Public Opinion on Foreign Aid."

112. David Morawetz, *Twenty-Five Years of Economic Development, 1950–1975* (The World Bank, 1977).

113. US Congress, Congressional Research Service, *Development Assistance Policy: A Historical Overview*, by Theodor W. Galdi, 12–16.

114. Richard L. Hough, *Economic Assistance and Security: Rethinking US Policy* (Washington, DC: National Defense University Press, 1982), 84.

115. Schuh, et al., *International Cooperation for Sustainable Economic Growth*, 17–19.

CHAPTER 6

1. Carter, *The Agency for International Development*, 10–11.

2. US Library of Congress, Congressional Research Service, *US Agency for International Development (AID): Background, Operations, and Issues*, by Curt Tarnoff, 6.

3. Cyrus Vance, *Hard Choices: Critical Years in America's Foreign Policy* (New York: Simon & Schuster, 1983), 429–31.

4. John J. Gilligan, "Statement of Hon. John J. Gilligan, Administrator, Agency for International Development," to the House of Representatives, Committee on International Relations, Subcommittee on International Development, *Hearing on Rethinking United States Foreign Policy toward the Developing World: A Critical Review of AID*, August 4, 1977.

5. Butterfield, *US Development Aid*, 197–98.

6. Gilligan, *Hearing on Rethinking United States Foreign Policy toward the Developing World: A Critical Review of AID.*

7. US Congress, Commission on Security and Economic Assistance, *A Report to the Secretary of State* (November 1983), Frank Charles Carlucci, 39.

8. US Congress, Congressional Budget Office, *Assisting the Developing Countries: Foreign Aid and Trade Policies of the United States* (September 1980), 66–67, 77.

9. Commission on Security and Economic Assistance, *A Report to the Secretary of State*, 39.

10. Norris, "The Cold War and Its Aftermath."

11. Governor John J. Gilligan, "Strengthening Missions and Streamlining Operations," in *Fifty Years in AID: Stories from the Front Lines*, eds. Janet C. Ballantyne and Maureen Dugan (Arlington, VA: Arlington Hall Press, September 2012).

12. Ibid.

13. US Congress, House of Representatives, Committee on International Relations, Subcommittee on International Development, *Hearing on Rethinking United States Foreign Policy toward the Developing World: Administration Activities in the Foreign Aid Field*, October 12, 1977.

14. Norris, "The Cold War and Its Aftermath."

15. Nooter, interview by W. Haven North, 72–75.

16. Ibid.

17. David Shear, interview by W. Haven North, January 13, 1998, ADST Oral History, 50, 54–58, 70, https://adst.org/wp-content/uploads/2013/12/Shear-David.pdf.

18. Parker W. Borg, *Experiences with American Assistance Programs* (December 2017), 8.

19. US Agency for International Development, *A History of Foreign Assistance* (Washington, DC, April 3, 2002), http://pdf.AID.gov/pdf_docs/Pnacp064.pdf.

20. Alexander Shakow, "PPC and Policy Making in the 1970s," in *Fifty Years in AID: Stories from the Front Lines*, eds. Janet C. Ballantyne and Maureen Dugan (Arlington, VA: Arlington Hall Press, September 2012).

21. Stuart E. Eizenstat, *President Carter: The White House Years* (New York: St. Martin's Press, 2018), 243–44.

22. US Agency for International Development, "From Tragedy to Action: USAID's Environmental Trajectory," *Frontlines* (November/December 2011), https://2012-2017.usaid.gov/news-information/frontlines/50-years-and-food-security/tragedy-action-usaid's-environmental.

23. US Agency for International Development, *AID's Legacy in Agriculture Development*, 23–24.

24. US Congress, Congressional Budget Office, *Bilateral Development Assistance Background and Options* (February 1977), 15.

25. Steven W. Sinding, interview by W. Haven North, February 27, 2001, ADST Oral History, 24–25, http://adst.org/wp-content/uploads/2013/12/Sinding-Steven-W.pdf.

26. Carol A. Peasley, interview by Kenneth Brown, January 29, 2015, ADST Oral History, 42, http://adst.org/wp-content/uploads/2013/12/Peasley-Carol-A.pdf.

27. Reimert Thorolf Ravenholt, interviewed by Rebecca Sharpless, July 18–20, 2002, Population and Reproductive Health Oral History Project, Sophia Smith Collection, 186, https://www.smith.edu/libraries/libs/ssc/prh/transcripts/ravenholt-trans.pdf.

28. Ibid., 188–89.

29. Duff Gillespie, interview by Rebecca Sharpless, May 19–20, 2003, Population and Reproductive Health Oral History Project, Sophia Smith Collection, 33, https://www.smith .edu/libraries/libs/ssc/prh/transcripts/gillespieduff-trans.pdf.

30. Sinding, "Population Programs and Problems."

31. Ravenholt, interview by Rebecca Sharpless, 198–99.

32. Charles Wallace, "Indonesia Serves as Example of How US Foreign Aid, Support for Contraceptives Can Lift Nations Out of Poverty," *Los Angeles Times*, September 27, 1993.

33. Allison Butler Herrick, interview by W. Haven North, April 1, 1996, ADST Oral History, 43, http://adst.org/wp-content/uploads/2013/12/Herrick-Allison-Butler.pdf.

34. W. W. Rostow, Memorandum to the President, May 21, 1966, LBJ Presidential Library.

35. Bradshaw Langmaid, interview by W. Haven North, July 14, 1998, ADST Oral History, 43–46, http://adst.org/wp-content/uploads/2013/12/Langmaid-Bradshaw.pdf.

36. House of Representatives, Committee on International Relations, Subcommittee on International Development, *Hearing on Rethinking United States Foreign Policy Toward the Developing World: A Critical Review of AID*.

37. Norris, "The Cold War and Its Aftermath."

38. Himelfarb, *50 Years of Global Health*, 27.

39. Owen Cylke, interview by W. Haven North, November 6, 1996, ADST Oral History, 35, 41–43, https://adst.org/wp-content/uploads/2013/12/Cylke-Owen.pdf.

40. The CBO notes, "The Economic Support Fund is a descendant of the Marshall Plan "defense support" funds of the 1940s. In 1961, with the enactment of the Foreign Assistance Act (FAA), this type of aid was formally designated as Supporting Assistance. In 1971 it was renamed Security Supporting Assistance and placed under the FAA title concerned with military, rather than economic, aid, thus emphasizing its different goals as compared with development assistance. . . . The intention is that ESF be used for development projects wherever possible, but only 30 percent of the funds distributed between 1975 and 1979 were directly for such projects." US Congress, Congressional Budget Office, *Assisting the Developing Countries: Foreign Aid and Trade Policies of the United States* (September 1980), 13.

41. Ruttan, *United States Development Assistance Policy*, xvii.

42. Bill Peterson and David S. Broder, "Gilligan Resigns as Foreign Aid Chief," *Washington Post*, February 1, 1979, https://search-proquest-com.dclibrary.idm.oclc.org/docview/147132350/A3424EAD31C64817PQ/1?accountid=46320.

43. Nooter, interview by W. Haven North, 72–75.

44. Norris, "The Cold War and Its Aftermath."

45. Eizenstat, *President Carter*, 575–77.

46. David S. McLellan, *Cyrus Vance*, (New Jersey: Rowman & Allanheld, Totowa, 1985), 75–76.

47. Lion, interview by W. Haven North, 39–40.

48. Sullivan, interview by W. Haven North, 45.

49. Lion, interview by W. Haven North, 39–40.

50. Schuh, et al., *International Cooperation for Sustainable Economic Growth*, 17–19.

51. Frederick E. Gilbert, interview by W. Haven North, September 4, 1997, ADST Oral History, 115, http://adst.org/wp-content/uploads/2013/12/Gilbert-Frederick-E.pdf.

52. Norris, "The Cold War and Its Aftermath."

CHAPTER 7

1. Juan de Onis, "Test for Haig Seen in Dispute Over Aid," *New York Times*, February 1, 1981.

2. Ruttan, *United States Development Assistance Policy,* 129–30.

3. Ann Van Dusen, interview by Alex Shakow, October 2017, ADST Oral History, 10, http://adst.org/wp-content/uploads/2018/01/Van-Dusen-Ann-1.pdf.

4. Peter Khiss, "Man in the News: US AID Director in Lebanon," *New York Times*, June 20, 1982.

5. Butterfield, *US Development Aid,* 199.

6. Ruttan, *United States Development Assistance Policy*, 311.

7. William Chapman, "Foreign Aid Puts GOP in Alien Territory," *Washington Post*, December 6, 1981, https://www.washingtonpost.com/archive/politics/1981/12/06/foreign-aid-puts-gop-in-alien-territory/fcfa02af-16ff-4ad5-89c0-be10b800e31b1/.

8. John Norris, "Five Myths About Foreign Aid," *Washington Post*, April 28, 2011, https://www.washingtonpost.com/opinions/five-myths-about-foreign-aid/2011/04/25/AF00z05E_story.html?utm_term=.fd84a8ee8763.

9. Howell Raines, "Reporter's Notebook: Insulating a President," *New York Times*, August 5, 1981.

10. Elisabeth Kvitashvili, interview by John Pielemeier, December 5, 2016, ADST Oral History, 14–15, http://adst.org/wp-content/uploads/2018/01/Kvitshavili-Elizabeth-1.pdf.

11. Pillsbury, *Secret Successes of AID*, 12–13.

12. Lou Cannon, *President Reagan: The Role of a Lifetime* (New York: Public Affairs, 1991), 411–12.

13. Peter McPherson, "Business Forum: Foreign and Under Fire; We Weren't Looking for a Quick Fix," *New York Times*, November 23, 1986, available at http://www.nytimes.com/1986/11/23/business/business-forum-foreign-aid-under-fire-we-weren-t-looking-for-a-quick-fix.html.

14. Ibid.

15. Barbara Crossette, "US to send AID Teams to Scout Third World," *New York Times*, October 20, 1981, http://www.nytimes.com/1981/10/20/world/us-to-send-aid-teams-to-scout-third-world.html.

16. Butterfield, *US Development Aid*, 201.

17. Allison Butler Herrick, interview by W. Haven North, April 1, 1996, ADST Oral History, 76–78, http://adst.org/wp-content/uploads/2013/12/Herrick-Allison-Butler.pdf.

18. M. Peter McPherson, Oral History, interview by Alex Shakow, April 8, 2018, 88.

19. Andrew Natsios, *The Clash of the Counter-Bureaucracy and Development*, Center for Global Development (July 2010), 10.

20. Krueger and Ruttan, "The Development Impact of Economic Assistance to LDCs," 2.

21. The Commission on Security and Economic Assistance, *A Report to the Secretary of State*, 2–4.

22. Nicholas D. Kristof, "The Third World: Back to the Farm," *New York Times*, July 28, 1985.

23. The Phoenix Group, *The Convergence of Interdependence and Self-Interest: Reforms Needed in US Assistance to Developing Countries* (February 1989), 10.

24. Stephen Solomon, "The Controversy Over Infant Formula," *New York Times*, December 6, 1981.

25. Ibid.

26. Ibid.

27. UN's Standing Committee on Nutrition's SCN News, No. 40, 121–34, 2013, "Visionary at the Conception: An Interview with Alan Berg, International Nutrition Pioneer," by James Levinson.

28. Robert Reinhold, "A.I.D. Officials Say They'll Resign if US Rejects Baby-Formula Code," *New York Times*, May 19, 1981.

29. Richard S. Olson, *FINAL REPORT: The Office of US Foreign Disaster Assistance (OFDA) of the United States Agency for International Development (AID): A Critical Juncture Analysis, 1964–2014*, for Macfadden & Associates (June 9, 2015), 21.

30. Ibid., 9.

31. Riley, *The Political History of American Food Aid*, 431.

32. Ibid., 427.

33. Michael Massing, "Does Democracy Avert Famine?" *New York Times*, March 1, 2003, https://www.nytimes.com/2003/03/01/arts/does-democracy-avert-famine.html.

34. Peter McPherson, note from Peter McPherson based on conversations with Ray Love, Julia Chang Bloch, and Ted Morse, July 22, 2020.

35. Riley, *The Political History of American Food Aid*, 42.

36. McPherson, interview by Alex Shakow, 41.

37. Hariadene Johnson, interview by W. Haven North, September 8, 1998, ADST Oral History, 133–34, http://adst.org/wp-content/uploads/2013/12/Johnson-Hariadene.pdf.

38. Olson, *FINAL REPORT: A Critical Juncture Analysis*, 33.

39. "Food for Ethiopia Brings US Dispute," *New York Times*, March 4, 1984, http://www.nytimes.com/1984/03/04/world/food-for-ethiopia-brings-us-dispute.html.

40. Alexander Ray Love, interview by W. Haven North, February 10, 1998, ADST Oral History, 78, http://adst.org/wp-content/uploads/2013/12/Love-Alexander-Ray.pdf.

41. Riley, *The Political History of American Food Aid*, 438.

42. McPherson, note from Peter McPherson based on conversations with Ray Love, Julia Chang Bloch, and Ted Morse.

43. Associated Press, "Ethiopia Links US and Soviet Relief Efforts," *New York Times*, November 19, 1984.

44. Riley, *The Political History of American Food Aid*, 434.

45. McPherson, note from Peter McPherson based on conversations with Ray Love, Julia Chang Bloch, and Ted Morse.

46. Olson, *FINAL REPORT: A Critical Juncture Analysis*, 41.

47. Ibid., 42–43.

48. US Agency for International Development, *AID's Legacy in Agriculture Development*, 76–77.

49. Butterfield, *US Development Aid*, 123.

50. Himelfarb, *50 Years of Global Health*, 36–37.

51. McPherson, interview by Alex Shakow, 74.

52. Himelfarb, *50 Years of Global Health*, 45.

53. US Agency for International Development, "Special Issue: Why Foreign Aid," *Front Lines* 36.2 (March 1996): 1–11.

54. Sinding, "Population Programs and Problems."

55. Ambassador Frank S. Ruddy, interview by Charles Stuart Kennedy, September 9, 1991, ADST Oral History, 19–20, https://www.adst.org/OH%20TOCs/Ruddy,%20Francis%20_Frank_%20S.toc.pdf.

56. Richard Elliott Benedick, interview by Raymond Ewing, August 31, 1999, ADST Oral History, 45, https://adst.org/wp-content/uploads/2013/12/Benedick-Richard-Elliott-1.pdf.

57. Steven W. Sinding, interview by W. Haven North, February 27, 2001, ADST Oral History, 40–43, http://adst.org/wp-content/uploads/2013/12/Sinding-Steven-W.pdf.

58. McPherson, interview by Alex Shakow, 32.

59. Sinding, interview by W. Haven North, 46–51.

60. Stephen Engelberg, "Conservatives Hope to Link Abortion with Overseas Aid," *New York Times*, June 24, 1984.

61. Alan Riding, "Battleground in Colombia: Birth Control," *New York Times*, September 5, 1984.

62. Susan F. Rasky, "Reagan Restrictions on Foreign Aid for Abortion Programs Lead to a Fight," *New York Times*, October 14, 1984.

63. Sinding, interview by W. Haven North, 46–51.

64. Clifford D. May, "Washington Talk: Anti-Abortion Policy; Mincing No Words, or Pictures, on Birth Control," *New York Times*, July 29, 1987.

65. Philip Shenon, "Conservative Groups Press for the Ouster of A.I.D. Chief," *New York Times*, April 10, 1985, http://www.nytimes.com/1985/04/10/world/conservative-groups-press-for-the-ouster-of-a-i-d-chief.html.

66. Butterfield, *US Development Aid*, 104.

67. Lynn Bennett, Meena Acharya, et al., *The Status of Women in Nepal* (Katmandu: Centre for Economic Development and Administration, Tribhuvan University, 1982).

68. Butterfield, *US Development Aid*, 270.

69. Allison Butler Herrick, interview by W. Haven North, April 1, 1996, ADST Oral History, 73, http://adst.org/wp-content/uploads/2013/12/Herrick-Allison-Butler.pdf.

70. Lawrence K. Altman, "New Homosexual Disorder Worries Health Officials," *New York Times*, May 11, 1982.

71. Janet C. Ballantyne and Maureen Dugan, eds., in *Fifty Years in AID: Stories from the Front Lines* (Arlington, VA: Arlington Hall Press, September 2012).

72. Duff Gillespie, interview by Rebecca Sharpless, May 19–20, 2003, Population and Reproductive Health Oral History Project, Sophia Smith Collection, 64, 77–78, https://www.smith.edu/libraries/libs/ssc/prh/transcripts/gillespieduff-trans.pdf.

73. Van Dusen, interview by Alex Shakow, 15.

74. Cannon, *President Reagan*, 731–33.

75. General Accounting Office, *Progress in Implementing the Development Fund for Africa* (April 1991), 8.

76. Richard Podol, interview by W. Haven North, September 12, 1996, ADST Oral History, 50–51, http://adst.org/wp-content/uploads/2013/12/Podol-Richard.pdf.

77. Philip Birnbaum, interview by W. Haven North, February 22, 1996, ADST Oral History, 69–70, https://adst.org/wp-content/uploads/2013/12/Birnbaum-Philip.pdf.

78. Harvey E. Gutman, interview by Stuart Van Dyke, August 26, 1997, ADST Oral History, 28–29, http://adst.org/wp-content/uploads/2013/12/Gutman-Harvey-E.pdf.

79. Helen Suzman, "What America Should Do About South Africa," *New York Times Magazine*, August 3, 1986.

80. Ruttan, *United States Development Assistance Policy*, 127.

81. US Congress, Congressional Research Service, *Development Assistance Policy: A Historical Overview*, by Theodor W. Galdi, 17.

82. Correspondence with author, June 15, 2019.

83. Marshall "Buster" Brown, "A Career Retrospect: Home and Abroad," in *Fifty Years in AID: Stories from the Front Lines*, eds., Janet C. Ballantyne and Maureen Dugan (Arlington, VA: Arlington Hall Press, September 2012).

84. Donald S. Brown, interview by W. Haven North, 39–41, 44–47.

85. Marshall D. Brown, interview by W. Haven North, December 4, 1996, ADST Oral History, 60, https://adst.org/wp-content/uploads/2013/12/Brown-Marshall-D.pdf.

86. McPherson, interview by Alex Shakow, 67.

87. Christopher S. Wren, "US Is Reorienting Aid to Egypt," *New York Times*, August 31, 1986, http://www.nytimes.com/1986/08/31/world/us-is-reorienting-civil-aid-to-egypt.html.

88. Pillsbury, *Secret Successes of AID*, 217–24.

89. Fox, *Applying the Comprehensive Development Framework to AID Experiences*, 1, 25–26.

90. US Congress, Congressional Budget Office, *The Role of Foreign Aid in Development*, 51–52.

91. Anne Dammarell, interview by Charles Stuart Kennedy, June 10, 2013, ADST Oral History, 40–41, 44–46, 50, http://adst.org/wp-content/uploads/2013/12/Dammarell-Anne-1.pdf.

92. Bernard Gwertzman, "Reagan Calls Bombing Cowardly," *New York Times*, April 19, 1983.

93. Cannon, *President Reagan*, 385–87.

94. Ruttan, *United States Development Assistance Policy*, 126.

95. "Key Sections from Study of Latin Region by Kissinger Panel," *New York Times*, January 12, 1984.

96. Butterfield, *US Development Aid*, 209.

97. Stephen Kinzer, "Strategic Goals Often Appear to Loom Behind Assistance for Latin Region," *New York Times*, January 12, 1984, http://www.nytimes.com/1984/01/12/world/strategic-goals-often-appear-to-loom-behind-assistance-for-latin-region.html.

98. Philip Taubman, "Abuses Disclosed in Aid Programs in Latin Nations," *New York Times*, February 20, 1984, http://www.nytimes.com/1984/02/20/world/abuses-disclosed-in-aid-programs-in-latin-nations.html?pagewanted=all.

99. Juan Carlos Hidalgo, *Growth Without Poverty Reduction: The Case of Costa Rica*, Cato Institute, *Economic Development Bulletin* 18 (January 23, 2014), https://www.cato.org/publications/economic-development-bulletin/growth-without-poverty-reduction-case-costa-rica.

100. James W. Fox, *Real Progress: Fifty Years of AID in Costa Rica* (Washington, DC: US Agency for International Development, 1998), 25–26.

101. Butterfield, *US Development Aid*, 209–10.

102. US Congress, Congressional Budget Office, *The Role of Foreign Aid in Development*, 54.

103. Raymond Bonner, "The Political Harvest Also Grows When Peasants Rule," *New York Times*, January 11, 1981.

104. James LeMoyne, "After Parades and Promises, Duarte Flounders in Salvador," *New York Times*, February 16, 1987.

105. Ruttan, *United States Development Assistance Policy*, 510.

106. C. Stuart Callison and John G. Stovall, "How Do You Spell Development? A.I.D.'s Identity Crisis," *Foreign Service Journal* (January 1992): 34.

CHAPTER 8

1. Irvin Molotsky, "Soviets Accept US Aid for First Time Since '40s," *New York Times*, December 10, 1988.

2. Olson, *FINAL REPORT: A Critical Juncture Analysis*, 45.

3. Alexander Ray Love, interview by W. Haven North, February 10, 1998, ADST Oral History, 104–5, http://adst.org/wp-content/uploads/2013/12/Love-Alexander-Ray.pdf.

4. Linda Feldman, "US World Aid Chief Calls for Reforms," *Christian Science Monitor*, February 21, 1989, https://www.csmonitor.com/1989/0221/adev.html/%28page%29/2.

5. Alan Woods, *A US Model for Progress in the Developing World*, The Heritage Foundation (1989), https://pdf.usaid.gov/pdf_docs/PNABF168.pdf.

6. Alan Woods, *Development and the National Interest: US Economic Assistance into the 21st Century* (February 1989), 111–13.

7. Ibid., 113.

8. Ibid., 111–13.

9. C. Stuart Callison, "Development and the National Interest," *Foreign Service Journal* (January 1990): 28–31.

10. Woods, *Development and the National Interest*, 79–81.

11. Ibid., 114.

12. Ibid., 61.

13. Ibid., 75.

14. Schuh et al., *International Cooperation for Sustainable Economic Growth*, 47.

15. Michael J. Crosswell, "The Development Record and the Effectiveness of Foreign Aid," US Agency for International Development, Staff Discussion Paper No. 1, June 1998, 3.

16. Schuh et al., *International Cooperation for Sustainable Economic Growth*, 47.

17. Lawrence H. Summers, *Investing in All the People, Educating Women in Developing Countries*, EDI Seminar Paper No. 45 (Washington, DC: Economic Development Institute of the World Bank, 1994), 1, 7.

18. Butterfield, *US Development Aid*, 136–37.

19. James W. Fox, *Gaining Ground: World Well-Being 1950–95*, AID Evaluation Special Study No. 79 (November 1998), 12.

20. Ibid., 9.

21. Ruttan, *The Future of US Foreign Economic Assistance*, 5–10.

22. Gerald F. Hyman, *Foreign Policy and Development: Structure, Process, Policy, and the Drip-by-Drip Erosion of AID*, Center for Strategic and International Studies (September 2010), 7–10.

23. Rogers Worthington, "Secrecy in University Firing Fuels Anger," *Chicago Tribune*, October 26, 1989, https://www.chicagotribune.com/news/ct-xpm-1989-10-26-8901250578-story.html.

24. Schuh et al., *International Cooperation for Sustainable Economic Growth*, 41–42.

25. Callison and Stovall, "How Do You Spell Development?" 32.

26. Pillsbury, *Secret Successes of AID*, 86.

27. Hyman, *Foreign Policy and Development*, 7–10.

28. US Agency for International Development, *20 Years of AID Economic Growth Assistance in Europe and Eurasia* (Washington, DC, July 24, 2013), 19, https://www.usaid.gov/sites/default/files/documents/1863/EE_20_Year__Review.pdf.

29. Ibid., 31.

30. In many ways, the DCA emerged out of the earlier Private Sector Revolving Fund and similar activities under the Private Enterprise Initiative and Micro Credit programs of the 1980s, as well as the even earlier Housing Guarantee Program.

31. Carol Adelman, "Albania After the Wall," in *Fifty Years in AID: Stories from the Front Lines*, eds., Janet C. Ballantyne and Maureen Dugan (Arlington, VA: Arlington Hall Press, September 2012).

32. Jacob J. Kaplan, interview by W. Haven North, March 22, 1999, ADST Oral History, 30, http://adst.org/wp-content/uploads/2013/12/Kaplan-Jacob-J..pdf.

33. US Congress, Congressional Research Service, *The Former Soviet Union and US Foreign Aid: Implementing the Assistance Program, 1992–1994*, by Curt Tarnoff (January 18, 1995), 17.

34. Barbara Turner, interview by Ann Van Dusen, September 26, 2017, ADST Oral History, 20–22, http://adst.org/wp-content/uploads/2018/01/Turner-Barbara.pdf.

35. *Foreign Assistance Act of 1961*, as amended, 22 USC. 2151n.

36. Ronald Reagan, "Address to Members of the British Parliament," London, UK, June 8, 1982, Ronald Reagan Presidential Library and Museum, https://www.reaganlibrary.gov/research/speeches/60882a.

37. The National Endowment for Democracies history of events can be found at: https://www.ned.org/about/history/.

38. See Tom Carothers, *Revitalizing US Democratic Assistance: The Challenge of USAID*, Carnegie Endowment for International Peace (2009), beginning at page 7, https://carnegieendowment.org/files/revitalizing_democracy_assistance.pdf.

39. Correspondence with author, August 15, 2020.

40. Carothers and Diane De Gramont, *Development Aid Confronts Politics*, 59.

41. The World Bank, *Sub-Saharan Africa: From Crisis to Sustainable Growth* (1989), http://documents1.worldbank.org/curated/en/498241468742846138/pdf/multi0page.pdf.

42. US Congress, Congressional Research Service, *US Foreign Aid in a Changing World: Options for New Priorities*, report prepared for the Subcommittee on Europe and the Middle East of the US House of Representatives Committee on Foreign Affairs (February 1991), 3, 6–7.

43. US Congress, Congressional Research Service, *Foreign Assistance and Congressional Debate: International Challenges, Domestic Concerns, Decisions Deferred*, by Larry Q. Nowels (April 17, 1992), 9, http://pdf.AID.gov/pdf_docs/PCAAA464.pdf.

44. Callison and Stovall, "How Do You Spell Development?" 31–36.

45. Reena Shah, "Foreign-Aid Foes Are Speaking Up," *St. Petersburg Times* (Florida), February 24, 1992.

46. US Congress, *Foreign Assistance and Congressional Debate*, by Larry Q. Nowels, 5–6.

47. Steven V. Roberts, "Congress Has Its Ways of Influencing Foreign Aid; A $14.5 Billion Package Was Adopted by Committee Last Week," *New York Times*, April 7, 1985, http://www.nytimes.com/1985/04/07/weekinreview/congress-has-its-ways-influencing-foreign-aid-14.5-billion-package-was-adopted.html.

48. Al Kamen, "AID Chief Hopes to Sell Agency's Reform to Senate Panel," *Washington Post*, May 7, 1991.

49. US Congress, Congressional Research Service, *US Foreign Aid in a Changing World: Options for New Priorities*, 10–11.

50. John S. Blackton, "Is US Foreign Aid Still Relevant?" International Development Conference, January 24, 1991.

51. US Congress, House of Representatives, *Report of the Task Force on Foreign Assistance to the Committee on Foreign Affairs*, 101st Cong., 1st Sess., 1989.

52. The President's Commission on the Management of AID Programs, *Critical Underlying Issues: Further Analysis* (December 22, 1992), 50.

53. Anne O. Krueger, "Economic Policies at Cross-Purposes," The Brookings Institution (1993).

54. Natsios, *The Clash of the Counter-Bureaucracy and Development*, 11–12.

55. Tracy Thompson, "Ex-Official Guilty of AID Theft; High-Level Appointee Falsified Expenses," *Washington Post*, April 18, 1991.

56. Kamen, "AID Chief Hopes to Sell Agency's Reform to Senate Panel."

57. Al Kamen, "Report Alleges Violations by Head of AID; White House, Congress Examining IG Charges," *Washington Post*, October 6, 1991.

58. Al Kamen, "Urging AID Boss Be Fired," *Washington Post*, October 2, 1992, https://www.washingtonpost.com/archive/politics/1992/10/02/urging-aid-boss-be-fired/6e3fece5-3e04-4e9a-a901-6ab53bc69b38/.

59. Kamen, "AID Chief Hopes to Sell Agency's Reform to Senate Panel."

60. Ken Schofield, personal communication, May 5, 2010, as cited in Natsios, *The Clash of the Counter-Bureaucracy and Development*.

61. Patricia Sullivan, "General Herbert L. Beckington," *Washington Post*, November 14, 2007.

62. John M. Goshko, "At AID, General and Troops Don't See Eye to Eye," *Washington Post*, July 30, 1992, https://www.washingtonpost.com/archive/politics/1992/07/30/at-aid-general-and-troops-dont-see-eye-to-eye/7847dd66-97c3-4a0e-a015-d4e6ccba726d/?utm_term=.1b7c7a0da90e.

63. Al Kamen, "Ethical Fine Lines and Employee Financial Disclosures," *Washington Post*, October 12, 1992, https://www.washingtonpost.com/archive/politics/1992/10/12/ethical-fine-lines-and-employee-financial-disclosures/fe44ffb7-a7d6-4a13-8fd0-cb5c37cd0ae9/?utm_term=.14371f2879d0.

64. Kamen, "AID Chief Hopes to Sell Agency's Reform to Senate Panel."

65. David Mills, "TV Preview; CNN's 'A.I.D.': Muckraking Made Easy," *Washington Post*, December 28, 1991.

66. Walter Goodan, "TV Weekend; Examining the Scandals at a US Relief Agency," *New York Times*, December 27, 1991.

67. Barbara Presley Noble, "At Work; Mapping Offshore Migration of Jobs," *New York Times*, October 18, 1992, http://www.nytimes.com/1992/10/18/business/at-work-mapping-offshore-migration-of-jobs.html.

68. Doyle McManus, "US Aid Agency Helps to Move Jobs Overseas," *Los Angeles Times*, September 28, 1992, https://www.latimes.com/archives/la-xpm-1992-09-28-mn-98-story.html.

69. Norris, "The Cold War and Its Aftermath."

70. *New York Times*, "The 1992 Campaign: In Dispute; Quayle and Gore Battle Devolves into a Hand-to-Hand Fight about 4 Issues," October 14, 1992.

71. Keith Bradsher, "Congress Set to Rein in Foreign Aid Agency," *New York Times*, October 4, 1992, http://www.nytimes.com/1992/10/04/world/congress-set-to-rein-in-foreign-aid-agency.html.

72. Don Oberdorfer, "'Isolated' AID Should Be Merged with State Dept., Study Panel Says," *Washington Post*, March 3, 1992.

73. The President's Commission on the Management of AID Programs, *Report to the President: An Action Plan* (April 16, 1992), 4–6.

74. Oberdorfer, "'Isolated' AID Should Be Merged with State Dept."

75. The President's Commission on the Management of AID Programs, *Report to the President: An Action Plan*, 11–12.

76. The President's Commission on the Management of AID Programs, *Report to the President: An Action Plan*, 16–17, 19, and The President's Commission on the Management of A.I.D. Programs, *A Progress Report* (September 30, 1992), 11–12.

77. The President's Commission on the Management of AID Programs, *Report to the President: An Action Plan*, 11–12.

78. Oberdorfer, "'Isolated' AID Should Be Merged with State Dept."

79. The President's Commission on the Management of A.I.D. Programs, *A Progress Report*, 11–12.

CHAPTER 9

1. John W. Sewell, "US Foreign Aid Priorities in the Post–Cold War World," *Looking Ahead* XVI.1 (April 1994), 11–14, http://pdf.AID.gov/pdf_docs/PBAAC885.pdf.

2. Thomas L. Friedman, "The World; Is a Diplomacy of Dollars Really Enough?" *New York Times*, December 12, 1993, http://www.nytimes.com/1993/12/12/weekinreview/the-world-is-a-diplomacy-of-dollars-really-enough.html.

3. Curt Tarnoff, "Aid and Development: Reform and Realities," *Looking Ahead* XVI.1 (April 1994), 15–18, http://pdf.AID.gov/pdf_docs/PBAAC885.pdf.

4. Hyman, *Foreign Policy and Development*, 11–15.

5. John Norris, "The Clashes of the 1990s," *Devex*, July 23, 2014, https://www.devex.com/news/the-clashes-of-the-1990s-83341.

6. Marilyn Greene, "Foreign Aid Faces Clinton Budget Knife," *USA Today*, December 3, 1993.

7. US General Accounting Office, *Foreign Assistance: Status of AID's Reforms*, briefing report to the Chairman, Committee on International Relations House of Representatives (September 1996), 7.

8. Ibid., 7.

9. The Task Force to Reform A.I.D. and the International Affairs Budget, *Preventive Diplomacy: Revitalizing A.I.D. and Foreign Assistance for the Post–Cold War Era* (September 1993), iii.

10. Ibid., 29–30.

11. US General Accounting Office, *Foreign Assistance: Status of AID's Reforms*, 13.

12. Norris, "The Clashes of the 1990s."

13. US General Accounting Office, *Foreign Assistance: Status of AID's Reforms*, 13.

14. Hyman, *Foreign Policy and Development*, 11–15.

15. *New York Times*, "Foreign Aid: Better, but Threatened," November 28, 1993, http://www.nytimes.com/1993/11/28/opinion/foreign-aid-better-but-threatened.html.

16. Bill Clinton, *My Life* (New York: Vintage Books, 2005), 551–54.

17. Carnegie Corporation of New York, *Preventing Deadly Conflict: Final Report* (1997), 11–17, https://www.carnegie.org/publications/preventing-deadly-conflict-final-report/.

18. Ibid., xiv.

19. Madeleine Albright, *Madam Secretary*, with Bill Woodward (New York: Miramax Books, 2003), 147–52.

20. Colum Lynch, "Exclusive: Rwanda Revisited," *Foreign Policy*, April 5, 2015, https://foreignpolicy.com/2015/04/05/rwanda-revisited-genocide-united-states-state-department/.

21. Carnegie Corporation of New York, *Preventing Deadly Conflict*, 3.

22. J. Brian Atwood, "Suddenly, Chaos," *Washington Post*, July 31, 1994, https://www.washingtonpost.com/archive/opinions/1994/07/31/suddenly-chaos/6b7780ac-09dc-4f6d-95ab-44427fcda40b/.

23. Brian Atwood, interview with author, June 18, 2020.

24. Andrew Natsios, *The Great North Korean Famine: Famine, Politics, and Foreign Policy* (Washington, DC: United States Institute for Peace Press, 2001).

25. John F. Harris, *The Survivor: Bill Clinton in the White House* (New York: Random House, 2005), 191–97.

26. US Agency for International Development, *Making a World of Difference: Celebrating 30 Years of Development Progress* (Washington, DC, 1998), 14.

27. Glenn Slocum, interview by W. Haven North, November 18, 1998, ADST Oral History, 104–5, https://adst.org/wp-content/uploads/2013/12/Slocum-Glenn.pdf.

28. US Congress, Congressional Research Service, *US Assistance to the Former Soviet Union 1991–2001: A History of Administration and Congressional Action*, by Curt Turnoff (updated January 15, 2002), 10.

29. Clinton, *My Life*, 505–8.

30. US Congress, Congressional Research Service, *The Former Soviet Union and US Foreign Aid: Implementing the Assistance Program, 1992–1994*, by Curt Tarnoff, 1–2.

31. Ibid., 18–19.

32. James Norris, "Privatization Success in Russia," in *Fifty Years in AID: Stories from the Front Lines*, eds., Janet C. Ballantyne and Maureen Dugan (Arlington, VA: Arlington Hall Press, September 2012).

33. Desaix "Terry" Myers, interview by Alexander Shakow.

34. Stephen Giddings, "Housing Sector Reform in Russia," in *Fifty Years in AID: Stories from the Front Lines*, eds., Janet C. Ballantyne and Maureen Dugan (Arlington, VA: Arlington Hall Press, September 2012).

35. US Congress, Congressional Research Service, *The Former Soviet Union and US Foreign Aid: Implementing the Assistance Program, 1992–1994*, by Curt Tarnoff, 24.

36. Ibid., 37–38.

37. Charles Flickner, "The Russian Aid Mess," *National Interest* (Winter 1994).

38. Desaix "Terry" Myers, interview by Alexander Shakow, 63, 67.

39. US Congress, Congressional Research Service, *US Assistance to the Former Soviet Union 1991–2001: A History of Administration and Congressional Action*, by Curt Tarnoff, 17.

40. US Agency for International Development, *20 Years of AID Economic Growth Assistance in Europe and Eurasia*, v.

41. Ibid., 69, 71.

42. US General Accounting Office, *Foreign Assistance: Status of AID's Reforms*, 11.

43. Philip-Michael Gary, interview by Carol Peasley, January 9, 2017, ADST Oral History, 38–39, http://adst.org/wp-content/uploads/2013/12/Gary-Philip.pdf.

44. Butterfield, *US Development Aid*, 221; and US Agency for International Development, *Report to Congress on Title XII: Famine Prevention and Freedom from Hunger, December 1998* (Washington, DC: US Agency for International Development, 1998), 7.

45. Fox, *Applying the Comprehensive Development Framework to AID Experiences*, 17–18.

46. Tina Rosenberg, "Editorial Observer: America Finds Democracy a Difficult Export," *New York Times*, October 25, 1999.

47. Gary, interview by Carol Peasley, 48.

48. Hyman, *Foreign Policy and Development*, 11–15.

49. Barbara Turner, interview by Ann Van Dusen, September 26, 2017, ADST Oral History, 45–46, http://adst.org/wp-content/uploads/2018/01/Turner-Barbara.pdf.

50. James W. Fox, *Gaining Ground: World Well-Being 1950–95*, AID Evaluation Special Study No. 79 (November 1998), 13.

51. Himelfarb, *50 Years of Global Health*, 39.

52. Fox, *Applying the Comprehensive Development Framework to AID Experiences*, 13–14.

53. J. Joseph Speidel, interviewed by Rebecca Sharpless, October 10–11, 2002, Population and Reproductive Health Oral History Project, Sophia Smith Collection, 43, https://www.smith.edu/libraries/libs/ssc/prh/transcripts/speidel-trans.pdf.

54. US Agency for International Development, "Special Issue: Why Foreign Aid."

55. Albright, *Madam Secretary*, 195–96.

56. US Agency for International Development, "Statement by J. Bryan Atwood, Administrator, US Agency for International Development (AID). Gender Plan of Action. March 12, 1996," as cited in Butterfield, *US Development Aid*.

57. US Department of State, *Formulation and Administration of US Foreign Economic Policy*, by Joseph D. Coppock (Washington, DC, July 10, 1962).

58. Gaud, "William Gaud Oral History Interview I," 8.

59. Owen Cylke, interview by W. Haven North, November 6, 1996, ADST Oral History, 38, https://adst.org/wp-content/uploads/2013/12/Cylke-Owen.pdf.

60. Carol A. Peasley, interview by Kenneth Brown, January 29, 2015, ADST Oral History, 100, http://adst.org/wp-content/uploads/2013/12/Peasley-Carol-A.pdf.

61. Ibid., 104.

62. Brian Atwood, interview with author, June 18, 2020.

63. Neil A. Levine, *Legislation Reflects the Tenor of the Times: Reorganizing US Government Foreign Affairs Agencies, 1994–1998* (National Defense University, National War College, February 13, 2008), 2–3.

64. Miles Pomper, "Agencies Targeted for Consolidation Stew on Congress' Back Burner," *CQ Weekly*, April 18, 1998.

65. Steven Greenhouse, "Gore Rules Against Merger of A.I.D. and Others into State Dept.," *New York Times*, January 26, 1995, http://www.nytimes.com/1995/01/26/world/gore-rules-against-merger-of-aid-and-others-into-state-dept.html.

66. Juan J. Walte, "Foreign Aid May Go Way of Cold War," *USA Today*, May 2, 1995.

67. Levine, *Legislation Reflects the Tenor of the Times*, 5–7.

68. As cited in Michael J. Crosswell, *The Development Record and the Effectiveness of Foreign Aid*, US Agency for International Development, Staff Discussion Paper No. 1 (June 1998), 1, 4.

69. Marilyn Greene, "New Congress to Decide Who's Worthy of US Foreign Aid," *USA Today*.

70. Steven Greenhouse, "It's a Hard Job Saving Foreign Aid (but the Job Is Still There)," *New York Times*, February 19, 1995, http://www.nytimes.com/1995/02/19/world/it-s-a-hard-job-saving-foreign-aid-but-the-job-is-still-there.html.

71. US Congress, Congressional Research Service, *Foreign Policy Agency Reorganization in the 105th Congress,* by Susan B. Epstein, Larry Q. Nowels, and Steven A. Hildreth (May 28, 1998), 4.

72. Judy Mann, "Budget Cuts that Go Too Deep," *Washington Post,* May 10, 1995.

73. US Agency for International Development, "Special Issue: Why Foreign Aid."

74. Ibid.

75. Robert Pear, "Imperiled Agencies Mount Life-Saving Efforts," *New York Times,* May 21, 1995, http://www.nytimes.com/1995/05/21/us/imperiled-agencies-mount-life-saving -efforts.html.

76. US Agency for International Development, "Special Issue: Why Foreign Aid."

77. Fox, *Gaining Ground,* 1.

78. Amartya Sen, *Development as Freedom* (New York: Anchor Books, 1999).

79. Ambassador Harriet C. Babbitt, interview by Charles Stuart Kennedy, November 21, 2002, ADST Oral History, 37, https://www.adst.org/OH%20TOCs/Babbitt,%20Harriet %20C.toc.pdf.

80. Hariadene Johnson, interview by W. Haven North, September 8, 1998, ADST Oral History, 159–60, http://adst.org/wp-content/uploads/2013/12/Johnson-Hariadene.pdf.

81. Robert Lester, interview by Ann Van Dusen, November 15, 2016, ADST Oral History, 39–42, http://adst.org/wp-content/uploads/2013/12/Lester-Robert.pdf.

82. Norris, "The Clashes of the 1990s."

83. Levine, *Legislation Reflects the Tenor of the Times,* 5–7.

84. Presidential Veto Message, "Clinton: Bill Would Undercut US Leadership Abroad," *CQ Weekly Report,* April 20, 1996.

85. Margaret Carlson, "The Love Connection," *Time,* August 4, 1997.

86. US Congress, Congressional Research Service, *Foreign Policy Agency Reorganization in the 105th Congress,* by Susan B. Epstein, Larry Q. Nowels, and Steven A. Hildreth, 17.

87. Lester, interview by Ann Van Dusen, 43.

88. North and North, "Transformations in US Foreign Economic Assistance," 291.

89. John Norris, "The Crucible: Iraq, Afghanistan and the Future of AID," *World Politics Review,* November 19, 2013, http://www.worldpoliticsreview.com/articles/13380/ the-crucible-iraq-afghanistan-and-the-future-of-AID.

90. North and North, "Transformations in US Foreign Economic Assistance," 292.

91. Butterfield, *US Development Aid,* 15.

92. Borg, *Experiences with American Assistance Programs,* 9–10, 16.

93. Philip Shenon, "Departing Foreign Aid Chief Says Cuts Are Dangerous," *New York Times,* July 6, 1999, http://www.nytimes.com/1999/07/06/world/departing-foreign-aid-chief -says-cuts-are-dangerous.html.

94. Ibid.

CHAPTER 10

1. Ben Barber, "Andrew Natsios: Getting AID on Its Feet," *Foreign Service Journal* (September 2002), 20–27.

2. US Agency for International Development, *Foreign Aid in the National Interest: Promoting Freedom, Security, and Opportunity* (Washington, DC, 2002), 13.

3. Ibid.

4. Hyman, *Foreign Policy and Development*, 18.

5. Natsios, *The Clash of the Counter-Bureaucracy and Development*, 24–25.

6. John Norris, "Sept. 11 and Beyond," *Devex*, July 23, 2014, https://www.devex.com/news/sept-11-and-beyond-83342.

7. Natsios, *The Clash of the Counter-Bureaucracy and Development*, 24–25.

8. Stephen Seplow, "Whither Foreign Aid? What Was Once a Flash Point Has Become Largely a Nonissue. One Likely Reason: So Little Is Given," *Philadelphia Inquirer*, April 22, 2001.

9. Andrew Natsios, interview with Carol Peasley, April 24, 2018, ADST Oral History.

10. Ibid.

11. US Congress, Congressional Research Service, *US Assistance to the Former Soviet Union 1991–2001: A History of Administration and Congressional Action*, by Curt Tarnoff, 56.

12. Kathy Kiely, "Importance of Foreign Aid Is Hitting Home," *USA Today*, December 4, 2001.

13. Hyman, *Foreign Policy and Development*, 15.

14. Andrew S. Natsios, Foreword to *Foreign Aid in the National Interest: Promoting Freedom, Security, and Opportunity* (US Agency for International Development, 2002).

15. US Agency for International Development, *Foreign Aid in the National Interest: Promoting Freedom, Security, and Opportunity* (2002), 1.

16. Ibid., 7–9.

17. Ibid., 30.

18. Ibid., 10.

19. Kiely, "Importance of Foreign Aid Is Hitting Home."

20. Barber, "Andrew Natsios: Getting AID on Its Feet," 20–27.

21. Elisabeth Kvitashvili, interview by John Pielemeier, December 5, 2016, ADST Oral History, 47, http://adst.org/wp-content/uploads/2018/01/Kvitshavili-Elizabeth-1.pdf.

22. George W. Bush, *Decision Points* (New York: Crown Publishers, 2010), 334–35.

23. Hyman, *Foreign Policy and Development*, 20–21.

24. Natsios, interview by Carol Peasley.

25. Ibid.

26. Elisabeth Bumiller, "Bush, in Monterrey, Speaks of Conditional Global Aid," *New York Times*, March 23, 2002.

27. John Norris, "President Bush and His Development Legacy," *Devex*, July 5, 2016, https://www.devex.com/news/president-bush-and-his-development-legacy-87725.

28. Bush, *Decision Points*, 334–35.

29. Peter Baker, *Days of Fire: Bush and Cheney in the White House* (New York: Doubleday, 2013), 234–36.

30. Natsios, interview by Carol Peasley.

31. Baker, *Days of Fire*, 234–36.

32. Bob Herbert, "In America; Refusing to Save Africans," *New York Times*, June 11, 2001, https://www.nytimes.com/2001/06/11/opinion/in-america-refusing-to-save-africans.html.

33. This account is drawn from: Natsios, interview by Carol Peasley; and, Celia W. Dugger, "Planning to Fight Poverty from Outside the System," *New York Times*, January 14, 2006.

34. Norris, "President Bush and His Development Legacy."

35. Jean Edward Smith, *Bush* (New York: Simon & Schuster, 2016), 557–62.

36. Norris, "President Bush and His Development Legacy."

37. Natsios, *The Clash of the Counter-Bureaucracy and Development*, 28.

38. Randall Tobias, interview by author, June 16, 2020.

39. Ibid.

40. Smith, *Bush*, 557–62.

41. Bush, *Decision Points*, 331–34.

42. Norris, "President Bush and His Development Legacy."

43. Ibid.

44. Barbara Turner, interview by Ann Van Dusen, September 26, 2017, ADST Oral History, 54–55, http://adst.org/wp-content/uploads/2018/01/Turner-Barbara.pdf.

45. Laurie Garrett, "The Challenge of Global Health," *Foreign Affairs* (January/February 2007).

46. Natsios, *The Clash of the Counter-Bureaucracy and Development*, 30.

47. Norris, "President Bush and His Development Legacy."

48. Himelfarb, *50 Years of Global Health*, 75.

49. Ibid.

50. US Congress, Senate Committee on Foreign Relations, *Embassies Grapple to Guide Foreign Aid* (November 16, 2007), 1–2.

51. Hyman, *Foreign Policy and Development*, 20–21.

52. With thanks to John Sanbrailo for providing the historical perspectives on US anti-malaria efforts.

53. William S. Gaud, "The Role of Foreign Aid in US Foreign Policy," August 25, 1966, Presentation to the Cabinet, LBJ Presidential Library.

54. Himelfarb, *50 Years of Global Health*, 65–68.

55. US Agency for International Development, Centers for Disease Control, and Department for Health and Human Services, *A Decade of Progress: The President's Malaria Initiative*, Tenth Annual Report to Congress (April 2016), 7, https://www.pmi.gov/docs/default-source/default-document-library/pmi-reports/pmi-tenth-annual-report-congress.pdf.

56. Himelfarb, *50 Years of Global Health*, 65–68.

57. Philip-Michael Gary, interview by Carol Peasley, January 9, 2017, ADST Oral History, 70, http://adst.org/wp-content/uploads/2013/12/Gary-Philip.pdf.

58. Natsios, interview by Carol Peasley.

59. Natsios, *The Clash of the Counter-Bureaucracy and Development*.

60. Ibid., 27.

61. John Norris, "The Crucible: Iraq, Afghanistan and the Future of USAID," *World Politics Review*, November 19, 2013, https://www.worldpoliticsreview.com/articles/13380/the-crucible-iraq-afghanistan-and-the-future-of-usaid.

62. Jane Perlez, "A Nation at War: Care Packages; Pentagon and State Department in Tug-of-War Over Aid Disbursal," *New York Times*, April 1, 2003, http://www.nytimes.com/2003/04/01/world/nation-war-care-packages-pentagon-state-department-tug-war-over-aid-disbursal.html.

63. Keith Brown and Jill Tirnauer, *Trends in US Foreign Assistance Over the Past Decade* (Washington, DC: US Agency for International Development, August 17, 2009), 11, https://pdf.usaid.gov/pdf_docs/PNADQ462.pdf.

64. Natsios, interview by Carol Peasley.

65. Rajiv Chandrasekaran, "Who Killed Iraq?" *Foreign Policy*, October 15, 2009, https://foreignpolicy.com/2009/10/15/who-killed-iraq/.

66. Eamon Javers, "NY Fed's $40 Billion Iraq Money Trail," *CNBC*, October 25, 2011, http://www.cnbc.com/id/45031100.

67. Norris, "President Bush and His Development Legacy."

68. James Fallows, "Invading Iraq: What We Were Told at the Time," *The Atlantic*, March 19, 2003, https://www.theatlantic.com/politics/archive/2013/03/invading-iraq-what-we-were-told-at-the-time/274179/.

69. Andrew Natsios, "AID in the Post-9/11 World," *Foreign Service Journal* (June 2006), 23.

70. Himelfarb, *50 Years of Global Health*, 72.

71. Norris, "The Crucible."

72. Natsios, "AID in the Post-9/11 World," 23.

73. This account is drawn from: Brown and Tirnauer, *Trends in US Foreign Assistance Over the Past Decade*, 25; Center for Global Development, "Reorganizing US Development Assistance: For Better or Worse? A Debate," event held March 17, 2006; Natsios, interview by Carol Peasley; and, Hyman, *Foreign Policy and Development*, 22–24.

74. Norris, "Sept. 11 and Beyond."

75. Celia W. Dugger, "Planning to Fight Poverty from Outside the System," *New York Times*, January 14, 2006.

76. Ibid.

77. Hyman, *Foreign Policy and Development*, 22–24.

78. Brown and Tirnauer, *Trends in US Foreign Assistance Over the Past Decade*, 25–26.

79. Norris, "President Bush and His Development Legacy."

80. Steven R. Weisman, "Rice to Group Foreign Aid in One Office in State Dept.," *New York Times*, January 19, 2006, http://www.nytimes.com/2006/01/19/politics/rice-to-group-foreign-aid-in-one-office-in-state-dept.html.

81. M. Peter McPherson, interviewed by Alex Shakow, April 8, 2018, 30.

82. Randall Tobias, interview with author, June 16, 2020.

83. US Congress, Senate, Committee on Foreign Relations *Embassies Grapple to Guide Foreign Aid* (Washington, DC: US Government Printing Office, November 16, 2007), 1–2.

84. CNN, "State Department Official Resigns Over 'DC Madam,'" April 28, 2007, https://www.cnn.com/2007/POLITICS/04/27/dc.madam/index.html.

85. Randall Tobias oral history available at: https://tobiascenter.iu.edu/research/oral-history/audio-transcripts/tobias-randall.html.

86. Norris, "The Crucible."

87. Natsios, "AID in the Post-9/11 World."

88. Norris, "The Crucible."

89. OECD, "Endorsements to the Paris Declaration and Accra Agenda for Action," https://www.oecd.org/dac/effectiveness/countriesterritoriesandendorsementstotheparisdeclarationandaaa.htm; Brown and Tirnauer, *Trends in US Foreign Assistance Over the Past Decade*, 18.

90. The HELP Commission, *Beyond Assistance: The HELP Commission Report on Foreign Assistance Reform* (December 7, 2007), 7–8, 11–13.

CHAPTER 11

1. Barack Obama, "Obama's Foreign Policy Speech," *The Guardian*, July 16, 2008, http://www.guardian.co.uk/world/2008/jul/16/uselections2008.barackobama?gusrc=rss&feed=worldnews.

2. Robert M. Gates, "Remarks by Secretary of Defense Robert M. Gates at USGLC Tribute Dinner," July 15, 2008, US Global Leadership Campaign, http://www.usglc.org/ USGLCdocs/USGLC_Remarks_by_Defense_Secretary_Gates.pdf.

3. US Congress, Congressional Research Service, *Foreign Aid Reform, National Strategy, and the Quadrennial Review*, by Susan B. Epstein (April 12, 2010), 3.

4. Howard La Franchi, "Economy Forces Obama to Rein in Foreign-Aid Goals," *Christian Science Monitor*, March 23, 2009.

5. Brown and Tirnauer, *Trends in US Foreign Assistance Over the Past Decade*, iii–v.

6. US Agency for International Development, *AID's Legacy in Agriculture Development*, 11–12.

7. Justin Gillis, "A Warming Planet Struggles to Feed Itself," *New York Times*, June 5, 2011, https://www.nytimes.com/2011/06/05/science/earth/05harvest.html.

8. Feed the Future, *Feed the Future Guide: A Summary*, 1, https://feedthefuture.gov/sites/ default/files/resource/files/FTF_Guide_summary.pdf.

9. Feed the Future, *2015 Results Summary—Achieving Impact: Leadership and Partnership to Feed the Future* (2016), 10.

10. US Agency for International Development, Bureau for Food Security, *AID's Legacy in Agriculture Development* (Washington, DC, 2013, 2016), 11–12, https://www.usaid.gov/sites/ default/files/documents/1867/USAID-Legacy-in-Agricultural-Development.PDF.

11. Feed the Future, *2015 Results Summary*, 5.

12. Ibid., 10.

13. John Norris, "Five Myths About Foreign Aid," *Washington Post*, April 28, 2011, https:// www.washingtonpost.com/opinions/five-myths-about-foreign-aid/2011/04/25/AF00z05E _story.html?utm_term=.fd84a8ee8763.

14. Riley, *The Political History of American Food Aid*, 491.

15. Ibid., i, xxii.

16. US Congress, Congressional Research Service, *Foreign Aid Reform, National Strategy, and the Quadrennial Review*, by Susan B. Epstein, 9.

17. Hillary Clinton, *Hard Choices* (New York: Simon & Schuster, 2014), 534–35.

18. Brown and Tirnauer, *Trends in US Foreign Assistance Over the Past Decade*, iii–v.

19. US Library of Congress, Congressional Research Service, *US Agency for International Development (AID): Background, Operations, and Issues*, by Curt Tarnoff, 19.

20. John Norris, "President Obama and His Development Legacy," *Devex*, July 12, 2016, https://www.devex.com/news/president-obama-and-his-development-legacy-87853.

21. Ibid.

22. Mary Beth Sheridan, "Haiti's Earthquake Damage Estimated Up to $14 Billion," February 17, 2010, *Washington Post*, available at https://www.washingtonpost.com/wp-dyn/ content/article/2010/02/16/AR2010021605745.html.

23. Debarati Guha-Sapir, et al., *Independent Review of the US Government Response to the Haiti Earthquake* (Washington, DC: US Agency for International Development, March 28, 2011), https://pdf.usaid.gov/pdf_docs/pdacr222.pdf.

24. Ibid.

25. Philip Rucker, "Officials Hail USAID Administrator's Crisis Management Skills," January 15, 2010, *Washington Post*, www.washingtonpost.com/wp-dyn/content/article/ 2010/01/14/AR2010011402961.html.

26. Mark Landler, "Curing the Ills of America's Top Foreign Aid Agency," October 23, 2010, *New York Times*, https://www.nytimes.com/2010/10/23/world/23shah.html.

27. Clinton, *Hard Choices*, 535–36.

28. Olson, *FINAL REPORT: A Critical Juncture Analysis*, 61-65.

29. US Government Accountability Office, "Haiti Reconstruction: USAID Infrastructure Projects Have Had Mixed Results," June 25, 2013, https://www.gao.gov/products/GAO-13-558.

30. Barack Obama, "Remarks by the President at the Millennium Development Goals Summit in New York, New York," September 22, 2010, The White House, Office of the Press Secretary, https://obamawhitehouse.archives.gov/the-press-office/2010/09/22/remarks-president-millennium-development-goals-summit-new-york-new-york.

31. Himelfarb, *50 Years of Global Health*, 76.

32. US Agency for International Development, Centers for Disease Control, and Department for Health and Human Services, *A Decade of Progress: The President's Malaria Initiative*, 5.

33. Norris, "President Obama and His Development Legacy."

34. Hyman, *Foreign Policy and Development*, 1.

35. Charles Kenny, *Technology and AID: Three Cheers and a Thousand Cautions*, Center for Global Development (July 2011), 3–4.

36. Rajiv Shah, "Remarks by USAID Administrator Dr. Rajiv Shah at the Center for Global Development," January 19, 2011, https://2012-2017.usaid.gov/news-information/speeches/remarks-usaid-administrator-dr-rajiv-shah-center-global-development.

37. US Library of Congress, Congressional Research Service, *US Agency for International Development (AID): Background, Operations, and Issues*, by Curt Tarnoff, 34.

38. Justin Sandefur, *Here's the Best Thing the United States Has Done in Afghanistan*, Center for Global Development (October 15, 2013), http://www.cgdev.org/publication/here-best-thing-united-states-has-done-afghanistan.

39. Gwen Thompkins, "In Kenya, Obama Win Sparks Celebration," *NPR*, November 5, 2008, http://www.npr.org/templates/story/story.php?storyId=96670528.

40. Todd Moss, *My Fridge Versus Power Africa*, Center for Global Development (September 9, 2013), https://www.cgdev.org/blog/my-fridge-versus-power-africa.

41. UNDESA, *Electricity and Education: The Benefits, Barriers, and Recommendations for Achieving the Electrification of Primary and Secondary Schools* (The United Nations, December 2014), https://sustainabledevelopment.un.org/content/documents/1608Electricity%20and%20Education.pdf.

42. US Agency for International Development, *Leveraging Partnerships to Increase Access to Power in Sub-Saharan Africa* (April 28, 2015), http://www.usaid.gov/sites/default/files/documents/1860/About_Power%20Africa_04_28_2015%20(Final).pdf.

43. Tal Kopan, "Leahy: Cuban Twitter Plan 'Dumb,'" *Politico*, April 3, 2014, https://www.politico.com/story/2014/04/patrick-leahy-cuba-twitter-105348.

44. Manuel Roig-Franzia, "USAID Effort to Undermine Cuban Government with Fake 'Twitter' Another Anti-Castro Failure," *Washington Post*, April 4, 2014, https://www.washingtonpost.com/lifestyle/style/usaid-effort-to-undermine-cuban-government-with-fake-twitter-another-anti-castro-failure/2014/04/03/c0142cc0-bb75-11e3-9a05-c739f29ccb08_story.html.

45. Colby Itkowitz, "USAID Head Raj Shah Tells Staff He's Leaving (Which We All Knew)," *Washington Post*, December 17, 2014, https://www.washingtonpost.com/blogs/in-the-loop/wp/2014/12/17/usaid-head-raj-shah-to-tell-staff-hes-leaving-which-we-all-knew/.

46. Ron Nixon, "Chief of Agency for International Development to Step Down," *New York Times*, December 17, 2014, https://www.nytimes.com/2014/12/17/us/politics/chief-of -agency-for-international-development-to-step-down.html.

47. Eliza Anyangwe, "Who Is the 'Gayle-Force Wind' Picked Up by Obama to Lead USAID?" *The Guardian*, May 8, 2015, https://www.theguardian.com/global-development -professionals-network/2015/may/08/gayle-smith-obama-usaid-senate.

48. Norris, "President Obama and His Development Legacy."

CHAPTER 12

1. WOTR Staff, "Open Letter on Donald Trump from GOP National Security Leaders," *War on the Rocks*, March 2, 2016, https://warontherocks.com/2016/03/open-letter-on-donald -trump-from-gop-national-security-leaders/.

2. David Francis, John Hudson, and Dan De Luce, "Will Foreign Aid Get Cut on Trump's Chopping Block?" *Foreign Policy*, November 23, 2016, http://foreignpolicy.com/2016/11/23/ will-foreign-aid-get-cut-on-trumps-chopping-block/.

3. Andrew Kaczynski, Nathan McDermott, and Em Steck, "From AIDS to COVID-19: Trump's Decades of Spreading Dangerous Misinformation about Disease Outbreaks," CNN, May 30, 2020, https://www.cnn.com/2020/05/30/politics/kfile-trump-history-of-medical -misinformation/index.html.

4. Donald J. Trump, Twitter post, August 1, 2014, 9:22 p.m., https://twitter.com/ realDonaldTrump/status/495379061972410369.

5. Gabriel Schoenfeld, "Trump Tweeted Heartlessly about Ebola in 2014. He's Ill-Equipped to Handle the 2019 Outbreak," *USA Today*, July 22, 2019, https://www.usatoday .com/story/opinion/2019/07/22/trump-tweets-show-germaphobe-ill-equipped-for-us-ebola -crisis-column/1779930001/.

6. Chris Akor, "Donald Trump and Africa," *Business Day*, March 2, 2017.

7. Nina Brooks, Eran Bendavid, and Grant Miller, "USA Aid Policy and Induced Abortion in Sub-Saharan Africa: An Analysis of the Mexico City Policy," *The Lancet* 7.8 (August 1, 2019), https://www.thelancet.com/journals/langlo/article/PIIS2214-109X(19)30267-0/ fulltext.

8. Nurith Aizenman, "Study Looks at Impact of Trump Policy on Abortion Rate in Sub-Saharan Africa," NPR, June 27, 2019, https://www.npr.org/sections/goatsandsoda/ 2019/06/27/736574110/study-u-s-ban-on-aid-to-foreign-clinics-that-promote-abortion -upped-abortion-rat.

9. Daniele Selby and Jana Sepehr, "Fact-Checking President Trump's Statements about Foreign Aid," *Global Citizen*, January 4, 2019, https://www.globalcitizen.org/en/content/ trump-cabinet-meeting-foreign-aid/.

10. Akor, "Donald Trump and Africa."

11. Jessica Taylor, "Trump Unveils 'Hard Power' Budget that Boosts Military Spending," NPR, March 16, 2017, https://www.npr.org/2017/03/16/520305293/trump-to-unveil-hard -power-budget-that-boosts-military-spending.

12. Sylvan Lane, "GOP Senator: Trump Budget 'Dead on Arrival,'" *The Hill*, February 28, 2017, http://thehill.com/policy/finance/321576-gop-senator-trump-budget-dead-on-arrival.

13. US Global Leadership Coalition, "Letter to Paul Ryan, Nancy Pelosi, Mitch McConnell, and Chuck Schumer," February 2017, http://www.usglc.org/downloads/2017/02/FY 18_International_Affairs_Budget_House_Senate.pdf.

14. Conor Finnegan, "Tillerson Spent $12 Million on Consultants for State Department Redesign," ABC News, April 6, 2018, http://abcnews.go.com/Politics/ tillerson-spent-12-million-consultants-state-department-redesign/story?id=54275966.

15. Jason Beaubien, "Trump's Proposed USAID Head Knows AID—and Politics," *NPR*, May 11, 2017, https://www.npr.org/sections/goatsandsoda/2017/05/11/527995708/ trumps-proposed-usaid-head-knows-aid-and-politics.

16. Reuters Staff, "Senate Confirms New USAID Administrator Mark Green," Reuters, August 3, 2017, https://www.reuters.com/article/us-usa-aid-green/senate-confirms-new-usaid -administrator-mark-green-idUSKBN1AK01D.

17. US Congress, Senate, Committee on Foreign Relations, "Nomination Hearing for the Honorable Mark Green," June 15, 2017, https://www.foreign.senate.gov/hearings/ nominations-061517.

18. Sarah Rose and Erin Collinson, *Mark Green's Legacy and Priorities for the Next USAID Administrator*, Center for Global Development (April 10, 2020), https://www.cgdev.org/blog/ mark-greens-legacy-and-priorities-next-usaid-administrator#.XpYuPtt5mps.email.

19. Ali Vitali, Kasie Hunt, and Frank Thorp V, "Trump Referred to Haiti and African Nations As 'Shithole' Countries," NBC News, January 12, 2018, https://www.nbcnews.com/ politics/white-house/trump-referred-haiti-african-countries-shithole-nations-n836946.

20. Michael D. Shear and Julie Hirschfeld Davis, "Stoking Fears, Trump Defied Bureaucracy to Advance Immigration Agenda," *New York Times*, December 23, 2017, https://www .nytimes.com/2017/12/23/us/politics/trump-immigration.html?rref=collection%2Fsection collection%2Fpolitics&action=click&contentCollection=politics&region=rank&module =package&version=highlights&contentPlacement=1&pgtype=sectionfront.

21. Colum Lynch, "Hayley: Vote with US at U.N. Or We'll Cut Your Aid," *Foreign Policy*, March 15, 2018, http://foreignpolicy.com/2018/03/15/haley-vote-with-u-s-at-u-n-or-well -cut-your-aid/.

22. Nahal Toosi, "Trump Plan Would Steer Foreign Aid to 'Friends and Allies,'" *Politico*, September 6, 2019, https://www.politico.com/story/2019/09/06/trump-foreign-aid-allies -1483788.

23. USAID, *The Journey to Self-Reliance: Country Roadmaps*, https://selfreliance.usaid.gov/.

24. Michael Igoe, "USAID chief unveils major organizational shakeup," *Devex*, April 9, 2018, https://www.devex.com/news/exclusive-usaid-chief-unveils-major-organizational-shakeup -92493.

25. Michael Igoe, "USAID Chief Lays Out a Trump Development Doctrine," *Devex*, December 6, 2018, https://www.devex.com/news/usaid-chief-lays-out-a-trump-development -doctrine-93973.

26. Michael Igoe, "With Approval for 'Almost All' Reforms, USAID Announces Key Leadership," *Devex*, September 4, 2019, https://www.devex.com/news/with-approval-for-almost -all-reforms-usaid-announces-key-leadership-95539.

27. Kathryn Watson, "A Timeline of What Trump Has Said on Coronavirus," *CBS News*, April 3, 2020, https://www.cbsnews.com/news/timeline-president-donald-trump-changing -statements-on-coronavirus/.

28. Ibid.

29. Deb Riechman, "Trump Disbanded NSC Pandemic Unit that Experts Had Praised," *AP News*, March 14, 2020, https://apnews.com/ce014d94b64e98b7203b873e56f80e9a.

30. Edward Luce, "Inside Trump's Coronavirus Meltdown," *Financial Times*, May 14, 2020, https://www.ft.com/content/97dc7de6-940b-11ea-abcd-371e24b679ed.

31. Jenny Lei Ravelo, "World Calls Trump's Funding Freeze to WHO 'Foolish,' 'Dangerous,'" *Devex*, April 15, 2020, https://www.devex.com/news/world-calls-trump-s-funding-freeze-to-who-foolish-dangerous-97002.

32. Luce, "Inside Trump's Coronavirus Meltdown."

33. Andrew Soergel, "ADP: More than 20 Million People Lost Their Jobs in April," *US News*, May 6, 2020, https://www.usnews.com/news/economy/articles/2020-05-06/adp-more-than-20-million-people-lost-their-jobs-in-april.

34. Daniel Gerzon, et al., "The Impact of COVID-19 (Coronavirus) on Global Poverty: Why Sub-Saharan Africa Might Be the Region Hardest Hit," *World Bank Blogs*, April 20, 2020, https://blogs.worldbank.org/opendata/impact-covid-19-coronavirus-global-poverty-why-sub-saharan-africa-might-be-region-hardest.

35. Robbie Gramer, "Outgoing USAID Chief Says Pandemic Underscores Importance of Foreign Aid," *Foreign Policy*, April 13, 2020, https://foreignpolicy.com/2020/04/13/usaid-coronavirus-pandemic-foreign-aid-trump-mark-green-development-global-health/.

36. Yeganh Torati, "US Foreign Aid Agency Defends Political Appointees Who Wrote Anti-LGBT, Anti-Islam Posts," *ProPublica*, June 9, 2020, https://www.propublica.org/article/u-s-foreign-aid-agency-defends-political-appointees-who-wrote-anti-lgbt-anti-islam-posts.

CHAPTER 13

1. See, *e.g.,* Robert Cassen, *Does Aid Work?* (Oxford: Clarendon Press, 1994); Carol Lancaster, *Foreign Aid: Diplomacy, Development, Domestic Politics* (Chicago: University of Chicago Press, 2007); Steven Radelet, *The Great Surge: The Ascent of the Developing World* (New York: Simon & Schuster, 2015); Raj Kumar, *The Business of Changing the World: How Billionaires, The Disrupters, and Social Entrepreneurs are Transforming the Global Aid Industry* (Boston: Beacon Press, 2019).

2. Edward C. Banfield, "American Foreign Aid Doctrine," in *Why Foreign Aid?* ed. Robert A. Goldwin (Chicago: Rand McNally, 1963), 10–31; P. T. Bauer, *Equality, the Third World, and Economic Delusion* (Cambridge: Harvard University Press, 1981), 24.

3. "Deaton on Poverty and Foreign Aid: An Appraisal," *The Financial Express* (Bangladesh), October 27, 2015.

4. The World Bank, "Fertility Rate, Total (Births per Woman)," https://data.worldbank.org/indicator/SP.DYN.TFRT.IN, last accessed February 2020.

5. The World Bank, "Life Expectancy at Birth, Total (Years)," https://data.worldbank.org/indicator/SP.DYN.LE00.IN, last accessed February 2020.

6. The World Bank, "GDP Per Capita (Current US $)," https://data.worldbank.org/indicator/NY.GDP.PCAP.CD?end=2015&start=1960, last accessed February 2020.

7. The World Bank, "GDP Per Capita (Current US $), Least Developed Countries: UN Classification," https://data.worldbank.org/indicator/NY.GDP.PCAP.CD?end=2015&locations=XL&start=1960, last accessed February 2020.

8. UN Inter-Agency Group for Child Mortality Estimation, *Levels & Trends in Child Mortality* (2019), https://childmortality.org/reports.

9. Food and Agriculture Organization of the United Nations, *The State of Food Insecurity in the World* (2015), http://www.fao.org/3/a-i4646e.pdf. Food and Agriculture Organization of the United Nations, "Prevalence of Undernourishment," http://www .fao .org/sustainable -development-goals/indicators/211/en/, last accessed February 2020.

10. The World Bank, "Decline of Global Extreme Poverty Continues but Has Slowed," September 19, 2018, https://www.worldbank.org/en/news/press-release/2018/09/19/ decline-of-global-extreme-poverty-continues-but-has-slowed-world-bank.

11. The World Bank, "Literacy Rate, Adult Total (% of People Ages 15 and Above)," https://data.worldbank.org/indicator/SE.ADT.LITR.ZS, last accessed February 2020 and, The World Bank, "Literacy Rate, Adult Female (% of Females Ages 15 and Above)," https:// data.worldbank.org/indicator/SE.ADT.LITR.FE.ZS, last accessed February 2020.

12. The World Bank, "Literacy Rate, Adult Total (% of People Ages 15 and Above)," https://data.worldbank.org/indicator/SE.ADT.LITR.ZS, last accessed February 2020.

13. The World Bank, "Literacy Rate, Adult Female (% of Females Ages 15 and Above)," https://data.worldbank.org/indicator/SE.ADT.LITR.FE.ZS, last accessed February 2020.

14. US Congress, Congressional Research Service, *Global Trends in Democracy: Background, US Policy, and Issues for Congress* (Washington, DC: Congressional Research Service, 2018), https://crsreports.congress.gov/product/pdf/R/R45344; Steven E. Finkel, Aníbal Pérez-Liñán, Chris Belasco, and Michael Neureiter, *DRG Learning, Evaluation, and Research Activity Tasking N048: Effects of US Foreign Assistance on Democracy Building—Report on Phase III Activities* (USAID, 2018).

15. "The Role of Foreign Aid in US Foreign Policy: Summary of Mr. Gaud's Presentation," August 25, 1966, LBJ Presidential Library.

16. Natsios, *The Clash of the Counter-Bureaucracy and Development*, 9.

Select Bibliography

Acemoglu, Daron, and James Robinson. *Why Nations Fail: The Origins of Power, Prosperity, and Power.* New York: Crown Business, 2012.

Albright, Madeleine, with Bill Woodward. *Madam Secretary.* New York: Miramax Books, 2003.

Baker, Peter, *Days of Fire: Bush and Cheney in the White House* New York: Doubleday, 2013.

Ballantyne, Janet C., and Maureen Dugan, eds. *Fifty Years in AID: Stories from the Front Lines.* Arlington, VA: Arlington Hall Press, September 2012.

Banerjee, Abhijit, and Esther Duflo. *Poor Economics: A Radical Rethinking of the Way to Fight Global Poverty.* Washington, DC: Public Affairs, 2011.

Barnett, Robert W. "Population: Policy and Program," March 25, 1966, College of Physicians and Surgeons at Columbia University, LBJ Presidential Library.

Bass, Gary J. *The Blood Telegram: Nixon, Kissinger, and a Forgotten Genocide.* New York: Alfred Knopf, 2013.

Behrman, Greg. *The Most Noble Adventure: The Marshall Plan and the Time When America Helped Save Europe.* New York: Simon & Schuster, 2007.

Berg, Alan. "AID's Nutrition History (The Early Years)." Unpublished paper written to contribute to "Nourishing Lives and Building the Future: The History of Nutrition at USAID," June 2019.

Butterfield, Samuel Hale. *US Development Aid—An Historic First: Achievements and Failures in the Twentieth Century.* Westport, CT: Praeger, 2004.

Cannon, Lou. *President Reagan: The Role of a Lifetime.* New York: Public Affairs, 1991.

Carothers, Thomas, and Diane de Gramont. *Development Aid Confronts Politics: The Almost Revolution.* Washington, DC: Carnegie Endowment for International Peace, 2013.

Cassen, Robert. *Does Aid Work?* Oxford: Clarendon Press, 1994.

Clay, L. D. *The Scope and Distribution of US Military and Economic Assistance Programs.* Washington, DC: US Department of State, 1963.

Clinton, Bill. *My Life.* New York: Vintage Books, 2005.

Clinton, Hillary. *Hard Choices.* New York: Simon & Schuster, 2014.

Conway, Gordon. *One Billion Hungry: Can We Feed the World?* Ithaca, NY: Cornell University Press, 2012.

Crosswell, Michael J. "The Development Record and the Effectiveness of Foreign Aid," US Agency for International Development, Staff Discussion Paper No. 1, June 1998.

Dallek, Robert. *An Unfinished Life: John F. Kennedy, 1917–1963.* New York: Back Bay Books, 2003.

Donovan, Robert J. *The Second Victory: The Marshall Plan and the Postwar Revival of Europe.* Lanham, MD: Madison Books, 1987.

Easterly, William. *The White Man's Burden: Why the West's Efforts to Aid the Rest Have Done So Much Ill and So Little Good.* New York: The Penguin Group, 2007.

Eizenstat, Stuart E. *President Carter: The White House Years.* New York: St. Martin's Press, 2018.

Ermarth, Fritz. *The Soviet Union in the Third World: Purpose in Search of Power.* Santa Monica, CA: Rand Corp, 1969.

Farrell, John A. *Richard Nixon: The Life.* New York: Random House, 2017.

Fisher, Paul. *A Short History of the US Aid Program: The Development of Key Aid Concepts.* Washington, DC: Agency for International Development, 1963.

Fox, James. *Applying the Comprehensive Development Framework to AID Experiences.* Washington, DC: World Bank, 2000.

Goodman, Jimmy. "Happy Birthday, Herbert Hoover: The Lost Legacy of a Hated President," *The Atlantic,* August 10, 2011.

Hagen, James M., and Vernon W. Ruttan. *Development Policy Under Eisenhower and Kennedy.* Minneapolis: University of Minnesota, Economic Development Center, 1987.

Harris, John F. *The Survivor: Bill Clinton in the White House.* New York: Random House, 2005.

Himelfarb, Tanya. *50 Years of Global Health: Saving Lives and Building Futures.* Washington, DC: US Agency for International Development, June 2014.

Hyman, Gerald F. *Foreign Policy and Development: Structure, Process, Policy, and the Drip-by-Drip Erosion of AID.* Washington, DC: The Center for Strategic and International Studies, September 2010.

Jacobs, Seth. *Cold War Mandarin: Ngo Dinh Diem and the Origins of America's War in Vietnam, 1950–1963.* Lanham, MD: Rowman & Littlefield, 2006.

Krueger, Anne O. "Economic Policies at Cross-Purposes," The Brookings Institution, 1993.

Krueger, Anne O., and Vernon W. Ruttan. "The Development Impact of Economic Assistance to LDCs, Volume 1," Prepared for the Agency for International Development and the Department of State, 1983.

Kumar, Raj. *The Business of Changing the World: How Billionaires, the Disrupters, and Social Entrepreneurs Are Transforming the Global Aid Industry.* Boston: Beacon Press, 2019.

Lancaster, Carol. *Foreign Aid: Diplomacy, Development, Domestic Politics.* Chicago: University of Chicago Press, 2007.

Lederer, William J., and Eugene Burdick. *The Ugly American.* Greenwich, CT: Crest Giant, 1960.

Leuchtenburg, William E. *Herbert Hoover: The American Presidents Series: The 31st President, 1929–1933.* New York: Henry Holt & Company, 2009.

Levinson, Jerome, and Juan de Onis. *The Alliance that Lost Its Way.* Chicago: Quadrangle Books, 1970.

Lewis, John P. "Reviving American Aid to India: Motivation, Scale, Uses, Constraints," in *India: A Rising Middle Power*, ed. John W. Mellor. Boulder, CO: Westview Press, 1979.

———. *India's Political Economy*. Oxford: Oxford University Press, 1997.

Lyman, Princeton. "Building a Political-Economic Approach to Development," American Political Science Association, 1970.

Mann, Charles C. *The Wizard and the Prophet: Two Remarkable Scientists and Their Dueling Visions to Shape Tomorrow's World*. New York: Alfred A. Knopf, 2018.

McGee, Gale W. *Personnel Administration and Operations of Agency for International Development: Report of Senator Gale W. McGee to the Committee on Appropriations*. Washington, DC: US Government Printing Office, 1963.

Morss, Elliott R., and Victoria A. Morss. *US Foreign Aid: An Assessment of New and Traditional Development Strategies*. Boulder, CO: Westview Press, 1982.

Moyo, Dambisa. *Dead Aid: Why Aid Is Not Working and How There Is a Better Way for Africa*. New York: Farrar, Straus and Giroux, 2009.

Myrdal, Gunnar. *Asian Drama: An Inquiry into the Poverty of Nations*, Volumes I, II, and III. New York: Pantheon, 1968.

Natsios, Andrew. *The Great North Korean Famine: Famine, Politics, and Foreign Policy*. Washington, DC: United States Institute for Peace Press, 2001.

———. *The Clash of the Counter-Bureaucracy and Development*. Washington, DC: Center for Global Development, July 2010.

Neese, Harvey C., and John O'Donnell, eds. *Prelude to Tragedy: Vietnam, 1960–1965*. Annapolis, MD: Naval Institute Press, 2001.

North, W. Haven, and Jeanne Foote North. "Transformations in US Foreign Economic Assistance," in *Foreign Aid and Foreign Policy: Lessons for the Next Half-Century*, eds. Louis A. Picard, Robert Groelsema, and Terry F. Buss. New York: M. E. Sharpe, 2008.

Oliphant, Thomas, and Curtis Wilkie. *The Road to Camelot: Inside JFK's Five-Year Campaign*. New York: Simon & Schuster, 2017.

Olson, Richard S. *FINAL REPORT: The Office of US Foreign Disaster Assistance (OFDA) of the United States Agency for International Development (AID): A Critical Juncture Analysis, 1964–2014*, for Macfadden & Associates, June 9, 2015.

Owens, Edgar. *Development Reconsidered: Bridging the Gap between Government and People*. Washington: DC: Lexington Books, 1972.

Phillips, Rufus. *Why Vietnam Matters: An Eyewitness Account of Lessons Not Learned*. Annapolis, MD: Naval Institute Press, 2008.

Pillsbury, Dr. Michael. *Secret Successes of AID: With Declassified Documents on Economic Policy Reforms in Asia*. Washington, DC: National Defense University Press, 1999.

Piotrow, Phyllis Tilson. *World Population Crisis: The United States Response*. Westport, CT: Praeger, 1973.

Rabe, Stephen G. *The Most Dangerous Area in the World: John F. Kennedy Confronts Communist Revolution in Latin America*. Chapel Hill: University of North Carolina Press, 1999.

Radlet, Steven. *The Great Surge: The Ascent of the Developing World*. New York: Simon & Schuster, 2015.

Reiff, David. "Where Hunger Goes: On the Green Revolution," *The Nation*, February 17, 2011.

Riley, Barry. *The Political History of American Food Aid: An Uneasy Benevolence*. Oxford: Oxford University Press, 2017.

Rostow, W. W. "The Stages of Economic Growth," *Economic History Review*, New Series, vol. 12, no. 1, 1959.

Rubin, Jacob A. *Your Hundred Billion Dollars: The Complete Story of American Foreign Aid.* Philadelphia: Chilton Company, 1964.

Ruttan, Vernon W. *United States Development Assistance Policy: The Domestic Politics of Foreign Economic Aid.* Baltimore, MD: Johns Hopkins University Press, 1996.

Sanbrailo, John. "Extending the American Revolution Overseas: Foreign Aid, 1789–1850," *Foreign Service Journal*, March 2016.

Schlesinger, Arthur M. Jr. *A Thousand Days: John F. Kennedy in the White House.* Boston: Mariner Books, 1965, 2002.

Schuh, G. Edward, et al. "International Cooperation for Sustainable Economic Growth: The US Interest and Proposals for Revitalization," Report of a Task Force on Development Assistance and Economic Growth, 1992.

Schulzinger, Robert D. *US Diplomacy since 1900.* New York: Oxford University Press, 1998.

Sen, Amartya. *Development as Freedom.* New York: Anchor Books, 1999.

Todaro, Michael P., and Stephen C. Smith. *Economic Development*, 8th ed. Boston: Addison Wesley, 2003.

US Agency for International Development. *Foreign Aid in the National Interest: Promoting Freedom, Security, and Opportunity.* Washington, DC: AID, 2002.

———. *20 Years of AID Economic Growth Assistance in Europe and Eurasia.* Washington, DC, July 24, 2013.

———. *AID's Legacy in Agriculture Development: 50 Years of Progress.* Washington, DC: AID, November 2013.

US Congress, Commission on Security and Economic Assistance. *A Report to the Secretary of State*, Frank Charles Carlucci, November 1983.

US Congress, Congressional Budget Office. *Assisting the Developing Countries: Foreign Aid and Trade Policies of the United States*, September 1980.

US Congress, Congressiohal Research Service. *A Concise Survey of US Foreign Aid*, by Allan S. Nanes, February 26, 1975.

———. *Development Assistance Policy: A Historical Overview*, by Theodor W. Galdi, April 6, 1988.

———. *Foreign Assistance and Congressional Debate: International Challenges, Domestic Concerns, Decisions Deferred*, by Larry Q. Nowels, April 17, 1992.

———. *The Former Soviet Union and US Foreign Aid: Implementing the Assistance Program, 1992–1994*, by Curt Tarnoff, January 18, 1995.

———. *US Agency for International Development (AID): Background, Operations, and Issues* by Curt Tarnoff, 2015.

US Department of State. *Highlights of President Kennedy's New Act for International Development.* Washington, DC: US Government Printing Office, 1961.

Vance, Cyrus. *Hard Choices: Critical Years in America's Foreign Policy.* New York: Simon & Schuster, 1983.

Woods, Alan. *Development and the National Interest: US Economic Assistance into the 21st Century*, February 1989.

World Bank. *Sub-Saharan Africa: From Crisis to Sustainable Growth.* Washington, DC, 1989.

Yergin, Daniel, and Joseph Stanislaw. The Commanding Heights: The Battle between Government and the Marketplace that is Remaking the Modern World. New York: Simon & Schuster, 1998.

Index

About the Author

John Norris worked at AID during the 1990s both as a speechwriter and field disaster specialist. Since that time, he has served in a variety of senior roles at the State Department, United Nations, and nonprofits. Norris resides with his family on Bainbridge Island outside of Seattle, and he currently works at the Bill and Melinda Gates Foundation—although the views expressed here are entirely his own.

CPSIA information can be obtained
at www.ICGtesting.com
Printed in the USA
BVHW091830160521
607232BV00003B/3